ZAGATSURVEY®

2000

NEW YORK CITY RESTAURANTS

Published and distributed by
ZAGAT SURVEY, LLC
4 Columbus Circle
New York, New York 10019
Tel: 212 977 6000
E-mail: zagat@zagatsurvey.com
Web site: zagat.com

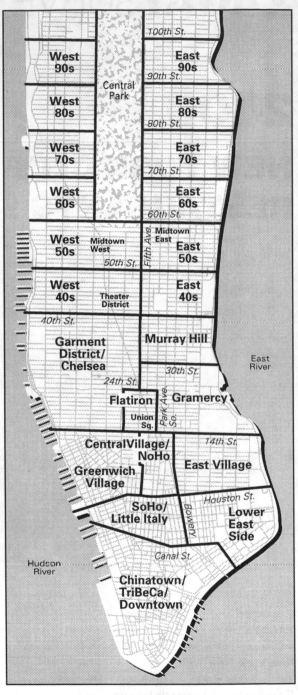

Menu

Introduction

Here are the results of our *2000 New York City Restaurant Survey* covering some 1,808 restaurants in what we believe is the best and most varied restaurant scene in the world, including London, Paris and Tokyo, for which we also do *Surveys*.

By annually surveying large numbers of local restaurant-goers, we think we have achieved a uniquely current and reliable guide. We hope you agree. This year, a record 19,227 people participated in this *Survey*, eating over 3.2 million restaurant meals, an average of 1,800 meals per restaurant surveyed. Since the participants dined out an average of 3.24 times per week, this *Survey* is based on more than 8,800 meals per day.

Of our surveyors, 20% are in their 20s, 27% in their 30s, 20% in their 40s, 20% in their 50s and 13% are 60 or above. We thank each respondent. They are a most diverse group in every respect but one – they are food lovers all. This book is really "theirs."

To help guide you to NYC's best meals and best buys, we have prepared a number of lists. See, for example, New Yorkers' Most Popular Restaurants (page 11), Top Ratings (pages 13–19), Best Buys (page 20) and Prix Fixe Menus (pages 21–22). We have also included a Traffic Report (page 12) listing the restaurants most frequently visited by our surveyors in the past year. On the assumption that most people want a "quick fix" on the places at which they are considering eating, we have tried to be concise and to provide handy indexes by cuisine type, neighborhoods and special features and appeals. We publish a NYC dining map as a companion to this guide, and early next year will release our *NYC Nightlife Survey*, a guide to bars, clubs and lounges.

To be a reviewer in our 2001 *Survey*, simply send a stamped, self-addressed, business-size envelope to ZAGAT SURVEY, 4 Columbus Circle, New York, NY 10019, so that we can contact you. Each participant will receive a free copy of our *2001 New York City Restaurant Survey* when published.

Your comments, suggestions and even criticisms of this *Survey* are also solicited. There should always be room for improvement in the next millennium, but as always we depend on your help.

New York, New York   Nina and Tim Zagat
October 27, 1999

What's New

The past year witnessed the continuing boom of the New York dining scene:

1. Spending Increases: Surveyors' spending per meal increased from $31.68 to $33.17, i.e. by 4.7%, this year. This is significantly higher than the 2.5% annual inflation in restaurant tabs that we have observed over the past 20 years. Whether this is a sign of good times or a cause for concern is for economists and, most probably, gourmands to say. Our surveys in other cities show this is part of a nationwide pattern, e.g. Boston 7.4%, San Francisco 5.7%, Los Angeles 5.7% and Las Vegas, which is up 23.6% over a three-year period.

2. Comparative Dining Costs: New York continues to be the nation's most expensive city in which to dine. In comparison to $33.17 per meal here, the average in other major US cities surveyed is $23.43. In contrast, dining is far more expensive in London ($46.75 per meal) and in Paris ($46.21). Comparing the 20 most expensive restaurants, the difference is even greater: New York ($70.06); London ($96.29) and Paris ($113.74).

3. Tipping is Up: With more money in their pockets thanks to the strong economy, New Yorkers have become increasingly generous when it comes to tipping. This year the average tip is just shy of 18%, with almost half of our surveyors tipping 20% or more. Astonishingly, fully 72% of our surveyors have *never* refused to give a tip even in the face of poor service.

4. Dining Frequency: This year our 19,227 surveyors reported dining out 3.24 times per week on average, an imperceptible drop from last year's 3.27 figure. In what will surely come as a surprise to most New Yorkers, the national average is 3.7, with Houston leading at 4.9 meals per week. However, when it comes to takeout, New York is the nation's leader at 3.8 meals per week. This brings the total number of lunches and dinners eaten at New York restaurants or taken out to 7.1.

5. Openings vs. Closings: Once again, the number of noteworthy openings (274) easily exceeded closings (96) as they have in every year this decade. In comparison, the prior year's ratio was 277 to 117 – i.e. nearly the same number of openings but 21 less closings. Among the newcomers, there have been some truly important arrivals, e.g. Atlas, Beacon, Cello, Danube, Five Points, Local, Nobu Next Door, Veritas and ViceVersa; moreover, few, if any, of the closed restaurants will be greatly missed or long remembered. 1999 will also mark the spectacular revival and expansion of the Russian Tea Room, fittingly in time to celebrate the arrival of the new millennium.

6. Top Performers: Le Bernardin, which earned NY's Top Food ranking for the first time last year, retains that title and also adds Top Service honors, while Lespinasse is No. 1 for Decor. Other chart-toppers include Aureole (Top American), Il Mulino (Top Italian) and Peter Luger, the No. 1 steakhouse for 16 years running. And in the most remarkable performance of all, restaurateur Danny Meyer has four restaurants in the Most Popular rankings: Union Square Cafe remains No. 1 for the fourth year, Gramercy Tavern rises up a notch to No. 2, and Eleven Madison Park and Tabla both break into the list (No. 37

and 38 respectively) in their first rated years. There's no mystery to Meyer's success: his emphasis on fine food, warm hospitality and good value has obviously struck a chord with surveyors.

7. Major Projects by Leading Players: A number of leading restaurateurs have undertaken major new projects, some already open and some scheduled to open soon. These include: Joe Bastianich and Mario Batali (Lupa); David Bouley (Danube); London's Sir Terence Conran (Guastavino and Club Guastavino); David Emil and Waldy Malouf (Beacon); Peter and Penny Glazier (Michael Jordan's); Steve Hanson (Ruby Foo's); André and Rita Jammet (Sono); Danny Meyer (Eleven Madison Park and Tabla); the Santo family (Bolivar, Cibi Cibi and the upcoming Little Dove); and David and Karen Waltuck (Le Zinc).

8. Minor Trends: Besides the changes reported above, there have been a number of smaller, but still noteworthy, changes:

• a new wave of theme restaurants (ESPN Zone, Joe Franklin's Memory Lane, Mars 2112 and WWF-NY);

• the introduction of more elaborate wine lists (Bayard's, Cello, Lespinasse, Oceana, Union Pacific, Veritas and Wild Blue to name just a few);

• the expansion of the Belgian moules/frites formula (Belgo Nieuw York, B. Frites and Markt);

• more than ever big-ticket prix fixes offered instead of à la carte (Patria plus newcomers Cello and Scalini Fedeli), as well as multicourse tasting menus instead of the traditional appetizers and entrées (March and Peacock Alley);

• the weakening of the soup segment, with closings of Souperdog, Soup Pot, a branch of Souperman and the Soup Nutsy – the imitator of Al's Soup Kitchen International, which once again beat some of the major players with its 26 food rating.

9. The Service Deficit: Service continues to be the weak link in the dining industry, garnering 62% of all complaints in our cross-country surveys. In New York, the pattern is somewhat different, with 43% of complaints applying to service, but with other factors such as noise (14%), crowding (17%) and prices (17%) playing a far higher role than elsewhere. Only 1% of New Yorkers' complaints relate to food while the national average is 11%.

10. Men and Women: If the problems of service weren't enough of a concern, four out of five of our surveyors report that men get treated better than women when dining out. Whether that's true or false, given the fact that half of all customers are women, it is clearly in the industry's self-interest to redress this impression.

11. The Future Looks Bright: Since the factors that have made the NYC restaurant scene so dynamic over the past 20 years remain in place, we have every reason to expect that as we move into the new millennium, the city will retain its status as home to the most varied and exciting high-quality dining in the world.

New York, New York   Nina and Tim Zagat
October 27, 1999

Dining Tips

Over our 20-plus years of surveying restaurant-goers, we've heard from hundreds of thousands of people about their dining-out experiences. Most of their reports are positive – proof of the ever-growing skill and dedication of the nation's chefs and restaurateurs. But inevitably, we also hear about problems.

Obviously, there are certain basics that everyone has the right to expect when dining out: 1. Courteous, hospitable, informative service; 2. Clean, sanitary facilities; 3. Fresh, healthful food; 4. Timely honoring of reservations; and 5. Smoke-free seating.

Sadly, if these conditions aren't met, many diners simply swallow their disappointment, assuming there's nothing they can do. However, the truth is that diners have far more power than they may realize. Every restaurateur worth his or her salt wants to satisfy customers, since happy clients equal a successful business. Rather than the adversaries they sometimes seem to be, diners and restaurateurs are natural allies – both want the same outcome, and each can help the other achieve it. Towards that end, here are a few simple but sometimes forgotten tips that every restaurant-goer should bear in mind:

1) Speak up: If dissatisfied by any aspect of your experience – from the handling of your reservation to the food, service or physical environment – tell the manager. Most problems are easy to resolve at the time they occur – but not if management doesn't know about them until afterward. The opposite is also true: if you're pleased, speak up.

2) Spell out your needs ahead of time: If you have specific dietary requests, wish to bring your own wine, want a smoke-free (or smoking) environment, or have any other special needs, you can avoid disappointment by calling ahead to make sure the restaurant can satisfy you.

3) Do your part: A restaurant's ability to honor reservations, for example, is largely dependent on diners honoring reservations and showing up on time. Make it a point to cancel reservations you're unable to use and be sure to notify the restaurant if you'll be late. The restaurant, in turn, should do its best to seat parties promptly, and, if there are delays, should keep diners informed (a free drink doesn't hurt either).

4) Vote with your dollars: Most people tip 15 to 19%, and often 20% or more at high-end restaurants. Obviously, you have the right not to tip at all if unhappy with the service; but in that case, many simply leave 10% to get the message across. If you like the restaurant, it's worth accompanying the low tip with a word to the management. Of course, the ultimate way to vote with your dollars is not to come back.

5) Put it in writing: Like it or not, all restaurants make mistakes. The best ones distinguish themselves by how well they acknowledge and handle mistakes. If you've expressed your complaints to the restaurant management but haven't gotten a satisfactory response, write to your local restaurant critic, with a copy to the restaurant, detailing the problem. That really gets the restaurateur's attention. Naturally, we also hope you'll express your feelings, pro and con, by voting on zagat.com.

Key to Ratings/Symbols

This sample entry identifies the various types of information contained in your Zagat Survey.

(1) Restaurant Name, Address & Phone Number

(2) Hours & Credit Cards

(3) ZAGAT Ratings

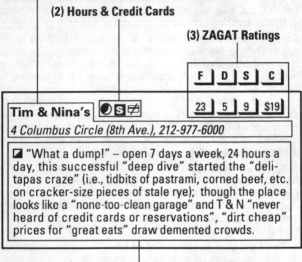

F	D	S	C
23	5	9	$19

Tim & Nina's ◑ Ⓢ ⊄

4 Columbus Circle (8th Ave.), 212-977-6000

◪ "What a dump!" – open 7 days a week, 24 hours a day, this successful "deep dive" started the "deli-tapas craze" (i.e., tidbits of pastrami, corned beef, etc. on cracker-size pieces of stale rye); though the place looks like a "none-too-clean garage" and T & N "never heard of credit cards or reservations", "dirt cheap" prices for "great eats" draw demented crowds.

(4) Surveyors' Commentary

The names of restaurants with the highest overall ratings, greatest popularity and importance are printed in **CAPITAL LETTERS**. Address and phone numbers are printed in *italics*.

(2) Hours & Credit Cards

After each restaurant name you will find the following courtesy information:

◑ .... *serving after 11 PM*

Ⓢ .... *open on Sunday*

⊄ .... *no credit cards accepted*

(3) ZAGAT Ratings

Food, **Decor** and **Service** are each rated on a scale of **0** to **30**:

F	D	S	C

F	....	*Food*
D	....	*Decor*
S	....	*Service*
C	....	*Cost*

23	5	9	$19

0 - 9	....	*poor to fair*
10 - 15	....	*fair to good*
16 - 19	....	*good to very good*
20 - 25	....	*very good to excellent*
26 - 30	....	*extraordinary to perfection*

▽ 23	5	9	$19

▽ .... *Low number of votes/less reliable*

The **Cost (C)** column reflects the estimated price of a dinner with one drink and tip. Lunch usually costs 25% less.

A restaurant listed without ratings is either an important **newcomer** or a popular **write-in**. The estimated cost, with one drink and tip, is indicated by the following symbols.

–	–	–	VE

I	....	*$15 and below*
M	....	*$16 to $30*
E	....	*$31 to $50*
VE	....	*$51 or more*

(4) Surveyors' Commentary

Surveyors' comments are summarized, with literal comments shown in quotation marks. The following symbols indicate whether responses were mixed or uniform.

◪ .... *mixed*
◼ .... *uniform*

Most Popular Restaurants

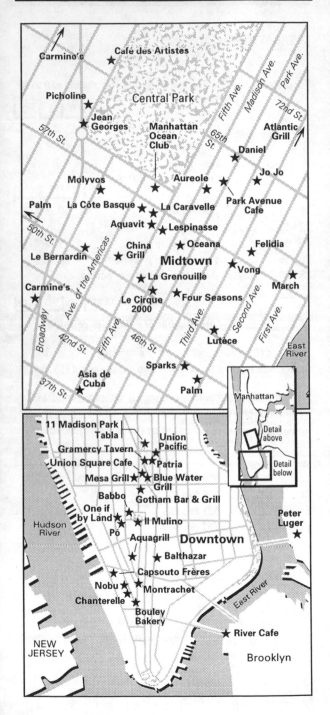

Most Popular Restaurants

Each of our reviewers has been asked to name his or her five overall favorite restaurants. The 50 spots most frequently named (and their opening dates), in order of popularity, are:

1. Union Square Cafe ('85)
2. Gramercy Tavern ('94)
3. Gotham Bar & Grill ('84)
4. Aureole ('88)
5. Le Bernardin ('86)
6. Jean Georges ('97)
7. Four Seasons ('59)
8. Peter Luger (1887)
9. Café des Artistes ('17)
10. Nobu ('94)
11. Daniel ('93)
12. Chanterelle ('79)
13. Le Cirque 2000 ('74)
14. Lespinasse ('91)
15. La Côte Basque ('57)
16. Blue Water Grill ('96)
17. Picholine ('93)
18. Bouley Bakery ('97)
19. Babbo ('98)
20. One if by Land, TIBS ('72)
21. Balthazar ('97)
22. Il Mulino ('80)
23. Aquavit ('87)
24. La Grenouille ('62)
25. Vong ('92)

26. River Cafe ('77)
27. Carmine's ('90)
28. Mesa Grill ('91)
29. Patria ('94)
30. Asia de Cuba ('97)
31. Union Pacific ('97)*
32. La Caravelle ('60)
33. Oceana ('92)
34. Park Avenue Cafe ('92)
35. Aquagrill ('96)
36. Montrachet ('85)
37. Eleven Madison Park ('98)
38. Tabla ('98)
39. Felidia ('81)
40. Lutèce ('61)
41. March ('90)
42. Palm ('26)
43. Sparks ('69)
44. Atlantic Grill ('98)
45. Capsouto Frères ('80)
46. Jo Jo ('91)
47. China Grill ('87)
48. Manhattan Ocean Club ('84)
49. Molyvos ('97)
50. Pó ('93)

It's obvious that most of the above restaurants are expensive, but New Yorkers also love a bargain. Fortunately, our city has an abundance of wonderful ethnic restaurants and other inexpensive spots that fill the bill. Thus, we have listed 90 "Best Buys" on page 20 and both Prix Fixe and Pre-Theater Bargains on pages 21–22. In fact, despite New York's reputation as an expensive place to live, its vast size and less pricey outer boroughs offer far more affordable and diverse dining options than any other US city.

---

* Tied with the restaurant listed directly above it.

Most Visited Restaurants

This list indicates the 50 spots most often visited by our surveyors, and the number of visits in the past year:

4,874	Union Square Cafe	2,775	Le Bernardin
4,494	Carmine's	2,659	Le Cirque 2000
4,320	Café des Artistes	2,622	Redeye Grill
4,303	Gotham Bar & Grill	2,509	Second Avenue Deli
4,117	Blue Water Grill	2,508	America
4,069	Balthazar	2,490	Cafe Un Deux Trois
3,949	Peter Luger	2,478	Mesa Grill
3,941	Gramercy Tavern	2,470	China Grill
3,856	Carnegie Deli	2,457	Penang
3,762	Starbucks	2,432	Atlantic Grill
3,622	John's Pizzeria	2,422	Jean Georges
3,577	EJ's Luncheonette	2,404	Zen Palate
3,403	Aureole	2,391	Oyster Bar (Gr. Cent.)
3,331	Docks Oyster Bar	2,372	La Côte Basque
3,272	Tavern on the Green	2,367	Vong
3,268	Krispy Kreme	2,313	Katz's Deli
3,213	Cosi Sandwich Bar	2,293	Rain
3,198	Four Seasons	2,267	Bouley Bakery
3,128	California Pizza Kitchen	2,265	One if by Land, TIBS
3,021	Jackson Hole	2,242	Palm
3,014	Sarabeth's	2,225	Asia de Cuba
2,996	Aquavit	2,180	Trattoria Dell'Arte
2,922	Smith & Wollensky	2,178	Bryant Park Grill
2,896	Ollie's	2,168	Dallas BBQ
2,819	Nobu	2,165	Lemongrass Grill

The above numbers represent simple volume, i.e. the number of our reviewers who have gone to these places in the past year. Since surveyors visited each restaurant 8.85 times on average, the number of meals eaten in the above restaurants is enormous – over 43,000 meals at Union Square Cafe, or roughly 118 people a day!

It's clear that these restaurants are not high traffic spots solely for their food; many have been bashed by the media or simply ignored. What this report reflects is that other features besides food, such as ambiance, convenience and value, often determine where people elect to eat. Our Teflons index confirms this.

Top Ratings*

Top 50 Food Ranking**

28 Le Bernardin
   Daniel
   Peter Luger
   Nobu
   Chanterelle
   Jean Georges
   Aureole
27 Lespinasse
   La Grenouille
   Nobu, Next Door
   Il Mulino
   Union Square Cafe
   Gotham Bar & Grill
   Gramercy Tavern
   Café Boulud
   La Côte Basque
   Tomoe Sushi
   Montrachet
   Oceana
26 Four Seasons
   Picholine
   March
   Lutèce
   Bouley Bakery
   Babbo

   La Caravelle
   Le Cirque 2000
   Sushi of Gari
   Blue Ribbon Sushi
   Soup Kitchen Int'l, Al's
   Milos
   Sushisay
   Tabla
   Felidia
   Grimaldi's
25 Kuruma Zushi
   Yama
   Aquagrill
   Veritas
   Jo Jo
   Union Pacific
   Periyali
   Manhattan Ocean Club
   Le Perigord
   Nick's
   Patria
   Aquavit
   Sparks
   Vong
   Pearl Oyster Bar

Top Spots by Cuisine

American
28 Aureole
27 Union Square Cafe
   Gotham Bar & Grill
   Gramercy Tavern
26 March
25 Veritas

American Regional
24 Cooking with Jazz/Cajun
   Mesa Grill/SW
   Coach House/NE
23 Hudson River Club/NY
   An American Place/NE
22 Tropica/FL

Breakfast
24 Payard Pâtisserie
   Mark's
23 Fifty Seven Fifty Seven
   Barney Greengrass
   Carlyle
20 Regency (540 Park)

Brunch
25 Aquagrill
24 Park Avenue Cafe
   River Cafe
   Le Régence
   Chez Michallet
   Café des Artistes

Caviar & Champagne
25 Petrossian
24 Caviar Russe
23 Caviarteria
21 FireBird
20 O'Nieal's Grand St.
19 King Cole Bar

Chinese
25 Canton
24 Shun Lee Palace
   Tse Yang
   Shun Lee
23 Mr. K's
   Chin Chin

---

* Excluding restaurants with low voting.
** These lists are all in order of ranking. Thus, Le Bernardin at 28.21
   came in ahead of Daniel at 27.68.

Top Food

Coffeehouses/Desserts
23 Emack & Bolio's
Veniero's
22 Cupcake Cafe
City Bakery
21 Sant Ambroeus
Once Upon a Tart

Continental
26 Four Seasons
25 Petrossian
24 One if by Land, TIBS
23 Two Two Two
Carlyle
22 Leopard

Delis
23 Barney Greengrass
22 Second Avenue Deli
20 Carnegie Deli
Katz's Deli
19 Stage Deli
18 Pastrami Queen

French
28 Le Bernardin
Daniel
Chanterelle
Jean Georges
27 Lespinasse
La Grenouille

French Bistros
27 Montrachet
25 Jo Jo
24 Alison on Dominick
Chez Michallet
23 Capsouto Frères
La Bouillabaisse

Greek
26 Milos
25 Periyali
24 Elias Corner
23 Molyvos
Telly's Taverna
Ithaka

Hamburgers
22 Wollensky's Grill
Corner Bistro
'21' Club
21 City Hall
Island Burgers
19 Cal's

Hotel Dining
28 Jean Georges/Trump Int'l
27 Lespinasse/St. Regis
26 La Caravelle/Shoreham
Le Cirque 2000/NY Palace
24 Le Régence/Plaza Athénée
Roy's NY/Marriott Fin. Ctr.

Improved
23 Mr. K's
22 Thai House Cafe
Holy Basil
Sirabella's
Corner Bistro
21 Da Tommaso

Indian
23 Dawat
22 Salaam Bombay
Jackson Diner
Shaan
21 Haveli
Raga

Italian
27 Il Mulino/Aquila
26 Babbo/multi
Felidia/Trieste
25 Pic. Venezia/Venice
Il Giglio/Rome
Da Umberto/Florence
Gennaro/Lipari
Don Peppe/multi
24 Rao's/Naples
Il Nido/Lucca
Il Tinello/Florence
Tuscany Grill/Florence
Cucina/Florence
Pó/Pistoia
Roberto's/Naples

Japanese
28 Nobu
27 Nobu, Next Door
Tomoe Sushi
26 Sushi of Gari
Blue Ribbon Sushi
Sushisay

Korean
24 Kum Gang San
23 Hangawi
21 Won Jo
Woo Chon
20 Kang Suh
Dok Suni's

14

Kosher
22 Second Avenue Deli
Tevere 84
21 Haikara Grill
Pongal
Levana
20 Le Marais

Late Dining
25 Blue Ribbon
23 Raoul's
22 Wollensky's Grill
Balthazar
First
21 NY Noodle Town

Mediterranean
26 Picholine
24 Verbena
23 Savoy
22 Il Buco
21 Gus' Figs Bistro
Spartina

Mexican/Tex-Mex
24 Maya
23 Rosa Mexicano
22 Zarela
Mi Cocina
Zócalo
21 Rocking Horse

Middle Eastern
22 Oznot's Dish
21 Moustache
Salam Cafe
20 Layla
19 Al Bustan
Persepolis

Newcomers/Rated
27 Nobu, Next Door
Café Boulud
26 Babbo
Tabla
25 Veritas
Eleven Madison Park

Newcomers/Unrated
Atlas
Beacon
Cello
Danube
Five Points
Local

Noodle Shops
25 Honmura An
21 NY Noodle Town
Big Wong
20 Sweet-n-Tart Cafe
Onigashima
Sobaya

People-Watching
27 La Grenouille
Nobu, Next Door
26 Babbo
25 Blue Ribbon
24 Bond Street
22 Balthazar

Pizza
26 Grimaldi's
25 Nick's
Lombardi's
23 Denino's
21 Little Italy Pizza
Totonno

Power Scenes
28 Daniel
26 Four Seasons
24 Rao's
23 Patroon
22 '21' Club
20 Regency (breakfast)

Private Rooms
28 Le Bernardin
27 La Grenouille
Gramercy Tavern
La Côte Basque
Oceana
26 Four Seasons

Pub Dining
22 Wollensky's Grill
Corner Bistro
21 Keens Steakhouse
20 O'Nieal's Grand St.
18 Waterfront Ale House
17 Neary's

Quick Fixes
26 Soup Kitchen Int'l, Al's
25 Pearl Oyster Bar
22 Second Avenue Deli
Blue Ribbon Bakery
20 Carnegie Deli
Cosi Sandwich Bar

Top Food

Seafood
28 Le Bernardin
27 Oceana
26 Milos
25 Aquagrill
   Manhattan Ocean Club
   Pearl Oyster Bar

Sleepers
25 Ponticello
24 S'Agapo
23 Kam Chueh
   Istana
   Zula
22 Veronica

South American
25 Patria/Nuevo Latino
23 Calle Ocho/Latin Am.
21 Chur. Plataforma/Brazilian
   Pampa/Argentinean
   Chimichurri/Argentinean
20 Cabana/Cuban-Carib.

Southern/Soul
20 Shark Bar
   Jezebel
   Lola
   Soul Fixins'
   Virgil's Real BBQ
19 Mardi Gras

Spanish
23 Bolo
22 Toledo
   Marichu (Basque)
   El Cid
   El Charro
21 Solera

Steakhouses
28 Peter Luger
25 Sparks
   Palm
24 Post House
23 Morton's of Chicago
   Smith & Wollensky

Sunday Dinner
28 Peter Luger
   Nobu
27 Union Square Cafe
   Gotham Bar & Grill
   Café Boulud
26 Picholine

Tasting Menus
28 Daniel ($105 & up)
   Nobu ($60)
   Chanterelle ($89)
   Jean Georges ($115)
27 Lespinasse ($125)
   La Grenouille ($110)

Thai
25 Vong
23 Planet Thailand
   Thailand
   Q, a Thai Bistro
22 Thai House Cafe
   Holy Basil

Trips to the Country*
29 Xaviar's, NY
28 Restaurant du Village, CT
   La Panetière, NY
   Cavey's, CT
   Jeffrey's, NJ
27 Mill River Inn, LI

24-Hour
24 Kum Gang San
21 Won Jo
   Woo Chon
20 Kang Suh
   Uncle George's
18 Florent

Vegetarian
27 Café Boulud
23 Hangawi
21 Josie's
   Pongal
   Vatan
   Mavalli Palace

Vietnamese
23 Vietnam
22 Saigon Grill
   Le Colonial
   Nha Trang
21 Rain
   Indochine

Wild Cards
25 Aquavit/Scandinavian
   Blue Ribbon/Eclectic
23 China Grill/Eclectic
22 Blue Ribbon Bakery/Eclectic
   Nyonya/Malaysian
   Pão!/Portuguese

---

* See our just-published *Zagat Long Island*, *New Jersey* and
  Connecticut/Southern New York State Surveys which cover nearly
  2,500 restaurants.

Top Food by Neighborhood

Chelsea/Garment Dist.
25 Da Umberto
24 Kum Gang San
23 Tonic
22 Le Madri
   El Cid
   Gascogne

Chinatown
25 Canton
23 Thailand
   Vietnam
22 Joe's Shanghai
   Wong Kee
   Nha Trang

East Village
24 Iso
   Il Bagatto
23 Hasaki
   Veniero's
22 Second Avenue Deli
   I Coppi

Flatiron/Union Sq.
27 Union Square Cafe
   Gramercy Tavern
25 Veritas
   Periyali
   Patria
24 Mesa Grill

Gramercy/Madison Park
26 Tabla
25 Yama
   Union Pacific
   Eleven Madison Park
24 Verbena
23 I Trulli

Greenwich Village
27 Il Mulino
   Gotham Bar & Grill
   Tomoe Sushi
26 Babbo
25 Pearl Oyster Bar
   Taka

Midtown – East 40s & 50s
27 Lespinasse
   La Grenouille
   Oceana
26 Four Seasons
   March
   Lutèce

Midtown – West 40s & 50s
28 Le Bernardin
27 La Côte Basque
26 La Caravelle
   Milos
25 Manhattan Ocean Club
   Aquavit

Murray Hill
24 Coach House
23 Hangawi
22 Asia de Cuba
   Toledo
   Sonia Rose
   Water Club

Outer Boroughs
28 Peter Luger/Bklyn
25 Pic. Venezia/Qns
   Don Peppe/Qns
24 Kum Gang San/Qns
   River Cafe/Bklyn
   Cooking with Jazz/Qns

SoHo/Little Italy
26 Blue Ribbon Sushi
25 Aquagrill
   Blue Ribbon
   Honmura An
24 Alison on Dominick
   Quilty's

TriBeCa/Downtown
28 Nobu
   Chanterelle
27 Nobu, Next Door
   Montrachet
26 Bouley Bakery
25 Il Giglio

Upper East Side – 60s & Up
28 Daniel
   Aureole
27 Café Boulud
26 Sushi of Gari
25 Jo Jo
24 Park Avenue Cafe

Upper West Side – 60s & Up
28 Jean Georges
26 Picholine
25 Gennaro
24 Café des Artistes
   Terrace
   Shun Lee

Top 50 Decor Ranking

28 Lespinasse
27 La Grenouille
River Cafe
Le Bernardin
Four Seasons
Windows on the World
One if by Land, TIBS
King Cole Bar
Le Régence
Café des Artistes
FireBird
26 Tabla
Water's Edge
Aureole
La Côte Basque
Chanterelle
Daniel
Café Botanica
Box Tree
View
Park View at Boathouse
Chez Es Saada
Terrace
Le Cirque 2000
Hudson River Club

Gramercy Tavern
Top of the Tower
Jean Georges
Carlyle
Kings' Carriage House
Nirvana
25 Aquavit
Café Pierre
Union Pacific
Eleven Madison Park
Hangawi
Fifty Seven Fifty Seven
La Caravelle
Tavern on the Green
Vong
Palio
Water Club
March
Morgan Court Cafe
Mark's
Gotham Bar & Grill
Casa La Femme
Mr. K's
Palm Court
Asia de Cuba

Gardens

Barbetta
Barolo
Bottino
Bryant Park
Dolphins
Gascogne
Grove
I Coppi
I Trulli

La Nonna
Le Jardin Bistro
Marichu
Metropolitan Cafe
Surya
Tavern on the Green
Va Tutto!
Verbena
Vittorio Cucina

Old NY

1716 Historic Old Bermuda
1726 One if by Land, TIBS
1794 Bridge Cafe
1868 Landmark Tavern
1868 Old Homestead
1879 Gage & Tollner

1885 Keens Steakhouse
1892 Old Town Bar
1907 Palm Court
1913 Oyster Bar (Gr. Cent.)
1920 Ye Waverly Inn
1929 '21' Club

Romantic

Box Tree
Café des Artistes
Candela
Casa La Femme
Cello
Erminia
Jezebel
King Cole Bar
La Belle Epoque
La Grenouille
Le Refuge

Mark's
Mercer Kitchen
Mr. K's
One if by Land, TIBS
Rafaella
River Cafe
Temple Bar
Terrace
Torch
ViceVersa
Water's Edge

Rooms

Aquavit	Hudson River Club
Aureole	Jean Georges
Babbo	La Côte Basque
Balthazar	La Fourchette
Bouley Bakery	La Grenouille
Calle Ocho	Le Bernardin
Carlyle	Le Cirque 2000
Chez Es Saada	Lespinasse
Circo	Lutèce
FireBird	March
Four Seasons	Milos
Fressen	Palio (bar)
Gage & Tollner	Ruby Foo's
Gotham Bar & Grill	Union Pacific
Gramercy Tavern	Zen Palate/Union Sq.

Views

American Park	River Cafe
Bateaux NY	Spirit Cruises
Bryant Park Grill	Tavern on the Green
Foley's Fish House	Terrace
14 Wall Street	Top of the Tower
Grill Room	View
Harbour Lights	Water Club
Hudson River Club	Water's Edge
Michael Jordan's	Wild Blue
Nirvana	Windows on the World
Park View at Boathouse	World Yacht

Top 50 Service Ranking

28 Le Bernardin	Café Pierre
27 Lespinasse	Carlyle
Chanterelle	Nobu
Jean Georges	Hangawi
26 Daniel	Mark's
Four Seasons	Picholine
La Grenouille	Volare*
Aureole	Aquavit
La Côte Basque	Il Tinello
Gramercy Tavern	Union Pacific
Union Square Cafe	La Réserve
Lutèce	Mr. K's
March	Erminia
25 La Caravelle	Acappella
Café Boulud	Roy's NY
Le Cirque 2000	Babbo
Oceana	*23* Café des Artistes
Gotham Bar & Grill	River Cafe
Veritas	Terrace
Le Perigord	Petrossian
Eleven Madison Park	Fifty Seven Fifty Seven
Tabla	Nobu, Next Door
Le Régence	Leopard
24 Montrachet	Il Mulino
One if by Land, TIBS	Bouley Bakery

---

* Tied with the restaurant listed directly above it.

Best Buys

Top Bangs For The Buck*

These lists reflect the best dining values in our *Survey*. They are produced by dividing the cost of a meal into the combined ratings for food, decor and service.

Full-Service Restaurants

1. Mama's Food Shop/*American*
2. Sweet-n-Tart Cafe/*Chinese*
3. Rose of India/*Indian*
4. Big Wong/*Chinese*
5. Planet Thailand/*Thai*
6. Bo-Ky/*Vietnamese*
7. Rice/*Eclectic*
8. Veselka/*East European*
9. Lamarca/*Italian*
10. Moustache/*Middle Eastern*
11. Excellent Dumpling/*Chinese*
12. Thai House Cafe/*Thai*
13. Angelica Kitchen/*Vegetarian*
14. Jackson Diner/*Indian*
15. Dojo/*Health Food*
16. Kitchenette/*American*
17. Flor de Mayo/*Peruvian*
18. Route 66 Cafe/*Eclectic*
19. Tsampa/*Tibetan*
20. Burger Heaven/*American*
21. Vegetarian Paradise/*Chinese*
22. Wong Kee/*Chinese*
23. L'Annam/*Vietnamese*
24. New Pasteur/*Vietnamese*
25. Sam's Noodle/*Chinese*
26. Noodles on 28/*Chinese*
27. O Padeiro/*Portuguese*
28. Thailand/*Thai*
29. Old Devil Moon/*Southern*
30. ABC Parlour Cafe/*American*
31. El Pollo/*Peruvian*
32. Vietnam/*Vietnamese*
33. Teresa's/*Polish*
34. Odessa/*East European*
35. Kum Gang San/*Korean*
36. Yaffa's/*Eclectic*
37. Tea Box/*Japanese*
38. Cafe Asean/*Pan-Asian*
39. Nha Trang/*Vietnamese*
40. Quantum Leap/*Vegetarian*
41. Chez Brigitte/*French*
42. Saigon Grill/*Vietnamese*
43. Sammy's Noodle/*Chinese*
44. Chanpen/*Thai*
45. Nyonya/*Malaysian*
46. Radio Perfecto/*American*
47. Mamá Mexico/*Mexican*
48. Good Enough to Eat/*American*
49. Stingy Lulu's/*American*
50. Katz's/*Deli*

Single Item Specialty Shops

1. Emack & Bolio's/*ice cream*
2. Krispy Kreme/*doughnuts*
3. Amy's Bread/*baked goods*
4. Ess-a-Bagel/*deli*
5. Daily Soup/*soup*
6. Little Italy/*pizza*
7. Papaya King/*hot dogs*
8. Peanut Butter & Co./*sandwiches*
9. Dt•ut/*coffeehse.*
10. Gray's Papaya/*hot dogs*
11. Eisenberg/*sandwiches*
12. Hale & Hearty Soups/*soup*
13. Grey Dog's Coffee/*coffeehse.*
14. Cosi/*sandwiches*
15. Veniero's/*Italian pastry*
16. Cupcake Cafe/*pastry*
17. Soul Fixins'/*Southern*
18. Once Upon a Tart/*pastry*
19. City Bakery/*American*
20. Joe's/*pizza*
21. Freddie & Pepper's/*pizza*
22. Thé Adoré/*sandwiches*
23. Souperman/*soup*
24. Cafe Lalo/*coffeehse.*
25. Emerald Planet/*wraps*
26. Island Burgers/*burgers*
27. Soup Kitchen Int'l, Al's/*soup*
28. Nick's/*pizza*
29. Grimaldi's/*pizza*
30. Ferrara/*Italian pastry*
31. Vinnie's/*pizza*
32. Corner Bistro/*burgers*
33. Edgar's Cafe/*coffeehse.*
34. Two Boots/*pizza*
35. Columbus Bakery/*American*
36. Fresco on the Go/*Italian*
37. Pintaile's/*pizza*
38. Tossed/*salads*
39. La Taza de Oro/*Puerto Rican*
40. Burritoville/*Mexican*

---

* We have excluded the coffeehouse chains from the above lists.

Under $40 Prix Fixe Menus*

• Lunch •

Ambassador Grill	$20.00	La Réserve	$32.00
Anche Vivolo	13.95	L'Ecole	17.99
Angelo & Maxie's	20.00	Le Perigord	32.00
Arqua	20.00	Le Quercy	21.00
Artos	18.50	Le Régence	26.00
Aureole	33.00	Les Pyrénées	19.00
Becco	16.95	Levana	20.00
Bellew	20.00	Le Veau D'Or	19.95
Bistro du Nord	12.95	Lutèce	38.00
Bouley Bakery	35.00	Manhattan Grille	17.95
Café Boulud	29.00	Mark's	20.00
Café des Artistes	23.00	Montrachet (Fri. only)	20.00
Cafe Luxembourg	20.00	Mr. K's	25.00
Capsouto Frères	20.00	Nirvana	16.95
Captain's Table	24.00	Nobu	20.00
Cent'Anni	14.95	Novitá	20.00
Chanterelle	35.00	Palm	20.00
Chez Suzette	11.95	Park Bistro	24.50
Chianti (Manh.)	20.00	Patria	24.95
Chin Chin	20.00	Petrossian	25.00
Chur. Plataforma	27.95	Picholine	24.00
Cinquanta	26.00	Quatorze Bis	16.00
Duane Park Cafe	21.00	Quilty's	20.00
Felidia	29.50	René Pujol	28.00
Ferrier	19.95	Sardi's (Wed. & Sat.)	29.50
Gemelli	15.50	Shaan	15.95
Giambelli	27.00	Shun Lee Palace	20.00
Gotham Bar & Grill	20.00	Sonia Rose	27.00
Gramercy Tavern	33.00	Tavern on the Green	20.00
Halcyon	20.00	Toscana	14.95
Hangawi	24.95	Tribeca Grill	19.98
Honmura An	18.00	Trois Jean	20.00
Il Menestrello	30.00	Tse Yang	25.75
Istana	25.00	Turkish Kitchen	13.95
Jean Georges (Nougatine)	28.00	'21' Club	29.00
Jo Jo	28.00	Ulrika's	21.00
Kings' Carriage House	12.95	Union Pacific	29.99
La Caravelle	36.00	Veritas	29.00
La Côte Basque	35.00	Vong	28.00
La Mediterranée	15.95	Water Club	20.00
La Petite Auberge	22.95		

---

* This list shows the lowest prix fixe menus available; there may be higher-priced options. Since prix fixe prices may change or be canceled at any time, check on them when reserving. Nearly all Indians serve an AYCE (all-you-can-eat) buffet lunch for $15 or less.

• Dinner •

Restaurant	Price	Restaurant	Price
Alison on Dominick*	$20.00	Le Colonial*	$24.00
Ambassador Grill	30.00	Lenox Room*	19.95
Anche Vivolo*	21.95	Le Quercy**	25/30
Aquavit*	39.00	Les Pyrénées	28.00
Arqua	25.00	Le Tableau*	18.00
Artos*	25.00	Levana	18.00
Atlantic Grill*	18.98	Le Veau D'Or	19.95
Bar Six*	18.50	Manhattan Grille*	28.95
Bay Leaf*	20.95	Mark's*	32.00
Becco	21.95	Michael's*	32.50
Bombay Palace*	19.95	Mi Cocina*	20.00
Brasserie Julien*	12.50	Montebello*	26.75
Café Botanica*	38.00	Montrachet	34.00
Cafe Centro	26.00	Nino's	24.95
Café des Artistes	37.50	Nirvana*	29.90
Cafe du Pont*	20.00	Park Bistro*	24.50
Cafe Luxembourg	35.00	Pasha*	22.95
Café Pierre*	34.00	Payard Pâtisserie*	30.00
Cent'Anni*	23.95	Petrossian	35.00
Charlotte	36.50	Pitchoune	20.00
Chelsea Bistro & Bar*	28.50	René Pujol	39.00
Chez Michallet*	21.95	Riodizio	28.95
Chianti (Manh.)*	27.50	Russian Samovar*	25.00
Christer's*	27.00	San Domenico*	32.50
Chur. Plantation	29.00	Screening Room	30.00
Chur. Plataforma	32.95	Shaan*	21.95
Cibo	27.95	Supper Club*	25.00
Cinquanta	26.00	Table d'Hôte*	19.95
Cooking with Jazz*	15.00	Tapika*	26.00
Demi*	19.99	Tavern on the Green*	31.50
Ferrier*	19.95	Torre di Pisa*	26.95
FireBird*	36.50	Toscana*	22.00
Gascogne*	27.00	Trois Canards*	19.95
Halcyon**	36/40	Trois Jean*	25.00
Hangawi	30.00	Tropica	29.00
Henry's End*	20.00	Turkish Kitchen	27.50
Il Menestrello	30.00	'21' Club*	33.00
Indochine*	25.00	Two Two Two*	30.00
Kings' Carriage House	39.00	Vatan	19.95
La Boite en Bois**	29/32	Vivolo*	21.95
La Mediterranée**	25/29	Vong*	38.00
La Petite Auberge	22.95	Water Club	28.00
La Réserve*	39.50	Wilkinson's Seafood	22.00
Le Beaujolais	21.00	Willow*	20.00
L'Ecole	25.95	Windows on the World*	40.00

* Pre-theater only.
** Prices divided by a slash are for pre-theater and normal hours.

Alphabetical Directory of Restaurants

F | D | S | C

ABC Parlour Cafe [S] — 15 | 21 | 13 | $20

38 E. 19th St. (bet. B'way & Park Ave. S.), 212-677-2233

◪ Takeout options extend to "the tables and chairs" at this Flatiron furniture store cafe with "quaint", "Martha Stewart redux" decor (all for sale); the New American "nibbles" and desserts are fine "for casual eats", but beware "where's my waitress?" service.

Abigael's [S] — 18 | 16 | 17 | $36

9 E. 37th St. (bet. 5th & Madison Aves.), 212-725-0130
1407 Broadway (bet. 38th & 39th Sts.), 212-575-1407

■ "Not for the nosher", this "comfortable" Murray Hill kosher "surprise" (with a big new Garment District sibling) offers "creative" New American fare that's "upscale" in style and price; a few insist it's "nothing remarkable", but "if you gotta go kosher", it's a good bet.

Acacia [S] — – | – | – | E

217 E. 59th St. (bet. 2nd & 3rd Aves.), 212-751-5557

Try this undiscovered new East Side brasserie for one of the best and biggest burgers around (buffalo, ostrich or sirloin) and flavorful, if a tad pricey, French fare; besides, it's warm, friendly and handy as a post-Bloomie's pit stop.

Acadia Parish Cajun Cafe (Bklyn) **[S]** — 18 | 12 | 17 | $25

148 Atlantic Ave. (bet. Clinton & Henry Sts.), 718-624-5154

■ The "bayou meets Brooklyn" at this "crowded as hell" Cajun where "major portions" of "tasty" "N'Awlins eats" ("try the alligator tips") come at "decent" prices with "fast, witty" service; despite "charmless" decor, BYO helps "let the good food roll."

Acappella — 24 | 21 | 24 | $49

1 Hudson St. (bet. Chambers St. & W. B'way), 212-240-0163

■ "Overlooked" but "one of the better Downtown places", this "romantic" TriBeCa Northern Italian has "superattentive" service and "delicious food, if you can see it" in the "dark" setting; the tab hits "too high a note" for some, but it's in tune with the quality.

Acquario ◐[S]⊄ — ▽ 21 | 18 | 18 | $33

5 Bleecker St. (bet. Bowery & Elizabeth St.), 212-260-4666

■ This "low-key" NoHo newcomer "feels like a cozy little corner of a European town" and has an "interesting menu" of "reasonably priced" Mediterranean fare including "superb seafood"; though "cramped" and "noisy", it's making a good start.

Adrienne [S] — 22 | 24 | 23 | $56

Peninsula Hotel, 700 Fifth Ave. (55th St.), 212-903-3918

■ A "real sleeper", this "beautifully renovated" hotel dining room is a "quiet" "retreat" from Midtown mayhem, offering American-French prix fixe menus and "attentive service"; if a few claim you pay "lots to be bored", more call it "a winner" and wonder "where is everybody?"

Aesop's Tables (Staten Island) **[S]** — 21 | 19 | 19 | $35

1233 Bay St. (Maryland Ave.), 718-720-2005

■ It's not a fable: this very "charming" place offers "unique" New American–Med fare, moderate prices and "friendly service" in a "most unlikely neighborhood" (that's Manhattanese for Staten Island); the interior can feel "cramped", but there's a "lovely garden."

Afghan Kebab House — 17 | 10 | 15 | $18

1345 Second Ave. (bet. 70th & 71st Sts.), 212-517-2776 [S]
764 Ninth Ave. (bet. 51st & 52nd Sts.), 212-307-1612 ⊄
155 W. 46th St. (bet. 6th & 7th Aves.), 212-768-3875 [S]
74-16 37th Ave. (bet. 74th & 75th Sts.), Queens, 718-565-0471 [S]

◪ "No kabull", these "bare-bones", dress-down Afghans may look "scary" and some are "just wide enough" for a kebab, but they're "tasty", "cheap" and "quick", so BYO, "close your eyes" and dig in.

Agora [S] 17 | 13 | 16 | $29
1586 First Ave. (bet. 82nd & 83rd Sts.), 212-452-2752
■ "A nice variation in Italianville" is how Upper Eastsiders describe this "tasty" Turkish option; it's "comfortable", "low-key" and "trying very hard to please" with "no airfare."

Alaia ◐[S] 19 | 20 | 17 | $45
59 Fifth Ave. (bet. 12th & 13th Sts.), 212-242-9709
◪ "Baldwins in black", "Elton John at the next table", "attitude" all over – yes, it's "a trendy new bar scene", but there's also "surprisingly good" (if "a tad expensive") Med-American food at the Baldwin brothers' "cool" bi-level Villager; hipsters scoff: "people from Staten Island."

Al Bustan [S] 19 | 16 | 19 | $34
827 Third Ave. (bet. 50th & 51st Sts.), 212-759-5933
■ "Great appetizers" make for "an exotic tasting party" at this Midtown Lebanese; prices are "reasonable" and service is "attentive", but creamy decor that's "attractive" to some seems "sterile" to others.

Al Di La Trattoria (Brooklyn) **[S]** – | – | – | M
248 Fifth Ave. (Carroll St.), 718-783-4565
Behind an unmarked facade, this Park Slope yearling "find" has a simple but tasteful setting and "simply delicious" Northern Italian fare that's fairly "cheap"; its rep is growing fast, so come early or wait.

Alex & Max's ▽ 17 | 17 | 18 | $30
38 W. 39th St. (bet. 5th & 6th Aves.), 212-398-0350
■ "Very good for the neighborhood" is the early word on this Garment District newcomer with a seafood-focused New American menu; "service is friendly", there's a "lively bar" and it's handy for lunch.

Algonquin Hotel [S] 16 | 21 | 19 | $43
Algonquin Hotel, 59 W. 44th St. (bet. 5th & 6th Aves.), 212-840-6800
◪ Dorothy Parker and Co. might hoot to hear that after a big-bucks revamp, their old Theater District haunt is "still stodgy", though it's "better-looking" with a "slight improvement" in the American food; as always, it's "great for drinks", "nostalgia" and Oak Room cabaret acts and "the busloads from NJ love it."

Alison on Dominick Street [S] 24 | 22 | 23 | $53
38 Dominick St. (bet. Hudson & Varick Sts.), 212-727-1188
■ Finding this SoHo "hideaway" is the tough part, but it's worth it to enjoy "superb" Country French fare in a "velvety, romantic" setting that's "better than 1-800-Flowers" when you want results.

Alley's End [S] 19 | 20 | 19 | $33
311 W. 17th St. (bet. 8th & 9th Aves.), 212-627-8899
■ A "sense of 'noboby else knows'" adds charm to this "hidden" Chelsea basement with "fantasy" decor, a glassed-in garden and "solid" if "not memorable" New American fare; a "great date place", it feels "like you've stumbled into another world."

Alouette [S] 21 | 16 | 17 | $38
2588 Broadway (bet. 97th & 98th Sts.), 212-222-6808
■ "What's a classy bistro like this doing on Upper B'way?" ask those surprised by this "much-needed" "haven" offering "creative", "good value" French fare and "casually stylish" decor; despite "tight" quarters and service "lapses", it's "a real asset" north of 96th Street.

Alva ◐ 19 | 17 | 18 | $37
36 E. 22nd St. (bet. B'way & Park Ave. S.), 212-228-4399
◪ It's "a little cramped and curiously dark" given its namesake (Thomas *Alva* Edison) and lightbulb decor, but there's "enlightening" New American fare on the "limited menu" of this Flatiron fave; the bar up front is "great if you like cigars and strong drinks" while conversing.

F | D | S | C

Amaranth ◐[S] ▽ 14 | 15 | 14 | $43

21 E. 62nd St. (bet. 5th & Madison Aves.), 212-980-6700

◪ Where Arcadia used to be, this "trendy", "very Euro" new East Side "scene" with a "kissy-kissy", dancing-on-tables, noisy crowd and nearly irrelevant Mediterranean food is keeping the neighbors up with its bustling sidewalk tables; "forget good service unless you're a celeb" or a model, which almost everyone seems to be.

Amarone ◐[S] 20 | 15 | 19 | $31

686 Ninth Ave. (bet. 47th & 48th Sts.), 212-245-6060

■ "Excellent for pre-theater" and the "presentation of fresh pastas is a show in itself" at this Hell's Kitchen "bargain for homemade Italian" with simple but "cheering" decor and an "eager-to-please staff"; the "wine is fine" too.

Ambassador Grill [S] 19 | 20 | 20 | $45

Regal UN Plaza Hotel, 1 UN Plaza (44th St., bet. 1st & 2nd Aves.), 212-702-5014

◪ Critics find it "as stimulating as a Non-Aligned Movement meeting", but this "brass and glass" hotel New American by the UN is "quiet, comfortable" and "expensive", thus "perfect for diplomats"; P.S. its bountiful brunch could inspire "world peace."

America ◐[S] 13 | 14 | 14 | $25

9 E. 18th St. (bet. B'way & 5th Ave.), 212-505-2110

◪ With a "jack of all trades, master of none" menu stretching "from sea to shining sea", this "enormous", pulsating, stadium-sized Union Square American can be "headache-producing", but the food and prices are "decent" and it's "terrific for the PB&J set", "large groups" and "Aunt Minnie from Peoria."

American Park at The Battery [S] 20 | 23 | 18 | $41

Battery Park (opp. 17 State St.), 212-809-5508

■ "Go" for the "amazing" view, "stay" for the "delicious seafood" at this Battery Park "gem" with "sleek" decor and a "wonderful" patio; despite "spotty" service and "sticker-shock" prices, it's a "great way to escape Manhattan."

Amy's Bread [S] 23 | 12 | 16 | $12

672 Ninth Ave. (bet. 46th & 47th Sts.), 212-977-2670 ⌧

Chelsea Mkt., 75 Ninth Ave. (bet. 15th & 16th Sts.), 212-462-4338

■ "Give us this day our Amy's bread" chant worshipers of the "zesty", "interesting" loaves, "good sandwiches" and treats at these "cute", low-budget bakery/cafes; "go early for choices and seats."

An American Place [S] 23 | – | 21 | $47

Benjamin Hotel, 565 Lexington Ave. (bet. 50th & 51st Sts.), 212-888-5650

◪ Larry Forgione's American "classic" moved post-*Survey* to a handsome, wood-paneled Midtown space; fans "pledge allegiance" to Forgione's "first-class" fare, but critics cite "absentee chef syndrome", which is particularly noticeable given the open kitchen.

Anche Vivolo ◐ 18 | 16 | 19 | $35

222 E. 58th St. (bet. 2nd & 3rd Aves.), 212-308-0112

■ This "cozy", "blessedly quiet" East Side Italian draws an "older" crowd, but that's because they know "value" when they see it in the form of "solid" food, "attentive" service and prix fixe "bargains."

André [S] – | – | – | M

242 W. 56th St. (bet. B'way & 8th Ave.), 212-307-0700

Located in West Midtown, this new, moderately tabbed duplex French bistro has an unprepossessing, work-in-progress interior, but chef-owner André Lincy unquestionably knows how to cook, based on his years of experience behind the stove at Pierre au Tunnel.

	F	D	S	C
Andrusha [S]	17	15	18	$34

1370 Lexington Ave. (bet. 90th & 91st Sts.), 212-369-9374
◪ Fans of this Russian–Central European cafe tout it for "good Mittel Europa" fare in "modest" digs near the 92nd Street Y; it may be "a bit heavy" and "pricey", but it's "different" and "trying hard."

	F	D	S	C
Angelica Kitchen [S]⊅	19	14	16	$19

300 E. 12th St. (bet. 1st & 2nd Aves.), 212-228-2909
◪ "When you repent and go healthy", try this East Village vegan's "dream" serving "creative", "tasty" dishes in a "comforting wood" setting; cynics speak of "punishment food" and "too much money for steamed kale", but they're outvoted by those who "feel saintly."

	F	D	S	C
Angelina's (Staten Island) [S] ▽	21	18	19	$43

26 Jefferson Blvd. (Annadale Rd.), 718-227-7100
■ A Staten Island strip mall "surprise", this "Manhattan-type" Italian offers "excellent food and service" in a "warm", "spacious" setting; prices are Manhattan-ish too, but even so it's "always jammed."

	F	D	S	C
Angelo & Maxie's ◐[S]	20	18	17	$42

233 Park Ave. S. (19th St.), 212-220-9200
◪ "Testosterone oozes" from this "trader-filled" Flatiron steakhouse where everything is "big": the steaks, cigars, drinks, noise and "bar scene"; the food's "good", but some say the place feels like "a chain" and "belongs on Long Island."

	F	D	S	C
Angelo's Coal Oven Pizza [S]	20	12	15	$18

117 W. 57th St. (bet. 6th & 7th Aves.), 212-333-4333
■ "Fine" coal-oven pizzas, "huge salads" and a cheerful setting make this a welcome option in a Midtown stretch lacking "reasonable", "quick" eats; it's handy "before Carnegie Hall" too.

	F	D	S	C
Angelo's of Mulberry Street ◐[S]	19	14	17	$34

146 Mulberry St. (bet. Grand & Hester Sts.), 212-966-1277
◪ It's "touristy" and you may "wait for a table", but "if garlic and pasta are your thing", this Little Italy "old-timer" with flowing "red sauce" can satisfy; critics claim it's "40 years past its peak."

	F	D	S	C
Anglers & Writers ◐[S]	17	20	18	$24

420 Hudson St. (St. Luke's Pl.), 212-675-0810
■ Many a West Villager spends "Sunday AM angling for a table" at this "cozy" cafe with "country cottage" decor and "homey" American fare that's "not special but fine" especially for brunch or tea; in sum, a "pleasant spot to sit, relax and see what's biting."

	F	D	S	C
Annie's [S]	16	15	15	$24

1381 Third Ave. (bet. 78th & 79th Sts.), 212-327-4853
◪ The East Side "stroller set" ("borrow a baby if without one") rolls into Jim McMullen's "upscale coffee shop" for "good brunch" and American "basics" in a "bright, bustling" setting; if "nothing special", it's "easier than cooking at home" and almost cheaper.

	F	D	S	C
Antonio [S]	19	17	21	$35

140 W. 13th St. (bet. 6th & 7th Aves.), 212-645-4606
■ Something of a "secret", this "tranquil" West Village Italian offers "big portions" of "good food" and service that "couldn't be nicer"; while a few feel "something's missing" (maybe it "needs a decorator" and lower prices), most have no complaints.

	F	D	S	C
AQUAGRILL [S]	25	19	21	$44

210 Spring St. (6th Ave.), 212-274-0505
■ "Makes other seafooders look like guppies" say fans of this SoHo "star", a "delight for the price" given its "fresh, innovative" dishes, "awesome oysters" and "great brunch", all graciously served in a chicly "funky" setting with a terrace; no wonder it gets "noisy" and "crowded."

AQUAVIT ⬧

25 | 25 | 24 | $55

13 W. 54th St. (bet. 5th & 6th Aves.), 212-307-7311

■ Chef Marcus Samuelsson "makes magic" at this "Scandinavian paradise" in Midtown, where the "exquisite" fare ("salmon more ways than you can imagine") is as "crisp and pure" as the "dramatic" atrium space with birch trees and a "mesmerizing waterfall"; it's far from cheap ($64 prix fixe dinner), but the upstairs cafe is a "great deal."

Archives (Brooklyn) ⬧

▽ 20 | 21 | 20 | $36

NY Marriott Brooklyn, 333 Adams St. (Willoughby St.), 718-222-6543

■ "You forget you're in Brooklyn" at this Downtown yearling with "interesting" Eclectic food, "concerned service" and a "civilized" ambiance; it's a "well-meaning" effort, even if some find it "expensive."

Areo (Brooklyn) ◗⬧

23 | 18 | 19 | $38

8424 Third Ave. (85th St.), 718-238-0079

■ An "all-star" on Bay Ridge's "restaurant row" that's "always packed" with a "foxy"/"studly" crowd enjoying "delicious" Italian food and "flirty service" in a "pretty room"; expect noise and "long" weekend waits.

Arqua ⬧

22 | 20 | 20 | $44

281 Church St. (White St.), 212-334-1888

■ "Are we in Tuscany?" ask diners transported by the "always good, sometimes transcendent" food and "simple" yet "elegant" yellow-walled setting at this TriBeCa Northern Italian; it's pricey and "can be noisy" but generally makes for a "lovely, leisurely" meal.

Arté ⬧

19 | 19 | 19 | $36

21 E. Ninth St. (bet. 5th Ave. & University Pl.), 212-473-0077

☑ The "fireplace adds a romantic touch" and there's an "adorable" garden at this "cozy" Village Italian; though some report "uneven" food and service, most find it a "charmer" that's "very good for the price."

Artos

20 | 21 | 19 | $39

307 E. 53rd St. (bet. 1st & 2nd Aves.), 212-838-0007

■ "One of the best-kept secrets on the East Side", this "chic" Midtown Greek offers "super fish", "sensational" brick-oven breads and other "fab" fare plus "warm service" in a "spacious, airy" setting; so why is it "never packed"?

Arturo's Pizzeria ◗⬧

19 | 11 | 14 | $18

106 W. Houston St. (Thompson St.), 212-677-3820

☑ "Dark" and "divey" "Village joint" serving some of "NYC's best" coal-oven pizzas in a "beatnik" atmosphere with live jazz some nights; it can be "way too crowded", but that's part of its "unique charm."

Artusi

20 | 18 | 21 | $39

36 W. 52nd St. (bet. 5th & 6th Aves.), 212-582-6900

■ With "first-rate" food, "excellent service" and "classy, understated decor", this "upscale" Midtown Italian is "perfect" for business lunch or a "quiet dinner"; still, a few find it "overpriced and unexceptional."

ASIA DE CUBA ◗⬧

22 | 25 | 19 | $47

Morgans Hotel, 237 Madison Ave. (bet. 37th & 38th Sts.), 212-726-7755

■ Murray Hill's "white wonder" remains a "sexy" scene with a hot crowd ("be prepared to feel inadequate") sipping "cool drinks" in a "sleek" Philippe Starck setting, but it also serves "very original and good" Asian-Cuban fare; dissenters cite "trendarama" "attitude."

Asti ◗⬧

– | – | – | M

13 E. 12th St. (bet. 5th Ave. & University Pl.), 212-741-9105

You can have Puccini with your pasta at this Village Italian fixture where opera and show tunes are belted out by the staff as well as pro singers; the food and ambiance may make you feel you've "crashed a wedding reception", but for most people it's a "fun" affair.

Astray Café 🖪
▽ 19 | 15 | 18 | $30
59 Horatio St. (Greenwich St.), 212-741-7030
■ "You don't have to be gay to feel welcome" at this "cozy" Village bistro that "keeps regulars happy" with "creative", well-priced American fare, "very friendly" service and "mega martinis" – after one of them, "everything seems good!"

ATLANTIC GRILL ◑🖪
22 | 19 | 19 | $41
1341 Third Ave. (bet. 76th & 77th Sts.), 212-988-9200
■ Wear your "Chanel suit" to this "upbeat", "classy" Eastsider where locals feed on "excellent", "imaginative" seafood including "chichi sushi"; the "price is right" too, hence it's "always jammed"; P.S. a "good deal of fishing goes on" at the teeming bar.

Atlas ◑🖪
– | – | – | VE
40 Central Park S. (bet. 5th & 6th Aves.), 212-759-9191
On a prime Central Park South site, this attractive, low-key Global American (i.e. New American with accents from around the world) newcomer with ruddy, muted decor has a pricey, limited menu that has captivated our early reporters; the wine list is an excellent value.

Au Mandarin 🖪
19 | 15 | 17 | $29
World Financial Ctr., 200 Vesey St. (West St.), 212-385-0313
☑ Many a Wall Streeter has this "upscale" Chinese programmed into their speed dial since it's "great for takeout" that's a "cut above" the norm; it's also "good for a business lunch", but some find the food "heavy on the grease" and "overpriced."

AUREOLE
28 | 26 | 26 | $68
34 E. 61st St. (bet. Madison & Park Aves.), 212-319-1660
■ "Deserves its halo" say devotees of Charles Palmer's East Side paragon that's "still one of the tops", offering "wondrous", albeit pricey, New American food (rated No. 1 for that cuisine), architectural desserts worthy of "MoMA" and "superb service" in a duplex townhouse that's lovelier than ever after a post-*Survey* update by Adam Tihany; if some find it "a bit crowded" and "stuffy", far more call it a "dining dream", especially the prix fixe lunch; dinner is $65 prix fixe only.

Au Troquet 🖪
20 | 19 | 20 | $40
320 W. 12th St. (Greenwich St.), 212-924-3413
■ Straight out of the "back alleys of Paris", this "cozy" far West Village bistro offers "romance, serenity" and "solid" food in a lace-curtained setting with "helpful" service; despite a few grumbles ("expensive", "needs sprucing up"), most are quite content.

Avenue ◑🖪
20 | 15 | 15 | $34
520 Columbus Ave. (85th St.), 212-579-3194
☑ "Love the food, but not the tight squeeze or ditsy" service typifies reactions to Scott Campbell's "noisy", "crowded" Upper West Side French-American bistro; still, it's a "welcome" option for "good value", "everyday" dining, including breakfast.

Avenue A ◑🖪
18 | 14 | 14 | $25
103 Ave. A (bet. 6th & 7th Sts.), 212-982-8109
☑ "Equal parts club, party and sushi" joint, this "hip" Japanese East Villager provides "fresh fish at good prices" in a "dark", "funky" setting staffed by "waiters with nose rings" and a "better DJ than in most clubs"; critics say "sushi and strobe lights are not a winning combo."

Azuri Cafe 🖪⇗
▽ 21 | 7 | 13 | $15
465 W. 51st St. (bet. 9th & 10th Aves.), 212-262-2920
☑ It's more "hole-in-the-wall" than cafe and service can be "abrupt", but you get "heaps" of "fresh, tasty" food at "low prices" at this Midtown West Middle Eastern; given the decor, takeout is popular.

	F	D	S	C
Ba Ba Malaysian ☾[S]≠ ▽	19	15	17	$22

53 Bayard St. (bet. Bowery & Mott Sts.), 212-766-1318
■ "Finally a Malaysian place with good food and decor" is the early word on this Chinatown newcomer with "generous portions" of "tasty", "innovative" fare; the staff is "ultra-friendly" and tabs are "cheap."

	F	D	S	C
BABBO ☾[S]	26	23	24	$56

110 Waverly Pl. (bet. MacDougal St. & 6th Ave.), 212-777-0303
■ "An instant hit for good reason", this Village Italian owned by Joe Bastianich (Becco, Frico Bar) and chef Mario Batali (Pó) was voted the most popular newcomer in the *Survey*; "absolutely delicious, inventive cuisine", "perfectly choreographed service" and a "beautiful" bi-level setting give rise to only one complaint – "too bad it's hard to get a table."

	F	D	S	C
Bacco ☾[S]	19	18	17	$36

150 Spring St. (bet. W. B'way & Wooster St.), 212-334-2338
◩ SoHo Tuscan country tavern with a wine cellar where fans find "fine food at a good price" served by "gorgeous waiters" in a "cozy ambiance"; dissenters dub the scene "loud and crowded."

	F	D	S	C
Baci Italian Restaurant (Bklyn) [S] ▽	21	17	19	$31

7107 Third Ave. (bet. 71st & 72nd Sts.), 718-836-5536
■ "Intimate" Bay Ridge Italian with "tasty", moderately priced food "accompanied by entertainment – the chef-owner sings" romantic classics in English, Italian and Spanish.

	F	D	S	C
Bagatelle [S] ▽	18	17	17	$26

12 St. Marks Pl. (bet. 2nd & 3rd Aves.), 212-674-1011
◩ East Village yearling offering New American cooking with an Irish accent (think Guinness stew) in a spacious, high-ceilinged setting; there's a plethora of boutique beers to choose from, as well as live jazz Sunday and Monday.

	F	D	S	C
Bali Nusa Indah [S]	18	11	17	$21

651 Ninth Ave. (bet. 45th & 46th Sts.), 212-265-2200
■ "Exotic" Indonesian Hell's Kitchen "hole-in-the-wall" that's "perfect for a cheap, pre-theater dinner"; most choose to overlook the "dark, depressing decor" in order to "go with the prix fixe sampler deal."

	F	D	S	C
BALTHAZAR ☾[S]	22	23	19	$47

80 Spring St. (bet. B'way & Crosby St.), 212-965-1414
■ "Amazingly still hot after two years", SoHo's "beautiful" brasserie for "beautiful people" (alas, "I'm just too old") and "celebrity-spotting" ("I sat next to Woody and Soon-Yi") remains a boisterous "scene" thanks to "Paris in NY" atmosphere plus "surprisingly good food and service"; don't miss the plateau de fruits de mer.

	F	D	S	C
Baluchi's [S]	19	15	15	$24

1565 Second Ave. (bet. 81st & 82nd Sts.), 212-288-4810
1149 First Ave. (63rd St.), 212-371-3535
283 Columbus Ave. (bet. 73rd & 74th Sts.), 212-579-3900
240 W. 56th St. (bet. B'way & 8th Ave.), 212-397-0707
361 Sixth Ave. (bet. Washington Pl. & W. 4th St.), 212-929-2441 ☾
104 2nd Ave. (6th St.), 212-780-6000 ☾
193 Spring St. (bet. Sullivan & Thompson Sts.), 212-226-2828
■ "Better-than-average Indian" chain serving "decent, reliable" food, including a popular half-price lunch; surveyors debate the service: "friendly" vs. "slow."

	F	D	S	C
Bambou [S]	21	23	19	$42

243 E. 14th St. (bet. 2nd & 3rd Aves.), 212-358-0012
■ "Montego Bay on 14th Street", this Caribbean throbs with a "sexy", "tropical" "treat for the senses" setting and "delicious" "island-flavored food"; "potent drinks" make the "expensive" tabs easier to swallow.

Bamonte's (Brooklyn) 🅂
21 | 16 | 20 | $34
32 Withers St. (bet. Lorimer St. & Union Ave.), 718-384-8831
■ "Old-fashioned, family-run", 99-year-old Williamsburg Southern Italian "institution" serving "terrific meat sauce and pastas"; it's a "great neighborhood joint full of characters", so "you can wait forever for a table even with reservations."

Bangkok Cuisine ●🅂
17 | 13 | 16 | $25
885 Eighth Ave. (bet. 52nd & 53rd Sts.), 212-581-6370
☑ Fans of this Midtown Thai "staple" laud the "tasty", "fresh" fare, "bargain lunch buffet" (Wednesday–Friday) and "kind, unobtrusive service"; but critics call the food "unremarkable" and the decor "lousy."

Baraonda ●🅂
18 | 17 | 15 | $36
1439 Second Ave. (75th St.), 212-288-8555
☑ Northern Italian "Eurotrash haven" whose "wild scene" includes "pickups", "pricey pasta", "dancing on tables" and outside "seats to watch the Upper East Side strut" by; foes say: "loud", "pretentious."

Barbetta ●🅂
19 | 23 | 20 | $49
321 W. 46th St. (bet. 8th & 9th Aves.), 212-246-9171
☑ A "beautiful townhouse and garden" is the "patrician" setting for this "sumptuous" Theater District Northern Italian with consistently good food and extraordinary wines; still, a few insist it "needs Viagra"; P.S. summer lunch in the garden is a delight.

Bar Cichetti 🅂
18 | 18 | 17 | $34
220 W. Houston St. (bet. 6th & 7th Aves.), 212-229-0314
■ "Go grazing" on the namesake Venetian appetizers at this pleasant West Village "sleeper"; despite "good" food, "great wine" and "charm", it's surprisingly uncrowded.

Bardolino 🅂
19 | 15 | 18 | $24
1496 Second Ave. (bet. 77th & 78th Sts.), 212-734-9050
■ The "best inexpensive pasta on the East Side" and "great early birds" (at lunch and dinner) are the draws at this "cramped", "candlelit" Italian "hole-in-the-wall"; if "smaller than my studio apartment", it's "cheaper, easier and better than eating at home."

Bari 🅂
– | – | – | M
529 Broadway (Spring St.), 212-431-4350
Long valued by SoHo locals and weary tourists as an easy stop for sandwiches, lattés and people-watching, this bustling corner cafe recently added a (too new to call) spacious, upstairs Mediterranean dining room; downstairs morphs into a bar at night.

Barking Dog Luncheonette ●🅂⇗
16 | 14 | 15 | $19
1678 Third Ave. (94th St.), 212-831-1800
■ BYOS (Bring Your Own Stroller) to this *enfant*-amiable Upper East Side American serving big portions of "comfort food" and "good brunches"; the main growl is that it's "too popular", but critics snap "skip this dog."

Barney Greengrass 🅂⇗
23 | 7 | 13 | $21
541 Amsterdam Ave. (bet. 86th & 87th Sts.), 212-724-4707
■ "Oy gevelt" – "despite snarling waiters and peeling walls", this Upper West Side Jewish deli (top-rated in its category) offers the "best sturgeon this side of the Caspian" and "luscious lox"; "Barney is no interior decorator" ("tenement chic"), but that doesn't keep this "institution" from being a "Sunday brunch staple."

Barolo ●🅂
19 | 21 | 17 | $43
398 W. Broadway (bet. Broome & Spring Sts.), 212-226-1102
☑ "Pretty room, pretty people" – "decent" food and service is the word on this "pricey" SoHo Northern Italian; nonetheless, its "wonderful garden" is a "favorite" "when doing the art scene" or on a "first date."

Bar Pitti ◐🖪≠
20 | 14 | 16 | $29
268 Sixth Ave. (bet. Bleecker & Houston Sts.), 212-982-3300
■ "It's always crowded, but for good reason" at this "affordable" West Village Tuscan with sidewalk seating and "consistently good", "honest food"; the "great people-watching" includes "star sightings galore."

Bar Six ◐🖪
17 | 17 | 14 | $28
502 Sixth Ave. (bet. 12th & 13th Sts.), 212-691-1363
☑ "Gen X must make way for Gen Y" at this "loud", "smoky", "cool, candlelit" West Village bistro "with a hopping bar" that's a "haven for fashionistas"; surprisingly, the French-Moroccan food is "pretty good."

Basta Pasta 🖪
17 | 15 | 17 | $30
37 W. 17th St. (bet. 5th & 6th Aves.), 212-366-0888
☑ Italian food "cooked by Japanese chefs" ("linguine with flying fish roe") is the "interesting concept" driving this Flatiron District pioneer; but paisans protest that this "kind of fusion" leads to confusion.

Bateaux New York 🖪
▽ 19 | 24 | 20 | VE
Chelsea Piers, Pier 61, W. 23rd St. & Hudson River, 212-352-9009
■ Since its three-hour cruise around Lower Manhattan offers superb sights, a New American menu from consulting chef Scott Bryan (Veritas) and a wine list devised by sommelier John Gilman (Picholine), it's not surprising that this sleek replica of a Parisian *bateau-mouche* is *très cher* – $60 brunch, $100 and up dinner prix fixe.

Bayard's
24 | 22 | 21 | $49
1 Hanover Sq. (bet. Pearl & Stone Sts.), 212-514-9454
■ "Just opened and has great potential" is the word on this pricey New French Wall Street "hideout" in a "beautiful old building" that housed the famous India House club; the new place remains "elegant" and "clublike", with mahogany and maritime memorabilia.

Bay Leaf 🖪
20 | 17 | 18 | $32
49 W. 56th St. (bet. 5th & 6th Aves.), 212-957-1818
■ "Upper-end Indian" in Midtown serving "aromatic, flavorful" fare and what many say is the "best buffet lunch in town"; the atmosphere is "serene", the service "spiffy."

Beacon ◐
– | – | – | E
25 W. 56th St. (bet. 5th & 6th Aves.), 212-332-0500
Handsome Midtown American newcomer boasting three levels, an open kitchen and a large wood-burning oven; as expected, star chef Waldy Malouf (ex Rainbow Room and the Hudson River Club) is drawing a chic Uptown clientele that continues to praise his work.

Becco ◐🖪
20 | 17 | 19 | $36
355 W. 46th St. (bet. 8th & 9th Aves.), 212-397-7597
■ "Busy" Restaurant Row Northern Italian whose "bargain" AYCE three-pasta prix fixe dinner ($21.95), including "bathtubs of pasta", makes it a favorite "pre-theater place"; even doubters concede "you'll never leave hungry."

Belgo Nieuw York ◐🖪
17 | 18 | 16 | $30
415 Lafayette St. (bet. Astor Pl. & E. 4th St.), 212-253-2828
☑ "Lively" new Central Villager "jumping on the Belgian bandwagon" with "mussels galore" and an "amazing beer selection" served by a "spacey" "staff in monks' robes"; but critics predict "it may not hold the in crowd too long", especially if they keep the "trappist waiters."

Bella Blu ◐🖪
18 | 18 | 17 | $36
967 Lexington Ave. (bet. 70th & 71st Sts.), 212-988-4624
☑ Fans of this "cute", "crowded", "trendy" East Side Northern Italian like its "good pizza and seafood"; but foes call the cooking only "ok", the setting "cramped" and the tab "overpriced."

Bella Donna
| 18 | 10 | 15 | $21 |

1663 First Ave. (bet. 86th & 87th Sts.), 212-534-3261 S
307 E. 77th St. (bet. 1st & 2nd Aves.), 212-535-2866 S ⊄
18 E. 23rd St. (Madison Ave.), 212-505-3678
■ "Basic", "reliable" Italians serving "huge salads and above-average pasta and pizza"; "tables are tight" ("leave your elbows at home"), but they're "fun and cheap date places."

Bella Luna S
| 18 | 16 | 17 | $29 |

584 Columbus Ave. (bet. 88th & 89th Sts.), 212-877-2267
◪ "Bring the kids and go for the outdoor setting" at this "reasonable" West Side Northern Italian; but what some see as a "comfortable neighborhood" "standby", detractors dis as a "fading fixture."

Bellavista (Bronx) S
∇ | 20 | 19 | 18 | $30 |

554 W. 235th St. (bet. Johnson & Oxford Aves.), 718-548-0719
■ It's "Riverdale's best in a restaurant wasteland", so no wonder locals love to have this Italian around; specialties like "delicate-crust pizza" and "good" homemade pasta come with a "warm atmosphere."

Bellew
∇ | 23 | 23 | 21 | $45 |

167 E. 33rd St. (3rd Ave.), 212-685-1466
■ "A welcome addition" to Murray Hill, this slightly pricey, duplex New American with an Irish accent offers "well-prepared" dishes, many wood-grilled; the ambiance is "pleasant" and staff "friendly and attentive" to the few customers on hand.

Bellini
| 22 | 20 | 21 | $46 |

208 E. 52nd St. (bet 2nd & 3rd Aves.), 212-308-0830
■ "Bellini is *bellissimo*" is the word on this pricey Midtown Italian with Neapolitan specialties and "first-class food, service and decor"; "chic patrons" and "charming" owner Donatella Arpaia add appeal.

Bello
| 21 | 17 | 20 | $37 |

863 Ninth Ave. (56th St.), 212-246-6773
■ A "good bet when going to Lincoln Center", this "dependable" Hell's Kitchen Northern Italian features "fresh, nothing fancy" fare; the setting is "homey", staff "friendly" and "free parking a plus."

Belluno
∇ | 23 | 20 | 23 | $37 |

340 Lexington Ave. (bet. 39th & 40th Sts.), 212-953-3282
■ "Undiscovered" Murray Hill Northern Italian offering "creative" dishes, an "intimate atmosphere" and "extremely attentive" service; the only quibble is it's "expensive for the neighborhood."

Bel Villagio ●S
∇ | 17 | 15 | 16 | $38 |

228 Bleecker St. (bet. Carmine St. & 6th Ave.), 212-924-9717
■ The few surveyors who know this West Village yearling call it a "tiny gem" with "solid" Italian cooking; the interior exudes "old-world charm" and the "congenial" staff will "downright spoil a regular."

Ben Benson's S
| 22 | 17 | 20 | $50 |

123 W. 52nd St. (bet. 6th & 7th Aves.), 212-581-8888
■ "Suits", "solid" steaks and "wonderful side dishes" dominate at this "big boys' club" that's a "reliable" Midtown meat mecca; "you can bet your ascot" that the "testosterone" and "haze of smoke and noise" here won't keep the "corporate clientele" from coming.

Bendix Diner S
| 14 | 10 | 13 | $17 |

219 Eighth Ave. (21st St.), 212-366-0560
167 First Ave. (bet. 10th & 11th Sts.), 212-260-4220
◪ The food is "standard", service is "dysfunctional" and there's "less atmosphere than on Mars"; so why are these Asian-accented American diners "crowded and rushed?"; 'cause it's "cheap" and filling.

Benihana of Tokyo 🅂
16 | 15 | 18 | $33

120 E. 56th St. (bet. Lexington & Park Aves.), 212-593-1627
47 W. 56th St. (bet. 5th & 6th Aves.), 212-581-0930
☑ "Cheesy but still fun" for the kids, these Japanese "dinosaurs" divert with their chefs' "chop-chop" act that's "all for the show of it"; as for the food, it "varies in quantity and quality."

Benny's Burritos ◗🅂
17 | 10 | 12 | $16

113 Greenwich Ave. (Jane St.), 212-727-3560
93 Ave. A (6th St.), 212-254-2054 🍴
☑ "Burritos so large they have their own zip codes" distinguish these Mexicans where generally young amigos crowd in for "cheap, filling" fare; critics say the "heavy, unimaginative food", "best eaten after two or three margaritas", "will take years off your life."

Ben's Kosher Delicatessen 🅂
18 | 12 | 15 | $19

209 W. 38th St. (7th Ave.), 212-398-2367
Bay Terrace, 211-37 26th Ave. (Bell Blvd.), Queens, 718-229-2367
☑ "Bring a big mouth for the oversized sandwiches" at these "authentic kosher" offshoots of a Long Island chain; still, some opine "quantity not quality" – the "meat is as tough as the service."

Berkeley Bar & Grill
▽ 20 | 18 | 19 | $49

Sony Plaza Atrium, 550 Madison Ave. (bet. 55th & 56th Sts.), 212-833-7800
☑ Drew Nieporent's newest baby, an homage to Berkeley chef Alice Waters and California cuisine, draws mixed reviews: pros call it a "hit" and a "reason to come to Midtown"; foes dub it "noisy", "expensive" and "disappointing", adding "Alice doesn't live here anymore."

Bice Ristorante ◗🅂
20 | 20 | 18 | $47

7 E. 54th St. (bet. 5th & Madison Aves.), 212-688-1999
☑ "The '80s" still thrive at this "pricey" Midtown Northern Italian serving "power pastas" to "beautiful people on expense account" and "Eurotrash" ("lap dog optional"); it's a "stylish if no longer trendy" "scene" that critics call "overpriced, overhyped, over everything."

Bienvenue
20 | 15 | 20 | $33

21 E. 36th St. (bet. 5th & Madison Aves.), 212-684-0215
■ "Cozy", "charming", "old-fashioned French bistro sans attitude" in Murray Hill with "motherly waitresses" and "simple" cooking; it's "reasonably priced" ("best duck for the buck") to boot.

Big Wong 🅂🍴
21 | 5 | 10 | $13

67 Mott St. (bet. Bayard & Canal Sts.), 212-964-0540
■ "Cheap", "excellent Chinese Soul Food" makes for the "best jury duty lunch" at this "rowdy" Mott Street Cantonese noodle house; there's "no decor" and "no service", so just "keep your eyes closed and eat."

Billy's ◗🅂
17 | 13 | 17 | $36

948 First Ave. (bet. 52nd & 53rd Sts.), 212-753-1870
☑ Surveyors split over this atmospheric, vintage 1870 Sutton Place steakhouse: the majority insists "anything lasting 125-plus years has got to be good", but dissenters say it's "seen time and taste pass it by."

Biricchino
19 | 13 | 17 | $31

260 W. 29th St. (8th Ave.), 212-695-6690
■ A "convenient place to go before you watch the Knicks", this "dependable" Northern Italian near Madison Square Garden offers the "best [homemade] sausages" in town to go with its pasta.

Bistro du Nord 🅂
19 | 17 | 18 | $39

1312 Madison Ave. (93rd St.), 212-289-0997
☑ French bistro that's a Carnegie Hill "favorite" featuring a "good value prix fixe" for lunch, brunch and pre-theater; locals find it a "charming" "dollhouse", but for some that means "cramped."

F	D	S	C

Bistro Latino 18 | 18 | 16 | $37

1711 Broadway, 2nd fl. (54th St.), 212-956-1000

■ Midtown second-floor South American with Latin bands that's a "fun place to eat, drink and dance" and a "blast if you're in the mood for something different"; the midpriced food's "above average" and you can "watch salsa while you dine."

Bistro Les Amis ◐[S] 19 | 17 | 19 | $33

180 Spring St. (Thompson St.), 212-226-8645

■ "SoHo gem" that's a "fine French bistro" with a "diverse menu", "cute setting", "friendly staff" and "fair prices"; it's also a good spot for lunch while "gallery-hopping."

Bistro Le Steak ◐[S] 18 | 15 | 17 | $36

1309 Third Ave. (75th St.), 212-517-3800

◪ "Busy, busy, busy" Upper East Side bistro with "decent" "steaks you can sink your teeth into without taking a bite out of your wallet"; the less enthused shrug: "not prime or choice, but not to be chucked."

Bistro Metro (Queens) [S] ▽ 20 | 21 | 19 | $40

107-21 Metropolitan Ave. (Ascan Ave.), 718-263-5444

◪ An "oasis in Queens", this Forest Hills French bistro is a good choice "after the US Open"; while some say it's "overpriced", a sidewalk cafe and a pianist Thursday–Saturday help compensate.

Bistrot Margot [S]⊄ 18 | 16 | 16 | $29

26 Prince St. (bet. Elizabeth & Mott Sts.), 212-274-1027

■ "Cramped" but "cozy" and "cute" SoHo French bistro with "basic", "authentic" fare that's "well presented"; the "adorable garden" in the back is the "perfect spot for a light, romantic brunch."

Black & White ◐[S] – | – | – | M

86 E. 10th St. (bet. 3rd & 4th Aves.), 212-253-0246

Step under the checkered (black and white, of course) Central Village awning and get into Kelly (Spy Bar) Cole's midpriced Y2K rendition of American homestyle fare gone swank; staff frigidity may cause some to see red, but most of its cell-phone-toting clients feel right at home.

Black Betty (Brooklyn) ◐[S] – | – | – | M

366 Metropolitan Ave. (Havemeyer St.), 718-599-0243

Decadent dark red decor sets the stage for tantalizing spices at this modestly priced Williamsburg Mideastern; after dark, Brooklyn bohemia's hottest late-late show picks up in the adjoining lounge.

Blackbird 20 | 18 | 20 | $44

60 E. 49th St. (bet. Madison & Park Aves.), 212-692-9292

■ "Cocktails reign supreme" at this "hopping" new Midtowner from the Baum/Emil team, where the "best bartender in NY" (Dale DeGroff, ex Rainbow Room) presides over the "mellow" piano bar; the "inventive" New American menu also earns kudos.

Bleu Evolution [S] ▽ 16 | 19 | 15 | $27

808 W. 187th St. (bet. Ft. Washington & Pinehurst Aves.), 212-928-6006

■ "SoHo has nothing over Ft. Washington here" swear boosters of this "quirky" Eclectic Washington Heights yearling near the Cloisters; with "flavorful" food and a garden that's "tops", it's a "good reason to come way Uptown."

BLUE RIBBON ◐[S] 25 | 18 | 20 | $43

97 Sullivan St. (bet. Prince & Spring Sts.), 212-274-0404

■ Though the "line is just impossible", an appealing young "crowd waits hours for the impeccable fare and delightful service" at this "phenomenal" SoHo "late-night" Eclectic gem; it "lives up to the hype", but more than a few "wish they took reservations."

		F	D	S	C

Blue Ribbon Bakery ◐[S] — 22 | 18 | 20 | $33
33 Downing St. (Bedford St.), 212-337-0404
■ "The Brombergs strike again" at this "cute", "casual" bi-level Village bakery/cafe with a Eclectic menu of "simple", "fresh" fare ranging from "great lite bites to full-course meals"; bonus: you "can still get in."

BLUE RIBBON SUSHI ◐[S] — 26 | 19 | 19 | $42
119 Sullivan St. (bet. Prince & Spring Sts.), 212-343-0404
■ "It swims to your plate but you pay for the laps" jokes one wag about the "very fresh" but "expensive" sushi at this "cramped" Blue Ribbon SoHo spin-off; look for "fab", "creative" food plus "killer waits."

BLUE WATER GRILL ◐[S] — 23 | 22 | 20 | $42
31 Union Sq. W. (16th St.), 212-675-9500
■ Some prefer the "cool jazz room", others the "outdoor seats" with a view of Union Square, but either way, Steve Hanson's "seafood haven" in a converted bank is "quite the scene", offering "amazing" American fare and an "excellent raw bar" to "young Downtowners"; the only downside: it's often "noisy" at this "yuppie" "Grand Central of dining."

Bobby Van's Steakhouse — 21 | 18 | 20 | $48
230 Park Ave. (46th St.), 212-867-5490
◪ There's a "power-crowd scene but wonderful service" at this "middle-of-the-pack" Midtown steakhouse; "convenient to Grand Central" but "as good as its Bridgehampton counterpart", it's a "safe bet" for a "business lunch", with "tremendous portions" and much cigar puffing; however, dissenters say there's "nothing special but the check."

Boca Chica [S] — 19 | 14 | 15 | $24
13 First Ave. (1st St.), 212-473-0108
■ "Ay caramba!" – the "funky food fits the funky vibe" at this "cheap, lively", "colorful" East Village South American; with big portions and "killer drinks", it's fun for groups – just plan "to crawl to work" the next day.

Bo-Ky [S]₡ — 19 | 5 | 10 | $13
80 Bayard St. (bet. Mott & Mulberry Sts.), 212-406-2292
■ It's a "mess" with "cramped, shared tables", "slippery floors" and "surly service", but there's "nothing better on a winter day than a bowl of noodle soup" from this "dirt cheap" Chinatown Vietnamese.

Bolivar [S] — 19 | 17 | 17 | $42
206 E. 60th St. (bet. 2nd & 3rd Aves.), 212-838-0440
◪ There's a mixed vote on this East Side redo of Arizona 206: critics knock "small, pricey portions" and service that "can only get better", while converts find "potential" in Larry Kolar's "interesting" Pan-Am menu.

Bolo [S] — 23 | 21 | 21 | $46
23 E. 22nd St. (bet. B'way & Park Ave. S.), 212-228-2200
■ "Bobby Flay's greatest to date" rave aficionados of this Flatiron Contemporary Spaniard, where the celeb chef and "helpful" staff present "fantastic paella and sangria" in a most attractive room; though some warn you'll "get flayed by the prices", most feel it's well "worth it" – especially if "you can sit next to one of Bobby's old flames."

Bombay City [S] — ▽ 19 | 15 | 17 | $27
29 Seventh Ave. S. (bet. Bedford & Morton Sts.), 212-414-0931
■ Kudos greet this Villager serving "excellent Indian cuisine" that's "more expensive" than some, but also more "authentic"; "the owner takes time to help novices and guide experts."

Bombay Palace [S] — 19 | 18 | 18 | $30
30 W. 52nd St. (bet. 5th & 6th Aves.), 212-541-7777
■ "Awesome Indian food" draws a following to this "comfy", "peaceful" Midtown stalwart that may be a "bit dated" and "expensive", but is highly touted for its "bargain lunch buffets."

F	D	S	C

Bondí Ristorante [S] 20 | 18 | 20 | $36

7 W. 20th St. (bet. 5th & 6th Aves.), 212-691-8136

■ Though well-regarded anytime, it's "best when one sits outside" at this "unique and tasty" Flatiron Sicilian "oasis" with a "cozy" back garden; despite a "chichi clientele", it's "very friendly" and "relaxed."

Bond Street ◐[S] 24 | 22 | 18 | $50

6 Bond St. (bet. B'way & Lafayette St.), 212-777-2500

■ "Check all nonblack clothes at the door" of this "beyond trendy" NoHo Japanese where the "best fashion-conscious sushi" and Nobu-style "hot stuff" is delivered by an "intimidating Gucci-clad staff" to a "cool", "anorexic" crowd; most surveyors swoon over the "beautiful people, beautiful lighting, beautiful food", but a few complain "I'm still paying it off and I'm still hungry."

Bongo ◐[S] – | – | – | E

299 10th Ave. (bet. 27th & 28th Sts.), 212-947-3654

New England lobster rolls, daily oyster selections, champagnes by the glass and a designer martini list have led Chelsea gallery-owners and loft-dwellers to welcome this petite but attractive nightspot with a raw bar; it would be even more welcome if it cost a bit less.

Boom ◐[S] 16 | 16 | 14 | $35

152 Spring St. (bet. W. B'way & Wooster St.), 212-431-3663

◪ Trendoids may sneer ("Boom is a bust", "so over"), but the "Euro bar scene" – "late-night drinks, dancing on tables" – carries on at this SoHo Eclectic; though "not really the best place to eat", it's still a "fun" "after-hours" "hangout" "with a group."

Bop ◐[S] 17 | 19 | 16 | $31

325 Bowery (2nd St.), 212-254-7887

◪ "Tasty Korean fusion in a swanky setting" is the positive take on this NoHo bi-level space offering "delicious" "nouveau" Korean BBQ ("the best part") and bibimbop in an "ultrachic" setting; but purists decry "bland", "pseudo" fare.

Borgo Antico ◐[S] 18 | 19 | 20 | $36

22 E. 13th St. (bet. 5th Ave. & University Pl.), 212-807-1313

■ The "staff is welcoming and helpful" and the "lovely", "quiet" upstairs dining room with "big tables" feels "like eating at a friend's place" at this "very tasty" Village Tuscan "neighborhood secret"; locals beg "please don't tell anyone."

Bottino ◐[S] 20 | 20 | 18 | $40

246 10th Ave. (bet. 24th & 25th Sts.), 212-206-6766

■ With what some call the "best garden in NYC", this "scene in the newly chic West Chelsea" art world serves Northern Italian fare that's "great after gallery-hopping"; still, some yawn over a menu of "the usual suspects" and "too much hype."

Boughalem, Restaurant [S] 21 | 20 | 18 | $39

14 Bedford St. (bet. Downing & Houston Sts.), 212-414-4764

■ Diners tout this "small" West Village "jewel" for its New American fare (but the post-*Survey* departure of chef James Rafferty puts a question mark next to our Food rating); it's a "romantic hideaway" and should be less "cramped" with the addition of a garden.

BOULEY BAKERY ◐[S] 26 | 21 | 23 | $55

120 W. Broadway (Duane St.), 212-964-2525

■ "It's not the original, but what is?" note fans of David Bouley's nonetheless "extraordinary", elegantly "casual" (and recently expanded) TriBeCa bakery/restaurant with "wonderful breads baked on premises", "delightful" New French fare and what most call "impeccable" service; of course it's "pricey", but fans call Bouley "the Houdini of food since everything he cooks is magical."

Bouterin 🅂
23 | 24 | 22 | $54

420 E. 59th St. (bet. 1st Ave. & Sutton Pl.), 212-758-0323

■ This "corner of Provence" is filled with "lovely florals" and "Sutton Place regulars"; while it's a "favorite just for the looks of it", most say the food is "delicious" as well, with the only quibbles over "uneven" service; N.B. no lunch.

Box Tree 🅂
23 | 26 | 23 | VE

250 E. 49th St. (bet. 2nd & 3rd Aves.), 212-758-8320

☑ Fans dub this "wonderfully romantic" Midtown French "jewel box" (with ornately decorated guestrooms upstairs) the "best place for a special occasion"; but strident critics rail at "unfounded arrogance" and find it "overpriced" ($65 or $86 prix fixe dinner) and "overdone."

Brasilia 🅂
18 | 14 | 17 | $32

7 W. 45th St. (bet. 5th & 6th Aves.), 212-869-9200

☑ "If you like red meat, the supply is endless" at this "friendly" Midtown Brazilian "standby"; there's "no atmosphere", but the food is "good, plentiful" and moderately priced.

Brasserie Americaine ◐🅂
17 | 17 | 17 | $36

51 W. 64th St. (bet. B'way & CPW), 212-721-8271

☑ Westsiders call this French–New American bistro a "welcome addition to the Lincoln Center area", offering a "big, reasonable" menu of "not extraordinary" but generally "tasty" food.

Brasserie Julien ◐🅂
19 | 17 | 18 | $40

1422 Third Ave. (bet. 80th & 81st Sts.), 212-744-6327

☑ "Off to a good start", this new Upper East Side brasserie offers "well-prepared" French "bistro stuff, sensibly priced", earning special praise for its game; some "love the room", others wish it were "warmer."

Bravo Gianni ◐🅂
22 | 17 | 20 | $52

230 E. 63rd St. (bet. 2nd & 3rd Aves.), 212-752-7272

■ "Loyal patrons" agree this "classy but pricey" East Side Italian is "worth the money" for the "comfortable" digs and "delicious" food; it's a place for "gusto and good cheer", especially if you "go with a regular."

Brawta Caribbean Café (Bklyn) 🅂
19 | 13 | 14 | $20

347 Atlantic Ave. (Hoyt St.), 718-855-5515

■ This "funky", "friendly" Caribbean offering a "delightful mélange" of island fare and homemade drinks earns nods as the "best place to eat pre-BAM"; however, "laid-back" to some equals "slow" to others.

Briam ◐🅂
– | – | – | M

322 E. 14th St. (bet. 1st & 2nd Aves.), 212-253-6360

This East Village Greek newcomer's casual ambiance, friendly service and modest prices mean it's already packed weeknights; the namesake dish, a grilled vegetable casserole, is interesting, but the strengths are its other traditional dishes, not to mention the nine types of killer ouzo.

Bricco Ristorante
19 | 17 | 18 | $32

304 W. 56th St. (bet. 8th & 9th Aves.), 212-245-7160 🅂
46 W. 22nd St. (bet. 5th & 6th Aves.), 212-727-3362

☑ A "reliable" Italian duo turning out "perfect" brick-oven pizzas and "very good" Southern Italian fare at "affordable" prices; despite drawbacks (the "personable" staff can be "slow" and the "pretty" settings "cramped"), most consider them "neighborhood" "standouts."

Bridge Cafe ◐🅂
21 | 17 | 19 | $36

279 Water St. (Dover St.), 212-227-3344

■ For "one of the few very good meals near Wall Street", try this "charming, quaint" "Downtown secret" in "ancient" brick-walled quarters "snuggled under" the Brooklyn Bridge; given the "inventive" New American fare, "it's a shame it's not bigger."

	F	D	S	C

Bright Food Shop [S]⊭ 19 | 11 | 15 | $22
216 Eighth Ave. (bet. 21st & 22nd Sts.), 212-243-4433
■ The "bright" Mex-Asian fusion food and staff make up for the "drab" setting at this "creative", "affordable" Chelsea stop; "everything is good", but try the "lovely sangria", catfish tacos or cornmeal pancakes.

Brio [S] 18 | 15 | 17 | $34
786 Lexington Ave. (bet. 61st & 62nd Sts.), 212-980-2300
■ "After Bloomie's, it's a given" say fans of this "cozy" Italian, a "not innovative but reliable" "standby" for a "plate of pasta"; for "great pizza" try Brio Forno around the corner.

Broadway Diner [S]⊭ 13 | 11 | 13 | $19
590 Lexington Ave. (52nd St.), 212-486-8838
1726 Broadway (55th St.), 212-765-0909
◪ "Reliable diner food at B'way prices" sums up the plot at these "noisy", "slightly upscale" Midtown "neighborhood coffee shops"; though "nothing special", they're "satisfying" for "a quick bite."

Brooklyn Diner USA ◐[S] 15 | 15 | 15 | $26
212 W. 57th St. (bet. B'way & 7th Ave.), 212-977-2280
■ "Diner goes upscale" at this "oasis of kitsch" where they have "maintained the megaportions" but at "Midtown prices"; fans like the "sophisticated" "comfort food", especially the "gargantuan desserts."

Broome Street Bar ◐[S] 15 | 14 | 15 | $21
363 W. Broadway (Broome St.), 212-925-2086
■ "There before the trendy onslaught", this dark, brick-walled "ghost of SoHo past" hangs on as a "relaxed", "friendly" "neighborhood favorite" for "simple" burgers and beer – "God bless it."

Brother Jimmy's BBQ ◐[S] 15 | 10 | 13 | $21
1644 Third Ave. (92nd St.), 212-426-2020
1461 First Ave. (76th St.), 212-288-0999
428 Amsterdam Ave. (bet. 80th & 81st Sts.), 212-501-7515
■ "Loud music", a "frat crowd" and "beautiful waitresses" "take you back to college" at these "raging" "dives for drinks" and "heaping portions" of "great value" BBQ; they're "noisy and greasy, but fun" – unless you're "sober or over 30."

Brothers BBQ [S] 15 | 12 | 13 | $22
225 Varick St. (Clarkson St.), 212-727-2775
■ "If you went to Duke you'll probably feel at home" at this low-budget "Southern BBQ joint" serving the "best pulled pork and collard greens north of NC"; most of its "loud, beer-drinking" clients like its "comfy" West Village digs: just "bring earplugs."

Brown's 16 | 19 | 16 | $42
33 E. 61st St. (bet. Madison & Park Aves.), 212-888-9127
◪ Replacing Gertrude's, this "crowded" American newcomer in a townhouse caters to an "Upper East Side crowd" including Fabio look-alikes and Euros who turn here more for the "happening bar" than for the only "pretty good" food; foes say "oh please, too much attitude."

Bruculino [S] ▽ 16 | 16 | 19 | $30
225 Columbus Ave. (bet. 70th & 71st Sts.), 212-579-3966
◪ "Love it for local Upper West Side pasta" say those pleased to have "ordinary" but "good" Italian fare and "friendly service" in the nabe; but some fret about the "jinxed locale (multiple restaurant failures)."

Brunelli, Ristorante [S] 19 | 17 | 20 | $34
1409 York Ave. (75th St.), 212-744-8899
■ "Great big artichokes" are standouts on the "hearty" menu at this Upper East Side Italian yearling, a "gem" prized for its food and for the "caring" staff that "makes the place shine"; it's already a "favorite."

Bruno Ristorante ●

21	19	21	$47

240 E. 58th St. (bet. 2nd & 3rd Aves.), 212-688-4190
■ This "polished" Midtown Italian is a "throwback" for "mellowed folk" who appreciate the "elegant surroundings", "deferential service", "excellent wines and food" and "upstairs piano bar that's strictly NY."

Bryant Park Grill ●S

18	22	17	$37

25 W. 40th St. (behind NY Public Library), 212-840-6500

Bryant Park Cafe ●S

16	21	16	$33

25 W. 40th St. (behind NY Public Library), 212-840-6500
☑ A "little bit of heaven" for "dining alfresco", this New American combo behind the Public Library offers casual (the Cafe) or more formal (the Grill) dining in "one of the prettiest gardens in NY"; both food and service draw mixed reviews, but "brunch is excellent" and the bar scene is a big hit – "get there early for the hottest guys."

B. Smith's ●S

18	17	17	$37

771 Eighth Ave. (47th St.), 212-247-2222
■ A "slick" "buppie" crowd turns up for "creative" Eclectic–Soul Food at this "delightful" Theater District "best bet"; "smooth, cool jazz" in the rooftop cafe "satisfies the late crowd" – delightful owner Barbara Smith satisfies everyone.

Bubby's S

19	14	16	$23

120 Hudson St. (N. Moore St.), 212-219-0666
■ Popular TriBeCa brunch spot where "hip babies in strollers" and "famous people" (add Julia Roberts and Robert De Niro to the list) line up weekends for "amazing" comfort chow; though it's "worth the wait", locals lament the "invasion of Uptown folks" while admitting "my bubbe never cooked this well."

Bukhara Grill S

–	–	–	E

217 E. 49th St. (bet. 2nd & 3rd Aves.), 212-888-2839
Showcasing the fiery flavors of Northwest India, this new Midtown restaurant/lounge is an intimate, upscale oasis with woodsy decor, an indoor waterfall and ornate tableware; the copious $12.95 lunch buffet is a good option for those wanting to sample more for less.

Bull & Bear ●S

18	19	19	$44

Waldorf-Astoria, 570 Lexington Ave. (49th St.), 212-872-4900
☑ A "civilized" "CEO's hangout", this "competent" Waldorf steakhouse offers a "good kitchen but an even better place to talk business" in a "testosterone- and cigar-filled room"; a few bears growl about high prices – "leave it for the big boys."

Burger Heaven S

14	9	13	$14

536 Madison Ave. (bet. 54th & 55th Sts.), 212-753-4214
9 E. 53rd St. (bet. 5th & Madison Aves.), 212-752-0340
20 E. 49th St. (bet. 5th & Madison Aves.), 212-755-2166
291 Madison Ave. (bet. 40th & 41st Sts.), 212-685-6250
☑ These recently "spruced-up" "lunchtime gathering spots" offer good burgers and other "reliable" coffee shop fare; they're the "only option in Midtown" for a "cheap, sit-down" meal, but heavenly? – no way! say nonfans: "McYawn", "where burgers go when they die."

Burritoville

15	6	11	$12

1606 Third Ave. (bet. 90th & 91st Sts.), 212-410-2255 S
1489 First Ave. (bet. 77th & 78th Sts.), 212-472-8800 S
451 Amsterdam Ave. (bet. 81st & 82nd Sts.), 212-787-8181 ●S
166 W. 72nd St. (bet. Amsterdam & Columbus Aves.), 212-580-7700 ●S
625 Ninth Ave. (bet. 44th & 45th Sts.), 212-333-5352 ●S
352 W. 39th St. (bet. 8th & 9th Aves.), 212-563-9088 ●S
264 W. 23rd St. (bet. 7th & 8th Aves.), 212-367-9844 ●S
298 Bleecker St. (bet. Grove St. & 7th Ave. S.), 212-633-9254 ●S

Burritoville (Cont.)
141 Second Ave. (bet. 8th & 9th Sts.), 212-260-3300 ◐[S]
20 John St. (bet. B'way & Nassau St.), 212-766-2020
36 Water St. (Broad St.), 212-747-1100 [S]
144 Chambers St. (bet. Greenwich St. & W. B'way), 212-571-1144 [S]
◪ "Burritos as big as your head" win converts to these "decent", "cheap" McMexicans functioning mainly for takeout ("no pretense at decor", "speedy delivery"); the unconverted ask "why is it so popular?"

Butterfield 81 [S] — 21 | 19 | 19 | $49
170 E. 81st St. (bet. Lexington & 3rd Aves.), 212-288-2700
■ There's been a "big improvement" since chef Tom Valenti ("a sure hand at work in the kitchen") arrived at this "dark", "clubby" Upper East Side New American; though "pricey", it's a "neighborhood gem" with more "attitude than an O'Hara novel."

Cabana ◐[S] — 20 | 18 | 18 | $30
1022 Third Ave. (bet. 60th & 61st Sts.), 212-980-5678
107-10 70th Rd. (bet. Austin St. & Queens Blvd.), Queens, 718-263-3600
■ "Like a cafe in Havana", these "cheery", cheap Cuban-Caribbeans offer "fine Nuevo Latino cooking", transporting Bloomie's groupies and Forest Hills "fiesta"-goers to "the islands."

Cabana Carioca [S] — 17 | 11 | 15 | $26
123 W. 45th St. (bet. 6th & 7th Aves.), 212-581-8088
◪ Gringos love to "overeat" at this "venerable Brazilian pig out" place, a "salty and salacious" Theater District "standby" for cheap eats with "tacky decor" and "mounds" of "heart attack" grub; increasingly, critics complain "you leave full, not satisfied."

Cafe Asean [S]⊄ — 19 | 15 | 17 | $21
117 W. 10th St. (bet. Greenwich & 6th Aves.), 212-633-0348
■ "Ultraspicy" Pan-Asian "hidden jewel" that sparkles with an "oh-so-romantic garden" and a $15 "early dinner special"; it's a candidate for "most affordable Village hangout."

Café Botanica [S] — 21 | 26 | 22 | $48
Essex House, 160 Central Park S. (bet. 6th & 7th Aves.), 212-484-5120
■ A "tranquil, elegant" hotel "oasis" with Central Park views that make you feel "you're in a Childe Hassam painting"; this Provençal delight "oozes charm", whether at the "magnificent brunch buffet", "pre–Carnegie Hall" or when treating awestruck "out-of-towners."

CAFÉ BOULUD [S] — 27 | 22 | 25 | $63
Surrey Hotel, 20 E. 76th St. (bet. 5th & Madison Aves.), 212-772-2600
■ "Any place associated with chef Daniel Boulud has to be great, and it is" say devotees of this "low-key", modern Upper East Side cafe, whose "minimalist" French-Eclectic fare inspires "bravos" from "food groupies"; it's pricey with "cheek-by-jowl" seating, but most would "love to eat like this all the time."

Cafe Centro — 19 | 18 | 18 | $38
MetLife Bldg., 200 Park Ave. (45th St. & Vanderbilt Ave.), 212-818-1222
■ A "haven" for commuters and suits, this midpriced, "masculine" French-Med brasserie is "convenient to Grand Central" and useful for a "predictable business lunch" or "pit stop" before the ride home; some feel its most memorable quality is noise ("Cafe Loud-o"), but that's a natural by-product of its popularity.

Cafe Colonial ◐[S] — 19 | 19 | 17 | $35
276 Elizabeth St. (Houston St.), 212-274-0044
◪ This "hip" little SoHo cafe offers "tasty" American-Brazilian fare in a "funky", "pretty" room with "mismatched" furniture; despite "deafening decibels", "snide service" and a crowd that's "too cool by half", it's a happening "hangout" and ideal for a "relaxed brunch."

[F] [D] [S] [C]

Cafe Con Leche [S] 16 | 11 | 14 | $19

726 Amsterdam Ave. (bet. 95th & 96th Sts.), 212-678-7000
424 Amsterdam Ave. (bet. 80th & 81st Sts.), 212-595-7000

◪ "Glorified rice-and-beans joints" serving "plain, plentiful" Cuban-Dominican chow and the namesake drink to West Side "intellectuals who can't afford Asia de Cuba"; since you pay "so little for so much", few mind the elemental decor and service.

Café Crocodile 21 | 18 | 20 | $45

354 E. 74th St. (bet. 1st & 2nd Aves.), 212-249-6619

■ "One of the last ma-and-pa places with good French-Mediterranean home cooking", Andrée and Charles Abramoff's East Side townhouse charmer offers "food for the soul" (brandade, couscous, cassoulet) in a "homey" (if "snug") setting; after two decades it remains a "favorite."

Café de Bruxelles ◐[S] 20 | 17 | 18 | $36

118 Greenwich Ave. (W. 13th St.), 212-206-1830

■ "Belgian before Belgian was hip", this "quaint", modestly priced Village bistro dishes up "great *moules et frites*" ("love the mayonnaise") plus other "dependable", "hearty, tasty" fare and "super" beers, prompting fans to declare "the original is still best."

Café de Paris [S] 18 | 16 | 17 | $37

924 Second Ave. (49th St.), 212-486-1411

◪ Take "a trip to a Paris bistro" via this Midtown French serving "good, simple" food (special kudos for the steak frites); critics may find it "ho-hum", but sidewalk seats and "reasonable" prix fixes help.

CAFÉ DES ARTISTES ◐[S] 24 | 27 | 23 | $55

1 W. 67th St. (bet. Columbus Ave. & CPW), 212-877-3500

■ Like dining "in a Valentine's card", George and Jenifer Lang's "romantic" "classic" near Lincoln Center makes diners "feel like they're in an opera before going to one" with its "lush", "nymph-filled" setting; even if the French food "weren't so good, you'd still have to love" this "timeless" "top choice" for celebrations and proposals.

Cafe du Pont [S] 20 | 15 | 19 | $36

1038 First Ave. (bet. 56th & 57th Sts.), 212-223-1133

■ This rather "small and plain" French-Continental cafe pleases "the Sutton Place set" with its "imaginative" food, "personal service" and "good value"; outvoted dissenters find it a bit too "minimal."

Cafe Español ◐[S] 20 | 14 | 18 | $28

63 Carmine St. (7th Ave. S.), 212-675-3312
172 Bleecker St. (bet. MacDougal & Sullivan Sts.), 212-505-0657

■ Olés for the "cheap lobster" and other "garlicky" Spanish eats at these unrelated Villagers offering "mucho" food for not mucho money; "warm" and "festive", they make "you feel you're in Spain" – if you feel anything after their "powerful sangria."

Café Fès ◐[S] 17 | 20 | 16 | $29

246 W. Fourth St. (Charles St.), 212-924-7653

■ "Just like in the medina in Fez", this "authentic Moroccan" "the size of your living room" is a "low-priced" Village "favorite" serving "subtly spiced" fare in a "semi-exotic" setting; the downside: "slow, slow service", so plan on "a long meal."

Cafe Fiorello ◐[S] 19 | 17 | 18 | $38

1900 Broadway (bet. 63rd & 64th Sts.), 212-595-5330

■ A "packed" Lincoln Center Italian "standby" that can be a "noisy" "madhouse" but "always gets you out in time for the curtain"; fans tout the antipasto bar as well as "reliable" pastas, salads and thin-crust pizzas, best enjoyed from prime people-watching sidewalk seats.

F	D	S	C

Café Frida [S] ▽ 17 | 16 | 16 | $28
368 Columbus Ave. (bet. 77th & 78th Sts.), 212-712-2929
◪ An "upscale" new West Side Mexican with a "different" menu, attractive decor and fair prices; a few find the food "just ok" and so slowly served "you'll think they walked to Mexico" and back.

Cafe Greco [S] 17 | 15 | 17 | $29
1390 Second Ave. (bet. 71st & 72nd Sts.), 212-737-4300
■ "Grandparents 'R' Us" is how some refer to this East Side Greek-Med, but while it's a "seniors' paradise", anyone with an Olympian appetite and spartan spending habits will enjoy its "best buy" lunch, early bird deals and "outstanding fish."

Café Guy Pascal [S] 19 | 16 | 16 | $28
1231 Madison Ave. (89th St.), 212-831-2340
■ The return of Guy Pascal's French cafe/pâtisserie to Carnegie Hill is cheered, though "service could be quicker" and prices may be as "flaky" as the croissants; still, it's always "good for a quick bite" and, *bien sûr*, "save room for dessert."

Café Habana ◐[S] 18 | 16 | 16 | $22
17 Prince St. (Elizabeth St.), 212-625-2001
■ They're singing 'Babaloo' over the "off-the-charts grilled corn" and "best Cuban sandwich" at this new SoHo Cuban–South American that pulls off a rare hat trick: "trendy, cute and cheap"; those who ask "when is it possible to get a table?" hope it "gets bigger."

Cafe Lalo ◐[S]⊄ 20 | 17 | 13 | $16
201 W. 83rd St. (bet. Amsterdam Ave. & B'way), 212-496-6031
■ "Way too crowded" "even before *You've Got Mail*", this "very caloric" "neo-'60s" West Side coffeehouse is a "yuppie dessert haven" and "great date place" ("just ask Meg and Tom"), but "good luck getting a seat" or service at peak hours.

Café Loup ◐[S] 20 | 18 | 19 | $37
105 W. 13th St. (bet. 6th & 7th Aves.), 212-255-4746
■ "Unpretentious" Village bistro "standby" that draws "returnees" thanks to "solid food at a good price", a "casually elegant" setting and "efficient" service – simple qualities, but "not a common thing."

Cafe Luxembourg ◐[S] 20 | 19 | 18 | $44
200 W. 70th St. (bet. Amsterdam & West End Aves.), 212-873-7411
■ It's "always buzzing" at this art deco, cream-colored West Side bistro that's "still in fashion"; "beautiful people wanna-bes" come for the "hearty French fare" and "boozy brunches" while craning to spot the "celeb tucked in the corner" ("bumped into Liam Neeson").

Café M [S] 17 | 19 | 18 | $45
Stanhope Hotel, 995 Fifth Ave. (81st St.), 212-717-0303
◪ Though well-located "near the Met" and "great for people-watching" on the terrace, this Matthew Kenney Mediterranean "needs a little pizazz" and may be "overpriced"; still, "on a beautiful night sitting on Fifth Avenue, who cares?"

Cafe Margaux ◐[S] 19 | 17 | 18 | $31
175 Ave. B (11th St.), 212-260-7960
◪ Fans love this East Villager's "tasty" French-Eclectic fare and "nice ambiance" (with garden), but foes cite "high prices for Avenue B."

Cafe Milou ◐[S] – | – | – | M
92 Seventh Ave. S. (bet. Bleecker & Grove Sts.), 212-414-9824
Gianni Lekic, the new owner at this bustling Village sidewalk cafe, has added better food (Italian plus some French) courtesy of exec chef Bruna Alessandria; when not hosting, Lekic likes to concoct oddly named exotic drinks.

	F	D	S	C
Cafe Mozart ◐[S]	15	15	14	$20

154 W. 70th St. (bet. B'way & Columbus Ave.), 212-595-9797
◪ To some, this West Side cafe is "a cultured experience" for "delightful desserts" and "light" Eclectic bites plus live classical music, but others say it's "a bit off-key", more like "a European version of a NJ diner."

Cafe Noir ◐[S]	16	18	14	$28

32 Grand St. (Thompson St.), 212-431-7910
■ An "aptly named", "dark", "funky", "late-night" SoHo scene where a "cool, international crowd" nibbles on "good" Med-Moroccan fare; just "don't go when you're trying to stop smoking."

Cafe Nosidam ◐[S]	18	17	17	$40

768 Madison Ave. (66th St.), 212-717-5633
◪ "Another cell-phone wonder", this "Euro chic" East Side Italian-American strikes critics as "pretentious" and "pricey", but most call it a good pit stop for "dependable" food and "glam" "people-watching."

Café Pierre [S]	23	25	24	$58

Pierre Hotel, 2 E. 61st St. (bet. 5th & Madison Aves.), 212-940-8195
■ "Quiet elegance" is the hallmark of this "sophisticated" East Side French hotel cafe that's lovely for anything from breakfast to a "beautiful high tea", unrushed dinner or "romantic drink", all enhanced by "old-world", "wait-on-you-hand-and-foot" service and delightful pianist Kathleen Landis at night; so what if it's costly.

Cafe S.F.A. [S]	18	17	17	$26

Saks Fifth Ave., 611 Fifth Ave., 8th fl. (bet. 49th & 50th Sts.), 212-940-4080
■ The line "snakes through the lingerie racks", but this New American cafe at Saks allows clotheshounds to "refuel" on "great salads", sandwiches, etc. while viewing "St. Pat's spires."

Cafe Spice [S]	20	17	16	$28

72 University Pl. (bet. 10th & 11th Sts.), 212-253-6999
■ A "refreshing break from humdrum curry houses", this Village Dawat sib offers "spicy", "nouveau Indian" fare in a colorful "modern" setting with a "Pottery Barn" look; though some call for "bigger" portions, lower prices and "better" service, it's a "busy" "new fave."

Cafe St. John ◐[S]	17	15	16	$28

500 W. 110th St. (Amsterdam Ave.), 212-932-8420
■ Though not supernal it's "better than most things" in the nabe, thus this bistro opposite St. John the Divine is praised for its "good" food, "homey, relaxed" feel and "reasonable prices."

Cafeteria ◐[S]	17	18	13	$29

119 Seventh Ave. (17th St.), 212-414-1717
◪ Whether "heaven or hell", this "sleek" white 24-hour Chelsea neo-cafeteria offers modestly priced, "jazzed-up" New American "basics" to "models" and other "trendy young" things who come to "be seen looking cool"; the staff is "cute, but clueless."

Cafe Trevi ◐	22	18	22	$43

1570 First Ave. (bet. 81st & 82nd Sts.), 212-249-0040
■ Owner/maître d' Primo Laurenti's "personal service" makes this charming, low-key Northern Italian a "home away from home" for smart, well-heeled Eastsiders; besides the "old-style welcome", there's "simple, perfectly prepared food."

Cafe Un Deux Trois ◐[S]	16	15	16	$35

123 W. 44th St. (bet. B'way & 6th Ave.), 212-354-4148
◪ "Doodle while you wait" ("crayons" are provided) for "decent" bistro fare at this big, "upbeat" Theater District "warhorse" that's "hectic" and "crowded" but "convenient", "reasonable" and "quick": "1, 2, 3 and you're out the door and can remove the earplugs."

Café Word of Mouth 🅂 18 | 11 | 13 | $25
1012 Lexington Ave., 2nd fl. (bet. 72nd & 73rd Sts.), 212-249-5351
■ "Deserving more word of mouth" and "worth a climb", this second-floor East Side "sleeper" offers "yummy" breakfasts and lunch plus other "imaginative" Eclectic edibles; but it's not big on space or decor and has "waiters evolved from snails."

Caffe Buon Gusto ◐🅂 17 | 13 | 16 | $24
236 E. 77th St. (bet. 2nd & 3rd Aves.), 212-535-6884 ⧓
1009 Second Ave. (bet. 53rd & 54th Sts.), 212-755-1476
151 Montague St. (bet. Clinton & Henry Sts.), Brooklyn, 718-624-3838
☑ "Good mix-and-match pasta" at "cheap" prices explains why these Italian siblings are "always busy"; though "basic", they're an easy "substitute for your own cooking."

Caffe Cielo ◐🅂 18 | 17 | 19 | $34
881 Eighth Ave. (bet. 52nd & 53rd Sts.), 212-246-9555
■ The "pretty" setting has a "heavenly" cloud motif, and if the Italian fare doesn't always soar, it's "solid" enough to make this "amiable" West Midtowner a "bustling theater and business" lunch spot.

Caffe Grazie 🅂 17 | 16 | 18 | $36
26 E. 84th St. (bet. 5th & Madison Aves.), 212-717-4407
■ A "best bet" "après the Met", this East Side Italian offers "good food" and "gracious service" in a "quiet" townhouse; to some it's "a little dull", but most find it a "pleasant" alternative to "fancier spots."

Caffé on the Green (Queens) 🅂 21 | 21 | 20 | $42
201-10 Cross Island Pkwy. (bet. Clearview Expy. & Utopia Pkwy.), 718-423-7272
■ "There's life after Manhattan" as proved by this Queens "oasis", once Rudolph Valentino's home and now a "delightful" Italian with "excellent food", a "beautiful view, twinkling lights and parking."

Caffe Rafaella ◐🅂⧓ 17 | 18 | 14 | $20
134 Seventh Ave. S. (bet. Charles & 10th Sts.), 212-929-7247
■ Refugees from the daily grind love to "sink into" a "comfy chair" at this "quaint" Village Italian coffeehouse to enjoy its "good salads", "super desserts" and "people-watching" from outside seats; it works just as well for "romance" or simple "coffee and conversation."

Caffe Rosso ◐🅂 20 | 18 | 19 | $31
284 W. 12th St. (bet. 8th Ave. & W. 4th St.), 212-633-9277
■ "Pretty Village Italian" with a "romantic", "cozy country setting" and "consistently good", modestly priced food served by "really nice" people who will "make you feel loved", even if your date doesn't.

California Pizza Kitchen 🅂 15 | 11 | 14 | $19
201 E. 60th St. (bet. 2nd & 3rd Aves.), 212-755-7773
☑ "Cheap" "designer" pizzas and salads draw throngs to this "bright", "loud", "kid-friendly" West Coast chain outpost; critics say "hello! this is NY" – we don't need pies as "plastic as Pamela Anderson."

Calle Ocho 🅂 23 | 24 | 20 | $40
446 Columbus Ave. (bet. 81st & 82nd Sts.), 212-873-5025
■ One of the "hottest places on the Upper West Side", this new Pan-Latino "winner" offers "a fix of South Beach", with "beautiful people" enjoying "exciting, vibrant" food in a "stylish", "high-energy" setting; there's a "cool bar scene" too.

Cal's ◐🅂 19 | 19 | 19 | $36
55 W. 21st St. (bet. 5th & 6th Aves.), 212-929-0740
■ Flatiron Med-Eclectic offering the "perfect mix of casual ambiance and savvy" cooking in a "lofty" space roomy enough for "privacy"; "not too expensive", it works for a "business lunch" or "first date."

CamaJe Bistro & Lounge ●⬛ ▽ 19 | 16 | 20 | $36
85 MacDougal St. (bet. Bleecker & Houston Sts.), 212-673-8184
■ Though this Village French-American bistro/lounge doesn't draw a big response, fans say it "deserves better business" as it offers very good, moderately priced food in an "intimate", date-worthy setting.

Cambodian Cuisine (Bklyn) ⬛ ▽ 21 | 7 | 16 | $18
87 S. Elliot Pl. (bet. Fulton St. & Lafayette Ave.), 718-858-3262
■ Three reasons to try this Fort Greene Cambodian "hole-in-the-wall": it offers "lots of new tastes and textures", is "incredibly cheap" and there's "nothing like it" around; service is "sweet" if "distracted."

Campagna ●⬛ 24 | 21 | 21 | $49
24 E. 21st St. (bet. B'way & Park Ave. S.), 212-460-0900
■ Though "still a scene of fashionistas, would-be moguls and air-kissers", Mark Strausman's "elegant" Northern Italian is more than just a "Flatiron hot spot" thanks to "sophisticated" food led by "stunning" antipasti; it's "pricey", but most call it "a class act all the way."

Campagnola ●⬛ 23 | 19 | 21 | $48
1382 First Ave. (bet. 73rd & 74th Sts.), 212-861-1102
■ "Let the waiters 'make it real nice' for you" at this packed, "old-style" East Side Italian (complete with piano music) where the food is "always excellent" and "service is king" – at least for regulars; high prices don't faze the moneyed clientele and their "molls."

Campo ⬛ 20 | 16 | 19 | $32
89 Greenwich Ave. (bet. Bank & W. 12th Sts.), 212-691-8080
■ "Original tastes" mark this Village yearling offering "inventive", affordable 'country cuisine of the Americas' in "homey", rustic digs; don't miss the "unusual" brunch ("the orange doughnuts are to die for").

Can ●⬛ 19 | 18 | 17 | $35
482 W. Broadway (Houston St.), 212-533-6333
☑ Can "can be a good choice" for "tasty" French-Vietnamese fare served in a "pretty", "somewhat romantic" minimalist setting, but a few feel this staid SoHo spot deserves to be "never crowded."

Canaletto ●⬛ 22 | 17 | 21 | $41
208 E. 60th St. (bet. 2nd & 3rd Aves.), 212-317-9192
■ A most welcome East Side addition, this Italian "close to the movies and Bloomie's" treats diners with "TLC", serving midpriced "hearty food in a homey atmosphere"; no surprise – it gets "crowded."

Canal House ●⬛ 19 | 21 | 19 | $43
SoHo Grand Hotel, 310 W. Broadway, 2nd fl. (Grand St.), 212-965-3588
■ "Black clothes are requisite" at this "trendy" "haunt in the SoHo Grand", but "never mind the hype" – the American food is "good"; "you can really impress a date" in this attractive room or at the busy bar.

Candela ●⬛ 20 | 22 | 18 | $36
116 E. 16th St. (bet. Irving Pl. & Park Ave. S.), 212-254-1600
■ There are some "winning dishes" at this big "yet somehow cozy" "medieval" Union Square New American with "candles everywhere" to aid the "young" crowd in their romantic crusades; just "watch out for dripping wax."

Candido Pizza ●⬛⇆ 19 | 8 | 11 | $17
1606 First Ave. (bet. 83rd & 84th Sts.), 212-396-9401
☑ "Yummy", "light as a feather" thin-crust pizzas with "classic toppings" are turned out by this Eastsider's coal oven, but candidly speaking, the decor gets a "zero" and service is not much better.

F | D | S | C

Candle Cafe [S] — 19 | 13 | 17 | $22

1307 Third Ave. (bet. 74th & 75th Sts.), 212-472-0970

◪ "Believers" in a "granola mood" praise the Vegetarian food and "hemp beer" at this "cozy", kitschy bit of "California" on the East Side, but cynics claim you walk out "hungry and confused as to what you ate"; P.S. their motto ('be kind to animals, don't eat them') says it all.

Canton [S]≠ — 25 | 13 | 20 | $38

45 Division St. (bet. Bowery & Market St.), 212-226-4441

■ The *Survey's* top-rated Chinese, this Chinatown Cantonese vet is at its best if you "ask Eileen [the manager]" for advice; pro service and "upscale" (for C-town) decor help justify the high (for C-town) cost.

Canyon Road [S] — 20 | 18 | 17 | $30

1470 First Ave. (bet. 76th & 77th Sts.), 212-734-1600

■ "Good-looking" Eastsiders "dress in their preppy best" to dig into "way above ordinary" SW fare and "get sloshed" on "the definitive margs" at this "cool adobe" "date place"; though it "feels like New Mexico", the "noise" and "crowds" are pure Manhattan.

Capital ◐[S] — ▽ 19 | 16 | 18 | $32

1425 Second Ave. (bet. 74th & 75th Sts.), 212-734-9940

■ A "welcome" East Side arrival in a sea of trattorias, this Mideastern offers "inventive" fare as well as "excellent" homemade bread; other extras – or minuses, depending on one's taste – include weekend belly dancing and 'hookahs available for your smoking pleasure.'

CAPSOUTO FRÈRES [S] — 23 | 23 | 22 | $49

451 Washington St. (Watts St.), 212-966-4900

■ Though it's "hard to find" among TriBeCa's warehouses, "persist", because the "sublime soufflés" aren't the only dishes that rise to a "special occasion" at this French "gem"; besides "fantastic" (if pricey) food, assets include a high-ceilinged, brick-walled setting, "gracious hosts" and, thank God, "easy parking."

Captain's Table, The — 19 | 16 | 18 | $41

860 Second Ave. (46th St.), 212-697-9538

◪ There are two schools of thought on this Midtown seafooder, but to most it's a "solid" choice for "fresh fish" in "dignified" if "stodgy" digs.

Cara Mia [S] — 20 | 16 | 17 | $27

654 Ninth Ave. (bet. 45th & 46th Sts.), 212-262-6767

■ Keep this "friendly", "affordable" little Hell's Kitchen Italian in mind for pre-theater since it offers "huge portions" of "nicely done" "fresh pastas" in a simple but "festive" room.

Caribe [S] — 17 | 15 | 15 | $25

117 Perry St. (Greenwich St.), 212-255-9191

◪ "Can't afford a trip to Jamaica?" – this Village Caribbean is a "cheap" stand-in with "spicy" food, a tropical, drink-fueled "party" feel and "palm trees galore"; it would be perfect if they added a tanning salon.

Carino Ristorante [S] — 19 | 12 | 18 | $30

1710 Second Ave. (bet. 88th & 89th Sts.), 212-860-0566

■ "Adorable Mama Carino" "is always there, watching and greeting everybody" at this tiny, "flavorful" Upper East Side Italian; the "tables are too close", but that adds to the "warm, family" feel.

Carlyle Restaurant [S] — 23 | 26 | 24 | $61

Carlyle Hotel, 35 E. 76th St. (Madison Ave.), 212-744-1600

■ An East Side "bastion of urbanity" that's "long on taste and Short [Bobby, of course] on music", this hotel French-Continental is an "elegant private escape" for its "carriage trade" clientele, offering "fine" food, "posh" decor and ultra-"polite service"; still, some can't imagine being "old enough or rich enough to really belong here."

F	D	S	C

CARMINE'S [S] — 19 | 15 | 17 | $29

2450 Broadway (bet. 90th & 91st Sts.), 212-362-2200
200 W. 44th St. (bet. B'way & 8th Ave.), 212-221-3800 ◐

■ Though "loud" and "crazy", this popular family-style Italian duo is "perfect" for "gluttonous" groups, offering "truckloads" of low-cost, "garlic-drenched" food; just "wear elastic" and figure on a long wait since reservations are limited to parties of six or more.

Carnegie Deli ◐[S]⇏ — 20 | 9 | 12 | $22

854 Seventh Ave. (55th St.), 212-757-2245

◪ At this renowned Midtown deli "institution", it's part of the shtick to "jostle tourists, fight with waiters" and "ignore" elbow-to-elbow seating to enjoy super "sandwiches so big, you need Mick Jagger's mouth to eat them"; plan on primo pastrami, corned beef, cheesecake and other "cholesterol" classics at this Woody Allen–style "only in NY" experience that will never be certified by the AHA.

Carol's Cafe (Staten Island) ▽ 25 | 19 | 21 | $43

1571 Richmond Rd. (bet. Four Corners Rd. & Seaview Ave.), 718-979-5600

■ "Should be in Manhattan" say those envious of chef-owner Carol Frazzetta's "superb" Staten Island Eclectic; the prices may belong in Manhattan too and some find the decor "a bit sparse" and the pace "slow", but "the best things in life are worth waiting", and paying, for.

Casa ◐[S] ▽ 19 | 17 | 20 | $33

72 Bedford St. (Commerce St.), 212-366-9410

■ "Cozy, simple" Brazilian Villager with moderately priced "down-home food", a "cute" setting and "enthusiastic" service; a few dissenters find the food "blah", but the same can't be said of the "leggy crowd."

Casa Di Meglio ◐[S] — 17 | 17 | 18 | $31

235 W. 48th St. (bet. B'way & Eighth Ave.), 212-582-6577

■ Maybe it's "not going to win any awards", but this "quiet" Italian is a Theater District "find" thanks to "reliable" food, "honest prices" ("great pre-theater" prix fixe) and service that "gets you out in time."

Casa La Femme ◐[S] — 17 | 25 | 16 | $43

150 Wooster St. (bet. Houston & Prince Sts.), 212-505-0005

◪ "Tented tables" make this "exotic" SoHo Med-Egyptian a "one-way ticket to nookieville", but foes balk at paying "a fortune" for fair food and "surly" service, "unless you've got model looks or a Prada" outfit.

Casa Mia [S] ▽ 20 | 19 | 21 | $28

225 E. 24th St. (bet. 2nd & 3rd Aves.), 212-679-5606

■ Gramercy locals "hope the world doesn't discover" this "cozy" family-run Italian; the food is "good", the ambiance "homey" and "you get a lot for your money"; some even find it "kinda romantic."

Casimir ◐[S] — 21 | 19 | 15 | $30

103-105 Ave. B (bet. 6th & 7th Sts.), 212-358-9683

■ When you're too "broke" for Balthazar, try this "hip" East Village bistro; it's "authentic" "in every way", with "hearty food" and "waiters who are a delight to look at", even if their "heads are still in France."

Castellano [S] — 21 | 19 | 21 | $45

138 W. 55th St. (bet. 6th & 7th Aves.), 212-664-1975

■ If a bit "staid", this wood-paneled Midtown Northern Italian is "good for a client lunch" or pre–City Center meal, offering "old-world courtesy" and "fine" food that's "pricey" but "worth every cent" to regulars.

Cavaliere [S] — 18 | 16 | 18 | $31

192 Third Ave. (bet. 17th & 18th Sts.), 212-228-9320

■ A "pleasant", "basic" Gramercy Northern Italian with "good food", "moderate prices" and a roomy, "not overly loud" setting; not a star, but by no means a slouch.

Caviar Russe S
24 | 23 | 22 | $64
538 Madison Ave., 2nd fl. (bet. 54th & 55th Sts.), 212-980-5908
■ Feel like "Dr. Zhivago" spooning "your favorite caviar" and sipping vodka at this "decadent" "upstairs den", a luxe Midtown roe house with an "aristocratic" ambiance and "gracious service"; go ahead and "splurge" – "get the tasting menu."

Caviarteria S
23 | 15 | 18 | $47
Delmonico Hotel, 502 Park Ave. (59th St.), 212-759-7410
SoHo Grand Hotel, 310 W. Broadway (bet. Canal & Grand Sts.), 212-925-5515 ●
■ Offering "indulgence without snobbery", these caviar places, besides having "wonderful" caviar, also provide "delicious" blini, smoked salmon and champagne; it helps to "have a lot of disposable income", even though they're fairly priced.

Celadon S
20 | 23 | 19 | $49
1167 Madison Ave. (bet. 85th & 86th Sts.), 212-734-7711
☑ Despite "uneven" early performance, this new Upper East Side Asian-American shows real "promise" with a "beautiful" bi-level setting and generally "very good" fusion fare; though pricey and in need of "more practice", it looks like a keeper.

Cellini
21 | 19 | 21 | $41
65 E. 54th St. (bet. Madison & Park Aves.), 212-751-1555
■ "For an evening in Tuscany" minus "jet lag", try this Midtown Italian that "looks and feels" like the real thing, providing "good food" and "attentive yet unobtrusive service"; most find it a "reliable expense-accounter" that's "charming all-around."

Cello S
– | – | – | VE
53 E. 77th St. (bet. Madison & Park Aves.), 212-517-1200
Had this handsome East Side French seafooder-cum-garden been open at the time of our *Survey*, it might well have rated as the best newcomer of 1999; as it is, well-heeled locals have kept it packed since opening day, so despite top-of-the-line prices, it's already one of the toughest tickets in town.

Cendrillon S
20 | 17 | 19 | $34
45 Mercer St. (bet. Broome & Grand Sts.), 212-343-9012
■ A "cultural adventure" awaits at this "calm", "airy" SoHo Filipino–Pan-Asian that fans feel "deserves broader acclaim" for its "exotic" ingredients and flavors; however, a few say its fusion is "more like confusion" and "not worthy of East or West."

Cent'Anni S
22 | 15 | 20 | $44
50 Carmine St. (bet. Bedford & Bleecker Sts.), 212-989-9494
■ To its "dedicated clientele", this "reliable" Village Northern Italian is a "civilized" "Downtown pleasure" despite "tight" quarters and decor that "needs help"; "let them order for you", then "close your eyes" and you're in Italy.

Chadwick's (Brooklyn) S
19 | 17 | 18 | $31
8822 Third Ave. (89th St.), 718-833-9855
☑ This "favorite" Bay Ridge "Saturday night place" is a very good New American serving some old standards like "amazing beef Wellington" in a "country-like atmosphere"; at worst it's "pleasant but nondescript."

Chanpen Thai S
20 | 15 | 19 | $23
761 Ninth Ave. (51st St.), 212-586-6808
■ Dubbed a "humble Thai heaven in Hell's Kitchen", this "bargain" spot comes with ingredients "so fresh" and "service so cheery" that they make up for the modest ambiance; try it for pre-theater.

CHANTERELLE
28 | 26 | 27 | VE

2 Harrison St. (Hudson St.), 212-966-6960

■ "Sheer perfection", "angels feast on lesser food" – the accolades flow for Karen and David Waltuck's "serene", now 20-year-old TriBeCa New French, where "every dish shows the creative mind behind it", the decor exudes "understated elegance" and service is "seamless" and welcoming "whether you come" for the "top value" prix fixe lunch ($35) or a blowout dinner ($75 prix fixe only); in sum, "one of NYC's very best."

Charley O's ●S
– | – | – | M

218 W. 45th St. (bet. B'way & 8th Ave.), 212-626-7300

A remnant of what used to be a Manhattan chain, this jumbo Times Square American pub packs in a mix of tourists and business folk who still seem to dig its upscale, but affordable, burger-and-brew format.

Charlotte S
20 | 20 | 20 | $45

Millennium Broadway Hotel, 145 W. 44th St. (bet. B'way & 6th Ave.), 212-789-7508

☑ Popular for its "good pre-theater" prix fixe, this "handsome" hotel New American near Times Square also suits "for business" dining or Sunday brunch; but beyond the set menus, it can be "pricey."

Chat 'n Chew S
16 | 14 | 14 | $20

10 E. 16th St. (bet. 5th Ave. & Union Sq. W.), 212-243-1616

☑ "Big portions" of "cheap" American "comfort food" draw a "noisy" "young crowd" to this Union Square venue; it has a "kitschy", "yard-sale feel" and "sassy", "overworked" staff.

Chelsea Bistro & Bar S
22 | 20 | 20 | $43

358 W. 23rd St. (bet. 8th & 9th Aves.), 212-727-2026

■ "Warm and welcoming" Chelsea French bistro with "high-quality" victuals ("homemade breads", a "fabulous goat cheese tart"), specialty infused-Lillet drinks and a "well-chosen wine list."

Chelsea Grill S
19 | 15 | 17 | M

135 Eighth Ave. (bet. 16th & 17th Sts.), 212-242-5336

■ Chelsea residents "love the garden" and "thick, juicy", "perfectly seasoned" burgers at this Eclectic-American; the "laid-back" bar atmosphere is ideal "for hanging out."

Chelsea Lobster Co. ●S
– | – | – | M

156 Seventh Ave. (bet. 19th & 20th Sts.), 212-243-5732

A far cry from a Cape Cod roadside shack, this Chelsea seafooder has a cave-like interior with garage-door walls that roll up in summer, plus a midpriced menu featuring the namesake crustacean (served steamed, baked or on a roll).

Chelsea Ristorante S
21 | 17 | 20 | $34

108 Eighth Ave. (bet. 15th & 16th Sts.), 212-924-7786

■ Chelsea Italian where an "accommodating staff" serves "delicious brick-oven pizza" and "perfect salads"; even if the decor is "tacky", overall it's an "underappreciated" "gem."

Chez Brigitte S⊅
17 | 10 | 17 | $19

77 Greenwich Ave. (bet. Bank St. & 7th Ave. S.), 212-929-6736

■ It's "fun to watch the cook" from the 11-seat lunch counter of this never-changing, "sweet" West Village French standby; it remains the "most un-yup" place in the area for a filling stew or "tasty omelet."

Chez Es Saada ●S
18 | 26 | 16 | $40

42 E. First St. (bet. 1st & 2nd Aves.), 212-777-5617

■ "Slip into something slinky" then head to this "dark", "romantic" East Village French-Moroccan, a "sexy", "late-night" "underground Casbah" where "gorgeous people" ("what language was that?") sip exotic cocktails and nibble tapas-like treats at "uncomfortable" "low tables."

F | D | S | C

Chez Gnagna Koty's [S] ▽ 23 15 21 $17
530 Ninth Ave. (bet. 39th & 40th Sts.), 212-279-1755
■ "Surprise" Senegalese near the Port Authority – of course, a Senegalese would be a surprise anywhere in NYC and in this case, given the low prices, it's a pleasant surprise; the elemental setting is dressed up with African fabrics and background music.

Chez Jacqueline [S] 21 18 19 $42
72 MacDougal St. (bet. Bleecker & W. Houston Sts.), 212-505-0727
■ "On a summer afternoon" "sit outside" at this West Village French bistro, an "old standby" where "unchanging simple dishes" ("delicious rabbit") "never fail to satisfy" and "nice hosts" ensure a return visit.

Chez Josephine ◐ 20 21 20 $42
414 W. 42nd St. (bet. 9th & 10th Aves.), 212-594-1925
■ "Adorable" owner Jean-Claude Baker makes it "a party" at this "red velvet" French, a Theater District tribute to his mother Josephine; "well-prepared food", "interesting memorabilia", a "great piano player" and an "attentive staff" add up to a "fun place."

Chez Louis ◐[S] 22 17 18 $44
74 W. 50th St. (6th Ave.), 212-333-3388
■ "Hurray, it's back" declare Midtown acolytes of David and Susan Liederman's revived French bistro; it's hard not to "love the roast chicken" and garlic potato pie, but the interior "needs a little warmth."

Chez Michallet [S] 24 21 23 $44
90 Bedford St. (Grove St.), 212-242-8309
■ "Fall in love again" at this "tiny gem of a bistro in the heart of the West Village" with "wonderful food", a room that "defines picturesque" and "warm, friendly" service; if the conversation starts to fizzle there's always "great people-watching."

Chez Napoléon 19 14 20 $37
365 W. 50th St. (bet. 8th & 9th Aves.), 212-265-6980
■ A 40-year-old Classic French Theater District "warhorse" with "robust" victuals, reasonable prices and "personal attention" from the "sweet" owner; so what if it's "cramped" and "needs refurbishing."

Chez Oskar (Brooklyn) **◐[S]** ▽ 18 19 17 $30
211 DeKalb Ave. (Adelphi St.), 718-852-6250
◪ "Sit outside and sip your wine" at this "colonial outpost of France in Fort Greene", a "fun, electric place" for not-exactly-starving artists, with a long, stylish bar and up-to-the-minute French fare.

Chez Suzette ◐[S] 17 15 18 $34
675B Ninth Ave. (bet. 46th & 47th Sts.), 212-581-9717
■ Owner Gerard "makes you feel part of the family" at this "dark", "congenial" Theater District "country bistro"; foodwise "you could do better, but also much worse."

Chiam ◐[S] 22 20 22 $40
160 E. 48th St. (bet. Lexington & 3rd Aves.), 212-371-2323
■ An "ambitious" Midtown "gourmet" Chinese with "great dim sum", "healthy choices", a "superior" wine list, a "sleek", mirrored setting and "great service from waiters who speak English."

Chianti [S] 20 17 18 $40
1043 Second Ave. (bet. 54th & 55th Sts.), 212-980-8686
■ Scott Conant's "creative" Italian fare "deserves a better setting" say regulars at this Midtown East "neighborhood place", but that doesn't stop them from flocking in, especially for the bargain pre-theater dinner.

Chianti (Brooklyn) ◑ S
21 | 18 | 18 | $32
8530 Third Ave. (86th St.), 718-921-6300
■ "Bring friends" because "couples have a problem" finishing the "bathtub-size pasta dishes" at this "newly renovated" and expanded Bay Ridge Italian, a "Carmine's copycat" that's equally "loud."

Chikubu
21 | 15 | 19 | $41
12 E. 44th St. (bet. 5th & Madison Aves.), 212-818-0715
■ This "traditional" Midtown Japanese with "polite", kimono-clad staff serves satisfying sushi in a serene environment that's "good for entertaining, especially in the tatami room."

Chimichurri Grill S
21 | 14 | 18 | $38
606 Ninth Ave. (bet. 43rd & 44th Sts.), 212-586-8655
■ "Another Atkins diet place", this "bare-bones" Theater District Argentine grill has "tasty" steaks, empanadas and a "chimichurri sauce that improves anything"; foes say "tender meat, tough staff."

China Fun ◑ S
15 | 8 | 12 | $19
1239 Second Ave. (65th St.), 212-752-0810
246 Columbus Ave. (bet. 71st & 72nd Sts.), 212-580-1516
1653 Broadway (51st St.), 212-333-2622
☑ "When you don't have time for dim sum in Chinatown", consider this chain of "cheap", "quick and easy" if "uneven" noodle shops; bashers say "zero ambiance" means they're "better for delivery."

CHINA GRILL ◑ S
23 | 21 | 19 | $43
CBS Bldg., 52 W. 53rd St. (bet. 5th & 6th Aves.), 212-333-7788
■ "Cell phone–happy" bicoastal "media" types on "expense accounts" flock to this Midtown Eclectic for the "power scene", "exciting" fusion food, "dark", "cool", high-ceilinged setting and "sultry vixens" at the "noisiest bar in NYC"; critics consider it all "big, cold and insincere."

Chin Chin ◑ S
23 | 19 | 21 | $40
216 E. 49th St. (bet. 2nd & 3rd Aves.), 212-888-4555
■ "Dynamite Grand Marnier shrimp" and "amazing Peking duck" are just two of the "real winners" on the menu of this stylish, "upscale" Midtown Chinese with "beautiful family photos on the walls" and "caring" service led by host-owner Jimmy Chin.

Cho Dang Gol S
▽ 22 | 14 | 16 | $23
55 W. 35th St. (bet. 5th & 6th Aves.), 212-695-8222
■ Almost "everything on the menu" of this "low-key" "country-style" Midtown Korean includes "tofu made on the premises"; while you "may not know what half" the meal is, most agree it's "good anyway", especially the casseroles come winter.

Choga ◑ S
▽ 18 | 13 | 16 | $22
145 Bleecker St., 2nd fl. (bet. La Guardia Pl. & Thompson St.), 212-598-5946
■ If it's 3 AM and you're hankering for hamachi after "hanging out" in the West Village, there's always this "go-to place for sushi" and Korean fare; at that hour, you may not notice that the decor "needs revamping."

Chola S
21 | 15 | 18 | $35
232 E. 58th St. (bet. 2nd & 3rd Aves.), 212-688-4619
■ "Tastes from all parts of India" (even Calcutta's Jewish quarter) await at this Midtown East venue that's "on a par with", and the same block as, perennial favorite Dawat; the lunch buffet is a best buy.

Cho-Sen Garden (Queens) S
▽ 21 | 16 | 19 | $30
64-43 108th St. (bet. 64th & 65th Sts.), 718-275-1300
■ Kosher Chinese-Japanese (with a sushi bar, no less) is hard to come by, even in NYC, so those cho-sen people who've been to this affordable Forest Hills venue are grateful for its food and solid service that's even better if you're a regular or a rabbi.

Choshi 🟥
77 Irving Pl. (E. 19th St.), 212-420-1419

18	12	15	$28

■ "In the shadow of Gramercy Park" lies this "small" Japanese that offers "decent", "fresh" fish and "relaxing" outdoor seating.

Christer's
145 W. 55th St. (bet. 6th & 7th Aves.), 212-974-7224

21	20	20	$45

■ Chef and "salmon king" Christer Larsson does wonders with seafood at this "tranquil", rustic Midtown Scandinavian furnished with model fishing boats and "lovely fireplaces"; it's a "terrific" pre-theater choice for City Center and Carnegie Hall ticketholders.

Christina's Country Kitchen 🟥   ▽ 19 | 18 | 17 | $18
491 10th Ave. (bet. 37th & 38th Sts.), 212-631-0617

☑ "Long live the log cabin" decor declare denizens of this "cute" Javits-area country diner where "scrumptious pancakes", real Southern grits and other breakfast favorites are served all day and the vegetables are grown, of all places, on the rooftop.

Christine's 🟥⇗
208 First Ave. (bet. 12th & 13th Sts.), 212-254-2474

16	8	13	$17

■ "You can always find a policeman" "filling up for pennies" on "hearty" Polish-American chow ("real blintzes", "best pierogi") at this "dingy" East Village diner with the genre's usual "glaring lights."

Christos Hasapo-Taverna (Queens) ◑🟥   ▽ 21 | 16 | 19 | $34
41-08 23rd Ave. (41st St.), 718-726-5195

■ Doubling as a daytime butcher shop, this "friendly" Astoria Greek steakhouse offers "very good appetizers" and modestly priced, high-quality beef – by some estimates, it's only a "15-minute car ride from the Upper East Side."

Churrascaria Plantation ◑🟥
150 Central Park S. (bet. 6th & 7th Aves.), 212-489-7070

20	18	20	$41

■ "More subdued than" its sibling Churrascaria Plataforma, this Central Park South Brazilian may be "the most elegant" of the new rodizio-style eateries around town, but that doesn't mean there isn't a bountiful buffet and skewered meats that "just keep coming."

Churrascaria Plataforma ◑🟥
Belvedere Hotel, 316 W. 49th St. (bet. 8th & 9th Aves.), 212-245-0505

21	18	20	$42

■ "Holy cow, pig and everything else" – "the diet starts tomorrow" swear "loud", caipirinha-fueled groups of "festive" carnivores descending on this "high-energy", high-quality Theater District AYCE Brazilian rodizio with a "terrific" salad bar and "succulent meats"; "you'll waddle out satisfied if you don't have a heart attack" first.

Ciao Europa ◑🟥
Warwick Hotel, 63 W. 54th St. (bet. 5th & 6th Aves.), 212-247-1200

19	18	18	$37

☑ "Splendid murals" add to the "European" feel at this Midtown hotel Italian where businesspeople and tourists like the "space between tables", rational decibel level and "good value" pre-theater dinner.

Cibi Cibi ◑🟥
200 E. 60th St. (3rd Ave.), 212-751-8615

16	16	16	$31

☑ Formerly Yellowfingers, this new Italian across from Bloomie's works best "if you have a cell phone and foreign accent"; it offers great people-watching and a DJ nightly, but some report "kinks."

Cibo 🟥
767 Second Ave. (bet. 41st & 42nd Sts.), 212-681-1616

21	20	20	$39

■ A "favorite of Tudor City locals" and "business diners", this "much-needed", "classy" New American–Italian has "original" dishes, an "accommodating" staff, a "spacious room" and a "nice brunch."

F | D | S | C

Cilantro ◐[S] 18 | 17 | 18 | $25

1712 Second Ave. (bet. 88th & 89th Sts.), 212-722-4242

■ Happy-hour-hunting Upper Eastsiders in their "20s and 30s" tout this "cute" Southwestern's "exceptional" homemade chips, "powerful margaritas", outdoor garden and friendly owner who "goes around to every table"; critics counter "don't go out of your way."

Cinquanta ◐[S] 18 | 16 | 19 | $43

50 E. 50th St. (bet. Madison & Park Aves.), 212-759-5050

◪ An "older", cinquanta-ish crowd gets a "warm welcome" from the "nice people" who run this "upscale" Midtown Italian, though a few feel the attentive service borders on "hovering."

Cinque Terre [S] 20 | 17 | 18 | $41

22 E. 38th St. (bet. Madison & Park Aves.), 212-213-0910

◪ Ya gotta "love those regional dishes" at this Murray Hill Northern Italian that "has its own flavors" and is the "closest thing to the Italian Riviera" in Manhattan.

Circa ◐[S] 20 | 20 | 17 | $36

103 Second Ave. (6th St.), 212-777-4120

■ "Beautiful" "hipsters" prefer to "get a booth" or sit outside this East Village Mediterranean, which has a "far better menu" than its address or "black-clad" staff would suggest; consider it "for brunch" or "late-night snacks" with DJ music ("bring earplugs").

Circo, Osteria del [S] 23 | 24 | 21 | $50

120 W. 55th St. (bet. 6th & 7th Aves.), 212-265-3636

◪ "P.T. Barnum meets Marcella Hazan" via the Maccioni siblings at this "witty" Tuscan where "mama [Eggi's] pastas", "whimsical desserts" and "playful" "circus decor" lighten the mood of Midtown expense-accounters; critics counter "send in the clowns."

Circus ◐[S] 21 | 20 | 20 | $41

808 Lexington Ave. (bet. 62nd & 63rd Sts.), 212-223-2965

■ On weekends, this "lively" East Side Brazilian bistro supplements its "imaginative", "nuevo" menu with traditional dishes such as feijoada; but at all times the "welcoming servers" and "amazing" caipirinhas make it a "second home" to Rio expats.

Cité ◐[S] 22 | 20 | 21 | $50

120 W. 51st St. (bet. 6th & 7th Aves.), 212-956-7100

◪ A "well-packaged" Midtown steakhouse where "corporate card"–carrying "suits" host clients amidst "beautiful fresh flowers" and "well-spaced" tables over "solid" beef and seafood; oenophiles find the post–8 PM "unlimited" wine dinner a "fab" deal – give it a "tumble."

Cité Grill ◐[S] 21 | 19 | 19 | $41

120 W. 51st St. (bet. 6th & 7th Aves.), 212-956-7262

◪ Cité's "lower-priced", "more casual" grill sibling has "great burgers", a "popular" "after-work bar scene", a "convenient" pre-theater menu and the same "outstanding" AYCD wine dinner.

Citrus Bar & Grill ◐[S] 18 | 18 | 16 | $30

320 Amsterdam Ave. (75th St.), 212-595-0500

◪ "Fresh juice margs by the liter" mean "trouble walking home" for "yuppies" leaving the "hot bar scene" at this West Side Southwestern, a "welcome addition" to the area, even given the "hit-or-miss" menu.

City Bakery 22 | 12 | 14 | $15

22 E. 17th St. (bet. B'way & 5th Ave.), 212-366-1414

■ Maury Rubin's "pretzel croissants keep us in the city" declare Union Square residents enamored of this "minimalist" bakery, where "to-die-for hot chocolate", "rich pastries", a "fancy-shmancy salad bar" and snazzy sandwiches lead ladies to ask "is he single?"

F | D | S | C

City Crab & Seafood Co. ◐[S] — 18 | 15 | 15 | $35

235 Park Ave. S. (19th St.), 212-529-3800

◪ "Downstairs for groups", "up for quiet" is the advice at this Flatiron seafooder, where there's more unanimity over the "bar scene" than the food; regulars say "stick to the raw bar", crabs and lobster.

City Grill ◐[S] — 15 | 14 | 15 | $24

269 Columbus Ave. (bet. 72nd & 73rd Sts.), 212-873-9400

■ For a "quick", "neighborhood bite" after a visit to the Museum of Natural History, consider this "affordable", "kid-friendly" Upper West Side American with standout mac 'n' cheese and Cobb salad.

City Hall — 21 | 23 | 20 | $46

131 Duane St. (bet. Church St. & W. B'way), 212-227-7777

◪ Set in a landmark 1863 TriBeCa building with "soaring ceilings" and "wonderful photos" of old NYC, chef-owner Henry Meer's "ambitious" Traditional American features steaks, fish, burgers and a raw bar; though it's "overpriced" to some, nostalgists call it a "great newcomer."

Ci Vediamo [S] — 18 | 17 | 17 | $32

1431 Third Ave. (81st St.), 212-650-0850

■ "Sit upstairs for a quiet", "cozy" meal at this Upper East Side Italian, a "great first date place" for "twentysomethings" featuring "reasonable prices" and food that's "better than most" of its "endless" competitors.

Clarke's, P.J. ◐[S] — 15 | 14 | 14 | $27

915 Third Ave. (55th St.), 212-759-1650

◪ It may be "slipping noticeably" in the bloodshot eyes of longtime barflies, but this atmospheric landmark Midtown tavern still leaves some singing "'I Love NY'" after a "rainy Sunday" or "2 AM" burger amidst "old-fashioned decor" and a rotating cast of local characters.

Clay ◐[S] — ▽ 19 | 20 | 18 | $27

202 Mott St. (bet. Kenmare & Spring Sts.), 212-625-1105

◪ "Korean + trendiness" = Clay, a pale green, seductively lit "welcome addition" to NoLita with a stylish bar, an "inexpensive" menu of "interesting" (if "not the most authentic") dishes and a clientele that lives by the motto 'you can never wear too much black.'

Clementine ◐[S] — 21 | 21 | 18 | $44

1 Fifth Ave. (8th St.), 212-253-0003

■ The hype may have died down, but the "ultrabusy", "young" bar scene is still "happening" at John Schenk's art deco Village New American, where the "bubbly fountain" reflects the exuberant, pricey "cutting-edge" food, including "out-of-this-world desserts."

Cloister Cafe, The ◐[S]≠ — 11 | 21 | 12 | $21

238 E. Ninth St. (bet. 2nd & 3rd Aves.), 212-777-9128

◪ "It's all about" the "amazing garden" at this East Village French-Italian, so "who cares" if the food and service "don't deserve" such a "magical" setting; for best results, "stick to coffee and dessert."

Club Macanudo ◐ — 13 | 21 | 17 | $39

26 E. 63rd St. (bet. Madison & Park Aves.), 212-752-8200

◪ It would be strictly a "man's place" but for all the women on the prowl for an investment banker at this "posh" Upper East Side club that works as a "hangout to smoke cigars, sip scotch" and pick at Eclectic snacks while celebrating the Dow's latest record.

Coach House, The [S] — 24 | 20 | 22 | $59

Avalon Hotel, 16 E. 32nd St. (bet. 5th & Madison Aves.), 212-696-1800

◪ Larry Forgione's Murray Hill reincarnation of the beloved old Village classic serves "excellent", but expensive, Regional American fare in a room decorated with photos of old NY; but some feel it "hasn't decided" what it wants to be and is a letdown given the price and all the hype.

Coco Marina 🆂
– | – | – | E

World Financial Ctr., 2 World Financial Ctr. (Liberty & West Sts.), 212-385-8080
This Downtown outpost of Pino Luongo's Coco empire draws quite a lunchtime crowd, but while surveyors like the "great atrium space", some feel the pricey Italian food "does not live up to it."

Coconut Grill ●🆂
16 | 14 | 15 | $27

1481 Second Ave. (77th St.), 212-772-6262
☑ "Still popular after many years", this East Side American attracts "neighborhood" yups who like its "easy", "standby" appeal, sidewalk seating, "amazing fries", salads and "good-bet" Sunday brunch.

Coco Opera 🆂
16 | 18 | 16 | $42

58 W. 65th St. (bet. Columbus Ave. & CPW), 212-873-3700
☑ "Handy to Lincoln Center", this Pino Luongo offshoot has farroto to go coco over, but is otherwise "overpriced" and "disappointing" compared to its siblings; recent menu and staff changes may improve matters.

Coco Pazzo ●🆂
22 | 21 | 20 | $52

23 E. 74th St. (bet. 5th & Madison Aves.), 212-794-0205
■ "There's always a celebrity" among the "international clientele" of this "plush", "roomy", "high-priced" East Side Tuscan with indisputably "excellent" cuisine; but those not a guest of Ronald Perelman say "it helps to be a regular."

Coco Pazzo Café ●🆂
20 | 19 | 19 | $45

7 E. 59th St. (bet. 5th & Madison Aves.), 212-935-3535
■ As expected, Coco Pazzo's Midtown Italian sibling draws a business lunch crowd, but with "consistently good" food, cozy banquettes and charming countryside murals, it shifts its sights to a hipper, come-as-you-are dinner crowd.

Coco Pazzo Teatro ●🆂
19 | 18 | 18 | $46

Paramount Hotel, 235 W. 46th St. (bet. B'way & 8th Ave.), 212-827-4222
☑ "Becoming a favorite" of pre-theater diners because of its "perfect location" next to the shows, this sprawling Coco satellite is inevitably "harried at peak times", so "arrive early" or go "after 8 PM."

Coco Reef (Brooklyn) 🆂
– | – | – | M

222 Seventh Ave. (5th St.), 718-788-5036
Towering palms, coral-lined walls and tropical aquariums define the cool South Seas decor at this Park Slope Malaysian-Singaporean whose modestly priced menu focuses on spicy seafood; shaded terrace seats let you watch the carefree natives drift by.

Coco Roco (Brooklyn) 🆂
21 | 11 | 17 | $22

392 Fifth Ave. (bet. 6th & 7th Sts.), 718-965-3376
■ "Finger-lickin' good" rotisserie chicken and "ethereal seviche" explain why this "cheap", recently renovated Peruvian has "replaced Chinese takeout" for Park Slope residents.

Coffee Shop ●🆂
15 | 14 | 11 | $25

29 Union Sq. W. (16th St.), 212-243-7969
☑ Despite being a "passé hot spot", this "loud" Union Square Brazilian-American with "the world's thinnest staff" (i.e. models) still draws a crowd with its sidewalk tables and "late-night" bar scene; ratings suggest that the staff needs a shot of caffeine and warmer shoulders.

Colina 🆂
∇ 19 | 23 | 16 | $47

ABC Carpet & Home, 35 E. 18th St. (bet. B'way & Park Ave. S.), 212-505-2233
■ It's no surprise that this pricey Union Square Italian looks "beautiful" since it's in a genuine reconstructed Brazilian farmhouse; but initial reports suggest that management needs to jack up the service and simplify the good but confusing menu.

F | D | S | C

Col Legno ◐[S] 20 | 13 | 17 | $31

231 E. Ninth St. (bet. 2nd & 3rd Aves.), 212-777-4650

■ "Honest", "well-prepared" Tuscan rules at this "steady" East Villager where the "grill is king", the wood-oven pizza is "excellent" and the thyme potatoes are "the best this side of Firenze."

Columbus Bakery [S] 19 | 13 | 12 | $15

957 First Ave. (bet. 52nd & 53rd Sts.), 212-421-0334
474 Columbus Ave. (bet. 82nd & 83rd Sts.), 212-724-6880

■ "Only mothers understand" how to navigate these East and West Side bakery/cafes where the "daily stroller slalom" is de rigueur before "nursing a cup of coffee" over "fab" pastries, sandwiches and salads.

Comfort Diner, The [S] 15 | 13 | 13 | $18

142 E. 86th St. (Lexington Ave.), 212-426-8600 ◐
214 E. 45th St. (bet. 2nd & 3rd Aves.), 212-867-4555

◪ "You feel like you're in a scene from *Happy Days*" at these "retro" East Side diners where you "come as you are" for comfort classics, e.g. meat loaf, mac 'n' cheese and "thick shakes"; the uncharmed find the prices "inflated" and victuals "ordinary" ("mom was a better cook").

Cooking with Jazz (Queens) [S] 24 | 14 | 20 | $35

1201 154th St. (12th Ave.), 718-767-6979

■ "Be prepared for a hot and spicy" "wonderful" taste of the Big Easy at this "authentic" corner Cajun in Whitestone, where a "marvelous early bird" shares top billing with jazz (Sunday–Thursday) and staffers make a "serious effort to please"; P.S. there's now a less "cramped" branch in Malverne, LI.

Cool House of Loo [S] – | – | – | M

1378 Third Ave. (bet. 78th & 79th Sts.), 212-585-3388

Zippy new Asian-French fusion Eastsider with a midpriced menu that's slanted toward things aquatic, courtesy of a chef who's done time at Lutèce and LI's Tupelo Honey; to stand out against its color-drenched, almost psychedelic interior you just wear white.

Copeland's [S] 19 | 12 | 16 | $26

547 W. 145th St. (bet. Amsterdam Ave. & B'way), 212-234-2357

◪ If Sylvia's is booked up with Japanese tour groups, head 20 blocks north to this other Harlem Southern specialist with a "bargain buffet", jazz pianist nightly and Sunday gospel brunch – even the most materialistic NYer can use a little soul.

Coppola's [S] 18 | 15 | 16 | $28

206 W. 79th St. (bet. Amsterdam Ave. & B'way), 212-877-3840
378 Third Ave. (bet. 27th & 28th Sts.), 212-679-0070

◪ "Reminds me of growing up in Brooklyn" say nostalgic voters commenting on these affordable, "nontrendy", "solid" West Side and Gramercy "neighborhood Italians", home to "oldies but goodies" such as the "best minestrone" and "veal parmigiana the way it should be."

Cornelia Street Cafe ◐[S] 18 | 16 | 17 | $28

29 Cornelia St. (bet. Bleecker & W. 4th Sts.), 212-989-9319

■ A "mellow" "place to linger" in the Village, this "throwback" "may not win any awards but is a safe bet" for "straightforward", modestly priced, "French-inspired fare"; to get the full "hippie-ish" effect, "slip downstairs" for jazz, drama and poetry readings.

Corner Bistro ◐[S]≠ 22 | 11 | 12 | $15

331 W. Fourth St. (Jane St.), 212-242-9502

■ "Get there by 5:30 PM or expect a wait" for the "incomparable", "hands-down" "best burger in town" served on "paper plates" at this "dark", "rustic", "zero-pretension" West Village pub; after 20 years, the NYC press discovered this place – since then, it's been so "overrun by yuppies" that "maybe they'll hire a second waiter."

Cosi Sandwich Bar
20 | 11 | 13 | $12

60 E. 56th St. (bet. Madison & Park Aves.), 212-588-0888
165 E. 52nd St. (bet. Lexington & 3rd Aves.), 212-758-7800
38 E. 45th St. (bet. Madison & Vanderbilt Aves.), 212-949-7400
Paramount Plaza, 1633 Broadway (51st St.), 212-397-2674 **S**
61 W. 48th St. (bet. 5th & 6th Aves.), 212-265-2674
11 W. 42nd St. (bet. 5th & 6th Aves.), 212-398-6660
3 E. 17th St. (bet. B'way & 5th Ave.), 212-414-8468 **S**
3 World Financial Ctr. (Vesey St.), 212-571-2001 **S**
54 Pine St. (William St.), 212-809-2674
55 Broad St. (bet. Beaver St. & Exchange Pl.), 212-344-5000
Plus other locations throughout the NY area.
■ "Long lines" form at lunch for the "fabulous", "handmade", smartly "salty" flatbread, filled with generally "tasty spreads", at these "ubiquitous" "Starbucks of sandwich shops"; before you know it they'll be opening branches in Seattle.

Coté Sud **S**
18 | 15 | 16 | $38

181 E. 78th St. (bet. Lexington & 3rd Aves.), 212-744-1800
☑ For Eastsiders who missed *A Year in Provence*, there's always this "charming" bistro where "authentic" bouillabaisse and sweetbreads come at rates that compare favorably to making a trip to Provence.

Country Cafe **S⊅**
21 | 18 | 19 | $33

69 Thompson St. (bet. Broome & Spring Sts.), 212-966-5417
■ A "sweet little surprise" where the "small quarters" allow you to "rub thighs with strangers" and "sexy" French waiters, this "adorable" SoHo cafe serves a "traditional selection" of midpriced Gallic dishes as well as "a few Moroccan" specialties; "the only downer is the smoke."

Coup **◑S**
▽ 20 | 23 | 19 | $39

509 E. Sixth St. (bet. Aves. A & B), 212-979-2815
☑ "Bring your architect friends" to marvel at the "cutting-edge" decor of this "sleek" East Village New American, with a "wonderful garden", "impressive" food and "capable staff"; since it's gaining "hipster" status, "get in before Leo."

Cowgirl Hall of Fame **S**
14 | 17 | 15 | $23

519 Hudson St. (W. 10th St.), 212-633-1133
■ "Where else can you find corn dogs", Frito pies and a host of other "fattening", Southern-SW "trailer park" vittles than at this "raucous", "kitschy", country music–playing West Village theme shop?; it's "fun for kids" or tourists looking to "kick back" with a mason jar margarita.

C3 **S**
21 | 18 | 19 | $32

Washington Sq. Hotel, 103 Waverly Pl. (MacDougal St.), 212-254-1200
☑ "NYU law profs" and other judicious diners find this hotel-based, basement-level New American a "low-key", "underrated", "friendly refuge from Washington Square Park"; consider it for Sunday brunch ("fairly priced") or the "appealing" prix fixe dinner.

Cub Room **◑S**
21 | 21 | 19 | $43

131 Sullivan St. (Prince St.), 212-677-4100
■ Raging "broker madness" at the up-front bar belies the "warm", "cozy" atmosphere in the "pretty", "Frank Lloyd Wright"–style back dining room of this SoHo New American, whose "delicious" cuisine is bound to "impress a date."

Cub Room Cafe **S**
19 | 16 | 17 | $29

183 Prince St. (Sullivan St.), 212-777-0030
☑ "Cheaper than its progenitor", this next-door sibling to SoHo's Cub Room is a "reliable neighborhood lunch spot" (burgers, sandwiches, salads) and popular brunch choice for "wonderful pancakes", especially at the sidewalk tables.

F | D | S | C

Cucina (Brooklyn) [S]
24 | 21 | 21 | $41
256 Fifth Ave. (bet. Carroll St. & Garfield Pl.), 718-230-0711
◪ "It's fun to talk to" "hands-on" chef-owner Michael Ayoub at this Park Slope Italian "gem" with "candlelit" tables, flowers and "great antipasti"; while it may be a "shade overrated" "by locals", it's clearly the borough's "finest" ("light years beyond the average pastaria").

Cucina Della Fontana [S]
15 | 19 | 16 | $25
368 Bleecker St. (Charles St.), 212-242-0636
◪ Even lifelong NYers "feel like a tourist" or "Long Islanders doing the Village" at this bi-level Italian where the "generic" fare is offset by a downstairs atrium ("lovely fountain") that's "kinda tacky, but charming."

Cucina di Pesce ◑[S]≠
19 | 14 | 17 | $24
87 E. Fourth St. (bet. 2nd & 3rd Aves.), 212-260-6800
◪ "Free mussels" "while you wait" for a table "make it all worthwhile" at this "cheap", elbow-to-elbow East Village Italian seafooder where the early bird costs less than many appetizers around town and young patrons tout dining "in the garden."

Cucina Stagionale ◑[S]≠
18 | 12 | 16 | $22
275 Bleecker St. (bet. 6th & 7th Aves.), 212-924-2707
◪ One of the few BYOs in the West Village, this Italian is "not much to look at", but regulars say it's so "economical" you'll still be able to go "when the stock market crashes"; "come early" to avoid "long lines."

Cucina Vivolo
20 | 16 | 18 | $29
138 E. 74th St. (bet. Lexington & Park Aves.), 212-717-4700
■ After an East Side visit to the Whitney, "meet a friend for lunch" at this "serviceable" Italian "grazing place", a relatively "inexpensive" sibling to Vivolo that also works for "quick" takeout or delivery.

Cuisine de Saigon [S]
18 | 12 | 17 | $27
154 W. 13th St. (bet. 6th & 7th Aves.), 212-255-6003
◪ Diners "always get a warm greeting" at this "low-key", family-owned Village Vietnamese forerunner, which may now seem "generic" but remains a "good value"; there's a separate appetizer bar where you can eat spring rolls while watching the Yankees on TV.

Cupcake Cafe [S]≠
22 | 8 | 14 | $13
522 Ninth Ave. (39th St.), 212-465-1530
■ "Delicious" cupcakes are the specialty of this Port Authority–area storefront bakery "hole-in-the-wall" that draws everyone from bike messengers to Park Avenue dowagers "bypassing the beggars" to order their daughter's $1,000 wedding cake.

Cupping Room Café ◑[S]
17 | 16 | 15 | $25
359 W. Broadway (bet. Broome & Grand Sts.), 212-925-2898
◪ In winter, hot chocolate–sipping SoHo residents "want to live" by the "potbelly stove" of this "cute", "rustic" Eclectic "brunch fave", despite "erratic" service by "alien waters" who were "beamed" in.

Cyclo [S]
21 | 16 | 17 | $27
203 First Ave. (bet. 12th & 13th Sts.), 212-673-3975
◪ This East Village "new wave" Vietnamese comes with a "limited" menu of "fresh", "invigorating" dishes ("go for the appetizers"); you may find your elbow "in the next person's" soup, but hey, "who needs Le Colonial's" comforts given these prices.

Da Andrea ◑[S]
▽ 20 | 18 | 21 | $25
557 Hudson St. (bet. Perry & W. 11th Sts.), 212-367-1979
■ "Like eating in Italy", this "small, personal, welcoming" West Village trattoria offers "good", well-priced food in an "unfussy setting"; add "attentive" service led by "charming owner-host Andrea" and you have a "great new neighborhood place."

Da Antonio Ristorante
21 | 18 | 20 | $47

157 E. 55th St. (bet. Lexington & 3rd Aves.), 212-588-1545
■ "Get to know Antonio" (Cerra) advise fans of his "upscale" Midtown Northern Italian – you'll be ravenous just hearing his descriptions of the "delicious" menu; it's "expensive", but there are now prix fixe deals.

Da Beco S
▽ 21 | 17 | 20 | $39

517 Second Ave. (bet. 28th & 29th Sts.), 212-448-9505
■ Kips Bay locals highly tout this "charming", hidden Tuscan with "well-priced wines" and "accommodating" ways; a few say it's "rather plain" and "a little pricey" for the nabe.

Da Ciro S
21 | 17 | 18 | $34

229 Lexington Ave. (bet. 33rd & 34th Sts.), 212-532-1636
☑ This town's "best stuffed Robiola cheese pizza" is the signature dish of this "agreeable" Murray Hill "hideaway" whose "heavenly" brick-oven products and "great pasta" are "worth the trip"; so what if it's "cramped and noisy."

Daily Soup ⊅
19 | 9 | 14 | $10

780 Third Ave. (bet. 48th & 49th Sts.), 212-828-7687
134 E. 43rd St. (bet. Lexington & 3rd Aves.), 212-949-7687
241 W. 54th St. (bet. B'way & 8th Ave.), 212-765-7687
686 Eighth Ave. (bet. 43rd & 44th Sts.), 212-869-7687 S
325 Park Ave. S. (bet. 24th & 25th Sts.), 212-531-7687
499 Seventh Ave. (bet. 36th & 37th Sts.), 212-532-7687
17 E. 17th St. (bet. B'way & 5th Ave.), 212-929-7687 S
2 Rector St. (Trinity Pl.), 212-945-7687
55 Broad St. (Beaver St.), 212-222-7687
41 John St. (bet. Dutch & Nassau Sts.), 212-791-7687
☑ The "Starbucks of soup", these sleekly "spartan" spots ladle out "tasty" creations "full of stuff", served with bread, fruit and a cookie; surveyors debate whether it's a "great deal" or like "cafeteria food at boarding school" – "wraparound lines" are the answer.

Dakshin Indian Bistro S
▽ 18 | 16 | 18 | $22

741 Ninth Ave. (50th St.), 212-757-4545
■ Early visitors say this new Hell's Kitchen Indian's $7 AYCE lunch buffet is one of the "best bargains in town", offering "very good" standards in an area that's short on good Indian fare; at dinner try a $14 thali (tasting).

Dallas BBQ ●S
14 | 9 | 12 | $18

1265 Third Ave. (bet. 72nd & 73rd Sts.), 212-772-9393
27 W. 72nd St. (bet. Columbus Ave. & CPW), 212-873-2004
132 W. 43rd St. (bet. B'way & 6th Ave.), 212-221-9000
21 University Pl. (8th St.), 212-674-4450
132 Second Ave. (St. Marks Pl.), 212-777-5574
☑ For "white trash comfort food", i.e. BBQ chicken, ribs, Texas-sized burgers and "drown-in-them" drinks, most consider these "indoor circuses" a "fairly good deal"; "go with 20 frat buddies" or teens whose arteries can handle "enough grease for 10 lube jobs."

da Mario S
▽ 19 | 14 | 18 | $38

883 First Ave. (bet. 49th & 50th Sts.), 212-750-1804
☑ "Sophisticated" Italian fare in a "warm", "no glitz" setting sums up this young Sicilian, which is finding its niche in Midtown East; there may be "dozens better" – but try finding them in this area at this price.

Danal S
21 | 21 | 17 | $31

90 E. 10th St. (bet. 3rd & 4th Aves.), 212-982-6930
■ "Cute", "quirky" and a bit "cramped", this Central Villager serves Country French food in a "rustic" "grandma's house" ambiance "charming" enough to overcome "distracted" service; P.S. it has "the perfect Sunday brunch, kitsch and all."

F	D	S	C

Da Nico [S] — 21 | 17 | 19 | $29

164 Mulberry St. (bet. Broome & Grand Sts.), 212-343-1212

◪ "'Da best' Italian in Little Italy", especially if you "insist on the garden"; it's "full of tourists and corny waiters" and you may need a "shoehorn to get in", but "you can't beat" the pizza, pastas or prices.

DANIEL ◐ — 28 | 26 | 26 | $75

60 E. 65th St. (bet. Madison & Park Aves.), 212-288-0033

■ "Heavenly is as Daniel [Boulud] does" sigh the many bec fins who find his "formal" Classic French "as great as ever" in its "spacious" new East Side home; acclaimed for his "creative perfection", this master chef's "superb" food (ranked No. 2) gets "better all the time" and is backed up by "service with finesse" and newly softened decor, making this a place to celebrate "life's special moments"; just be sure to book "months ahead" and save up in the interim, or try the bar, with a less pricey à la carte menu and same-day reserving.

Daniella Ristorante [S] — 22 | 17 | 20 | $41

320 Eighth Ave. (26th St.), 212-807-0977

◪ By most accounts, this Italian "gem in the dead zone south of Penn Station" and Madison Square Garden is a standout with "tasty" food, "well-organized" service and a recently redone setting that's like someone's home but more "crowded."

Dan Maxwell's Steakhouse [S] — 18 | 14 | 18 | $35

1708 Second Ave. (bet. 88th & 89th Sts.), 212-426-7688

◪ "Hidden among the bars and pizza places on the Upper East Side" is this "obliging", roomy "steak joint" offering "decent" beef at "a fair price"; it's "not Peter Luger", but meets most meat cravings.

Danube — – | – | – | VE

30 Hudson St. (Duane St.), 212-791-3771

Any restaurant run by David Bouley has to be a good bet and that's exactly what this elegant, high-ceilinged, 70-seat TriBeCa Viennese newcomer designed by renowned Parisian designer Jacques Garcia promises to be; the food is lighter than you'd expect (more Bouley than Austria), but the Austrian-based wine list is heavier.

Da Silvano [S] — 21 | 17 | 18 | $47

260 Sixth Ave. (bet. Bleecker & Houston Sts.), 212-982-2343

◪ "Real Tuscan cuisine with a dash of Hollywood" celeb-sighting is offered at this Village trattoria institution whose sidewalk seats and "flirty" ("somewhat distracted") waiters bring to mind dining by "the Spanish Steps in Rome"; "noise", "hype" and "high prices" come with the 'in' territory.

Da Tommaso ◐[S] — 21 | 15 | 20 | $39

903 Eighth Ave. (bet. 53rd & 54th Sts.), 212-265-1890

■ Midtown West standby whose better-than-ever, midpriced "classico Italian" food, "sweet" service and "convenience to B'way shows" make up for a "lackluster setting."

Da Umberto — 25 | 19 | 21 | $50

107 W. 17th St. (bet. 6th & 7th Aves.), 212-989-0303

■ "Great crowd, great food, good cellar – it all comes together" at this airy, rustic Chelsea Tuscan where "*abbondanza*" rules; it's "pricey", "noisy" and some say brace for "attitude if not a regular", but "*molto bene*" meals are the norm here.

Dawat [S] — 23 | 19 | 20 | $38

210 E. 58th St. (bet. 2nd & 3rd Aves.), 212-355-7555

◪ "Worth every rupee", this "upscale" Eastsider that always ranks among NYC's best Indians (No. 1 this year) offers "creative", "gourmet" food, "showy", "no water glass goes unfilled" service and a "civilized" setting; however, a small but vocal minority claims it's "not aging well."

Dazies (Queens) 🆂　　　▽ 20 | 19 | 21 | $34 |
39-41 Queens Blvd. (bet. 39th Pl. & 40th St.), 718-786-7013
■ A vintage '70s Sunnyside Italian with "delicious" ("not overly seasoned") cooking, pleasant ambiance and solicitous service; in sum, a "neighborhood standby" that's good "if your in-laws are visiting."

DeGrezia　　　　　　　22 | 21 | 22 | $47 |
231 E. 50th St. (bet. 2nd & 3rd Aves.), 212-750-5353
■ "Fresh flowers set the tone" at this "gracious" Italian whose "excellent" dishes seem to come "from Tuscan hills", though its prices and "attentive service" are very Midtown NYC; try it for a business lunch or a "delightful evening."

Delegates' Dining Room　　20 | 21 | 20 | $36 |
United Nations, 4th fl. (1st Ave. & 46th St.), 212-963-7626
☑ "Super" river views from "floor to ceiling windows", "cosmopolitan" people-watching and an "around the world" International buffet "impress guests" at this lunch-only UN dining room; "allow extra" time for the security hassle.

Delhi Palace (Queens) 🆂　　▽ 20 | 12 | 17 | $22 |
37-33 74th St. (bet. Roosevelt & 37th Aves.), 718-507-0666
■ "Ethnic at its best", "what a bang for the buck" cheer curry cultists who call this the "best Indian in Jackson Heights"; "consistently fine" food makes the basic decor "bearable" and "lines" worth braving.

Delícia 🆂　　　　　　　▽ 18 | 12 | 16 | $24 |
322 W. 11th St. (bet. Greenwich & Washington Sts.), 212-242-2002
■ "Delicious and reasonable", this "funky", inexpensive little Village kitchen "makes you feel Brazilian" and "right at home", but at times the "waiters seem to go to Brazil to get the food."

Della Femina　　　　　　－ | － | － | E |
135 E. 54th St. (bet. Lexington & Park Aves.), 212-752-0111
For better or worse, adman Jerry Della Femina has transplanted the East Hampton social scene to East Midtown with much the same chic crowd; chef Kevin Penner's globally influenced American menu, served in a cream-colored, understated, summery room, is as confident and assured as Jerry is.

Delmonico's　　　　　　20 | 22 | 20 | $47 |
56 Beaver St. (S. William St.), 212-509-1144
☑ "The market is back and so is Delmonico's" cheer those bullish on this handsome Wall Street "culinary landmark" with its "quite good" steakhouse fare and "elegant service"; bears retort "more effort is expended in leather and mahogany upkeep" than on the food.

Delphini 🆂　　　　　　　20 | 21 | 18 | $37 |
519 Columbus Ave. (85th St.), 212-579-1145
■ An "excellent place" to "begin a seduction" with "candles, rose petals" and "plates to share" – and the Mediterranean food "ain't bad either" at this "dark, sexy" West Side "surprise"; "if you don't turn him [or her] on" here, "nothing will help."

Delta Grill, The ●🆂　　　18 | 16 | 17 | $27 |
700 Ninth Ave. (48th St.), 212-956-0934
☑ You're "on the bayou" yet near Broadway at this Hell's Kitchen Louisianan serving "credible" po' boys, jambalaya, crawfish and gumbo in a "loud", "darkly authentic" space; still, it's "not quite N'Awlins."

Demarchelier ●🆂　　　　17 | 16 | 16 | $43 |
50 E. 86th St. (bet. Madison & Park Aves.), 212-249-6300
☑ Though this Upper Eastsider "really looks like a bistro" and its steak frites "hits the French spot", a pricey, "unsurprising" menu and "arrogant" service make it "very French with all the good and bad."

Demi S
19 | 20 | 19 | $45

1316 Madison Ave. (93rd St.), 212-534-3475

☑ "Intimate" Carnegie Hill brownstone offering very "decent" New American fare and service in a pretty sous-sol setting; it's good "for special occasions", but "a bit expensive" apart from the prix fixe menus.

Denino's Pizzeria/Tavern (Staten Island) ◐S╤
23 | 10 | 16 | $17

524 Port Richmond Ave. (bet. Hooker Pl. & Walker St.), 718-442-9401

■ Long lines at this Staten Island Italian vet prove "you don't need decor" if you serve the "best" "crisp" thin-crust pizza around, seasoned with "local flavor" and washed down by a pitcher of beer.

Denizen ◐S
▽ 19 | 19 | 19 | $38

73 Thompson St. (bet. Broome & Spring Sts.), 212-966-7299

☑ A "groovy clientele" frequents this "romantic" Soho HRC (home replacement center) because it serves "interesting" French-Italian fare until late at night and is "sceney without being a scene"; yet a few find the experience "average" and a bit "expensive."

Deniz Lounge & Restaurant ◐S (fka Deniz a la Turk)
20 | 17 | 18 | $42

400 E. 57th St. (bet. 1st Ave. & Sutton Pl.), 212-486-2255

☑ This vast if rather "stark"-looking Turk near Sutton Place is known for its "fresh, fresh" seafare, "excellent appetizers" and "enthusiastic" staff; N.B. new ownership puts our ratings in doubt.

Destinée
24 | 20 | 23 | $58

134 E. 61st St. (bet. Lexington & Park Aves.), 212-888-1220

■ "Elegant eating" takes on new dimensions thanks to "sculptured" French creations, "a terrific host" and relative value for the money at this "romantic" East Side jewel box; fans rate it "one step away" from the top, citing only minor flaws like neighbors "in your lap."

Diner (Brooklyn) ◐S
▽ 19 | 18 | 18 | $22

85 Broadway (Berry St.), 718-486-3077

■ With "comfort food in a fun *Mad Max*-ish setting", this "friendly", if "too hip for the 'hood", Williamsburg vintage diner keeps "busy" serving American-French fare to "paint-spattered artists"; it's really a "burger joint with Belgian-style mussels and frites, plus decent wines."

Dining Room on Columbus S
▽ 19 | 16 | 16 | $36

380 Columbus Ave. (78th St.), 212-724-0276

☑ "Potential" is the word on this Eclectic "new addition" to the West Side's "best block for outdoor dining", where chef John Tesar gives an "original twist to traditional dishes" and also whips up a "nice brunch"; noise and start-up glitches are no surprise.

Dishes
▽ 21 | 13 | 13 | $15

47 E. 44th St. (bet. Madison & Vanderbilt Aves.), 212-687-5511

■ "Wish my office were closer" say fans of this affordable new Midtown "cafeteria-style" Eclectic cafe/carryout with a "great gourmet salad bar", "scrumptious" soups and other lunch/breakfast fare.

Dish of Salt ◐
20 | 20 | 19 | $39

133 W. 47th St. (bet. 6th & 7th Aves.), 212-921-4242

☑ Popular for "corporate lunching, tourist dinners" and pre-theater meals, this Times Square–area Cantonese dishes up "fancy Chinese food" in fancy digs; critics find it "bland", "somewhat chilly" and pricey.

Diva ◐S
17 | 19 | 15 | $34

341 W. Broadway (bet. Broome & Grand Sts.), 212-941-9024

☑ There's "something heady" about this SoHo "Euro bar" with a "funky red setting", but while some say the Italian fare "warrants the attitude", others call the place "passé" and some staff too worthy of the name.

Divine Bar
17 | 20 | 14 | $26

244 E. 51st St. (bet. 2nd & 3rd Aves.), 212-319-9463 ◑⧓
55 Liberty St., 2nd fl. (Nassau St.), 212-791-9463
■ "Always packed" with "twentysomething bankers" and other "loud" "singles", these "cushy" wine bars are "smoky", "social" and "fun" for "after-work drinks" and Eclectic nibbles, with "comfy couches" and "nooks to chat" in.

Divino Ristorante ◑⧓
18 | 15 | 18 | $35

1556 Second Ave. (bet. 80th & 81st Sts.), 212-861-1096
☑ "Good pasta and piano" play a "relaxing" duet at this Italian East Side "staple", despite service that "depends on staff mood" and a need to "redecorate"; two doors away, the "take-out division is great."

Diwan Grill ⧓
20 | 17 | 18 | $31

148 E. 48th St. (bet. Lexington & 3rd Aves.), 212-593-5425
■ This spacious East Midtown Indian may be getting "a little tacky", but that doesn't stop "diplomats" and other locals from enjoying its "fine food" and "pro" service; try the "outstanding" lunch buffet or, "to beat the crowds", dinner.

Docks Oyster Bar ⧓
21 | 17 | 18 | $40

633 Third Ave. (40th St.), 212-986-8080
2427 Broadway (bet. 89th & 90th Sts.), 212-724-5588
■ "Solid" seafood houses that "burst at the seams with hungry fish lovers" lured by their raw bars and "flopping" fresh fare served in big, businesslike settings (with a "major" bar scene Midtown); on the downside, they're "a bit pricey", the "din detracts" and service can be "out to sea."

Dojo ◑⧓⇄
15 | 8 | 11 | $13

14 W. Fourth St. (bet. B'way & Mercer St.), 212-505-8934
24-26 St. Marks Pl. (bet. 2nd & 3rd Aves.), 212-674-9821
☑ In "NYU territory", these "very Village" "bohemian" "dives" satisfy "granola quotients" and "student budgets" with veggie burgers and other "healthy", "crunchy" fare; they're "suspiciously cheap" and "quick", so "don't expect too much."

Dok Suni's ◑⧓⇄
20 | 15 | 14 | $25

119 First Ave. (bet. 7th St. & St. Marks Pl.), 212-477-9506
☑ This "hip", "dark", "small" ("read: smoking allowed") East Village Korean has "tasty" (if "Westernized") "homestyle" fare served by "ice princess waitresses"; "order right and it's [bargain] heaven", but a purgatory-like "wait" may come first.

Dolphins ◑⧓
▽ 21 | 24 | 23 | $34

35 Cooper Sq. (bet. 5th & 6th Sts.), 212-375-9195
■ A "pretty" garden, "tasteful" interior, "attentive" manners and "good" seafood at a "low price" have fans flipping for this Cooper Square new entry; it's early to say, but it seems a whale of a deal.

Domani Ristorante Glatt Kosher ⧓ ▽ 21 | 17 | 19 | $41

1590 First Ave. (bet. 82nd & 83rd Sts.), 212-717-7575
■ "Who would have thought kosher Italian could be this good?" kvell Upper Eastsiders impressed by this "small, delightful" yearling; besides "excellent" food and service, it even has "ambiance"; dinner only.

Domingo ⧓
18 | 20 | 20 | $46

209 E. 49th St. (bet. 2nd & 3rd Aves.), 212-826-8269
☑ "Classic Spanish food", a "great upstairs" room and summer terrace, "operatic waiters" and the buzz when owner Placido Domingo "drops by" are the fortes of this East Midtowner that's "improving with time"; dissenters say the "kitchen still needs work."

Dominick's (Bronx) 🅂⇥ | 23 | 9 | 16 | $30 |
2335 Arthur Ave. (187th St.), 718-733-2807
■ At this "family-style" Southern Italian Bronx "classic", you may hate the "lines", decor, "long row tables" and the "'we got shrimp', 'we got calamari', 'you wanna salad?'" nonmenu recited by no-nonsense staff, but the food's "awesome" and the place is "a kick", so "just go!"

Don Giovanni Ristorante ●🅂 | 17 | 13 | 14 | $22 |
358 W. 44th St. (bet. 8th & 9th Aves.), 212-581-4939
214 10th Ave. (bet. 22nd & 23rd Sts.), 212-242-9054
☑ "Casual" brick-oven pizza and pasta duo that fans sum up as "filling Italians without wallet-emptying"; outvoted foes write a different libretto ("average food", "variable" service).

Donguri 🅂   ▽ | 25 | 16 | 20 | $44 |
309 E. 83rd St. (bet. 1st & 2nd Aves.), 212-737-5656
■ While this "quaint" Upper East Side "hideaway" transports you "to Japan" with its "authentic food" and "attention to detail", such virtual travel is "expensive", albeit cheaper than an actual trip.

Don Peppe (Queens) 🅂⇥ | 25 | 13 | 18 | $37 |
135-58 Lefferts Blvd. (149th Ave.), 718-845-7587
■ "Wear loose pants and bring Binaca" when you visit this garlicky Italian "institution" in Ozone Park that's like a "scene from *The Godfather*", showing "what family-style is supposed to be"; a few call it "tired", but more say it's "not fancy, just good."

Downtown ●🅂 | 19 | 19 | 16 | $51 |
376 W. Broadway (bet. Broome & Spring Sts.), 212-343-0999
☑ Expect "good food and better people-watching" on the roof terrace or downstairs at Giuseppe Cipriani's Venice-in-SoHo "scene"; while most enjoy the "true Italian" cooking, critics target "laughable" prices, "indifferent" service and trying to be "too cool."

Drovers Tap Room ●🅂 | 19 | 17 | 17 | $32 |
9 Jones St. (bet. Bleecker & W. 4th Sts.), 212-627-1233
■ "Midwestern home cooking with a kick", "log cabin" decor and warm hospitality conjure up "another time and place" at this Villager; still, cynics can't fathom making a "big to-do over fried chicken."

Druids ●🅂   ▽ | 21 | 17 | 18 | $29 |
736 10th Ave. (bet. 50th & 51st Sts.), 212-307-6410
■ The "great back garden", Prohibition-era bar, art shows and jazz enhance some "really good" Eclectic eats at this "unpretentious" Hell's Kitchen western outpost; it's a "place to get away from it all."

DT•UT ●🅂⇥ | 17 | 19 | 13 | $12 |
1626 Second Ave. (bet. 84th & 85th Sts.), 212-327-1327
☑ Young friends "hang out", "fight over comfy chairs" and share s'mores and other sweets at this Upper East Side coffeehouse with "grandma's living room" decor and less service than even granny gave.

Duane Park Cafe | 24 | 20 | 22 | $45 |
157 Duane St. (bet. Hudson St. & W. B'way), 212-732-5555
■ "A rarity: an uncrowded, unhurried" place with "excellent" New American fare at "reasonable" (for the quality) prices; foodies have been exulting over this "unsung" TriBeCa treasure for years, calling it "worth the hike" Downtown "to feel so well fed and taken care of."

Due ●🅂⇥ | 20 | 17 | 19 | $34 |
1396 Third Ave. (bet. 79th & 80th Sts.), 212-772-3331
■ "There's first-class Italian food", "great wine" and "a cozy flavor of Italy" at this Upper Eastsider that's both "romantic" and "relaxing" while offering "very good value"; locals say it "keeps getting better", even if the decor hasn't.

	F	D	S	C

East Lake (Queens) ◐[S]⊘

F	D	S	C
20	9	12	$23

42-33 Main St. (Franklin Ave.), 718-539-8532

■ Ignore the old diner decor and "people sitting on top of each other" because this Flushing Chinese serves the "freshest fish" and "great dim sum"; it has to be good – "all the clientele is Chinese."

East of Eighth ◐[S]

F	D	S	C
17	17	17	$27

254 W. 23rd St. (bet. 7th & 8th Aves.), 212-352-0075

◪ "Gay-friendly" Chelsea Eclectic "neighborhood standby" that's a fine "anytime place" for a "cheap" brunch or a bite in the garden; critics call it "east of average" with staff that acts "surprised to be there."

East River Cafe [S]

F	D	S	C
19	18	18	$36

1111 First Ave. (61st St.), 212-980-3144

■ Locals like this "congenial" East Side Italian's "consistently good" food ("brunch is a treat") and "comfortable", "sedate" setting with piano music; it "looks like it should cost more", which makes its prix fixe "deals" even sweeter.

E.A.T. [S]

F	D	S	C
20	12	13	$32

1064 Madison Ave. (bet. 80th & 81st Sts.), 212-772-0022

◪ "Come back to E.A.R.T.H." typifies reactions to the tabs at Eli Zabar's East Side "glorified deli" "with attitude"; but as the crowds indicate, "for those in the right zip code", his "fine soups, breads, desserts" and other "haute nosh" makings are worth almost any price.

Ecco

F	D	S	C
22	19	19	$41

124 Chambers St. (bet. Church St. & W. B'way), 212-227-7074

■ They treat regulars "like old friends" at this reliably fine TriBeCa Italian that's "good for City Hall schmoozing" or a "casual Downtown dinner" in an "old NY" "saloon atmosphere."

Ecco-la ◐[S]

F	D	S	C
17	14	15	$23

1660 Third Ave. (93rd St.), 212-860-5609

■ Though its "dollhouse" setting is "cutesy", this East Side Italian's "close quarters" and "heaping mounds" of "bargain" pasta seem to satisfy a "noisy", "very young" crowd ("if over 30, you'll feel ancient").

Edgar's Cafe ◐[S]⊘

F	D	S	C
18	17	15	$17

255 W. 84th St. (bet. B'way & West End Ave.), 212-496-6126

◪ "Less crowded" than other West Side caffeine/carb/"conversation" stops, this cafe has "funky [Edgar Allan] Poe decor" plus "eye-popping", belt-busting desserts over which you can "linger for hours."

Edison Cafe [S]⊘

F	D	S	C
15	10	12	$17

Hotel Edison, 228 W. 47th St. (bet. B'way & 8th Ave.), 212-840-5000

◪ "A bit of *Broadway Danny Rose* in the new Times Square": you'll spot "B'way actors" and "borscht belt tummlers" at this "beloved" Theater District "dive coffee shop" that serves up a "NY experience" along with "first-class blintzes", matzo ball soup, etc.; it's "cheap", "greasy" and "oh so satisfying", except for the "surly" staffers.

Eighteenth & Eighth ◐[S]

F	D	S	C
18	15	16	$24

159 Eighth Ave. (18th St.), 212-242-5000

■ There's "always a wait" to get into this popular, "phone booth"–sized American serving affordable "comfort food"; it's a "staple for the Chelsea boys" but the "friendly" staff makes all feel "welcome."

Eisenberg Sandwich Shop ⊘

F	D	S	C
18	10	15	$11

174 Fifth Ave. (bet. 22nd & 23rd Sts.), 212-675-5096

■ At this Flatiron "prewar classic" coffee shop you can relive "the good ole days" and "satisfy cravings" for egg creams, chopped liver and "the best tuna salad in NYC", served by staff "as old as the original counter and stools"; "the lack of atmosphere *is* the atmosphere."

F | D | S | C

EJ's Luncheonette [S] — 16 | 12 | 14 | $18

1271 Third Ave. (73rd St.), 212-472-0600 ⊘
447 Amsterdam Ave. (bet. 81st & 82nd Sts.), 212-873-3444 ⊘
432 Sixth Ave. (bet. 9th & 10th Sts.), 212-473-5555

◪ These affordable, "kid-friendly", '50s-style diners dispense "decent" "truck stop" food in "sumo wrestler" portions to the "cell phone"/ "stroller" set; brunch is a favorite and thus can be a "mob scene."

Elaine's ◐[S] — 13 | 13 | 13 | $42

1703 Second Ave. (bet. 88th & 89th Sts.), 212-534-8103

◪ "It's who you see, not what you eat" that counts at this highly publicized East Side Italian watering hole favored by "the literati" and glitterati; "if you want to be sure of your unimportance, go once", or save your money and "just bang your head on the sidewalk outside."

El Charro Español ◐[S] — 22 | 15 | 20 | $33

4 Charles St. (bet. Greenwich Ave. & 7th Ave. S.), 212-242-9547

■ "You feel like family" at this Village Spanish "favorite" that's been serving "fab margaritas, yummy paella" and other "authentic" fare in a "homey, relaxed" setting for decades.

El Cid [S] — 22 | 14 | 18 | $30

322 W. 15th St. (bet. 8th & 9th Aves.), 212-929-9332

■ "Tiny" and "too crowded", this Chelsea Spanish "stalwart" doles out "top tapas" plus "killer sangria" that will "alter your perspective" on the "close quarters"; "make a reservation."

Elephant, The ◐[S] — 22 | 16 | 15 | $30

58 E. First St. (bet. 1st & 2nd Aves.), 212-505-7739

■ Expect "god-awful waits", "cramped" digs and herds of "hipsters" and "Euros", but the payoff at this "funky" East Village Thai-French bistro is "tantalizing" food, "kinky drinks" and "fanciful" tropical decor, all for peanuts.

ELEVEN MADISON PARK [S] — 25 | 25 | 25 | $58

11 Madison Ave. (24th St.), 212-889-0905

■ "Danny Meyer strikes again" with this "elegant" Madison Square Park "evocation of a bygone" era set in a "gorgeous" art deco space with "soaring ceilings"; most find chef Kerry Heffernan's New American fare equally "memorable", ditto Meyer's signature "superb" service, and if a few critics feel its early performance "falls a bit short", that's probably due to the "high expectations" his name inspires.

El Faro ◐[S] — 21 | 13 | 17 | $32

823 Greenwich St. (Horatio St.), 212-929-8210

■ Go to this "always jolly" West Village Spanish "landmark" for "huge portions" of "amazing paella" or "anything with garlic sauce"; the "dungeon" decor may need "a face-lift", but it's fine when you want to "get down and dirty."

Eliá (Brooklyn) [S] — ▽ 27 | 18 | 21 | $35

8611 Third Ave. (bet. 86th & 87th Sts.), 718-748-9891

■ Early reports on this Greek newcomer (whose chef/co-owner hails from Periyali) call it "a refreshing addition to Bay Ridge", offering "fresh, generous" food at "Brooklyn prices" in a soothing setting with flowers and whitewashed walls.

Elias Corner (Queens) ◐[S]⊘ — 24 | 10 | 16 | $29

24-02 31st St. (24th Ave.), 718-932-1510

■ Despite "long waits", "zero" decor and "no menu", it's "worth the schlep" to this "outstanding" Astoria taverna where the "fresh, well-prepared" grilled fish, modest prices and "outdoor dining in summer" are like returning to Athens.

F | D | S | C

Elio's ◐[S]
23 | 17 | 20 | $48

1621 Second Ave. (bet. 84th & 85th Sts.), 212-772-2242

■ "Pricey", a "little snooty" and "jammed" (busier than ever, if that's possible) with "chic" scene-makers (from "old money" to "Gwyneth"), this "noisy", "top-drawer" Upper East Side Northern Italian provides "consistently excellent" food and "pro" service; if it "caters to regulars", that's not so bad.

Eli's Manhattan [S]
20 | 15 | 14 | $23

1411 Third Ave. (80th St.), 212-717-8100

◪ Fine for "morning coffee" or a "quick lunch", this cafe in Eli Zabar's new East Side megamarket offers "fresh" (if fairly pricey) "designer" sandwiches, soups, etc.; there are plans to serve dinner in late '99.

Eli's Vinegar Factory [S]
20 | 14 | 14 | $25

431 E. 91st St., 2nd fl. (bet. 1st & York Aves.), 212-987-0885

◪ "Crowded with boomers" who say the French toast and pancakes are "worth fighting for", this weekend-only mezzanine cafe in a far East Side gourmet mart arguably has "NY's premier" brunch; to skeptics, it's a "cult" thing.

Ellen's Stardust Diner ◐[S]
12 | 14 | 13 | $21

1650 Broadway (51st St.), 212-956-5151

◪ "Food is not the point" at this "kitschy", "'50s-style" diner (owned by a former Miss Subways) near Times Square; "adults can stay home" since "the novelty wears off quickly" – even small fry find this "tourist mainstay" "silly but fun."

El Ombú [S]
– | – | – | M

1363 First Ave. (bet. 73rd & 74th Sts.), 212-861-6311

Argentine food has finally made an appearance on the Upper East Side; coming in the form of this friendly, casual grill with modest prices (e.g. skirt steak at $13.50) and a warm, rustic feel, it should be most welcome.

El Parador Cafe [S]
19 | 16 | 19 | $35

325 E. 34th St. (bet. 1st & 2nd Aves.), 212-679-6812

◪ "Better than the usual slop-of-beans Mexican", this Murray Hill "oldie but goodie" (circa 1959) remains a "standby" for "satisfying" fare and "courtesy"; it "could use redecorating", but is still "pleasant."

El Pollo [S]
19 | 9 | 13 | $17

1746 First Ave. (bet. 90th & 91st Sts.), 212-996-7810

■ "Muy delicioso!" chirp fans of the "heavenly roast chicken" at this bare-bones Upper East Side Peruvian; better yet, its "birdies" are high up in the "best buy" pecking order.

El Pote
20 | 12 | 18 | $31

718 Second Ave. (bet. 38th & 39th Sts.), 212-889-6680

■ Though "nothing to look at", this "unassuming", "small, crowded" Murray Hill vet "feels very Spanish" and tastes it too, offering "excellent paella" and other hearty, "fairly priced" fare; "friendly service" helps.

El Quijote ◐[S]
19 | 13 | 16 | $32

226 W. 23rd St. (bet. 7th & 8th Aves.), 212-929-1855

■ There's a nightly "garlic fest" at this "cheap", "kinda run-down" Chelsea Spanish "standby"; sangria-soaked surveyors swear by the "great lobster deal" and "anything in green sauce", but getting a table can be like tilting at windmills.

El Teddy's ◐[S]
17 | 19 | 15 | $32

219 W. Broadway (bet. Franklin & White Sts.), 212-941-7071

◪ Putting a "creative" spin on Mexican food, this "trendy" TriBeCa torchbearer still draws "scenesters" with its "trippy" designer-on-acid decor and "seat belts"–required margaritas; critics say service can be "nonexistent" and the bar is the best part.

Emack & Bolio's 🇸
23 | 8 | 14 | $8

389 Amsterdam Ave. (bet. 78th & 79th Sts.), 212-362-2747 ⊐
Macy's, 151 W. 34th St., 4th fl. (Herald Sq.), 212-494-5853
56 Seventh Ave. (bet. 13th & 14th Sts.), 212-727-1198 ◐⊐
■ "When that sweet tooth acts up", head to these Boston-import
"ice cream [and frozen yogurt] nirvanas" – they'll "make you forget
those guys from Vermont"; one complaint: "Manhattan needs more."

Embers (Brooklyn) 🇸⊐
21 | 13 | 17 | $35

9519 Third Ave. (bet. 95th & 96th Sts.), 718-745-3700
☑ Bay Ridge beef house that "packs them in" for "solid" steaks at
sensible prices; the downsides: "crowds", "waits" and "tight" quarters,
but "if you can't afford Luger", it does the job.

Emerald Planet 🇸
16 | 11 | 12 | $13

2 Great Jones St. (bet. B'way & Lafayette St.), 212-353-9727
■ This "healthy", low-budget "NoHo oasis" offers "fresh", "PC" food
à la "interesting wraps" and "awesome smoothies", but dissenters
recite its rap sheet: "distracted" staffers, "a bit pricey."

Emilio Ballato 🇸
18 | 14 | 16 | $32

55 E. Houston St. (bet. Mott & Mulberry Sts.), 212-274-8881
■ The new chef-owner of this SoHo Southern Italian stalwart has
changed the name, updated the menu and "spruced up the decor";
however, it remains a "dependable" "neighborhood" "standby."

Emily's ◐🇸
▽ 20 | 16 | 18 | $25

1325 Fifth Ave. (bet. 111th & 112th Sts.), 212-996-1212
■ "Forget your waistline" and dig into "super ribs", the "best fried
chicken" and other Southern food at this "friendly", "undiscovered"
Uptown "haven"; just a few consider it "hit-or-miss."

Empire Diner ◐🇸
15 | 15 | 13 | $22

210 10th Ave. (22nd St.), 212-243-2736
☑ "Not your typical diner", this 24-hour nouveau "deco" Chelsea
hangout is "best after midnight" with a side of "bizarre" night owl
"people-watching"; "surly" service is typical diner though.

Empire Szechuan ◐🇸
15 | 9 | 14 | $19

4041 Broadway (bet. 170th & 171st Sts.), 212-568-1600
2642 Broadway (100th St.), 212-662-9404
2574 Broadway (97th St.), 212-663-6005
251 W. 72nd St. (bet. B'way & West End Ave.), 212-496-8460
193 Columbus Ave. (bet. 68th & 69th Sts.), 212-496-8778
381 Third Ave. (bet. 27th & 28th Sts.), 212-685-6215
173 Seventh Ave. S. (bet. Perry & W. 11th Sts.), 212-243-6046
15 Greenwich Ave. (bet. 6th Ave. & W. 10th St.), 212-691-1535
☑ "Good to have around the corner" is the party line on this "churn it
out" Chinese chain that's growing "like weeds"; quality may be "middling",
but it's "fast, cheap and easy."

Ennio & Michael 🇸
21 | 17 | 21 | $39

539 La Guardia Pl. (bet. Bleecker & W. 3rd Sts.), 212-677-8577
■ A "Village favorite" that "defines 'neighborhood restaurant'" with
its "consistently good", midpriced "Italian comfort food", "pleasant"
if simple setting and "welcoming" service.

Enoteca I Trulli 🇸
23 | 20 | 21 | $42

124 E. 27th St. (bet. Lexington Ave. & Park Ave. S.), 212-481-7372
■ At this "delightful" adjunct to Gramercy's I Trulli, "wine is the star"
with "fabulous" by-the-glass choices, but the Tuscan food also shines
("like having Joe Montana as second-string QB").

Epices du Traiteur S
103 W. 70th St. (bet. B'way & Columbus Ave.), 212-579-5904

■ "Relaxed", "reasonable" and "reliable" describes this West Side Med-Tunisian "hidden gem"; with a "pretty garden" and "cute" if "cramped" setting, locals "couldn't ask for more."

EQ, Restaurant S
267 W. Fourth St. (Perry St.), 212-414-1961

■ Chef-owner "Dennis Foy has a winner on his hands" with this "intimate" French-American yearling that offers the best of "East Side dining in the West Village", i.e. it's "sophisticated", "delicious", "elegant" and definitely "not cheap."

Erminia
250 E. 83rd St. (bet. 2nd & 3rd Aves.), 212-879-4284

■ "Worth every penny for that much romance" swoon lovers of this "tiny", candlelit Upper East Side "hideaway" with "excellent" Italian food, "charming" service and, seemingly, "at least one engagement" per night; "book far in advance" so you can plan your wedding.

Ernie's ●S
2150 Broadway (bet. 75th & 76th Sts.), 212-496-1588

☑ It's easy to "fall into a bowl of pasta" – they're that large – at this West Side Italian where "so-so" food comes in "big portions" at middling prices; "kids and groups" don't make a dent in the din.

Eros ●
1076 First Ave. (bet. 58th & 59th Sts.), 212-223-2322

☑ Sporting a "Gothic" look, this "good" Sutton Place Greek sets a "seductive", "candlelit" scene; still, some see it as "unexceptional" and note: "dim lights are romantic, complete darkness is dangerous."

Esperides (Queens) ●S
37-01 30th Ave. (37th St.), 718-545-1494

■ Per admirers, "they prepare fish perfectly" and price it "reasonably" at this "upscale", spacious Greek that's "less discovered" than its Astoria brethren but equally worth "the trip to Queens."

ESPN Zone S
1472 Broadway (42nd St.), 212-921-3776

From the folks who brought us 24-hour sports TV comes this new Times Square mega–restaurant/entertainment complex; given its up-to-the-minute video technology, interactive game playing and gift shop, it probably won't be the ho-hum grill menu that draws in the sports fans.

Ess-a-Bagel S
831 Third Ave. (bet. 50th & 51st Sts.), 212-980-1010
359 First Ave. (21st St.), 212-260-2252

■ "Big, chewy" "bagels on steroids" are "thrown at you" by "crusty countermen", making for a "quintessential NY experience" at these elemental East Side shops also touted for "super" spreads and schmears; outvoted critics say "ess a shame" – "overrated."

Etats-Unis S
242 E. 81st St. (bet. 2nd & 3rd Aves.), 212-517-8826

■ A "tiny temple of temptation" on the East Side where a "solicitous" father-son team offers a "delectable", "market-driven" New American menu in a "cramped" but "charming" room; it's "pricey but worth it", especially the chocolate soufflé.

Europa Bar & Grill S
599 Lexington Ave. (53rd St.), 212-755-6622

This new Mediterranean from the Cafe Europa team aims to fill a host of Midtown needs: it has a stylish dining room, a take-out area that turns into a lounge at night, sidewalk seats and fairly priced pizzas, etc.

Evergreen Shanghai 🅂
19 | 11 | 15 | $22

10 E. 38th St. (bet. 5th & Madison Aves.), 212-448-1199
63 Mott St. (bet. Bayard & Canal Sts.), 212-571-3339 ●⇱

■ "Authentic" Shanghai cuisine (including "good soup dumplings") earns praise for this basic but "pleasant" duo; while the Murray Hill site is a welcome "oasis", it's "not up to par" with the C-town original.

Excellent Dumpling House 🅂⇱
18 | 5 | 11 | $13

111 Lafayette St. (bet. Canal & Walker Sts.), 212-219-0212

■ Focus on the (you guessed it) "excellent dumplings", not the decor, at this "brusque", "overcrowded" Chinatown "dump"; despite shared tables, it's almost a jury duty "duty."

Fanelli's Cafe ●🅂
14 | 16 | 14 | $22

94 Prince St. (Mercer St.), 212-431-5744

■ "Cheap", "down-to-earth" and "divey", this vintage 1800s SoHo pub serves "good" brews and burgers to locals and hungry shoppers; but hey, "where have all the artists gone?"

FELIDIA
26 | 23 | 23 | $58

243 E. 58th St. (bet. 2nd & 3rd Aves.), 212-758-1479

■ "Brava Lidia" cheer customers of Lidia Bastianich's classy (read: pricey) East Midtown Italian; its "refined" regional cooking, "divine wine list" and "elegant" decor make it an "impressive" place to "take clients"; still, a few find it "overrated", "cramped" and "cold."

Félix ●🅂
17 | 18 | 15 | $37

340 W. Broadway (Grand St.), 212-431-0021

☑ The food is pretty "good" but "irrelevant" at this "overpriced" SoHo French bistro with "actress/model waitresses"; the "hipper than thou" clients like its weekend brunch and sidewalk "people-watching."

Ferdinando's Focacceria (Bklyn) ⇱▽
22 | 12 | 16 | $19

151 Union St. (bet. Columbia & Hicks Sts.), 718-855-1545

■ A Carroll Gardens "throwback" that's been serving low-cost, "homemade" Sicilian specialties since 1904; the decor could use updating, but for now it's "so bad, it's kind of charming."

Ferrara 🅂
19 | 14 | 13 | $15

195 Grand St. (bet. Mott & Mulberry Sts.), 212-226-6150 ●
1700 Broadway (bet. 53rd & 54th Sts.), 212-581-3335 ●
363 Madison Ave. (bet. 45th & 46th Sts.), 212-599-7800

☑ "Little Italy is still alive" as long as this glitzed-up 1892 Italian pastry "heaven" is around; sure it's "touristy", but it's a "tradition" for cannoli and cappuccino, though purists say "forget the [Midtown] branches."

Ferrier ●🅂
18 | 16 | 15 | $40

29 E. 65th St. (bet. Madison & Park Aves.), 212-772-9000

☑ "Strike a pose" at this East Side bistro, a "cramped", "noisy", "people-watching" paradise filled with "size 4s" and "blondes having more fun"; the food is "good" and the prix fixe a "bargain", but that's not the point.

Fifty Seven Fifty Seven 🅂
23 | 25 | 23 | $57

Four Seasons Hotel, 57 E. 57th St. (bet. Madison & Park Aves.), 212-758-5757

■ "Lavish in looks and price", this elegant, marble-clad I.M. Pei–designed East Side American hotel dining room is a "who's who" "power scene", with "fine" food and "amazing" service; if better for "negotiation" than "hand-holding", you "can't go wrong" here.

F.illi Ponte
22 | 21 | 21 | $52

39 Desbrosses St. (West Side Hwy.), 212-226-4621

■ "Transformed" a few years ago from a "furs and pinkie rings" palace into a "beautiful" Downtown Italian showplace where you can "enjoy sunset" views or "watch brokers see who can spend more for wine"; most rate it "excellent from top to bottom", especially the free parking.

Fino [S] — 20 | 17 | 19 | $42

4 E. 36th St. (bet. 5th & Madison Aves.), 212-689-8040

■ "Dependable" Murray Hill Northern Italian that's "the highlight of the neighborhood" thanks to "excellent" food and "attentive" tuxedoed service; "you'll feel at home on the first visit" promise regulars.

Fiorentino's (Brooklyn) [S] — 20 | 12 | 16 | $27

311 Ave. U (bet. McDonald Ave. & West St.), 718-372-1445

■ "Long lines are the norm" at this "family-run" Gravesend "staple" for "cheap megaportions" of "basic" Southern Italian eats; it's "crowded", "noisy" and "doesn't have what you would call 'decor'", but you "can't beat the value."

FIREBIRD [S] — 21 | 27 | 22 | $52

365 W. 46th St. (bet. 8th & 9th Aves.), 212-586-0244

■ An "aristocratic Russian on Restaurant Row" that's aptly "theatrical", with "opulent" decor, "regal" service and "divine" vodkas that may inspire you to shout "bring back the czar", or at least "bring on the blini, caviar" and other "luscious", if "pricey", food; there's a cafe-cum-cabaret next door.

Fireman's of Brooklyn [S] — – | – | – | M

1081 Third Ave. (bet. 63rd & 64th Sts.), 212-838-7570

Brooklyn Diner owner Shelly Fireman waxes nostalgic again at this new East Side American with a 'Sheepshead Bay' raw bar plus good, well-priced fish, steaks, chops and chicken; life-size sculptures of Brooklyn Dodgers Johnny Podres and Roy Campanella keep watch.

Firenze ◐[S] — 21 | 18 | 21 | $41

1594 Second Ave. (bet. 82nd & 83rd Sts.), 212-861-9368

■ "What's not to love?" ask fans of this "quiet neighborhood" East Side Italian "secret" with "very good" food, a "pretty" if "tiny" room, "attentive service" and a "welcoming host"; it's a "good value" to boot.

First ◐[S] — 22 | 20 | 18 | $37

87 First Ave. (bet. 5th & 6th Sts.), 212-674-3823

■ This East Village New American backs up its "trendy" cachet with "delicious" food served in a "cool yet cozy" space ("get a booth"); it can be "raucous", but it's a "great late-night" "date place"; P.S. those "tiny tinis" can "leave you drunk as a skunk."

Fish ◐[S] — ▽ 21 | 16 | 17 | $35

280 Bleecker St. (bet. 6th & 7th Aves.), 212-727-2879

■ More "inventive" than its name, this "intimate" yet "comfortable" West Village seafooder does "tasty" things with "fresh" fin fare and serves it to a "hip crowd"; there's a good raw bar too.

Fish Restaurant [S] — 18 | 12 | 16 | $28

2799 Broadway (108th St.), 212-864-5000

■ Columbia types trolling for "no-frills", "good, fresh fish" tout this low-cost, "low-key" spot, but warn "come early or feel like a sardine."

Five Points ◐[S] — – | – | – | M

31 Great Jones St. (bet. Bowery & Lafayette St.), 212-253-5700

There's a lot of buzz about this NoHo newcomer; it reportedly has excellent Med-American fare prepared by Marc Meyer (a Larry Forgione disciple) and a striking modern setting featuring a 'stream' flowing through a tree trunk and a gently arched wooden ceiling.

Flea Market Cafe ◐[S] — 19 | 17 | 14 | $28

131 Ave. A (bet. 9th St. & St. Marks Pl.), 212-358-9282

■ A "magnet for boho French twentysomethings", this "funky", "cramped" East Village bistro with "cute" flea market decor serves "tasty" food at "low-end" prices; but it comes with "service in the French style – need one say more?"

Flor de Mayo ◐[S] 20 9 15 $18
2651 Broadway (bet. 100th & 101st Sts.), 212-595-2525
484 Amsterdam Ave. (bet. 83rd & 84th Sts.), 212-787-3388
■ Besides "amazing Peruvian chicken" and the "sweetest fried plantains", these Upper West Side Peruvian-Chinese "joints" provide a "reality check" in the form of "real people and real prices"; for best results, "stick to the Latin" dishes and "go early."

Flor de Sol ◐ 18 21 17 $34
361 Greenwich St. (bet. Franklin & Harrison Sts.), 212-334-6411
■ "They must save a fortune in electricity" at this "dark and sultry", "sophisticated" Spaniard in TriBeCa where the tapas, paella and the like are "good", but the "attractive" Gothic decor, "great sangria" and flamenco dancing are even better.

Florent ◐[S]💳̸ 18 15 15 $27
69 Gansevoort St. (bet. Greenwich & Washington Sts.), 212-989-5779
■ "Where else can you dine with artists, drag queens", "club" kids, "truckers" and "celebs" than at this "perpetually cool", late-night French bistro/diner in the Meatpacking District; it's "loud" and "funky", but happily the food's "tasty" and "price is right."

Flor's Kitchen [S] ▽ 19 8 16 $15
149 First Ave. (bet. 9th & 10th Sts.), 212-387-8949
■ An East Village yearling that's "tiny" but "packs a punch" with its "authentic", bargain Venezuelan fare; "the real thing takes time" so brace for "slow" service.

Flower Drum [S] 19 15 19 $29
856 Second Ave. (bet. 45th & 46th Sts.), 212-697-4280
■ It may be a "dinosaur" and "could use sprucing up", but "you're always well taken care of" at this Midtown Chinese with "better-than-average" food and "old-style service."

Focacceria ◐[S] ▽ 19 15 17 $25
87 MacDougal St. (bet. Bleecker & Houston Sts.), 212-253-8049
■ "Reasonably priced", "simple and good" focaccia sandwiches and pastas are the fortes of this "pleasant" West Village Italian cafe; if only there weren't "too many seats per square foot."

Focaccia Fiorentina [S] 18 13 16 $23
1166 First Ave. (64th St.), 212-593-2223
◪ "Fancy it's not", but this East Side Northern Italian cafe "keeps neighbors loyal" because it's "ok for a quick pasta", focaccia sandwich and other "cheap" if "sometimes uneven" basics.

Foley's Fish House [S] 20 23 20 $45
Renaissance Hotel, 714 Seventh Ave. (bet. 47th & 48th Sts.), 212-261-5200
■ "Location" is the bait at this seafooder with "amazing" Times Square views, but the "solid" menu (including "super crab cakes") also draws bites; it's "perfect" for theatergoers, though the scenery here is so good, it may be better than the show.

Follonico 23 20 21 $45
6 W. 24th St. (bet. 5th & 6th Aves.), 212-691-6359
■ A "darling of the publishing lunch bunch", this Flatiron Italian provides a "journey to Tuscany" via "earthy" food from the wood oven in a "casually elegant" room; service can be "slow", but most advise "linger and enjoy."

Fontana di Trevi [S] 19 16 19 $38
151 W. 57th St. (bet. 6th & 7th Aves.), 212-247-5683
◪ "Old-world graciousness by Carnegie Hall" is what one finds at this Northern Italian "'50s place" that's "reliable and convenient", if "nothing special" and a tad "pricey for what it is."

44 🅂 21 | 23 | 18 | $48

Royalton Hotel, 44 W. 44th St. (bet. 5th & 6th Aves.), 212-944-8844
■ There's "attitude to spare", along with expensive but "excellent" New American fare, a "hip" power crowd and "sleek" Philippe Starck decor (like "the starship Enterprise") at this hotel Midtowner; the "handsome staff" may be "lost in a fog", but that gives you "time to figure out" the must-see futuristic bathrooms.

FOUR SEASONS 26 | 27 | 26 | $67

99 E. 52nd St. (bet. Lexington & Park Aves.), 212-754-9494
■ "For all seasons" and all reasons, from the definitive "power lunch" in the Grill Room to celebrations in the "glorious" Pool Room, this "peerless" NY "classic" has "set the standard" for over 40 years with its "exceptional" Continental cuisine, "superb" service and Philip Johnson's "landmark" design; if you hesitate to blow your "child's college tuition" here, try the Grill Room's $59 prix fixe dinner.

14 Wall Street Restaurant, The 20 | 21 | 20 | $44

14 Wall St., 31st fl. (bet. Broad St. & B'way), 212-233-2780
■ "Take the elevator up and leave reality below" at this "sunny" Wall Street penthouse (J.P. Morgan's "old digs"), a "secret" spot with "good" French food, "robber baron" ambiance and "million-dollar views" – all enjoyed on credit cards.

Francisco's Centro Vasco 🅂 21 | 12 | 17 | $36

159 W. 23rd St. (bet. 6th & 7th Aves.), 212-645-6224
■ "Go with a group" and plan "to wait and wait" at this "crowded", "deafening" Chelsea Spaniard whose "monster-sized lobsters" come at "a very good price"; the rest of the menu is just "fair."

Frank ●🅂⊅ 22 | 13 | 16 | $24

88 Second Ave. (bet. 5th & 6th Sts.), 212-420-0202
■ Frank "can cook!" marvel those who've managed to get into this "cozy"-is-an-understatement East Villager offering "robust", bargain Italian fare and "homey" decor; but you may "age" waiting for a table and must "suck in your stomach" to fit.

Frankie & Johnnie's 21 | 14 | 18 | $43

269 W. 45th St. (bet. B'way & 8th Ave.), 212-997-9494 ●
194-05 Northern Blvd. (194th St.), Queens, 718-357-2444 🅂
☑ "The basics are done well" at this often "packed" and "noisy" mezzanine Italian Theater District steakhouse (with a Bayside sib); big portions, "moderate prices" and B'way convenience are pluses, but critics claim it's "living in and on the past."

Franklin Station Café 🅂 18 | 14 | 16 | $23

222 W. Broadway (Franklin St.), 212-274-8525
■ "Offbeat" TriBeCa French-Malaysian cafe with "fine" soups, noodle dishes and other "unusual" fare; prices are low, service sweet and decor "sparse", but there's a slide show for diversion.

Frank's Restaurant 🅂 20 | 16 | 19 | $45

85 10th Ave. (15th St.), 212-243-1349
☑ "At the intersection of cholesterol and testosterone" you'll find this sprawling, "cigars-welcome", "bachelor party–heaven" West Chelsea Italian steakhouse serving "huge hunks" of "beautiful" beef "with all the trimmings"; Wall Street brokers and bankers love it because it's right on the way Uptown.

Fraunces Tavern 15 | 21 | 17 | $37

54 Pearl St. (Broad St.), 212-269-0144
■ "George Washington wept here" say foes who impeach this 1760s Wall Streeter for nonrevolutionary, "overpriced" American fare and "slow service"; but "you gotta love" its "historic", "colonial" aura and it's a Downtown "power breakfast" staple.

Freddie & Pepper's ●S⇄
19 | 5 | 13 | $12
303 Amsterdam Ave. (bet. 74th & 75th Sts.), 212-799-2378
☑ For a slice of pizza with "excellent" "gourmet toppings", try this West Side "hole-in-the-wall" kindly described as "homely"; "order out" – it's too "depressing to eat inside."

Fred's S
18 | 17 | 18 | $27
476 Amsterdam Ave. (83rd St.), 212-579-3076
■ Dog fanciers dig this "cute" West Side "shrine to Fred" (the owner's black Lab), but even cat lovers purr over its "comforting" (in taste and price) American fare; still, it's "easier to get into Ft. Knox on Friday night."

Fred's at Barneys NY S
19 | 18 | 16 | $36
10 E. 61st St. (bet. 5th & Madison Aves.), 212-833-2200
■ Have a "civilized" lunch "among the liposuctioned elite" at this "handsome" East Side Italian that may be in Barneys' basement, but is no bargain; still, the food is "excellent" – if you can get served – and the "scene" is "chic" enough for good scoping.

French Roast ●S
14 | 14 | 11 | $21
2340 Broadway (85th St.), 212-799-1533
78 W. 11th St. (6th Ave.), 212-533-2233
☑ Caffeinating and "lounging" are the draws at these "24/7", "Left Bank"–style bistros with "standard" fare to appease "that 3 AM goat cheese omelet craving"; but you're lucky if you "actually see a waiter."

Fresco by Scotto
23 | 21 | 21 | $48
34 E. 52nd St. (bet. Madison & Park Aves.), 212-935-3434
■ The Scotto family's "upbeat" Midtown Italian "power spot" draws "TV celebs", honchos and others thanks to its "robust pizzas and pastas", "caring" staff and "cheery" decor; but it gets "crowded and noisy" and is best enjoyed "on a corporate card."

Fresco by Scotto on the Go
21 | 16 | 17 | $19
40 E. 52nd St. (bet. Madison & Park Aves.), 212-754-2700
■ "Are the Scottos geniuses or what?" ask those impressed by their new, less pricey Midtown take-out/eat-in branch with a "wonderfully creative salad bar", panini sandwiches, etc.; where next?

Fressen ●S
▽ 20 | 24 | 17 | $39
421 W. 13th St. (bet. 9th Ave. & Washington St.), 212-645-7775
■ Slicker than its name suggests, this Meatpacking District newcomer is getting lots of positive early buzz; the New American food (using organic ingredients) is reportedly quite good and the high-design, Mondrian-like setting and active bar scene also get praise.

Frico Bar ●S
20 | 17 | 18 | $37
402 W. 43rd St. (9th Ave.), 212-564-7272
☑ "A different kind" of Theater District Italian, this Bastianich venture serves "unusual" regional fare in a "good-looking" yet "casual" space; despite having upscaled its decor and prices, it "works well" pre- or post-B'way or for a quieter lunch.

Friend of a Farmer S
17 | 17 | 16 | $25
77 Irving Pl. (bet. 18th & 19th Sts.), 212-477-2188
☑ More like "friend of a yuppie", this "sweet" "country kitchen" charms most diners with its "homestyle" American fare and "bit of Vermont in Gramercy" setting; it's a brunch fave, but critics call it "blandness personified" with staff that can be a "friend of no one."

Frontière
21 | 20 | 20 | $42
199 Prince St. (bet. MacDougal & Sullivan Sts.), 212-387-0898
■ There's "imaginative" French-Italian 'border cuisine' and "romantic" ambiance at this "inviting" little SoHo bistro "without attitude"; it's best on a warm night with "the doors open."

F	D	S	C

Frutti di Mare ◐ [S] 🚫 — 18 | 14 | 16 | $24

84 E. Fourth St. (2nd Ave.), 212-979-2034

■ At peak hours, diners put up with "lines", "cramped" seating and "here's-your-food-now-get-out" service at this East Village Italian seafooder because it's still a "best buy" for "good, honest" eats; noise goes with the territory.

Fujiyama Mama ◐ [S] — 20 | 19 | 17 | $34

467 Columbus Ave. (bet. 82nd & 83rd Sts.), 212-769-1144

■ Expect "above-average" sushi at this "totally '80s" West Side "techno" Japanese with "wacky disco" decor (complete with DJ); it's "fun for groups" or "psychedelic birthdays", if you don't mind "rock concert decibel levels."

Gabriela's [S] — 20 | 12 | 17 | $23

685 Amsterdam Ave. (93rd St.), 212-961-0574

■ Upper Westsiders line up at this "family-friendly" "treasure" for "plentiful portions" of "gourmet Mexican" food at "coffee shop prices"; the "pleasingly tacky" room can be "a zoo", but few mind.

Gabriel's — 22 | 18 | 21 | $48

11 W. 60th St. (bet. B'way & Columbus Ave.), 212-956-4600

■ With its exciting Northern Italian food and "genuinely warm staff", this "Lincoln Center haven" strikes "the perfect balance between homey and upscale"; it "can get costly", but owner Gabriel Aiello works hard to please diners (including not a few celebs), and mostly succeeds.

Gage & Tollner (Brooklyn) — 21 | 23 | 21 | $43

372 Fulton St. (Jay St.), 718-875-5181

◪ Time travel seems plausible at this "magnificent" 1879 Brooklyn steak-and-seafood house, a true "landmark"; nostalgists "never tire" of its "gaslit" elegance, and if it's "not up to past" glory, most still rate it "excellent."

Galapagos ◐ [S] — – | – | – | M

126 First Ave. (bet. 7th & 8th Sts.), 212-353-1955

South American seafood docks in the East Village at this attractive, white-tablecloth space; it's open to the sidewalk in summer with a small back patio and a midpriced menu featuring seviche, paella, etc., plus such nonaquatic items as churrasco and arroz con pollo.

Gallagher's Steak House ◐ [S] — 21 | 16 | 18 | $48

228 W. 52nd St. (bet. B'way & 8th Ave.), 212-245-5336

◪ The dry-aged beef is "terrific" at this "old reliable" (if "touristy") Theater District vet, a "solid" player even if it is "a cut below the premier" chophouses; prices are up there, but you get a lot of old NY steakhouse character, and characters, for your money.

Gamut, The — ▽ 20 | 20 | 20 | $31

102 E. 25th St. (bet. Lexington Ave. & Park Ave. S.), 212-598-4555

■ New Gramercy Eclectic bistro with a 'distressed chic' look and a midpriced menu covering a range of dishes (with special theme nights Wednesdays); the cozy room opens onto the street in summer.

Garage Restaurant ◐ [S] — 16 | 17 | 17 | $28

99 Seventh Ave. S. (bet. Barrow & Grove Sts.), 212-645-0600

◪ Though the New American food isn't high octane, this "casual" West Villager pumps out "great jazz" in an "airy" space with "booths and a fireplace" upstairs, a raw bar below and sidewalk seats.

Garden Cafe [S] — ▽ 19 | 22 | 20 | $40

Kitano Hotel, 40 E. 38th St. (Park Ave.), 212-885-7123

◪ With its "quiet, Zen-like" ambiance, this Murray Hill hotel Euro-Japanese provides a "serene setting" for a "leisurely" business lunch; however, some suggest it can be garden variety.

Garden Cafe (Brooklyn) ▽ 23 | 18 | 22 | $35
620 Vanderbilt Ave. (Prospect Pl.), 718-857-8863
■ Near the Brooklyn Museum and Botanic Garden is this "tiny" townhouse "surprise" with a "limited" but lovely New American menu; the chef's "infectious" enthusiasm, coupled with "attentive" service and fair prices, make it a Prospect Heights "oasis."

Gargiulo's (Brooklyn) S 20 | 16 | 18 | $36
2911 W. 15th St. (bet. Mermaid & Surf Aves.), 718-266-4891
☑ Take a "nostalgia" trip to Coney Island for "gargantuan portions" of Neapolitan fare at this "big", "noisy", "old-time" pasta palace; critics call it "a banquet hall with food to match", but you eat free "if you win their lottery."

Garrick Bistro, The S 20 | 19 | 19 | $38
Mayfair Hotel, 242 W. 49th St. (bet. B'way & 8th Ave.), 212-489-8600
■ This "intimate" new Theater District bistro with an "elegant" "'40s" feel enhanced by rare show biz photos offers first-rate French fare and a "bargain pre-theater" deal; it's a bit "cramped" but "charming."

Gascogne S 22 | 20 | 19 | $43
158 Eighth Ave. (bet. 17th & 18th Sts.), 212-675-6564
■ "Authentic Gallic charm" permeates this "small" but "serious" Chelsea bistro showcasing "hearty" SW French fare (and "don't forget the Armagnac"); though its prices draw a few jabs, most tout it as a "romantic date place" with brunch in the garden as the best bet.

Gebhardt's (Queens) S ▽ 19 | 15 | 18 | $32
65-06 Myrtle Ave. (bet. 65th Pl. & 65th St.), 718-821-5567
■ "Go from Queens straight to Germany" not via JFK, but by this midpriced Glendale stalwart that's been serving "substantial portions of hearty German food" since 1933; how many places still offer "great sauerbraten" and *"gemütlichkeit"*?

Gemelli 16 | 16 | 16 | $36
4 World Trade Ctr. (bet. Church & Dey Sts.), 212-488-2100
☑ Besides its "good location" (for financial types and scenic outdoor dining), this World Trade Center trattoria's Neapolitan food can be "very good", but the place gets "noisy when crowded" and may feel "like eating in a cafeteria", albeit a "pretty" one.

Gene's S 17 | 14 | 18 | $32
73 W. 11th St. (bet. 5th & 6th Aves.), 212-675-2048
■ "Utterly unpretentious" Village Italian "time warp" that's been a "good value" neighborhood fixture since 1919; sure, it's "old-fashioned" and "drab", but try telling that to its loyal regulars.

Gennaro S⊅ 25 | 11 | 16 | $32
665 Amsterdam Ave. (bet. 92nd & 93rd Sts.), 212-665-5348
■ Though "hands down the best Italian" on the Upper West Side, this "impossibly small" storefront's "waits" and "frazzled" service can be annoying; still, "the price is right", so go "at 5:30" for a shot at getting in.

Ghenet S 20 | 12 | 17 | $23
284 Mulberry St. (bet. Houston & Prince Sts.), 212-343-1888
■ Definitely a "change of pace" in SoHo, from the "delightful" Ethiopian cuisine to the "plain" decor, "sweet" service and low prices; "go with a group" of people who don't mind eating with their fingers.

Giambelli ●S 21 | 17 | 20 | $48
46 E. 50th St. (bet. Madison & Park Aves.), 212-688-2760
☑ "Old hat, but it fits" sums up this Midtown Italian "warhorse" that's still in the running "on the expense-account circuit" thanks to "solid" food, "quiet" ambiance and "reliable, old-style" formal service.

Gigino Trattoria ◪
21 | 20 | 18 | $36

323 Greenwich St. (bet. Duane & Reade Sts.), 212-431-1112

■ The look is "relaxed" Tuscan "country kitchen", and this theatrical TriBeCa Italian lives up to its setting with "fab pizza" and "homey" entrees at fair prices; locals call it "fail-safe" for "everyday eating."

Gino ◪⊘
20 | 13 | 18 | $39

780 Lexington Ave. (bet. 60th & 61st Sts.), 212-758-4466

◪ "After all these years" (55), this East Side standby still draws an older, "semi-power" crowd and "celebs hiding from the masses" with "old-fashioned" Southern Italian fare served by "pros"; critics say it "needs a remake, starting with" that zebra wallpaper, but regulars "love it – can't help it!"

Giorgio's of Gramercy ◪
21 | 19 | 20 | $33

27 E. 21st St. (bet. B'way & Park Ave. S.), 212-477-0007

■ "Flatiron's best-kept secret", this "lovely hideaway" puts more expensive places to shame with its "small" but "delightful" midpriced New American menu; it's a "perfect date place" with fans wondering "why it isn't talked about more."

Giovanni ◪
21 | 18 | 21 | $42

47 W. 55th St. (bet. 5th & 6th Aves.), 212-262-2828

■ "Excellent" is the word on this Midtown Italian "sleeper" with "consistent" food, stylish space and "accommodating staff"; it's "great for lunch", but high-ish tabs may be why it's "uncrowded."

Giovanni's Atrium
19 | 16 | 18 | $35

100 Washington St. (Rector St.), 212-344-3777

■ This longtime "Wall Street hangout" comes with sturdy, midpriced Italian fare, a "warm staff" and "imaginative decor" (including a sparkly "ceiling with stars"); P.S. the food "travels well" too.

Girasole ●◪
21 | 18 | 20 | $47

151 E. 82nd St. (bet. Lexington & 3rd Aves.), 212-772-6690

■ "A pro crew that respects good food" runs this "notch above the usual" East Side Italian that treats its classy clientele to "dependable" quality in a "pretty", roomy townhouse; only price gives pause.

Global 33 ●◪
17 | 19 | 14 | $30

93 Second Ave. (bet. 5th & 6th Sts.), 212-477-8427

◪ "Amazing" Cosmopolitans, "way cool decor" and loud music keep a "very hip" crowd – and we mean crowd – packed into this "dark", "smoky" "epitome" of an East Village "scene"; the "multi-ethnic tapas" "add up fast", but they help absorb the alcohol.

Globe, The ◪
18 | 19 | 16 | $32

373 Park Ave. S. (bet. 26th & 27th Sts.), 212-545-8800

◪ "Happening" Gramercy New American serving good "upscale" takes on diner food in a "sleek space-age" setting with "cool booths"; critics find "trendiness, little else" and a "staff in outer space."

Go Fish ◪
17 | 16 | 16 | $28

1675 Third Ave. (bet. 93rd & 94th Sts.), 212-410-4900

■ "Bargain" Upper East Side seafooder with a "cute" "nautical" look and "pretty garden" view; critics find it "chain-like" with service listing towards "inept", but since it's "crowded", the locals are obviously biting.

Golden Monkey (Queens) ◪⊘
▽ 20 | 10 | 12 | $21

133-47 Roosevelt Ave. (Prince St.), 718-762-2664

◪ "The monkey rules" say fans of this "cheap" Flushing Szechuan and its "enormous range" of "authentic, tasty" eats (the "best this side of Chengdu"); decor and service also suggest monkeys ruled.

Golden Unicorn 🅂 20 11 12 $24
18 E. Broadway (Catherine St.), 212-941-0911
■ "Dim sum as in Hong Kong" awaits three floors up at this large, "chaotic" Chinatowner where "there's always a wait"; service, like the decor, leaves much to be desired, so plan to "holler and grab."

Good Enough to Eat 🅂 20 16 16 $22
483 Amsterdam Ave. (bet. 83rd & 84th Sts.), 212-496-0163
■ Getting in for brunch at this Vermont "country inn"–like Westsider is no small feat, but many willingly wait for its "homestyle" American "comfort food" and "cozy" decor – just "don't get run over by a stroller"; P.S. to avoid crowds, go weekdays.

Goodfella's Brick Oven Pizza 🅂 19 12 15 $20
96-06 Third Ave. (bet. 96th & 97th Sts.), Brooklyn, 718-833-6200
1718 Hylan Blvd. (Garretson & Seaview Aves.), Staten Island, 718-987-2422
☑ NYers never agree on who makes the "best pizza", but this unfancy Brooklyn and Staten Island brick-oven duo earns its share of votes, especially the vodka pie; the rest of the Italian menu gets less notice.

Goody's 🅂 21 8 15 $21
1 E. Broadway (Chatham Sq.), 212-577-2922
94-03B 63rd Dr. (bet. Booth & Saunders Sts.), Queens, 718-896-7159 ⊅
■ There's no need to shanghai anyone to go to these "no-atmosphere" siblings – just tell them about the "kick-ass soup dumplings" and other "cheap, terrific" Shanghai eats.

GOTHAM BAR & GRILL 🅂 27 25 25 $57
12 E. 12th St. (bet. 5th Ave. & University Pl.), 212-620-4020
■ Still "at the top of its game", this Village New American retains all the virtues that have made it a perennial Most Popular contender (No. 3 this year): Alfred Portale's "towering", "pure genius" cuisine, "tack-sharp service", a "beautiful", airy room and "glamorous crowd"; what's more, the $20 prix fixe lunch and special wine deal put this "rarefied" Gotham glory within everyone's reach.

Grace's Trattoria 🅂 16 16 16 $33
201 E. 71st St. (3rd Ave.), 212-452-2323
☑ Even though this East Side trattoria is "not as exciting" as the gourmet market to which it's attached, it's "pleasant for lunch" or a "relaxing" dinner; still, it "seems expensive for an informal setting."

GRAMERCY TAVERN 🅂 27 26 26 $60
42 E. 20th St. (bet. B'way & Park Ave. S.), 212-477-0777
■ "All the senses come alive" at Danny Meyer's masterpiece of "friendly elegance" (No. 2 for Popularity), which "opened big and has lasted" as a "star" of Flatiron/Gramercy; Tom Colicchio's food is "the essence of first-rate American" cuisine and finds a "perfect" home in the smartly "rustic" setting staffed by "gracious" pros; not surprisingly, all this care is costly ($62 prix fixe dinner), but "each meal is a new high" and the casual front tavern is "a steal" that doesn't require reserving.

Grande Mela ●🅂 – – – E
1409 Second Ave. (bet. 73rd & 74th Sts.), 212-327-0400
But for the television over the bar, this spacious, handsome East Side Italian newcomer gives all the signs of being a serious fine dining establishment; time will tell whether the screen or cuisine wins out.

Grand Sichuan 🅂⊅ 22 8 15 $21
125 Canal St. (Bowery), 212-625-9212
Grand Sichuan Int'l 🅂
229 Ninth Ave. (24th St.), 212-620-5200
■ Those seeking "bold", "serious" Szechuan fare say "you won't find better" than at the C-town original and its newer Chelsea branch; "ignore" the "drab decor" because the food is real, and a deal.

F	D	S	C

Grand Ticino [S] — 18 | 16 | 18 | $36
228 Thompson St. (bet. Bleecker & W. 3rd Sts.), 212-777-5922
■ Though featured in *Moonstruck,* this vintage 1919 "archetype" of Village Italian dining happily hasn't gone Hollywood – it's still "quiet, gentle" and "reliable"; that it's "been there forever" says a lot.

Grange Hall ◐[S] — 20 | 20 | 17 | $32
50 Commerce St. (Barrow St.), 212-924-5246
■ A "good deal" with a "New Deal" look, this "charming" Villager serves first-rate "homestyle" Midwest cooking but gets very "noisy"; the bar is "active" and brunch a "bargain", despite the "wait."

Grano Trattoria ◐[S] — ▽ 20 | 17 | 20 | $30
21 Greenwich Ave. (W. 10th St.), 212-645-2121
■ "Comfortable" digs, moderate prices, "friendly" staff and "creative" Italian food add up to a "pleasant escape from Village hysteria"; try the "great game dishes" and fresh pastas.

Gray's Papaya ◐[S]⊘ — 18 | 5 | 11 | I
2090 Broadway (72nd St.), 212-799-0243
402 Sixth Ave. (8th St.), 212-260-3532
◪ Always a "guilty pleasure", these 24-hour stand-up fast-fooders offer fab franks, fruit drinks and authentic seediness; some find the price hike to 75 cents a sign of "civilization's destruction", but they're still a bargain for a "nitrate rush" and ideal for those "4 AM and I'm drunk" munchies.

Great Jones Cafe ◐[S]⊘ — 19 | 14 | 15 | $21
54 Great Jones St. (bet. Bowery & Lafayette St.), 212-674-9304
■ This NoHo Cajun dive will "add spice to your life" with its "down-home" eats, martinis and jukebox; smoke and "tables micrometers apart" make it a "fire marshal's nightmare" but good "fun" for others.

Great Shanghai [S] — 21 | 12 | 16 | $25
27 Division St. (Bowery), 212-966-7663
■ "Go en masse or not at all" to take full advantage of the variety of "flavorful" fare at this "Chinatown fave"; the decor and service are "typical" C-town, but so are the prices – and the Peking duck is fab.

Green Field Churrascaria (Queens) [S] — 18 | 15 | 17 | $29
108-01 Northern Blvd. (108th St.), 718-672-5202
◪ Return from the "huge" salad bar and "unbutton those pants", because you're about to "overdose on grilled meat" at this Queens AYCE Brazilian; "go with a group" – everyone else does, and you'll feel less lost in the "noisy", football field–sized space.

Grey Dog's Coffee ◐[S]⊘ — 19 | 16 | 17 | $14
33 Carmine St. (bet. Bedford & Bleecker Sts.), 212-462-0041
■ "Good doggy karma" prevails at this "San Francisco–style" West Village coffeehouse "hangout" that raises sandwich-making to an "art form" but also doles out "good breakfasts"; if the "hippie" staff is "not so quick", who's in a hurry?

Grifone — 23 | 20 | 22 | $48
244 E. 46th St. (bet. 2nd & 3rd Aves.), 212-490-7275
■ "Small" and "secluded", ergo "good for affairs" (business or romantic), this Midtown Northern Italian "sleeper" is an "elegant" setting for "excellent", "expense-account" dining; the "splendid professional" staff is liked as much as the food.

Grill Room, The — 20 | 22 | 19 | $47
World Financial Ctr., 225 Liberty St. (West St.), 212-945-9400
◪ WFC "denizens" with "expense accounts" come to "power lunch" or sip cocktails at this "quiet" American with an "amazing" Hudson view that slightly outshines its steak and fish; though a "great watering hole", it may need to spend time "on the couch to figure out its personality."

GRIMALDI'S (Brooklyn) 🇸⌘   26 | 12 | 16 | $18
19 Old Fulton St. (bet. Front & Water Sts.), 718-858-4300
■ If ol' blue eyes "comes back for pizza", he'll come to this Brooklyn mecca that's "the best" (with ratings to prove it) for "no-nonsense" coal-oven pies that are a "revelation" for their "crisp crusts" and fresh toppings; with Frank on the jukebox, the waits are almost enjoyable.

Grove 🇸   19 | 19 | 17 | $33
314 Bleecker St. (Grove St.), 212-675-9463
■ The American-French bistro food is "fine", but dining in the "dreamy" garden "makes it divine" at this West Village brunch fave; inside is "mellow" and either way, it won't cost "an arm and a leg."

Gus' Figs Bistro 🇸   21 | 18 | 20 | $34
250 W. 27th St. (bet. 7th & 8th Aves.), 212-352-8822
■ An "oasis" near F.I.T., this Chelsea Med serves "imaginative" food at "decent" prices in a "warm" room where "you feel comfortable dressed up or in jeans"; in short, it "has everything going for it."

Gus' Place 🇸   20 | 18 | 20 | $34
149 Waverly Pl. (bet. Christopher St. & 6th Ave.), 212-645-8511
■ Still a Village "fave" thanks to "authentic", "reasonable" Greek-Med food, a "delightful" ambiance and "cordial" owner Gus, who oversees a "well-trained" staff – other "restaurateurs should train" with him.

Haikara Grill 🇸   21 | 19 | 18 | $40
1016 Second Ave. (bet. 53rd & 54th Sts.), 212-355-7000
■ "A thrill for [kosher] taste buds", this "upscale" East Midtown Japanese serves "good kosher sushi" ("who knew?") and other "delicious" fare, but as is the norm for both genres, it's "expensive."

Halcyon ◗🇸   22 | 23 | 22 | $49
Rihga Royal Hotel, 151 W. 54th St. (bet. 6th & 7th Aves.), 212-468-8888
☑ This "solid", "classy" Midtown hotel oasis serves "artistically designed" New American cuisine in a "serene" room that's "perfect for conversation"; though "expensive", its prix fixes are "great values" and brunch is "special"; on the other hand, some consider it "stuffy" and say "if they named it after the sedative they chose well."

Hale & Hearty Soups ⌘   20 | 9 | 13 | $11
849 Lexington Ave. (bet. 64th & 65th Sts.), 212-517-7600
22 E. 47th St. (bet. 5th & Madison Aves.), 212-557-1900
55 W. 56th St. (bet. 5th & 6th Aves.), 212-245-9200
49 W. 42nd St. (bet. 5th & 6th Aves.), 212-575-9090
462 Seventh Ave. (bet. 35th & 36th Sts.), 212-244-7687
Chelsea Mkt., 75 Ninth Ave. (bet. 15th & 16th Sts.), 212-255-2400 🇸
World Trade Ctr., 5 World Trade Ctr. (Vesey St.), 212-938-1473
32 Court St. (Remsen St.), Brooklyn, 718-596-5600
■ "Efficient soup factories" that come through with a "variety" of "darn good" if "pricey" potages; though big eaters feel like latter-day Oliver Twists begging for "more food" and "more space", "the lines say it all."

Hamachi   21 | 13 | 16 | $31
34 E. 20th St. (bet. B'way & Park Ave. S.), 212-420-8608
☑ For a nifty "neighborhood sushi choice", check out this "fairly priced" Flatiron Japanese, a popular "standby" despite its coffee shop decor; however, some wish they'd "dim the lights" and speed up the service.

Hangawi 🇸   23 | 25 | 24 | $39
12 E. 32nd St. (bet. 5th & Madison Aves.), 212-213-0077
■ You must "take off your shoes" to experience this "tranquil" Murray Hill Korean Vegetarian "nirvana"; fans say it's "more soothing than a massage", with "exotic" dishes, a "lovely", "meditative" setting and "attentive" staff; but a few claim it's "pricey for greens" and you'll "need a snack" afterward.

[F] [D] [S] [C]

Harbour Lights ◐[S] 17 | 22 | 17 | $40

South St. Seaport, Pier 17, 3rd fl. (Fulton & South Sts.), 212-227-2800

◪ "Don't go on a rainy day" because the "view is the thing" at this seafood-focused Seaport New American; though "touristy" and "a little overpriced" for "standard" food, the harbor vistas make it all worthwhile, even "romantic."

Hard Rock Cafe ◐[S] 12 | 18 | 13 | $25

221 W. 57th St. (bet. B'way & 7th Ave.), 212-489-6565

◪ Though this kid-friendly rock-themed chain now has outposts from Cleveland to Kowloon, its longtime Midtown outlet "rocks on" like the Energizer Bunny, dispensing "good burgers", T-shirts and noise; cynics find it "hard to believe there are enough tourists to keep it going."

Harley Davidson Cafe ◐[S] 11 | 16 | 12 | $25

1370 Sixth Ave. (56th St.), 212-245-6000

■ A "chaotic", eardrum-busting, "teens and tourists" Midtown theme mecca that's "fun" for motorcycle buffs and has a "decent", affordable American menu; critics claim the food "tastes like chrome extenders" and "would rather inhale Harley fumes."

Harry Cipriani [S] 21 | 20 | 20 | $61

Sherry Netherland, 781 Fifth Ave. (bet. 59th & 60th Sts.), 212-753-5566

◪ You'll "rub elbows with the rich", literally, at this "small", "celeb-oriented", elegant East Side scene; aided by "great Bellinis", the Venetian food is "excellent" but comes at "high prices" and some liken the normally smooth service to "arrogance in a silk glove."

Harry's at Hanover Square 17 | 16 | 18 | $39

1 Hanover Sq. (bet. Pearl & Stone Sts.), 212-425-3412

◪ "HQ for the old boys' club", this "comfortable", wood-paneled Wall Street "landmark" may serve "dated" Continental fare at "expense-account" prices, but its closing parties and wine cellar are "superb" and lunch is "packed" with bulls celebrating the latest market high.

Haru ◐[S] 23 | 16 | 17 | $32

1329 Third Ave. (76th St.), 212-452-2230

433 Amsterdam Ave. (bet. 80th & 81st Sts.), 212-579-5655

■ Some of "the biggest, freshest" sushi on either side of Central Park is served at these stylish Japanese "hot spots", but "expect a prime-time wait" of an "hour-plus", "abrupt" service and "cramped" seating amid "the highest concentration of cell phones outside of Japan."

Harvest (Brooklyn) [S] 17 | 15 | 17 | $24

218 Court St. (Warren St.), 718-624-9267

◪ An instant "neighborhood staple" in Cobble Hill, this "homey", "child-friendly", "jeans, greens, pass the beans" American serves "comfort food with Southern flair"; if some dishes are on "the bland side", you "can't beat its brunch."

Hasaki ◐[S] 23 | 15 | 17 | $34

210 E. Ninth St. (bet. 2nd & 3rd Aves.), 212-473-3327

■ If you endure the "killer" waits, this "tiny", no-reserving East Village Japanese "favorite" will come through with "pristine" sushi at "reasonable" prices; though it may be time to "renovate", that can't apply to the "comfy" garden.

Hatsuhana 24 | 17 | 20 | $44

17 E. 48th St. (bet. 5th & Madison Aves.), 212-355-3345

237 Park Ave. (46th St.), 212-661-3400

■ "Sparkling, standout sushi" keeps these "traditional" Japanese Midtowners swimming along; while "pricey" with "dull" decor, they're "great for business lunches" that are "one notch up from casual."

	F	D	S	C

Havana Chelsea [S] ▽ 20 | 6 | 13 | $16

190 Eighth Ave. (bet. 19th & 20th Sts.), 212-243-9421

For a crash course in "Cuban Basics 101", visit this low-budget Chelsea "greasy spoon"; besides an "awesome Cuban sandwich", it has what may be "the last rotary pay phone" in NYC, an artifact that compares favorably to the decor.

Haveli [S] 21 | 17 | 19 | $26

100 Second Ave. (bet. 5th & 6th Sts.), 212-982-0533

Serving "dependable", "authentic" Indian fare at "fair prices", this "upscale" East Villager qualifies as an all-around winner; service is so "attentive", it may be "a bit smothering."

Heartbeat [S] 20 | 22 | 19 | $47

W New York, 149 E. 49th St. (bet. Lexington & 3rd Aves.), 212-407-2900

Thanks to its "cool Miamish" David Rockwell decor, this pricey, health-oriented Midtown New American à la Drew Nieporent wins by a split decision: the majority praises "big flavors with little fat", while the minority bashes "thin", "soulless" food that "needs butter in a big way"; check out the eye candy in the adjacent lounge.

Heartland Brewery [S] 13 | 13 | 13 | $23

1285 Sixth Ave. (51st St.), 212-582-8244

35 Union Sq. W. (bet. 16th & 17th Sts.), 212-645-3400

"Drink more, eat less" might be the motto of the young, "loud" crowd at these "just-like-college" brewpubs in Midtown and Union Square; the brews are the draw, but if you "stick to the basic fare" you'll do ok.

Heidelberg [S] 17 | 15 | 16 | $29

1648 Second Ave. (bet. 85th & 86th Sts.), 212-628-2332

Take a "nostalgic" trip back to Yorkville's past via this midpriced German "survivor" serving "stick to your ribs" food and "fresh German beer"; it's great for brats, but service can be the wurst.

Heights Cafe (Brooklyn) [S] 16 | 16 | 16 | $27

84 Montague St. (Hicks St.), 718-625-5555

On a "pretty" Brooklyn Heights corner, this "attractive", affordable Eclectic has a lively "bar scene", "great" brunch and sidewalk "people-watching"; diners debate whether the menu offers "something for everyone" or is an "inconsistent" "hodgepodge."

Helianthus Vegetarian [S] ▽ 18 | 12 | 18 | $19

48 MacDougal St. (bet. Houston & Prince Sts.), 212-598-0387

Faux meat is served by "caring" staff at this "quiet" SoHo Asian-Vegetarian; as usual for such places, carnivores say "bland."

Henry's End (Brooklyn) [S] 23 | 14 | 21 | $36

44 Henry St. (Cranberry St.), 718-834-1776

"Exotic" seasonal game is the trademark of this "quirky, friendly" Brooklyn Heights New American, but year-round it has "seriously delicious" food and wine, even if it's seriously short on "square footage."

Henry's Evergreen [S] 18 | 13 | 17 | $24

(fka Evergreen Cafe)

1288 First Ave. (bet. 69th & 70th Sts.), 212-744-3266

Eastsiders turn to this "staple" for "better-than-average" Chinese food and "good dim sum", served at "decent" prices in a "bright" setting with a "perky" staff; owner Henry Leung promises 'a fresh new look this fall' with continued emphasis on fine wines.

Herban Kitchen [S] 20 | 15 | 17 | $26

290 Hudson St. (bet. Dominick & Spring Sts.), 212-627-2257

Vegetarians and carnivores coexist at this "not typical" SoHo organic American whose "tasty" fare ranges from wraps and salads to, yes, steak; it all comes with a garden and service that can be "zoned-out."

Historic Old Bermuda Inn (S.I.) 🇸 ▽   18 | 23 | 19 | $39
2512 Arthur Kill Rd. (Bloomingdale Rd. & Rossville Ave.), 718-948-7600
☑ The setting in a 1716 house lends this Staten Island standout "great charm", and though its "very good" Continental dining isn't making history, the "unique" locale keeps it "popular and crowded"; it's also a Sunday brunch favorite.

Hog Pit 🇸   17 | 11 | 14 | $22
22 Ninth Ave. (13th St.), 212-604-0092
☑ "Sawdust on the floor, pool table in back, ribs on the menu" and an often boisterous crowd define this Meatpacking District "lowbrow" "dive" with a "great jukebox"; basically, "the name says it all."

Holy Basil ◑🇸   22 | 17 | 18 | $26
149 Second Ave. (bet. 9th & 10th Sts.), 212-460-5557
■ At this "attractive" mezzanine East Village Thai, you'll find modestly priced, "sophisticated" food from a kitchen "unafraid to use spices"; since the word is out and a "cool clientele" omnipresent, you must book.

Home 🇸   21 | 16 | 18 | $33
20 Cornelia St. (bet. Bleecker & W. 4th Sts.), 212-243-9579
■ "Homey" West Villager dishing up "delicious" American comfort food "with a nouvelle twist" in a "darling" but way too "cozy" room and back garden; some find the service "like home" too.

Honmura An 🇸   25 | 24 | 23 | $44
170 Mercer St. (bet. Houston & Prince Sts.), 212-334-5253
■ "Japanese food both innovative and classic" is "graciously" served at this "lovely" SoHo bastion of "serenity" specializing in "spectacular" soba noodles; the menu may seem pricey at first, but those who have eaten here concur it's "worth" it.

Hourglass Tavern 🇸   17 | 16 | 18 | $25
373 W. 46th St. (bet. 8th & 9th Aves.), 212-265-2060
■ Tiny, "charming" Theater District standby whose "clever premise" ("in and out" in an hour) is backed up by "decent" Mediterranean food, "fair prices" and "friendly" service, albeit by "actor wanna-bes."

Houston's 🇸   19 | 17 | 18 | $27
CitiCorp Ctr., 153 E. 53rd St. (enter at 54th St. & 3rd Ave.), 212-888-3828
NY Life Bldg., 44 E. 27th St. (Park Ave. S.), 212-689-1090
■ "Amazing for a chain" is the word on this Midtowner (with a Gramercy branch to open at press time) whose "steady" American fare, modest prices and hopping bar produce "killer waits" at peak hours; "and on the seventh day, the Lord made Houston's spinach dip."

HSF ◑🇸   19 | 10 | 12 | $24
46 Bowery (bet. Bayard & Canal Sts.), 212-374-1319
☑ Join the crowds at this low-cost, "no-frills" Chinatowner for "good" dim sum and hot pots; however, "brush-off service" and "challenging bathrooms" can be turnoffs.

Hudson River Club 🇸   23 | 26 | 23 | $55
4 World Financial Ctr., 250 Vesey St. (West St.), 212-786-1500
■ "Spectacular" harbor views are the backdrop for "terrific" Hudson Valley cuisine and "first-class" service at this "clubby", "spacious" WFC standout; it's "wonderful" for business or "celebrations", but as you'd expect, this "class act" comes at "expense-account" prices.

Hunan Park ◑🇸   18 | 11 | 16 | $21
721 Columbus Ave. (95th St.), 212-222-6511
235 Columbus Ave. (bet. 70th & 71st Sts.), 212-724-4411
■ You "wouldn't do backflips for it", but this "solid if not extraordinary" duo serves some of the "best Chinese food on the Upper West Side"; service is "friendly" and prices refreshingly "realistic."

Hurricane Island 🅂
| | | 17 | 13 | 16 | $36 |

1303 Third Ave. (bet. 74th & 75th Sts.), 212-717-6600

☑ Get that "on vacation" feel at this Eastsider that's "like a shore fish shack", turning out "good", "fairly priced" lobsters and seafood; even those who say it's a "better bar than restaurant" concede it's "fun."

Hush ◐
| | | – | – | – | E |

17 W. 19th St. (bet. 5th & 6th Aves.), 212-989-4874

Scenemaster Steve Steckel has hired John Tesar (13 Barrow St.) to create a menu of New American 'fun' food in hopes of luring diners to his Flatiron newcomer; however, the multichambered space, dance floor and oversized bars make it a venue for the late-night club set.

I Coppi 🅂
| | | 22 | 22 | 20 | $41 |

432 E. Ninth St. (bet. Ave. A & 1st Ave.), 212-254-2263

■ "Delightful" East Villager that looks and tastes "more authentically Tuscan" than being in Florence; its "caring owners", lovely garden and "refined" food are, alas, "discovered", and "pricey, perhaps" too.

Ideya ◐🅂
| | ▽ | 19 | 15 | 17 | $36 |

349 W. Broadway (bet. Broome & Grand Sts.), 212-625-1441

■ This "festive" SoHo mojito mover offers very good, midpriced "Latin-inspired food and drinks in a cool ambiance"; while eaters are fully "satisfied", party-goers cheer: "good for groups" or "girls' night out."

Iguana 🅂
| | ▽ | 19 | 22 | 19 | $34 |

240 W. 54th St. (bet. B'way & 8th Ave.), 212-397-1254

■ The "West 50s are saved" by the "great" margs, Tex-Mex home cooking, "hopping bar scene" and "roomy" dance space at this rebirth of an '80s fun place; P.S. it's still "rough around the edges."

Ikeno Hana 🅂
| | ▽ | 21 | 11 | 17 | $32 |

1016 Lexington Ave. (bet. 72nd & 73rd Sts.), 212-737-6639

■ "Neighborhood" sushi "for the East 70s crowd"; this "worthy" (but "no ambiance") Japanese offers fairly priced, "well-prepared" fare with "quick service at the counter" and "slow" pacing otherwise.

Il Bagatto ◐🅂⇔
| | | 24 | 17 | 15 | $28 |

192 E. Second St. (bet. Aves. A & B), 212-228-0977

☑ Though "cramped and out of the way" in Alphabet City with often "unbearable" waits, this "diamond in the rough" with rhinestone prices is one of the "best" Italians around; "mama" "runs the show" – you'd better do what she says.

Il Buco ◐🅂
| | | 22 | 22 | 17 | $40 |

47 Bond St. (bet. Bowery & Lafayette St.), 212-533-1932

☑ With "delicious", "savory dishes" and a "romantic", "antique-filled" setting, this NoHo Mediterranean scores as an "ultimate date place" – or "shop", since everything is for sale; despite "self-impressed staff" and "not so tiny prices", it's a "fun 'in' place."

Il Cantinori ◐🅂
| | | 23 | 21 | 21 | $50 |

32 E. 10th St. (bet. B'way & University Pl.), 212-673-6044

■ A "Village celeb hangout", this "opulent" trattoria is at its best in summer "when they open the front"; year-round, its "delicious" Tuscan food, "intoxicating" flowers and smooth service seduce most, but not all – "too pricey", "chichi."

Il Corallo ◐🅂
| | | 20 | 14 | 16 | $23 |

172-176 Prince St. (bet. Sullivan & Thompson Sts.), 212-941-7119

■ There are "tons of pastas to choose from" at this "cute", good-value trattoria, all served "without the usual SoHo pretensions"; thus, it's "always crowded, with always a wait" at night and on weekends, but is "terrific" for midweek lunch.

F	D	S	C

Il Cortile ◐[S] 23 | 21 | 20 | $43
125 Mulberry St. (bet. Canal & Hester Sts.), 212-226-6060
■ In the "heart of Little Italy", year-round "romantic" indoor "garden dining" on the area's "best" Italian food keeps this vet's "witty" staff "overworked"; there's just one question: can you "survive the wait?"

Il Fornaio [S] 20 | 13 | 17 | $27
132A Mulberry St. (bet. Grand & Hester Sts.), 212-226-8306
■ Lauded as an "inexpensive", "solid Italian on a street full of wanna-bes", this Mulberry Street spot has old-fashioned virtues ("helpful", "clean") with "old-fashioned prices", but little in the way of decor.

Il Gatto & La Volpe [S] ▽ 20 | 15 | 19 | $34
1154 First Ave. (bet. 63rd & 64th Sts.), 212-688-8444
■ "Enjoyable little" East Side trattoria yearling with "creatively prepared" food and good service; some think it might do better with "lower prices" and a more skilled decorator.

Il Giglio 25 | 19 | 22 | $50
81 Warren St. (bet. Greenwich St. & W. B'way), 212-571-5555
◪ Many consider this formal, pink and pricey Downtown Il Mulino relative to be "just as good" (and "you can actually get a reservation"), with "attentive service" compensating for its "tight" space; critics say there's no comparison.

Il Menestrello 22 | 19 | 22 | $48
14 E. 52nd St. (bet. 5th & Madison Aves.), 212-421-7588
■ Set in Midtown "expense-account territory", this "steady" performer is "run like an Italian restaurant should be [with] experienced staff and well-prepared fish and pasta" in a "warm, gracious setting"; sure, the place "could use a little freshening up", but so could we all.

Il Monello [S] 23 | 20 | 22 | $51
1460 Second Ave. (bet. 76th & 77th Sts.), 212-535-9310
■ "They pamper guests with good food and service" and "great lighting" at this "class act" Upper East Side Northern Italian; it's no wonder so many stylish, well-heeled locals are regulars.

IL MULINO ◐ 27 | 19 | 23 | $60
86 W. Third St. (bet. Sullivan & Thompson Sts.), 212-673-3783
■ Perennially NYC's No. 1 Italian, this dark, "lively garlic madhouse" in the Village piles on a lot of "delicious", "very filling" food and almost too-"friendly" service; it's a "formidable" feast that "overshadows the noise, crowds and waits" ("even with a reservation") and is "worth every penny"; for a more leisurely meal, try lunch.

Il Nido 24 | 20 | 22 | $55
251 E. 53rd St. (bet. 2nd & 3rd Aves.), 212-753-8450
■ Offering "classy" Midtown East dining, this Northern Italian upholds "its tradition" of "great pasta cooked with flair", "beautiful flowers" and "solicitous service"; if a bit "stuffy" and "cramped", it's a "power" place for lunch and pulchritude site at night.

Il Palazzo ◐[S] ▽ 23 | 19 | 20 | $35
151 Mulberry St. (bet. Grand & Hester Sts.), 212-343-7000
■ Earning better food ratings and higher prices than most of its Little Italy neighbors, this "waiters in tux, patrons in jeans", "treat you like family" place serves "terrific pastas" and other Italian standards in a "romantic back garden" and storefront dining room.

Il Pellicano ◐[S] 18 | 17 | 18 | $36
401 E. 62nd St. (bet. 1st & York Aves.), 212-223-1040
◪ You can "sit upstairs and hold hands" or just have a quick pre-movie bite at this "small", "secluded" far East Side Italian; however, surveyors debate whether the food and service, though good, live up to its charm.

F | D | S | C

Il Postino ◐[S] 22 | 19 | 21 | $51

337 E. 49th St. (bet. 1st & 2nd Aves.), 212-688-0033

■ The lengthy "specials recitation" at this exuberant Midtown East Italian can be trying (one surveyor "took a nap"), yet its "excellent" food and "pro" service "come as a pleasure [given the] dearth of good eating in the neighborhood" – there's good people-watching too.

Il Riccio ◐[S] – | – | – | M

152 E. 79th St. (bet. Lexington & 3rd Aves.), 212-639-9111

If a full house of happily munching diners means anything, this warm yellow new East Side Italian (with a little garden in back) is already a success; whether it's cheap or good or both, there aren't many free seats left except at off-hours.

Il Tinello 24 | 21 | 24 | $52

16 W. 56th St. (bet. 5th & 6th Aves.), 212-245-4388

◪ There's "nothing innovative" about this "classic" Midtown Northern Italian's "excellent" service and food, or its "fine dining" setting; ergo, it's favored by an "older crowd" for business and special occasions.

Il Vagabondo ◐[S] 17 | 14 | 16 | $33

351 E. 62nd St. (bet. 1st & 2nd Aves.), 212-832-9221

◪ A popular East Side "throwback" where you go for hearty, "roll-up-your-sleeves" Italian grub and then "digest with a game of bocce" on its indoor court; kids and noisy groups love it, but dissenters say "it's a dive – even the bocce is poor."

Il Valentino [S] 20 | 20 | 20 | $49

Sutton Hotel, 330 E. 56th St. (bet. 1st & 2nd Aves.), 212-355-0001

■ "Solid second-tier" Sutton Place Italian with first-tier prices in an attractive hotel setting with well-spaced tables and "attentive" staff; critics call it "just another well-dressed Italian with nothing new to say."

Il Valletto, Sofia ◐ ▽ 20 | 19 | 19 | $50

133 E. 61st St. (bet. Lexington & Park Aves.), 212-838-3939

◪ Under its new owner, Frank Sofia, this fine dining East Side Italian standby carries on its "tradition" with "good food" and "cater-to-your-whim" service; sure, a few feel it's "too pricey", but that comes with the elegant territory.

Inagiku [S] 23 | 21 | 22 | $54

Waldorf-Astoria, 111 E. 49th St. (bet. Lexington & Park Aves.), 212-355-0440

■ A "great mix" of Japanese food, elegant quarters and exceptional service makes this a Midtown favorite, but it's priced accordingly.

Independent, The ◐[S] 18 | 17 | 16 | $41

179 W. Broadway (bet. Leonard & Worth Sts.), 212-219-2010

◪ "Fashionable" Downtown duplex "haunt" with "very good" American comfort food, a "beautiful" bar, "celeb-watching" and staff that can be "kooky", "friendly" or "TriBeCa rude"; "weeknight regulars" say it's just "fine" but nonregulars reply: "dark", "boring."

India Grill [S] ▽ 20 | 15 | 17 | $28

240 E. 81st St. (bet. 2nd & 3rd Aves.), 212-988-4646

■ With the "juiciest chicken tikka in Manhattan", a "delicate touch" with seasoning and "gentle, helpful" manners, this Upper East Side Indian leaves one wondering why it isn't busier.

Indigo [S] 22 | 19 | 19 | $36

142 W. 10th St. (bet. Greenwich Ave. & Waverly Pl.), 212-691-7757

■ "Everyone's comfortable" at this West Village American-Eclectic; it evokes applause not only for its "exciting", "inventive fusion cuisine", but also for its "peaceful" yet trendy atmosphere and "bargain", for the quality, prices; even though chef Scott Bryan is mostly at Veritas now, there's been no slippage here.

Indochine ●S
21 | 21 | 17 | $43

430 Lafayette St. (bet. Astor Pl. & 4th St.), 212-505-5111

☑ "Models 'R' Us" could be the name of this attractive, cosmopolitan French-Vietnamese opposite the Public Theater; patrons "feel so hip" here nibbling on "minuscule portions" of "tasty" exotica that they hardly notice the deficiencies of "the best-looking staff in NYC."

'ino ●S⇗
▽ 22 | 16 | 19 | $18

21 Bedford St. (bet. Downing St. & 6th Ave.), 212-989-5769

■ Hardly bigger than a "closet", this "incredible", low-budget "anti-Starbucks" Village wine bar makes "perfect" panini, bruschetta, etc.; an instant hit, it has one flaw – "portions are tino."

Ipanema S
20 | 15 | 19 | $31

13 W. 46th St. (bet. 5th & 6th Aves.), 212-730-5848

☑ Possibly the "best in 'Little Brazil'" thanks to its "relaxed Brazilian hospitality", modestly priced, hearty, flavorful cooking and "powerful" native drinks; however, the place "does not live up to [everyone's] expectations", especially the bland decor.

i Restaurant Lounge S
21 | 19 | 18 | $43

(fka 2 Seven 7 Church)

277 Church St. (bet. Franklin & White Sts.), 212-625-0505

☑ This "cool" TriBeCa Eclectic "discovery" has "excellent" food, "interesting decor" and a "sexy downstairs bar"; but to some it's just an "overpriced" place with a "superiority complex."

Isabella's ●S
20 | 19 | 18 | $33

359 Columbus Ave. (77th St.), 212-724-2100

■ Brunch at this "delightful", "good value" West Side Mediterranean is like "spending the day in Europe" – that is if you "arrive early enough to avoid the yuppie mob"; considering its "light", "satisfying" fare, "open, airy" interior and "great people-watching" from sidewalk seats, most surveyors say it's a "winner", thus it's usually "packed."

Island S
17 | 16 | 16 | $36

1305 Madison Ave. (bet. 92nd & 93rd Sts.), 212-996-1200

☑ A "popular" Hamptons-esque habitat of the "younger of Carnegie Hill's elite" for its stylish, casual setting and its New American food, especially its "lovely" brunch; however, it may have "lost its local cool under new management."

Island Burgers & Shakes S⇗
21 | 9 | 14 | $14

766 Ninth Ave. (bet. 51st & 52nd Sts.), 212-307-7934

☑ You can "fill up" on some of NYC's "best", "cheap" burgers, chicken sandwiches and frothy shakes at this "funky" Hell's Kitchen "carbo-fat heaven"; now if only they'd "sell french fries."

Island Spice
20 | 13 | 17 | $24

402 W. 44th St. (bet. 9th & 10th Aves.), 212-765-1737

☑ "The price is right" at this Hell's Kitchen islander, the folks are "nice", the spicing "flavorful" and atmosphere "laid-back"; it reminds many of their "trip to the Caribbean", though some say it's a "little tame."

Isle of Capri
17 | 15 | 17 | $38

1028 Third Ave. (61st St.), 212-223-9430

☑ Near Bloomie's, this Italian "museum" of "old-fashioned" food, "family feeling" and "soothing", if "outdated", decor "seldom disappoints" those taking a "walk down memory lane" – or "surprises, either."

Iso ●
24 | 14 | 16 | $33

175 Second Ave. (11th St.), 212-777-0361

■ There's often a wait to cram into this 40-seat East Village Japanese for what may be the "best sushi for the money in NYC"; when you see the Keith Haring paintings, you've reached the head of the line.

Istana 🟦
▽ 23 | 22 | 22 | $42

NY Palace Hotel, 455 Madison Ave. (51st St.), 212-303-6032

■ In the "marble lobby" below Le Cirque, this "fine", relatively unknown Midtown Mediterranean cafe is a "big surprise", with an affordable fixed price lunch and a "not to be missed" tapas "high tea."

Ithaka ●🟦
23 | 21 | 22 | $37

48 Barrow St. (bet. Bedford & Bleecker Sts.), 212-727-8886

■ It's a West Village brownstone, yet the back room and "lovely" garden take you "back to Greece", an illusion heightened by "excellent" grilled fish and being made to "feel like part of the family."

I Tre Merli ●🟦
17 | 18 | 15 | $37

463 W. Broadway (bet. Houston & Prince Sts.), 212-254-8699

☑ SoHo's Euro "chic" set makes the scene at this open-to-the-street Italian wine specialist; those who actually go to eat find the food "reasonable" and the "model-esque" waitresses "uninterested."

I Trulli
23 | 23 | 22 | $48

122 E. 27th St. (bet. Lexington Ave. & Park Ave. S.), 212-481-7372

■ "Everything works" at this "different" Italian, featuring "delicious", "hearty specialties from Apulia" in an "evocative, rustic", fireplace-warmed Gramercy room and "romantic" garden "hosted with charm."

Jackson Diner (Queens) 🟦⊅
22 | 11 | 15 | $19

37-47 74th St. (bet. Roosevelt & 37th Aves.), 718-672-1232

■ "Addicts" swear it's "worth the trek" to Jackson Heights for the "best Indian food in NYC" – "authentically delicious", "freshly spiced" and "cheap", especially the "superb" lunch buffet.

Jackson Hole 🟦
15 | 10 | 13 | $18

1270 Madison Ave. (91st St.), 212-427-2820
1611 Second Ave. (bet. 83rd & 84th Sts.), 212-737-8788 ●
232 E. 64th St. (bet. 2nd & 3rd Aves.), 212-371-7187 ●
517 Columbus Ave. (85th St.), 212-362-5177 ●
521 Third Ave. (35th St.), 212-679-3264 ●
69-35 Astoria Blvd. (70th St.), Queens, 718-204-7070 ●

☑ "Monstrous burgers" are the draw at these "joints" that "don't leave a hole in your wallet"; but many feel "bigger isn't always better" and quip "they got the name half right"; still, they're handy "for a quick bite."

Jacques' Bistro 🟦
20 | 16 | 20 | $35

204 E. 85th St. (bet. 2nd & 3rd Aves.), 212-327-2272

■ "Sure to please", this "charming" if "tight" "piece of Paris on the East Side" appeals with "gracious" service, "tasty" French bistro fare and a "lively" feel; the "warm host" makes up for any shortcomings.

Jade Palace (Queens) ●🟦
▽ 22 | 13 | 15 | $22

136-14 38th Ave. (Main St.), 718-353-3366

■ "Dim sum lovers rejoice" in all the "surprising interpretations" and "excellent value" at this palatial Flushing Chinese; as a result you must "be prepared to wait for a table", but insiders say it's "worth it."

Jade Plaza (Brooklyn) ●🟦
▽ 21 | 12 | 14 | $21

6022 Eighth Ave. (bet. 60th & 61st Sts.), 718-492-6888

■ "Fresh dim sum and seafood" make this Sunset Park Chinese "a popular destination", especially on weekends; despite a huge room, it's often "crowded" and thus "loud", so "go early to avoid a wait."

Jai Ya Thai ●🟦
20 | 10 | 14 | $25

396 Third Ave. (28th St.), 212-889-1330
81-11 Broadway (bet. 81st & 82nd Sts.), Queens, 718-651-1330

■ "Wonderful tastes" await at these "crowded" Siamese twins that are "among the most authentic" Thais in town; expect "socially challenged" (i.e. "rude") staff and "dingy decor", but the "food makes it worthwhile."

Japonica 🅂
23 | 15 | 18 | $35

100 University Pl. (12th St.), 212-243-7752

■ "People flock to this Japanese gem" in the Village for "generous portions" of "amazing, if pricey, sushi" ("order the Japonica Invention" – it's a "work of art"); despite "dated decor" and "rushed service", it's often "overcrowded", so try takeout" or "go early."

Jasmine 🅂
21 | 17 | 17 | $24

1619 Second Ave. (84th St.), 212-517-8854

■ For a "quieter", less expensive experience on the East Side, locals head to this "welcoming option" that's a "great find" for "tantalizing" "Thai with a twist"; a few skeptics say it "just misses."

JB Restaurant & Bar 🅂
– | – | – | M

202 Ninth Ave. (bet. 22nd & 23rd Sts.), 212-989-2002

At first glance, it looks like strictly boys' night out at this Chelsea American newcomer, but owner John Blair makes everyone feel welcome; early word is the tasty dishes won't bust the budget, and there's a terrific bar inherited from predecessor Sydney B.

Jean Claude ●🅂⌨
22 | 15 | 17 | $38

137 Sullivan St. (bet. Houston & Prince Sts.), 212-475-9232

■ It "feels like a real French bistro" at this "surprise" in SoHo that offers "delectable" "basic fare" at "bargain" prices; though the decor is "minimal" and service swings from "attentive" to "aloof", devotees say "who cares?" when you get such a "great meal for the money."

JEAN GEORGES 🅂
28 | 26 | 27 | $78

Trump Int'l Hotel, 1 Central Park West (bet. 60th & 61st Sts.), 212-299-3900

■ This "world-class" "dazzler" off Columbus Circle proffers chef Jean-Georges Vongerichten's "brilliantly" executed New French cuisine in an "elegant, contemporary setting" made all the more "comfortable" by an "impeccable" staff that pays "attention to all details"; you may need to "arrange financing" (dinner is $85 prix fixe), but most feel it's still a "small price to pay to know that for a few hours, life will be perfect"; the less formal front room, Nougatine, is more affordable and there's an outdoor terrace in summer.

Jekyll & Hyde ●🅂
11 | 21 | 14 | $25

1409 Sixth Ave. (bet. 57th & 58th Sts.), 212-541-9505

☑ Featuring "spooky props and performances", this Midtowner with a "haunted-house theme" may be "gimmicky" and "cheesy", but it's "campy fun"; the "low-end" American eats are surely "not the point."

Jeollado ●🅂⌨
▽ 20 | 15 | 17 | $24

116 E. Fourth St. (bet. 1st & 2nd Aves.), 212-260-7696

■ "Funky", "friendly" and "loud", this low-budget East Village Japanese newcomer serves very good sushi and house rolls, as well as Korean fare that's "kind of disappointing"; fortunately, the "owner is always welcoming" and there's a screening room that shows student films.

Jerry's 🅂
17 | 14 | 14 | $27

101 Prince St. (bet. Greene & Mercer Sts.), 212-966-9464

☑ "Casually" "hip" SoHo "upscale diner" that's usually "packed" with "artists, celebs, locals and tourists" who come for its "honest" American food, e.g. "tasty" salads, sandwiches and omelets; while some sniff "what's all the fuss about?", most get a kick out of this taste of Downtown "chic at a reasonable cost."

Jewel of India 🅂
20 | 19 | 19 | $33

15 W. 44th St. (bet. 5th & 6th Aves.), 212-869-5544

■ "Definitely a jewel" posit partisans of this "high-class" "oasis" that prepares "refined", "first-rate" Indian fare, including a "generous" lunch buffet that's one of the "best values in Midtown"; the "lovely", "comfortable" room makes a meal here even more of a "pleasure."

	F	D	S	C

Jezebel | 20 | 24 | 19 | $43

630 Ninth Ave. (45th St.), 212-582-1045
■ With "outrageous" – as in "fabulous" – decor evocative of "a New Orleans bordello", "flavorful" "down-home" cooking and a "kindly staff", this "unique" Theater District "Southern belle" provides "a romantic escape" to the "Deep South"; P.S. "love the porch swings!"

J.G. Melon ◐ [S] 💳̸ | 17 | 12 | 15 | $23

1291 Third Ave. (74th St.), 212-744-0585
■ "Grab a burger" – one of the "best in NYC" – and a side of "delicious cottage fries" and "hang with the locals" at this "crowded, smoky" "East Side landmark"; even if the "joint" is "cramped", the "casual" bar is "lively" and "sociable" enough to assure "a happy experience."

Jimmy's Bronx Cafe (Bronx) ◐ [S] | 19 | 16 | 17 | $32

281 W. Fordham Rd. (Major Deegan Expy.), 718-329-2000
◪ Dancing fools and half the Yankee team are "livin' *la vida loca*" at this huge, "festive" Bronx "scene" where salsa and merengue are featured Thursdays–Sundays amid "glitzy" "contrived opulence", while the kitchen turns out "interesting variations on Latin" fare.

Jing Fong [S] | 19 | 11 | 10 | $20

20 Elizabeth St. (bet. Bayard & Canal Sts.), 212-964-5256
◪ Join in a "dim sum orgy" at this C-town Cantonese "stadium" known for its "amazing" variety ("go before noon for the best selection") where you'll "share a table with strangers"; critics, however, object to the "disinterested" service and say it's "way too big."

Joanie's ◐ | ▽ 22 | 18 | 20 | $44

126 E. 28th St. (bet. Lexington Ave. & Park Ave. S.), 212-689-5656
■ "The friendly, eponymous owner mingles" and "puts care into everything" while the "inventive" New French menu (focusing on seafood) is "ambitious and mostly succeeds" at this Gramercy "find"; live salsa and jazz make this a "terrific" "place to celebrate."

Joanna's [S] | 19 | 17 | 20 | $41

30 E. 92nd St. (bet. 5th & Madison Aves.), 212-360-1103
◪ "Service couldn't be more pleasing" at this "cozy" Carnegie Hill Italian with a "townhouse-like setting" and "warm glow" that make it "good for intimate" meals; but while some say the menu is "wonderful", others dis it – the early-bird special is a fine way to decide for yourself.

Joe Allen ◐ [S] | 17 | 15 | 17 | $34

326 W. 46th St. (bet. 8th & 9th Aves.), 212-581-6464
■ "Famously filled day or night", this "casual", "brick-walled" Theater District American "classic" is always "enjoyable", especially after a show when the drama "elite" meet to "relax"; the "solid", "reliable" menu holds "no surprises, but no disappointments."

Joe's Pizza ◐ [S] 💳̸ | 20 | 7 | 12 | $12

7 Carmine St. (6th Ave.), 212-255-3946
233 Bleecker St. (Carmine St.), 212-366-1182
◪ "Surprisingly good for such a crappy-looking place", these Village Italians are "a must" for "thin, crispy-crust" pies that are among "the best in the city"; P.S. it's never unanimous when pizza is concerned.

Joe's Shanghai [S] | 22 | 8 | 13 | $22

24 W. 56th St. (bet. 5th & 6th Aves.), 212-333-3868
9 Pell St. (bet. Bowery & Mott St.), 212-233-8888 ◐ 💳̸
82-74 Broadway (bet. 45th & Whitney Aves.), Queens, 718-639-6888 💳̸
136-21 37th Ave. (bet. Main & Union Sts.), Queens, 718-539-3838 💳̸
◪ The "famous soup dumplings" are "the only reason to go" to this Chinese quartet – "but what a reason!", for they're "sublime"; however, "other dishes can be heavy" and, as ratings suggest, "don't look around" or "expect attention."

Johnny Rockets ●S
— | — | — | I

42 E. Eighth St. (bet. B'way & University Pl.), 212-253-8175
For some innocent "fun on Eighth Street", try this new, squeaky-clean chain "burger joint" with a '50s retro feel (e.g. free nickels for the jukebox) and soda jerks dispensing shakes along with cheap, basic eats.

John's of 12th Street S⊘
20 | 13 | 16 | $25

302 E. 12th St. (2nd Ave.), 212-475-9531
■ "Old as the hills, but still breathing", this dark, candlelit East Village Italian remains "perennially popular"; chow down on "huge portions" of "too-garlicky" "simple" "standards" – "red sauce *abbondanza*" – that are "dependable" and "nostalgic."

John's Pizzeria ●S
21 | 12 | 14 | $19

278 Bleecker St. (bet. 6th Ave. & 7th Ave. S.), 212-243-1680 ⊘
408 E. 64th St. (bet. 1st & York Aves.), 212-935-2895
48 W. 65th St. (bet. Columbus Ave. & CPW), 212-721-7001
260 W. 44th St. (bet. B'way & 8th Ave.), 212-391-7560
■ "A NYC institution", this "venerable" (even if "a little run-down") Village flagship and its trio of offshoots are justly renowned for "awesome" thin-crust, brick-oven pizza that legions feel "can't be beat"; a few cry "overrated", but for most the "only negative is you can't buy by the slice."

JO JO
25 | 21 | 23 | $55

160 E. 64th St. (bet. Lexington & 3rd Aves.), 212-223-5656
■ The "first of Jean-Georges Vongerichten's inventive" "gems", this "inspired" French bistro set in an East Side townhouse offers "fantastic food" served by a "terrific" staff; it's "a class act in every way" and for those who find "downstairs too crowded and noisy", the upstairs space is more "relaxing."

Josephina ●S
19 | 17 | 18 | $34

1900 Broadway (bet. 63rd & 64th Sts.), 212-799-1000
■ In an "airy", "roomy" setting, this "convenient" "Lincoln Center option" offers a "unique approach to healthy eating", with "well-executed", affordable American fare including "vegetarian delights."

Josie's ●S
21 | 16 | 17 | $29

300 Amsterdam Ave. (74th St.), 212-769-1212
■ "Always packed" with "yuppies grazing on organic fare", this West Side Eclectic "health food mecca" turns out dishes so good they "surprise non-granola types"; despite "cramped", "loud" quarters, the "innovative flavors will make you feel happy" and "virtuous."

Jubilee S
22 | 16 | 19 | $39

347 E. 54th St. (bet. 1st & 2nd Aves.), 212-888-3569
■ This "sweet little" French bistro near Sutton Place is an "ideal neighborhood spot" combining "friendly" service, "decent prices" and "genuine" fare; regulars tout the house specialty mussels and "perhaps NYC's best fries."

JUdson Grill
22 | 21 | 20 | $48

152 W. 52nd St. (bet. 6th & 7th Aves.), 212-582-5252
■ "Bill Telepan, a creative and wonderful chef", has put this "beautiful, spacious" Midtown New American "back on the map"; the "completely professional" staff makes it "heaven for power lunches" and the "cosmopolitan" ambiance guarantees "an after-work scene" at the "neat" circular bar.

Jules ●S
19 | 19 | 15 | $32

65 St. Marks Pl. (bet. 1st & 2nd Aves.), 212-477-5560
☑ "By now an East Village classic", this "hopping" French bistro has "simple, reliable" fare; despite "cramped" quarters and "service with attitude", the "cool" jazz hits the right notes with a "young" crowd.

Julian's ◐🅂   19 | 18 | 18 | $33
802 Ninth Ave. (bet. 53rd & 54th Sts.), 212-262-4800
■ Like "a Mediterranean resort", this "lively" "oasis" in Hell's Kitchen is "a good bet" for a "varied menu" of "satisfying" food delivered in "a pleasant setting" (including a "cute" "enclosed garden").

Junior's (Brooklyn) ◐🅂   17 | 11 | 14 | $21
386 Flatbush Ave. Ext. (DeKalb Ave.), 718-852-5257
☑ Just like it was in 1950, this Downtown "Brooklyn tradition" is "an institution built on cheesecake"; the rest of the American menu is only "a cut above the typical diner's", but it makes nostalgists happy.

Juniper Café 🅂   ▽ 19 | 18 | 19 | $28
185 Duane St. (bet. Greenwich & Hudson Sts.), 212-965-1201
■ A "really cute" spot with "really good food", this "out-of-the-way" TriBeCan serves affordable 'American bistro/trattoria' fare to a sometimes "noisy" "young crowd"; art exhibits, magazines and occasional jazz add interest.

Junno's 🅂   ▽ 23 | 22 | 22 | $27
64 Downing St. (bet. Bedford & Varick Sts.), 212-627-7995
■ "Slick and sexy" in a "minimalist space" with a "laid-back" feel, this petite West Village Japanese newcomer is already a "home away from home" for avid fans who say it's "like hanging at a very cool friend's place" with "great food" on hand; dinner only.

Justin's ◐🅂   17 | 19 | 17 | $36
31 W. 21st St. (bet. 5th & 6th Aves.), 212-352-0599
☑ "Don't mind the stares as you enter" this Flatiron "buppie place" – "we're all expecting Sean 'Puffy' Combs" (the owner) and hoping for other "celeb sightings"; "no hip-hop here, just a cozy, classy, fun spot" with "good", if declining, Caribbean–Soul Food.

Kabul Cafe 🅂   18 | 11 | 16 | $22
265 W. 54th St. (bet. B'way & 8th Ave.), 212-757-2037
■ "More people should discover" this bargain West Midtown "taste of Afghanistan" with "great kebabs, soup and lamb; decor (or lack of) aside, it's a "quiet, comfortable" place with "good service."

Kalio (Brooklyn) 🅂   20 | 18 | 19 | $33
254 Court St. (bet. Butler & Kane Sts.), 718-625-1295
■ "Cobble Hill's bit of elegance", this New American has "innovative dishes", a "welcoming" attitude and "warm", newly renovated setting; some say it's "kind of pricey", but feel "lucky" to have it nearby.

Kam Chueh ◐🅂⊉   ▽ 23 | 8 | 15 | $27
40 Bowery (Bayard St.), 212-791-6868
■ Let the ratings tell the story: this Chinese is a "cut above" most Chinatown joints in terms of cuisine (especially seafood), but the same can't be said of the decor or service; still, it's perfect for groups.

Kang Suh ◐🅂   20 | 9 | 13 | $27
1250 Broadway (32nd St.), 212-564-6845
☑ For a "treat" before MSG events, try this big, modestly tabbed, 24-hour Midtown Korean BBQ "staple" with grill-your-own tables and an "extensive", "authentic" menu; just plan on "dingy" decor and "smelling like a smokehouse" afterward.

Kaplan's at the Delmonico 🅂   16 | 8 | 13 | $22
59 E. 59th St. (bet. Madison & Park Aves.), 212-755-5959
☑ A case of "faded glory", this "old-fashioned" East Side Jewish deli "will do in a pinch" for an "overstuffed sandwich" and sour pickles; but "impossible seating", "rude" service and nondecor are minuses.

F | D | S | C

Karyatis (Queens) ◐[S] — 22 | 18 | 20 | $33
35-03 Broadway (bet. 35th & 36th Sts.), 718-204-0666
■ All the "usual Hellenic suspects" get "superior" treatment at this "upscale" Astoria Greek with "helpful" service, live music and decor that's more "elegant" than the norm; it's not expensive for what it is.

Katen ◐[S] — ▽ 21 | 18 | 21 | $39
Marriott Marquis Hotel, 1535 Broadway, 8th fl. (45th St.), 212-704-8900
■ The few surveyors who know this Times Square Japanese hidden on the Marriott Marquis' 8th floor say that Nobu vet Hiroshi Kani makes "some truly wonderful sushi" at "reasonable" prices.

Katsuhama [S] — ▽ 20 | 10 | 15 | $28
11 E. 47th St. (bet. 5th & Madison Aves.), 212-758-5909
■ Regulars report that this simple-looking Midtowner serves NY's "best katsu", proving "sushi isn't necessary for a delicious Japanese meal"; the lunch box is a "best buy."

Katz's Delicatessen [S] — 20 | 9 | 11 | $17
205 E. Houston St. (Ludlow St.), 212-254-2246
◪ "Meg Ryan wasn't faking" – "everyone should experience a hot pastrami" at this huge, often mobbed Lower East Side cafeteria-style deli "where Harry met Sally"; it's been dishing up hefty sandwiches, knishes, hot dogs and "NY attitude" for 111 years and looks the part; P.S. "don't forget to tip the sandwich man under the 'No Tipping' sign."

K.B. Garden (Queens) [S] — 22 | 14 | 13 | $22
136-28 39th Ave. (bet. Main & Union Sts.), 718-961-9088
◪ "Good for groups", this low-cost Flushing Cantonese hall has a "great variety" of dim sum, but "get there early" and plan to "point" since it can be "crowded" with "minimal" service; seafood is also a good bet.

Keens Steakhouse — 21 | 20 | 19 | $45
72 W. 36th St. (bet. 5th & 6th Aves.), 212-947-3636
■ "Venerable" 19th-century Garment-area steakhouse "filled with NY history", "killer" mutton chops and lots of suits; "they don't rush you", so linger over a single malt and check out the "cool" pipe collection (over 80,000); there's also an atmospheric bar and upstairs party rooms with museum-quality artifacts.

Keewah Yen [S] — 19 | 15 | 18 | $32
50 W. 56th St. (bet. 5th & 6th Aves.), 212-246-0770
◪ Though "nothing special", this recently renovated (post-*Survey*) Midtown Chinese has several valued qualities: it's "polite", "consistent", "reasonable" and convenient.

Kelley & Ping [S] — 18 | 16 | 13 | $22
127 Greene St. (bet. Houston & Prince Sts.), 212-228-1212
◪ This "hip and trendy" but also "cheap" and "yummy" SoHo Pan-Asian tearoom/shop feels like "prewar Shanghai", except for the "damn cell phones"; it gets "crowded", but the crowd is "sexy."

Khyber Pass ◐[S] — 18 | 14 | 15 | $23
34 St. Marks Pl. (bet. 2nd & 3rd Aves.), 212-473-0989
■ "In the heart of tatoo town", this "little-noticed" East Village Afghan is an "exotic", "reliable" "dining escape" offering "tasty dishes" at "bargain prices" in a funkily "romantic" setting; the "front window" seats are the place to be.

Kiev ◐[S]⊄ — 17 | 7 | 12 | $16
117 Second Ave. (7th St.), 212-674-4040
◪ To satisfy a "3 AM" blintz, borscht or pierogi craving, head to this 24-hour "East Village tradition" for "cheap" Slavic eats; the "decor needs help", ditto service, but being able to stumble in at any hour in any condition with "no questions asked" is a plus.

Kiiroi-Hana [S] — 20 | 11 | 16 | $31

23 W. 56th St. (bet. 5th & 6th Aves.), 212-582-7499

■ A "good Midtown resource" for "beautiful" "fresh sushi" and steaming Japanese noodle soups in a "relaxed, easy atmosphere"; if there's "not much flair", at least there's "good value."

Killmeyer's (Staten Island) [S] — ▽ 21 | 18 | 20 | $28

4254 Arthur Kill Rd. (Sharrotts Rd.), 718-984-1202

■ "You're in Deutschland", not Staten Island, when you dine at this Bavarian with otherwise hard-to-find "good German food" and a "rustic setting", complete with beer garden and live music.

KING COLE BAR ◐[S] — 19 | 27 | 21 | $41

St. Regis Hotel, 2 E. 55th St. (bet. 5th & Madison Aves.), 212-339-6721

■ For many, the "best bar in NYC" is this "classy" Midtowner that works for drinking, dating or deal-making due to its "elegant" ambiance ("love that Maxfield Parrish mural"), "killer" (in price and potency) cocktails and good light American fare.

Kings' Carriage House [S] — 22 | 26 | 22 | $47

251 E. 82nd St. (bet. 2nd & 3rd Aves.), 212-734-5490

■ You can "feel like a 19th-century aristocrat" when you dine on the "very good" Continental food at this "beautiful" English-style East Side townhouse; what's more, there's an "unbelievable bargain" lunch and a "perfect" tea too.

Kin Khao ◐[S] — 21 | 18 | 15 | $31

171 Spring St. (bet. Thompson St. & W. B'way), 212-966-3939

■ The "innovative", fairly priced, "consistently delicious" Thai food is worth the "crazy lines" and "crowded" conditions at this SoHo "scene"; now if someone could just "stifle the staff's 'tude."

Kismat ◐[S] — ▽ 19 | 15 | 18 | $22

603 Ft. Washington Ave. (187th St.), 212-795-8633

■ "Go to the Cloisters", then head to this good nearby Bangladeshi; though its setting is elemental, it's "cozy", "friendly" and reasonable.

Kitaro [S] — ▽ 21 | 12 | 17 | $29

1164 First Ave. (bet. 63rd & 64th Sts.), 212-317-9892

510 Amsterdam Ave. (bet. 84th & 85th Sts.), 212-787-9008

■ "So small you might walk right by it, but don't", because this East Side Japanese (with a new crosstown sibling) has "great sushi and rolls" at "good prices"; fans are generous "to share the secret."

Kitchen Club [S] — 20 | 18 | 19 | $38

30 Prince St. (Mott St.), 212-274-0025

■ "Interestingly exotic" Japanese-European fusion specialist and "date place" in NoLita with an "intimate", "arty setting" and "marvelously original" food from talented chef-owner Marja Samson; "add a point for decor" if her dog is around.

Kitchenette [S] — 20 | 12 | 13 | $18

80 W. Broadway (Warren St.), 212-267-6740

■ "Amazing breakfasts", "inventive" sandwiches and "pies and cakes from your childhood" star at this "cramped", "cute", "cheap" TriBeCa American that's like a "farmhouse table", except for the "funky club kids chowing down."

Knickerbocker Bar & Grill ◐[S] — 20 | 18 | 18 | $36

33 University Pl. (9th St.), 212-228-8490

■ A "long-standing" Village favorite for steaks and other "upscale" New American "comfort food" seasoned with "terrific jazz" and served in a casually "clubby", poster-adorned room; it's "not as fancy or trendy as some", just good.

Kokachin ◐[S] ▽ 21 | 21 | 20 | $51

Omni Berkshire Pl. Hotel, 21 E. 52nd St. (bet. 5th & Madison Aves.), 212-355-9300

■ Though few have tried this pricey hotel-based Midtown American, solid ratings suggest it's doing things right; a comfortable, quiet setting and "glacial service" make it a good place "to talk privately."

Korea Palace [S] 18 | 15 | 17 | $31

127 E. 54th St. (bet. Lexington & Park Aves.), 212-832-2350

■ It serves sushi, but the BBQ and other "traditional" Korean food is the way to go at this brightly lit East Side "businessman's lunch delight."

Kori ◐ – | – | – | M

253 Church St. (bet. Franklin & Leonard Sts.), 212-334-4598

An outpost of style on an unstylish TriBeCa block, this new Korean serves a well-priced menu of grills, bibimbop and more in a small but stylish space with rust-colored walls and pretty banquettes.

Krispy Kreme [S]≠ 22 | 7 | 11 | I

1497 Third Ave. (bet. 84th & 85th Sts.), 212-879-9111 ◐
280 W. 125th St. (bet. F. Douglass & Malcolm X Blvds.), 212-531-0111
141 W. 72nd St. (bet. Amsterdam & Columbus Aves.), 212-724-1100 ◐
Port Authority, 625 Eighth Ave. (bet. 40th & 41st Sts.), 212-290-8644
2 Penn Plaza (33rd St. on Amtrak rotunda level), 212-947-7175
265 W. 23rd St. (bet. 7th & 8th Aves.), 212-620-0111
38 E. Eighth St. (bet. Greene St. & University Pl.), 212-529-5111 ◐
5 World Trade Ctr. (Church St.), 212-432-6111
108-22 Queens Blvd. (Continental Ave.), Queens, 718-263-1121

■ NYers have succumbed to the "addictive as crack", "sugarcoated clouds" at these green-and-white "donut nirvanas" from down South; though "bad for the butt", most people eat six at a time.

Kum Gang San ◐[S] 24 | 19 | 18 | $25

49 W. 32nd St. (B'way), 212-967-0909
138-28 Northern Blvd. (bet. Main & Union Sts.), Queens, 718-461-0909

■ Both the "huge" new Herald Square outpost with its faux rock decor, waterfall and white piano, and its sprawling Flushing parent offer "excellent Korean BBQ" and other "authentic" fare in "upscale" settings; they're best "for groups", but fine even if dining alone.

KURUMA ZUSHI 25 | 17 | 22 | $61

7 E. 47th St., 2nd fl. (bet. 5th & Madison Aves.), 212-317-2802

■ "Extraordinary quality" sushi comes at "extraordinary" prices at this mezzanine Midtowner where the chef-owner teaches "the intricacies" of fine raw fish if you sit at the bar; since there's no "loan department" on-site, "go on an expense account."

La Baraka (Queens) [S] 22 | 18 | 23 | $36

255-09 Northern Blvd. (Little Neck Pkwy.), 718-428-1461

■ "No one is a stranger" at this "excellent", midpriced, "family-run" Little Neck French-Tunisian where "gracious" owners "make you feel at home"; its "charm" outweighs the "crowding" and "ride."

La Belle Epoque ◐[S] 16 | 23 | 17 | $37

827 Broadway (bet. 12th & 13th Sts.), 212-254-6436

◪ The room is *belle* ("Paris" via "New Orleans") and the jazz brunch and tango nights are "fab", so maybe it doesn't matter if other meals at this French-Creole Village showplace have been slipping.

La Bergamote [S]≠ ▽ 22 | 12 | 18 | $12

169 Ninth Ave. (20th St.), 212-627-9010

■ For the "best pain au chocolat this side of Saint-Germain", "flaky croissants" and "fresh berry tarts", try this drool-producing Chelsea cafe; pastry fanatics call it the "best thing to happen to Chelsea since the Piers"; decor? – doesn't matter.

F | D | S | C

La Boheme ◑ [S] — 18 | 16 | 17 | $37
24 Minetta Ln. (bet. Bleecker & W. 3rd Sts.), 212-473-6447
◪ Village "touch of France" serving "creative" Provençal fare (try the pizzas) in a "cozy" (or "cramped") room; critics call it "pricey for unexceptional food", but eat there anyway if headed to a nearby show.

La Boite en Bois [S] 🚫 — 21 | 18 | 20 | $44
75 W. 68th St. (bet. Columbus Ave. & CPW), 212-874-2705
◪ It's easy to join your "neighbors' conversation" at this "tiny", no-"tall"-folks-allowed Country French bistro near Lincoln Center; that said, most find it "charming" and "delicious", if a bit pricey.

La Bonne Soupe ◑ [S] — 16 | 13 | 14 | $24
48 W. 55th St. (bet. 5th & 6th Aves.), 212-586-7650
■ When you're "not flush", this Midtown French does the trick; it's been ladling out "good soups", salads, etc. plus "value" since long before those slick soup shops hit town; so what if it's a bit "shabby"?

La Bouillabaisse (Brooklyn) 🚫 — 23 | 13 | 18 | $31
145 Atlantic Ave. (bet. Clinton & Henry Sts.), 718-522-8275
■ "Amazing" bistro food (including the namesake dish), "low prices" and a "tiny space" lead to "ridiculous lines" at this simple Brooklyn Heights "charmer"; "go early" or plan to "rub hips" with strangers.

L'Absinthe [S] — 22 | 22 | 20 | $52
227 E. 67th St. (bet. 2nd & 3rd Aves.), 212-794-4950
■ "Paris doesn't come cheaply", thus the "chic crowd" pays a premium to enjoy the "*rive droite*" on the East Side via this bistro's "skilled" cooking and "authentic" ambiance; "off nights" are rare.

L'Acajou ◑ [S] — 20 | 14 | 18 | $38
53 W. 19th St. (bet. 5th & 6th Aves.), 212-645-1706
■ From the "smoke-filled bar" to the "high-fat entrees" and "boho" "media-fashion" crowd, this midpriced Flatiron bistro disguised as a "hip" diner is "authentically" French; regulars like its "edgy" feel.

LA CARAVELLE — 26 | 25 | 25 | $66
Shoreham Hotel, 33 W. 55th St. (bet. 5th & 6th Aves.), 212-586-4252
■ NYers have had "over 30 years of wonderful meals" at André and Rita Jammet's Midtown French grande dame; offering Cyril Renaud's "superb" food in an "elegant" room, it's that rare "formal" restaurant that extends "warm" "VIP" service to all, making it one of the city's "most civilized places to eat"; prix fixe only: dinner $68, lunch $38.

La Caridad 78 ◑ [S] 🚫 — 17 | 6 | 11 | $15
2197-2199 Broadway (78th St.), 212-874-2780
◪ Low prices for "huge portions" of "tasty" "peasant" eats make this West Side Chino-Cubano a favorite "taxi-driver" haunt; it's also good for a "cheap date", if "no decor" and "ornery service" don't turn you off.

La Cocina [S] — 18 | 14 | 16 | $22
2608 Broadway (bet. 98th & 99th Sts.), 212-865-7333
217 W. 85th St. (bet. Amsterdam Ave. & B'way), 212-874-0770
762 Eighth Ave. (bet. 46th & 47th Sts.), 212-730-1860
◪ "Good Mexican food", "not thrills", are what you get at this "plain" but "polite", well-priced trio; the margs make it all "more palatable."

LA CÔTE BASQUE [S] — 27 | 26 | 26 | $67
60 W. 55th St. (bet. 5th & 6th Aves.), 212-688-6525
■ "Traditional French at its best" sums up this renowned Midtown "beauty" whose murals "transport you" to the Basque coast while Jean-Jacques Rachou's "superior" cuisine and accompanying "silken" service recall haute dining as it "used to be"; if "a bit stuffy", most say "don't change a thing", surely not the "bargain" $35 lunch; dinner is $63 prix fixe.

F | D | S | C

Lady Mendl's [S] ▽ 21 | 26 | 21 | $33
The Inn at Irving Place, 56 Irving Pl. (bet. 17th & 18th Sts.), 212-533-4466
■ A "very Edith Wharton" Gramercy tearoom that "takes you back to a more graceful age" with its "elegant", "relaxing" feel and lovely afternoon tea; it suits our sippers to a T.

La Focaccia ◐[S] 20 | 18 | 18 | $31
51 Bank St. (W. 4th St.), 212-675-3754
■ A "first-date paradise", this West Village Italian offers "fantastic focaccia" and other "good" and "reasonable" food in a "candlelit" setting; even at its noisiest, it has "lots of charm."

La Forêt [S]🚫 22 | 14 | 17 | $35
1713 First Ave. (bet. 88th & 89th Sts.), 212-987-9839
■ Due to "terrific" French food, "fair prices" and no reserving, this Upper East Side "cubbyhole" comes with "long" waits; most think all they need is "a bigger place."

La Fourchette [S] 23 | 25 | 22 | $61
1608 First Ave. (84th St.), 212-249-5924
■ "Classy" decor, "delicious" New French food from Marc Murphy (ex Cellar in the Sky) and "wonderful" wines make this Yorkville yearling an exciting "surprise"; even if a bit "pretentious", it's "worth every $100" – if that's too rich for your blood, try the $25 brunch.

La Giara [S] 19 | 17 | 18 | $32
501 Third Ave. (bet. 33rd & 34th Sts.), 212-726-9855
◪ "Above-average" Italian that's a "needed" option in "restaurant-challenged" Murray Hill; its "comfortable" woody setting, "fair prices", fine wines and outdoor seats make most "happy to find it."

La Gioconda 22 | 17 | 20 | $34
226 E. 53rd St. (bet. 2nd & 3rd Aves.), 212-371-3536
■ This "cute" East Midtown Italian offers "good food" and "excellent value in an expensive" locale; given "the cramped space", the waiters may "trip all over you", but they're so "adorable", you may not mind.

La Gondola ◐[S] – | – | – | M
1427 Second Ave. (bet. 74th & 75th Sts.), 212-794-8700
Just what the East Side needs – another midpriced Italian; at least this newcomer has the sense to carve out a special niche (Venetian food) and a clever look, with mirrors designed to look like windows.

La Gould Finch ◐[S]🚫 – | – | – | M
93 Ave. B (6th St.), 212-253-6369
Pink neon signs declaring 'Way Open' greet you at this East Village Cajun storefront shrine to bordello chic, serving hearty, sloppy fare amid furry tablecloths, chintzy upholstery, tasseled lamps and gilded frames; a harpist adds to the down-home mood.

La Goulue ◐[S] 19 | 20 | 18 | $49
746 Madison Ave. (bet. 64th & 65th Sts.), 212-988-8169
◪ Candidate for "the new Mortimer's", this wood-paneled East Side bistro offers better "theater" than some B'way shows with its "kiss-kiss" Euro/socialite "scene", but behind the "attitude" is some "good French food", albeit at "hefty" prices.

LA GRENOUILLE ◐ 27 | 27 | 26 | VE
3 E. 52nd St. (bet. 5th & Madison Aves.), 212-752-1495
■ For elegant "big-deal" dining, few places match the Masson family's Midtown Classic French "showstopper", where one "sits among kings" and other VIPs enjoying "top-of-the-line" food and service in a flower-filled setting that's "what Paris wishes it looked like in the spring"; it's prix fixe and pricey ($45 lunch, $90 dinner), but it "doesn't get much better" and the upstairs private room is one of NY's secret treasures.

F	D	S	C

La Griglia [S] — | — | — | M
5 E. 20th St. (bet. B'way & 5th Ave.), 212-995-2482
As the name implies, grilled Italian fare stars at this charming little Flatiron newcomer whose main challenge may be its sleepy side-street location; hopefully its savory aromas and moderate prices will lure folks down the block.

La Grolla, Ristorante [S] ▽ 23 | 16 | 21 | $41
413 Amsterdam Ave. (bet. 79th & 80th Sts.), 212-496-0890
■ A "different" Northern Italian, this new, pricey (by neighborhood standards) Upper Westsider features the "sumptuous" food of the Val d'Aosta region; add a "warm, intimate" setting and "solicitous" service and its "rapid popularity" is no surprise.

Laight Street — | — | — | M
62 Laight St. (Greenwich St.), 212-334-2274
This trendy new seafooder is fishing for TriBeCa hipsters with its sleek, modern setting (complete with aquarium, communal table and exposed wine cellar) and a menu offering everything in full and half portions.

La Jumelle ◐[S] 19 | 17 | 15 | $30
55 Grand St. (bet. W. B'way & Wooster St.), 212-941-9651
■ "Classic" SoHo late-night bistro with "good, cheap" steaks, "funky" decor and a "cool Downtown" ambiance, despite an "aging clientele"; "service could be better", but who cares? – the staff is "gorgeous."

Lakruwana ◐[S] 17 | 16 | 16 | $25
358 W. 44th St. (bet. 8th & 9th Aves.), 212-957-4480
■ For something "different", try this "exotic" Theater District Sri Lankan that's "good", "spicy", "cheap" and "comfy"; "you can't beat the Sunday buffet – but what is that stuff?"

La Lanterna di Vittorio ◐[S]💳̸ ▽ 19 | 21 | 16 | $17
129 MacDougal St. (bet. 3rd & 4th Sts.), 212-529-5945
■ Sit by the "cozy fireplace" at this Village Italian coffeehouse and its cappuccino, desserts and snack fare taste even better; it's "dark", "quaint" and "romantic", "if you don't mind tourists."

La Lunchonette ◐[S] 21 | 15 | 18 | $36
130 10th Ave. (18th St.), 212-675-0342
■ An "odd" location in West Chelsea adds to the feeling that this "funky", "mellow" bistro is a "fabulous find" for "affordable" food; the crowd may "wear black and look French", but there's "no attitude."

La Mangeoire [S] 19 | 19 | 19 | $40
1008 Second Ave. (bet. 53rd & 54th Sts.), 212-759-7086
■ "Escape to the French countryside" via this East Midtown Provençal with a "rustic" flower-filled setting and "completely reliable" food and service; better yet, the prix fixes are a "bargain" and the chocolate mousse is "the next best thing to sex."

Lamarca 💳̸ 19 | 9 | 16 | $17
161 E. 22nd St. (3rd Ave.), 212-674-6363
■ "Tiny" Gramercy Southern Italian cafe with good "homemade pastas" at "shockingly low prices" – and you can take it home if you want decor; the neighbors have just one beef: "not open weekends."

La Mediterranée [S] 19 | 17 | 19 | $38
947 Second Ave. (bet. 50th & 51st Sts.), 212-755-4155
■ "A bit old-fashioned and just the way we like it" say locals who laud this "cozy" Midtown bistro for its "well-prepared food", "warm service" and "mellow" piano music; add "prix fixe value" and "what more" could you want?

La Mela 🆂
18 | 11 | 16 | $32 |

167 Mulberry St. (bet. Broome & Grand Sts.), 212-431-9493

☑ "Like Uncle Vinnie's birthday party", this "loud", "kitschy", "no-menu" Little Italy Italian "keeps the food coming" and "the wine flowing" until you shout "stop, I'm going to explode!"; it's "touristy", but with a group, it's also "a blast."

La Metairie 🆂
21 | 20 | 20 | $46 |

189 W. 10th St. (W. 4th St.), 212-989-0343

■ Village Provençal bistro that's "so cute, so French, so good" and so "tight" that you'd better "like your neighbors because they'll be sitting in your lap," or go "midweek" to best enjoy its "romantic" "farmhouse" feel; P.S. "when did charming get so expensive?"

La Mirabelle 🆂
21 | 18 | 21 | $40 |

102 W. 86th St. (bet. Amsterdam & Columbus Aves.), 212-496-0458

■ Having moved to a "more convenient" location, this West Side bistro still has the "same very good food" and "sweet" service (led by owner Annick Le Douran); it's "less *intime*" now, but remains a "solid value."

Lan ◐🆂
20 | 16 | 17 | $26 |

56 Third Ave. (bet. 10th & 11th Sts.), 212-254-1959

■ With "fresh-as-can-be sushi" plus other good choices, this Central Village Japanese pleases fans of the raw and the cooked – especially with its "great-value" early dinner specials.

Landmark Tavern 🆂
16 | 18 | 17 | $32 |

626 11th Ave. (46th St.), 212-757-8595

☑ A taste of "the old sod" seasoned with NY "history" awaits at this "wonderfully preserved" vintage 1868 West Midtown tavern; the "decent" Irish-English "pub grub" tastes best on a "frigid" night after you "hoist a pint" or two.

L'Annam ◐🆂
19 | 14 | 17 | $20 |

393 Third Ave. (28th St.), 212-686-5168

■ Despite debate over whether this Gramercy Vietnamese serves "delectably spiced" dishes or "Americanized" fare with "little zing", all agree it's "cheap", "quick" and "friendly", i.e. a good neighbor.

La Nonna 🆂
– | – | – | E |

133 W. 13th St. (bet. 6th & 7th Aves.), 212-741-3663

One of the Village's most appealing gardens (once part of the New Deal) now has fine food to match, thanks to chef-owner Massimo Felici (of Ribollita) and his Tuscan fare; the revamped interior, with restored brick walls, a brick oven and comfortable adjoining lounge, gives it more than just alfresco appeal.

Lanza Restaurant 🆂
17 | 13 | 17 | $28 |

168 First Ave. (bet. 10th & 11th Sts.), 212-674-7014

☑ Atmospheric 1904 Italian that's one of the few East Villagers where the word "trendy doesn't exist"; the "basic" food won't knock your fedora off, but it's a "good value" and there's a "great garden."

La Paella ◐🆂
19 | 16 | 16 | $28 |

214 E. Ninth St. (bet. 2nd & 3rd Aves.), 212-598-4321

■ "Better than Barcelona", or at least closer, this East Village Spanish provides "tasty tapas" in a dark, "cozy", often "loud", setting; it's "good date" material, if you "ignore the model waitresses."

La Petite Auberge 🆂
20 | 16 | 19 | $39 |

116 Lexington Ave. (bet. 27th & 28th Sts.), 212-689-5003

■ "A French bistro before French bistros were cool", this "old-style" Gramercy veteran gets all Cs: "cozy", "consistent", "caring" and comfortably priced; "wonderful soufflés" are a highlight.

F | D | S | C

La Pizza Fresca Ristorante [S] 21 | 16 | 16 | $29

31 E. 20th St. (bet. B'way & Park Ave. S.), 212-598-0141

■ "These guys know their pies" say those impressed by this Flatiron trattoria's "superior" brick-oven Neapolitan pizzas; pastas and salads also "shine", though service can be "slow."

La Primavera 19 | 17 | 19 | $39

234 W. 48th St. (bet. B'way & 8th Ave.), 212-586-2233

■ It may not bring the house down, but this "comfortable" Theater District Northern Italian gets you to your show "on time" and well fed with "no hassles"; the prix fixe makes the evening more affordable.

L'Ardoise [S] 19 | 12 | 17 | $37

1207 First Ave. (bet. 65th & 66th Sts.), 212-744-4752

■ Though "dreary" and "narrow", this East Side bistro provides a "genuine taste of France" at "fair prices" plus entertainment via its "eccentric" owner – he may be "cranky" but he'll "make your day."

La Réserve ◐ 24 | 24 | 24 | $58

4 W. 49th St. (bet. 5th & 6th Aves.), 212-247-2993

■ "Refined", "reserved" and rock-steady, this "formal" Midtown French is "first-class all the way", from its "fine" food and "meticulous" service to the "civilized", flower-filled setting; it's "not exciting", just "sure" and "solid", the way its moneyed clientele likes it; N.B. longtime owner/maître d' Jean-Louis Missud has handed over the reins to partner Georges Briguet of Le Perigord.

La Ripaille [S] 20 | 18 | 19 | $40

605 Hudson St. (bet. Bethune & W. 12th Sts.), 212-255-4406

■ "So small it feels like home", yet so French it feels like "Paris", this West Village bistro is a "cozy", "romantic" setting for good Gallic "comfort food"; but a few find it "pricey" and without "much flair."

La Rivista ◐ 19 | 15 | 18 | $41

313 W. 46th St. (bet. 8th & 9th Aves.), 212-245-1707

◪ Very good Restaurant Row Italian that's popular as a "steady, dependable" pre-theater choice; still, a few find it "somewhat pricey" for "pasta without panache."

La Rocchetta [S] ▽ 21 | 23 | 18 | $34

513 Columbus Ave. (bet. 84th & 85th Sts.), 212-799-5784

■ An "unusual", attractive "Byzantine design" sets the stage for "surprisingly good" Italian fare at this moderately priced West Side newcomer; there's a "good private room" too.

La Soirée d'Asie [S] ▽ 21 | 21 | 22 | $48

156 E. 64th St. (bet. Lexington & 3rd Aves.), 212-421-7899

■ "Lovely [family] owners" run this serene East Side townhouse Vietnamese with "delicate yet satisfying" fare; but some find it "expensive" for "small portions."

La Taza de Oro ◐💳 18 | 7 | 15 | $14

96 Eighth Ave. (bet. 14th & 15th Sts.), 212-243-9946

■ Storefront Chelsea Puerto Rican "cult classic" for "Latino soul food" that "tastes like home cooking"; "cheeky waiters" and "*café con leche* of the gods" are part of the grunge "bargain."

La Tour [S] – | – | – | M

1319 Third Ave. (bet. 75th & 76th Sts.), 212-472-7578

With the look and feel of a real Parisian bistro, this midpriced French newcomer has quickly won a loyal local following; write-ins say service can be spotty, but you can't beat the mussels or steak tartare and when it's on, it's electric; try the early bird.

F | D | S | C

Lattanzi ◐ 21 | 19 | 21 | $45

361 W. 46th St. (bet. 8th & 9th Aves.), 212-315-0980

■ "One of the better Restaurant Row performers", this "pretty" Italian is a "standout" pre-curtain and even "better after" when it's less crowded and they serve "unique" Roman-Jewish dishes; "don't miss the artichokes" or the garden.

L'Attitude ◐[S] – | – | – | M

470 Sixth Ave. (bet. 11th & 12th Sts.), 212-243-2222

If looking for 'tude, there's none to be had at this laid-back little West Village newcomer; what you'll find are the usual French bistro suspects like steak frites at pleasing prices, along with atmospheric ceiling fans, leather banquettes and a quieter crowd than normal for the locale.

Lavagna $̸ ▽ 22 | 17 | 19 | $30

545 E. Fifth St. (bet. Aves. A & B), 212-979-1005

■ "Tight-quartered but a bargain" for "excellent" Italian food with "Mediterranean flair" is the word on this rustic new East Villager; it gets "crowded", but the "cheerful staff" does its best to keep up.

La Vela [S] 18 | 15 | 18 | $30

373 Amsterdam Ave. (bet. 77th & 78th Sts.), 212-877-7818

■ "Good for dates" as well as a place "to bring children", this all-purpose West Side Italian is a "friendly", "low-key" neighbor that's "not outstanding", just "reliable", "reasonable" and "relaxing."

La Vineria [S] ▽ 18 | 15 | 18 | $29

19 W. 55th St. (bet. 5th & 6th Aves.), 212-247-3400

■ In a Midtown area lacking "moderately priced, decent food", this "intimate" Italian is most "welcome" for its brick-oven pizzas and other "good", "earthy" fare; that "Italians eat here" says a lot.

Layla [S] 20 | 22 | 18 | $45

211 W. Broadway (Franklin St.), 212-431-0700

■ Take "a magic carpet ride" at this Robert De Niro–owned TriBeCa Mideastern where the food, belly dancer and colorful decor are all "tantalizing"; it's "pricey", but a good show.

Le Bar Bat ◐ 13 | 17 | 13 | $33

311 W. 57th St. (bet. 8th & 9th Aves.), 212-307-7228

◪ It's "Halloween" year-round at this "Gothic"-style West Midtown disco/lounge/restaurant, in that order; the American food is a sideshow, and some say the "bridge-and-tunnel" crowd is scarier than the decor.

Le Beaujolais [S] 19 | 14 | 18 | $36

364 W. 46th St. (bet. 8th & 9th Aves.), 212-974-7464

■ "Nothing changes" (including the "tired but homey" decor) at this veteran Restaurant Row bistro; it's still a "dependable" pre-theater "good buy" with "solid" French food and "charming hosts."

LE BERNARDIN ◐ 28 | 27 | 28 | $75

155 W. 51st St. (bet. 6th & 7th Aves.), 212-489-1515

■ The pinnacle of "piscatory perfection", Maguy LeCoze's French seafood stunner nets Top Food and Top Service honors this year, making it NY's overall "king of the sea"; it's "expensive" (prix fixe only: $42 lunch, $72 dinner), but with chef Eric Ripert's works of "genius", a "soothingly elegant" Midtown setting and "polished" service, it's leagues above most and a sure bet when you "need to impress", business-wise or otherwise.

Le Biarritz 19 | 16 | 18 | $40

325 W. 57th St. (bet. 8th & 9th Aves.), 212-757-2390

◪ It "could use redecorating", but this West Midtown French is popular with an "older local clientele" for its "good, basic" food and "old-shoe" comfort; it's handy for Carnegie Hall and Lincoln Center too.

Le Bilboquet S | 19 | 17 | 15 | $44

25 E. 63rd St. (bet. Madison & Park Aves.), 212-751-3036

■ To enjoy this East Side French bistro, don your "best Euro outfit", take your "cigarets", "shades and cell phone" and "plan to crowd" in with "socialites, models" et al.; the food's "good", but it's "more about socializing", "air kisses and attitude."

Le Bistrot de Maxim's | 18 | 21 | 18 | $46

680 Madison Ave. (61st St.), 212-751-5111

◪ The decor is "beautiful", the French food "quite good" and the prix fixe menus offer "value" at this East Side bistro; still, some liken it to "Brigitte Bardot" – "quite something" once, but now "boring."

Le Boeuf à la Mode S | 20 | 19 | 21 | $46

539 E. 81st St. (bet. East End & York Aves.), 212-249-1473

■ It's been "around for umpteen years" – nothing à la mode about it – but this "quiet" East Side bistro is "still going strong" with locals who have "never had a bum meal" here; the prix fixe controls costs.

Le Bouchon S | ▽ 20 | 16 | 19 | $42

319 W. 51st St. (bet. 8th & 9th Aves.), 212-765-6463

■ Though it doesn't get a lot of notice, this "very French" Theater District bistro serves "generous" fare at not-ungenerous prices; "phenomenal blood sausage" and quenelles are specialties.

Le Charlot ◐ S | 21 | 18 | 18 | $43

19 E. 69th St. (bet. Madison & Park Aves.), 212-794-1628

◪ Some claim this "very small" East Side bistro is "all about the attitude, the smoke and the scene", but it's also about "good food" plus "people-watching galore"; either way, it's "always packed" and "lively."

LE CIRQUE 2000 S | 26 | 26 | 25 | $74

NY Palace Hotel, 455 Madison Ave. (bet. 50th & 51st Sts.), 212-303-7788

◪ It's not like "the old days", but this "Y2K-ready" version of Sirio Maccioni's NY legend, now in Midtown's Villard Houses, is still a "spectacle", with Sottha Khunn's "terrific" French food, Jacques Torres' superb desserts, Adam Tihany's must-see, if not must-like, "elegantly trippy" decor and, as always, electric people-watching; even given "attitude", "uneven" meals, high costs and "tourists", this "big top" is the town's best "show."

L'Ecole | 22 | 19 | 21 | $37

French Culinary Institute, 462 Broadway (Grand St.), 212-219-3300

■ "Tomorrow's culinary stars" are "learning the right stuff" from Pépin, Sailhac, Soltner and Co., judging by the "fine" French meals they produce at this "lovely" SoHo cooking school; "like Avis, they try harder" and succeed, resulting in a top "gourmet value."

Le Colonial ◐ S | 22 | 23 | 20 | $46

149 E. 57th St. (bet. Lexington & 3rd Aves.), 212-752-0808

■ In an "elegant, steamy", Saigon-meets-"Casablanca" East Side setting, "light", "upscale" Vietnamese fare draws "fashionable" types for whom "diet" portions are a plus and high prices painless; the upstairs lounge is still a "hot" scene.

Le Gamin ◐ S ⊄ | 18 | 15 | 10 | $20

183 Ninth Ave. (21st St.), 212-243-8864
536 E. 5th St. (bet. Aves. A & B), 212-254-8409
50 MacDougal St. (bet. Houston & Prince Sts.), 212-254-4678
1 Main St. (Plymouth St.), Brooklyn, 718-722-3010

◪ "Paris in every way" – "the food, the decor", the "attitudinal staff" – describes this cafe minichain; the crêpes, sandwiches and café au lait are "terrific", if the waiters can be convinced to bring them.

F | D | S | C

Le Gans ◐ [S] ▽ 19 | 20 | 16 | $41
46 Gansevoort St. (Greenwich St.), 212-675-5224
◪ Early visitors to this attractive, "upscale" new Village bistro say it offers "well-done" Provençal food in a "very European" ambiance with welcome late hours, but note room for service "improvement."

Le Gigot [S] 22 | 18 | 19 | $41
18 Cornelia St. (bet. Bleecker & W. 4th Sts.), 212-627-3737
■ Even "cramped as it is", this "teensy" West Village bistro is "always a pleasure" for its "authentic, homestyle" fare, "good service" and "charmingly French" aura; our advice: 'gee go!'

Le Jardin Bistro [S] 21 | 20 | 19 | $36
25 Cleveland Pl. (bet. Kenmare & Spring Sts.), 212-343-9599
■ On a "sunny day" in the garden, it's hard to beat this small, "sweet" SoHo bistro for charm, but inside or out, it makes for a "hearty", "romantic" meal; it's also quite affordable.

Le Madeleine [S] 19 | 19 | 19 | $37
403 W. 43rd St. (9th Ave.), 212-246-2993
■ One of the Theater District's long-running hits, this French bistro has a "delightful" garden room, "always good" food and "accommodating" service; it's ideal pre-curtain and "even better if you have time to linger."

Le Madri ◐ [S] 22 | 22 | 21 | $49
168 W. 18th St. (7th Ave.), 212-727-8022
■ "Everyone looks good", and by most accounts, "everything is good" at Chelsea's "super Tuscan", from the "fab" food to the "stylish", spacious room with "stargazing" potential; it's a "costly" but winning "combo of class and casual."

Le Marais ◐ [S] 20 | 15 | 16 | $41
150 W. 46th St. (bet. 6th & 7th Aves.), 212-869-0900
◪ "As good as it gets in kosher steaks", this Times Square–area French steakhouse comes with "authentic" bistro ambiance; a few find it "uneven", but since it's handy, expect "crowds" and "noise" pre-show.

Lemon, The ◐ [S] 14 | 17 | 13 | $33
230 Park Ave. S. (bet. 18th & 19th Sts.), 212-614-1200
◪ "Big on ambiance", "bodies" and "bar scene", this Lower Park Eclectic can't shake its rep as being "appropriately named" in terms of food; some say it's "getting better", but service is so "slow" you may never find out.

Le Monde ◐ [S] 17 | 19 | 14 | $27
2885 Broadway (bet. 112th & 113th Sts.), 212-531-3939
◪ The Columbia area's "own l'il Balthazar" is "really taking off", but whether that's due to affordable "good food" and bistro ambiance or "because we're desperate up here" is debated; it's not due to service.

Lemongrass Grill [S] 17 | 12 | 14 | $21
2534 Broadway (bet. 94th & 95th Sts.), 212-666-0888 ◐
494 Amsterdam Ave. (84th St.), 212-579-0344
138 E. 34th St. (bet. Lexington & 3rd Aves.), 212-213-3317
80 University Pl. (11th St.), 212-604-9870
37 Barrow St. (7th Ave. S.), 212-242-0606 ◐
53 Ave. A (4th St.), 212-674-3538 ◐
110 Liberty St. (Church St.), 212-962-1370
61A Seventh Ave. (bet. Berkeley & Lincoln Pls.), Brooklyn, 718-399-7100
◪ If it keeps growing, this low-budget chain of "reliable Thais" will soon be on every corner; though critics knock "assembly-line, timidly spiced" fare, their prices and "convenience" keep 'em "crowded."

Lenox Room S
22 | 21 | 21 | $52
1278 Third Ave. (bet. 73rd & 74th Sts.), 212-772-0404
■ A "high-class" "crowd-pleaser", this East Side American draws well-heeled neighbors who "dress nicely" to enjoy its "excellent" food, "clubby" setting and "attentive" service directed by maître d'/owner Tony Fortuna; there's a "terrific" jazz brunch too.

Lento's (Brooklyn) ●S
19 | 11 | 16 | $21
7003 Third Ave. (Ovington Ave.), 718-745-9197 ☞
833 Union St. (bet. 6th & 7th Aves.), 718-399-8782
■ This "old Italian joint (emphasis on old)" in Bay Ridge and its newer Park Slope branch offer "thin", "crispy" pizzas (aka "pizza on a saltine") and other "good, cheap eats"; otherwise they're "nothing special."

L'Entrecote
19 | 15 | 20 | $42
1057 First Ave. (bet. 57th & 58th Sts.), 212-755-0080
■ East Side bistro "standby" offering a "warm welcome", "good food" (including the namesteak) and "no surprises"; though short on space, it's fine for a "friendly", fairly fared French "fix."

Léon, Resto ●S
– | – | – | M
351 E. 12th St. (bet. 1st & 2nd Aves.), 212-375-8483
Hearty, midpriced French fare draws a young hipster crowd to this stylish new East Village bistro with open French doors, a vaulted ceiling and brick walls; service can be bumpy but has Gallic charm.

Leopard, The
22 | 21 | 23 | $56
253 E. 50th St. (bet. 2nd & 3rd Aves.), 212-759-3735
■ It may be a "'60s time warp", but this "unique" Midtown townhouse French-Continental delivers "quality and quantity at a prix fixe" price ($55 dinner) that includes "free-flowing wine"; service is "excellent" and it's "romantic", if a bit "shopworn."

Le Pain Quotidien S☞
20 | 16 | 14 | $21
1131 Madison Ave. (bet. 84th & 85th Sts.), 212-327-4900
100 Grand St. (Mercer St.), 212-625-9009
■ "Farmhouse"-like Belgian cafe near the Met (and now in SoHo too) with "super" breads, pastries and snacks in a "laid-back" ambiance; service, though, can be "a 'pain'" and "more choices" would help.

LE PERIGORD S
25 | 23 | 25 | $62
405 E. 52nd St. (bet. FDR Dr. & 1st Ave.), 212-755-6244
■ Owner Georges Briguet sets the "gracious" tone at this newly refurbished East Midtown haute French, "a favorite for years" of regulars who feel "cosseted" as they enjoy "outstanding" food in a "peaceful", "elegant" ambiance; if some find it a bit "dated", more like it precisely for its "classic", "old-time" ways; dinner is $52 prix fixe.

Le Pescadou ●S
21 | 16 | 19 | $43
18 King St. (6th Ave.), 212-924-3434
■ The "tables are too close" and the "noise level" climbs, but this "cozy", "Parisian-like bistro" is "one of the better fish places" in SoHo; it's "a bit pricey" and could use "bigger quarters", but it's reliable.

Le Petit Hulot S
18 | 17 | 18 | $42
973 Lexington Ave. (bet. 70th & 71st Sts.), 212-794-9800
■ "Charming French country ambiance", "dependable" bistro food and a "lovely" garden make this "quiet", "intimate" Eastsider a local "favorite", especially for lunch or the "bargain" dinner prix fixe.

Le Quercy S
20 | 16 | 19 | $39
52 W. 55th St. (bet. 5th & 6th Sts.), 212-265-8141
■ A Midtown "throwback" to when "real" bistros offering "real value" weren't a rarity; it's "not *extraordinaire*", just "very good" with old-fashioned comfort and prix fixe "bargains."

Le Refuge 🅂   22 | 21 | 21 | $49
166 E. 82nd St. (bet. Lexington & 3rd Aves.), 212-861-4505
■ "The name describes this cozy" East Side "retreat" that looks and tastes like "provincial France", with "miles of charm" and a "pretty" garden; the "only problem" is cost, but prix fixe deals are the solution.

Le Refuge Inn (Bronx) 🅂   23 | 22 | 22 | $51
Le Refuge Inn, 620 City Island Ave. (Sutherland St.), 718-885-2478
■ Like "a French corner of Cape Cod", this City Island inn is "charming inside and out", with "excellent" food, an "attentive" owner and the option of an "overnight stay"; brunch is an economical way to try it.

LE RÉGENCE 🅂   24 | 27 | 25 | $64
Hotel Plaza Athénée, 37 E. 64th St. (bet. Madison & Park Aves.), 212-606-4647
■ Marie Antoinette would adore the very "regal", robin's egg–blue "Versailles"-like decor at this haute French Eastsider where "everything purrs", including most diners, thanks to "exceptional" food and service plus a "bountiful" blowout brunch; gilt-edged prices are a given.

Le Rivage 🅂   19 | 16 | 19 | $38
340 W. 46th St. (bet. 8th & 9th Aves.), 212-765-7374
■ Restaurant Row French bistro "old faithful" that delivers a "good meal for the money", especially via its "best-buy" prix fixe deals; it's an "accommodating" place that gets a B'way evening off to a good start.

Les Deux Gamins ◑🅂   19 | 16 | 12 | $27
170 Waverly Pl. (Grove St.), 212-807-7357
■ "More French than the Eiffel Tower", this Village bistro offers a "cheek-by-jowl"-by-cigaret "Paris" scene where the "young and hip" come for "hearty", "cheap food" "*avec* supermodels"; "service? – they never heard of it."

Les Deux Lapins   ▽ 19 | 17 | 20 | $27
222 Thompson St. (bet. Bleecker & W. 3rd Sts.), 212-387-8484
■ This French-Caribbean bistro hopped from the East Village to new (but still small) West Village digs; the food is "filling" and cheap, and the owners "so sweet, you wish they were your relatives."

Les Halles ◑🅂   21 | 16 | 17 | $40
411 Park Ave. S. (bet. 28th & 29th Sts.), 212-679-4111
■ "*Authentique*" meats, frites and decor mark this Gramercy bistro/ butcher shop that "would be right at home in Paris"; but it can also resemble *le métro* given "noise" and tables so "tight" "you need the Jaws of Life" to get in or out.

Le Singe Vert ◑🅂   17 | 16 | 15 | $34
160 Seventh Ave. (bet. 19th & 20th Sts.), 212-366-4100
☑ Your "basic bistro and a little pricey" at that with "very French service", but Chelsea locals are happy to "sip" wine and dig into some decent standards while wondering "which way is the Seine?"

LESPINASSE   27 | 28 | 27 | $81
St. Regis Hotel, 2 E. 55th St. (bet. 5th & Madison Aves.), 212-339-6719
■ Though Gray Kunz is "missed", his talented successor, Christian Delouvrier, is "hardly a letdown" and this "gorgeous" Midtown French (No. 1 for Decor) remains a "sumptuous", "spacious" setting for "phenomenal meals" with "service fit for royalty" – "they do everything for you" in what can only be described as an "awesome" "indulgence", and $10,000 later you go home.

Les Pyrénées ◑🅂   19 | 17 | 19 | $41
251 W. 51st St. (bet. B'way & 8th Ave.), 212-246-0044
☑ When the tune running in your head is "Get Me to the Play on Time", this Theater District French is a "dependable" choice; the food is "solid", service well rehearsed and the prix fixe a "value."

Les Routiers [S] 20 | 16 | 18 | $40
568 Amsterdam Ave. (bet. 87th & 88th Sts.), 212-874-2742
■ A "cozy, warm" West Side bistro offering "good-quality food and wine" plus "gracious", "unhurried" service at an "affordable" price; it's something of a "secret", and locals whisper "let's keep it that way."

Les Sans Culottes ◐[S] 16 | 14 | 17 | $32
1085 Second Ave. (bet. 57th & 58th Sts.), 212-838-6660
329 W. 51st St. (bet. 8th & 9th Aves.), 212-581-1283
347 W. 46th St. (bet. 8th & 9th Aves.), 212-247-4284
■ "Damn the cholesterol" and dive into the sausage free-for-all that kicks off meals at these "friendly" "bargain" bistros "for the masses"; beyond that, they're sans thrills, just "decent", filling and "fun."

Le Tableau [S]≠ 21 | 16 | 18 | $32
511 E. Fifth St. (bet. Aves. A & B), 212-260-1333
■ Offering "French flair, East Village–style", this bistro can be a very "cacophonous, sardine scene", but its "inventive" menu is "surprisingly good" and the early bird is "reasonable", so squeeze on in.

Le Taxi [S] 17 | 17 | 16 | $44
37 E. 60th St. (bet. Madison & Park Aves.), 212-832-5500
◪ "Stylish" decor, a "Euro feel" and some "tasty" dishes distinguish this East Side French bistro, but overall it's "nothing special" and the meter runs rather high.

Le Train Bleu [S] 15 | 19 | 16 | $33
Bloomingdale's, 1000 Third Ave., 6th fl. (bet. 59th & 60th Sts.), 212-705-2100
◪ With its Orient Express decor and lack of crowds, this American cafe is a "refreshing" whistle-stop between buys at Bloomie's, even if the kitchen and service sometimes derail.

Levana [S] 21 | 18 | 19 | $44
141 W. 69th St. (bet. B'way & Columbus Ave.), 212-877-8457
■ Aka "the kosher Four Seasons", this Westsider serves "very imaginative" French–New American fare that would be good "in anyone's book", but which is "astonishing" for glatt kosher; it's "pricey" aside from the prix fixe.

Le Veau D'Or 18 | 14 | 18 | $43
129 E. 60th St. (bet. Lexington & Park Aves.), 212-838-8133
◪ "The clock has stopped" at this "been-there-forever", '30s-era French bistro near Bloomie's; plan on good, "old-style" food and service in a setting that isn't lying about its age.

L'Express ◐[S] 16 | 15 | 13 | $26
249 Park Ave. S. (20th St.), 212-254-5858
◪ "Open 24/7" and always "hopping", this "noisy" Flatiron French has that "generic bistro feel" down pat and its "basic" food is "not too pricey"; since its service is the inverse of its name, you'd better "relax" and check out the "wanna-be model" crowd.

Le Zie ◐[S]≠ – | – | – | M
172 Seventh Ave. (bet. 20th & 21st Sts.), 212-206-8686
Whimsically named as a low-rent knockoff of nearby Le Madri, this modest Chelsea storefront Italian got off to a fast start thanks to low prices and tasty food; it looks like a neighbors-supported keeper.

Le Zoo [S] 21 | 17 | 17 | $36
314 W. 11th St. (Greenwich St.), 212-620-0393
■ "Aptly named": at busy hours a "noisy" young crowd stampedes into this "chic", casual little West Village bistro hoping to bag a table and enjoy "inventive", hearty fare; at brunch, it seems like they feed "all the animals in the city."

F	D	S	C

Lhasa [S] ▽ 17 | 17 | 19 | $24

96 Second Ave. (bet. 5th & 6th Sts.), 212-674-5870

◪ A "peaceful" refuge from East Village craziness, this "soothing" Tibetan has "subtle" food, "hospitable service" and a "beautiful" patio; still, as its food and decor ratings indicate, it's too subtle for some.

Liebman's (Bronx) **[S]** ▽ 18 | 11 | 16 | $18

552 W. 235th St. (Johnson Ave.), 718-548-4534

■ You "wouldn't make a special trip for it", but this modestly priced Riverdale kosher deli is a neighborhood favorite, offering "good corned beef" and other "reliable quality" standards not found for miles around.

Lili's Noodle Shop & Grill ◐[S] – | – | – | I

1500 Third Ave. (bet. 84th & 85th Sts.), 212-639-1313

This bright new East Side noodle shop has more modern, Western-style decor than the standard Chinese but not so much more as to raise prices (the weekday lunch special is only $5.50); with 169 choices on the menu, you can come back again and again without getting bored.

Limoncello [S] 20 | 19 | 21 | $45

Michelangelo Hotel, 777 Seventh Ave. (51st St.), 212-582-1310

■ Very "doable" for a "business lunch" or pre-show dinner, this Theater District Italian tenders "rich pastas", game and other reliably good food in a "bright", roomy setting with "warm" service; still, a few feel it's "pricey" for "no big deal."

Little Basil [S] – | – | – | M

39 Greenwich Ave. (Charles St.), 212-645-8965

The new West Village sibling of the East Village's Holy Basil offers pleasingly spiced and priced Thai fare in a simple, somewhat cramped corner space with big windows, pillow-strewn banquettes and candlelight; decibels rise as young locals drift in.

Little Havana [S] ▽ 17 | 12 | 16 | $27

30 Cornelia St. (bet. Bleecker & W. 4th Sts.), 212-255-2212

■ Little is putting it mildly, but this "simple", 19-seat Village Cuban comes up with some big flavors on its "limited" menu; "friendly" people and "fair prices" also boost its stature.

Little Italy Pizza 21 | 6 | 11 | $9

65 Vanderbilt Ave. (bet. 45th & 46th Sts.), 212-687-3660
72 W. 45th St. (6th Ave.), 212-730-7575
182A Varick St. (bet. Charlton & King Sts.), 212-366-5566
11 Park Pl. (bet. B'way & Church St.), 212-227-7077

■ "Excellent for a standing slice" or "two to go", these decor-impaired thick-crust "pizza joints" are a "true salvation" for deli-weary lunchers.

Little Jezebel [S] ▽ 18 | 19 | 17 | $30

529 Columbus Ave. (86th St.), 212-579-4952

◪ Though "tiny", this Westsider manages to offer a "New Orleans" feel along with some "fine", "fattening" Southern food served by a "pleasant" staff; however, a few rebels say it's "too crowded" and the food sometimes heads South.

Little Szechuan [S] ▽ 19 | 9 | 15 | $19

5 E. Broadway (in front of Chatham Sq.), 212-732-0796

◪ "Supercheap, very good" C-town Chinese known for "great sesame noodles"; though decor is lacking, it's a comfy, fairly "warm" place.

Live Bait ◐[S] 14 | 12 | 12 | $23

14 E. 23rd St. (Madison Ave.), 212-353-2400

◪ Still wriggling, this Flatiron "frat boys' dream" done up as a "funky" Southern "dive" with "model/waitresses" as bait packs 'em in "like fish sticks" at the bar; despite reports of "tasty" "fried" grub, only carp would regularly eat here.

Lobster Box (Bronx) S
17 | 15 | 16 | $38
34 City Island Ave. (Belden St.), 718-885-1952
☑ "Good lobsters", "great views" and a "getaway" from Manhattan are reasons to make the "schlep" to this City Island seafood vet; but it's "not inexpensive" and for some, the "memories" are better.

Lobster Club S
22 | 19 | 20 | $50
24 E. 80th St. (bet. 5th & Madison Aves.), 212-249-6500
☑ You're "missing out" if you don't try the namesake sandwich and other "upscale down-home" fare at Anne Rosenzweig's "pretty" Upper East Side townhouse New American; given high tabs and her high rep, some are inevitably let down, but, as ratings show, most enjoy this reliably good "change of pace."

Local ●S
– | – | – | E
224 W. 47th St. (B'way), 212-921-2005
This ambitious Times Square newcomer has won early fans for chef Franklin Becker's New American menu, even though many items cost an arm and a leg in the elegant downstairs dining room; upstairs is more casual and much more affordable.

Lola ●S
20 | 20 | 19 | $40
30 W. 22nd St. (bet. 5th & 6th Aves.), 212-675-6700
■ "The bar is hot", as is the Eclectic food and rockin' gospel brunch at this "sexy" Flatiron spot (picture "Barry White turned into a restaurant"); though a few wish it would lower the prices, it's a "fab" party scene.

Lombardi's S⊅
25 | 11 | 15 | $19
32 Spring St. (bet. Mott & Mulberry Sts.), 212-941-7994
■ "One of the best" for "sit-down", thin-crust pizzas is the consensus on this "old NY–style" coal-oven joint in SoHo; you can "squeeze into" a booth, head for the deck or even eat "right in the kitchen."

Londel's Supper Club S
∇ 21 | 19 | 22 | $26
2620 Frederick Douglass Blvd. (bet. 139th & 140th Sts.), 212-234-6114
■ "Londel Davis is so welcoming" and his "hip", high-ceilinged Harlem Southern-Continental is a pleasing place to "have fine food and hear fine music"; however, given its high quality and moderate prices, it can get a bit "noisy."

London Lennie's (Queens)
21 | 16 | 18 | $34
63-88 Woodhaven Blvd. (63rd Dr.), 718-894-8084
■ "Excellent, fresh", "fairly priced" fish plus no reserving means this Rego Park seafooder can be "a zoo" at prime times, so go early or plan to "wait"; though "spartan"-looking, it's "roomy, well lit" and "friendly."

L'Orange Bleue ●S
18 | 18 | 17 | $35
430 Broome St. (Crosby St.), 212-226-4999
■ "Tasty" Moroccan-French fare, "interesting" decor, fair prices and "great energy" are reasons enough to try this "boho" SoHo bistro, but here are a few more: sidewalk seats and "NY's cutest waiters"; obviously, there's nothing blue about this place except the exterior.

Lotfi's Moroccan
19 | 16 | 18 | $31
358 W. 46th St. (bet. 8th & 9th Aves.), 212-582-5850
■ "Come to the Casbah" for a pre-curtain "change of pace" at this Restaurant Row Moroccan offering "exotic" food and "value"; if tables are "too close", at least you get "theater reviews from other diners."

Lot 61 ●S
16 | 21 | 13 | $39
550 W. 21st St. (bet. 10th & 11th Aves.), 212-243-6555
☑ Huge, arty, way West Chelsea "warehouse" filled with groovsters "taking themselves too seriously", ditto the model staff; "to fill up" on the Eclectic "tasty" tapas tends to take top tabs, but the "60 different martinis" are more of a draw anyway.

F | D | S | C

Louie's Westside Cafe ◐[S] — 16 | 14 | 16 | $30
441 Amsterdam Ave. (81st St.), 212-877-1900
◪ The "model of a neighborhood pleaser", this affordable West Side American is "nothing special", just a "comfy place" for a good meal that's as close to "home-cooked" as most kitchen-challenged NYers get.

Loui Loui ◐[S] — 16 | 15 | 15 | $32
1311 Third Ave. (75th St.), 212-717-4500
◪ "Reliable", if "standard", Italian fare, a room that "never feels crowded" and sidewalk seats make this affordable Eastsider "a good local place"; but it can be "noisy" and some say it's "like 100 others."

L-Ray ◐[S] — 18 | 17 | 17 | $34
64 W. 10th St. (bet. 5th & 6th Aves.), 212-505-7777
◪ "L-Ray ok!" – fans of this Village newcomer claim its "snappy" Gulf Rim eats (Tex-Mex, Cajun, etc.), "funky" "New Orleans" vibe and "cool bar" "guarantee a good time"; doubters say "not there yet."

Luca [S] — 21 | 14 | 19 | $33
1712 First Ave. (bet. 88th & 89th Sts.), 212-987-9260
■ "Luca and you shall find" a "gem" of an East Side Italian that's "the real thing" and a "terrific value"; but "no reserving" and "crammed tables" may add up to "aggravation" before your antipasto.

Luca Lounge ◐[S]≠ — ▽ 20 | 20 | 17 | $24
220 Ave. B (bet. 13th & 14th Sts.), 212-674-9400
■ "Swanky" yet "funky" Alpha City Italian with a "cozy" bar, "chic" little dining room and "fantastic" garden, plus a limited menu of "good" mini-pizzas, salads and "Italianesque tapas"; what's not to like?

Lucian Blue (Brooklyn) [S] — ▽ 21 | 24 | 20 | $35
63 Lafayette Ave. (Fulton St.), 718-422-0093
■ A "good addition to Fort Greene" and handy pre-BAM, this New American reportedly has "excellent food", "smart" decor (skylights, green-and-orange banquettes, a sleek bar) and a "pleasant" staff; locals are "pleased to be so pleased."

Lucien ◐[S] — 20 | 15 | 16 | $32
14 First Ave. (1st St.), 212-260-6481
■ "On the Left Bank of First Avenue" in the East Village is a fine new place to "wear your beret", "practice French with the staff" and dig into not-too-pricey, "vein-clogging" bistro basics in a simple "'40s Paris" setting; expect "cramped" seating, "attitude" and "smoke."

Lucky Cheng's ◐[S] — 12 | 17 | 16 | $32
24 First Ave. (bet. 1st & 2nd Sts.), 212-473-0516
◪ "Buckle up for a wild ride" at this East Village "transvestite party" with a "saucy" staff that puts on "quite a show"; if you must be told that the Asian-Eclectic food is "not the attraction", you probably shouldn't be allowed out at night; P.S. "bring your camera – you never know who or what will go down" here.

Lucky Strike ◐[S] — 17 | 16 | 14 | $29
59 Grand St. (bet. W. B'way & Wooster St.), 212-941-0479
■ "Way past its trendy days" but still "really cool", this SoHo "standby" provides bistro ambiance (complete with "smoke") and "dependable" Franco-American "comfort food" that's best "late-night", when the "people-watching" also peaks.

L'Ulivo Focacceria ◐[S]≠ — ▽ 21 | 16 | 19 | $28
184 Spring St. (bet. Sullivan & Thompson Sts.), 212-343-1445
■ "No pretense, just honest" Italian food, which jumped three points in ratings this year, is what you'll find at this low-key, low-cost SoHo focacceria offering "very good" pizzas, pastas and service plus an "in-Italy" feel; sidewalk seats are good for gallerygoer scoping.

[F] [D] [S] [C]

Lumi ◐[S] — 19 | 19 | 19 | $46

963 Lexington Ave. (70th St.), 212-570-2335
■ Necessarily well-heeled Eastsiders say you'll have "a good meal" at this "upscale" yet "casual" duplex townhouse Italian with "solid" fare, "careful service" and "pretty" decor; there's a summer patio too.

Luna Blu ▽ 19 | 17 | 19 | $37

246 E. 44th St. (bet. 2nd & 3rd Aves.), 212-681-6541
◪ This "quiet" little Midtown Italian doesn't get much reaction, but those who know it say it delivers a "creative", midpriced menu in a "pleasant" room; still, a few feel there's "not enough happening" here.

Luna Piena [S] — 20 | 17 | 19 | $33

243 E. 53rd St. (bet. 2nd & 3rd Aves.), 212-308-8882
■ "Eater-friendly" East Side "neighborhood pasta place" with "hearty" food at "moderate prices", "upbeat service", a "pretty" interior and "cute garden"; not surprisingly, it's "crowded regularly."

Lundy Brothers (Brooklyn) [S] — 15 | 16 | 14 | $35

1901 Emmons Ave. (Ocean Ave.), 718-743-0022
◪ "Not even close" say those who loved the original Lundy's, but this "noisy", "parking lot"-sized Sheepshead Bay seafooder does get nods for its shore dinner and brunch, and some report you no longer have to throw a "temper tantrum to get service."

Lupa ◐[S] — – | – | – | M

170 Thompson St. (bet. Bleecker & Houston Sts.), 212-982-5089
New, moderately priced Roman trattoria in the Village under the knowledgeable aegis of Jason Denton (of 'ino) and Babbo's Joe Bastianich and Mario Batali; near the bar is a salumeria that will sell meat and cheese during dining hours as well as after the kitchen closes.

Lupe's East L.A. Kitchen ◐[S]≠ ▽ 17 | 9 | 14 | $18

110 Sixth Ave. (Watts St.), 212-966-1326
■ "More NY than LA", this "no-frills" SoHo Mexican "hole-in-the-wall" dishes up "humble" "cheap eats" to an "artsy crowd" that likes the fact that it "feels homey, not chainy", assuming home isn't fancy.

Lusardi's ◐[S] — 23 | 18 | 22 | $48

1494 Second Ave. (bet. 77th & 78th Sts.), 212-249-2020
■ "Some things never change" and Eastsiders are glad this "classy" Northern Italian is one of them; with "excellent" food and "pro" service, it "captures a lot of hearts" and stomachs even if it's fairly "pricey."

LUTÈCE — 26 | 25 | 26 | $70

249 E. 50th St. (bet. 2nd & 3rd Aves.), 212-752-2225
■ While memories of the André Soltner glory years at this "elegant" East Midtown haute French duplex townhouse will never fade, this "old champ" "still shines" under another outstanding chef, Eberhard Mueller, who is leading it into the new millennium in "his own style", producing "sublime" food (largely grown at his wife's farm) served by an "outstanding" staff; it's "dining at its luxurious, unpretentious best", and well worth the prix fixe tabs (lunch $38, dinner $65).

Luxia ◐[S] — 19 | 17 | 18 | $35

315 W. 48th St. (bet. 8th & 9th Aves.), 212-957-0800
■ A "small", "sweet" Theater District "hideaway" with "good" Italian-Eclectic food, a "pretty garden", "unbeatable fruit martinis" and live jazz on some nights; if a few say "nothing special", more call it "a find."

Luzia's [S] — 17 | 14 | 17 | $29

429 Amsterdam Ave. (bet. 80th & 81st Sts.), 212-595-2000
■ "Portuguese comfort food" is the focus at this "homey", "cozy" (sometimes "too crowded") West Side "good deal"; brunch is "a great way to start the day", since there are "no lines" – "rare" in this area.

F | D | S | C

Lx ◐ [S] — – | – | – | E
45 E. 60th St. (bet. Madison & Park Aves.), 212-421-1234
Deep red tones give great warmth to this stylish new East Side Argentine; if the kitchen is even half as talented as the decorator (and that's the early word), it should turn out to be a great success.

Mad 28 ◐ [S] — 17 | 19 | 16 | $39
72 Madison Ave. (bet. 27th & 28th Sts.), 212-689-2828
◪ "Designer pizzas" and "thoughtfully crafted Italian fare" win admirers at this "large and airy" Gramercy yearling situated in an "area bereft of good restaurants"; but it "needs to work out some kinks" – "slow service", "high prices."

Maison ◐ [S] — ▽ 22 | 21 | 19 | $44
1477 Second Ave. (77th St.), 212-879-4824
■ Busy Upper East Side bees are "all abuzz" over this "welcome addition" to the nabe, a lovely art nouveau French-American winner that's refreshingly "without attitude" despite its Downtown feel; look for an on-premises bakery come late '99.

Malaga [S] — 20 | 11 | 17 | $32
406 E. 73rd St. (bet. 1st & York Aves.), 212-737-7659
■ "Tacky surroundings" are "part of the charm" of this East Side Spanish, where the "generous portions" of Iberian delights are "almost as good as in Newark"; "reasonable prices" ice the cake.

Malatesta Trattoria ◐ [S] 🚫💳 — ▽ 20 | 17 | 17 | $28
649 Washington St. (Christopher St.), 212-741-1207
■ It may be located "at the edge of nowhere", but this "cozy", candlelit West Village Italian is always "filled" thanks to "dependable" cooking, "hearty wines", "cute servers" and, not incidentally, "affordable" prices.

Maloney & Porcelli ◐ [S] — 22 | 20 | 20 | $52
37 E. 50th St. (bet. Madison & Park Aves.), 212-750-2233
■ "Big portions" meet "big egos" at this big Midtown steakhouse, a "testosterone-fueled" "he-man joint" where the signature "pork shank is kingpin" but the steaks are no slouches; the "cigar-and-suspender" set considers it a "great place to close a deal" – but not a romantic one.

Mamá Mexico ◐ [S] — 20 | 16 | 19 | $24
2672 Broadway (bet. 101st & 102nd Sts.), 212-864-2323
■ "Strong, tall margaritas" and huge sangrias fuel the "fiesta" feel of this winning Upper West Side Mexican that also showcases an "over-the-top" mariachi band on Fridays; *compadres* commend the "fab staff" and only "wish the place weren't so popular."

Mama's Food Shop 🚫💳 — 20 | 11 | 14 | $13
200 E. Third St. (bet. Aves. A & B), 212-777-4425
■ "Habit-forming", "downright tasty" eats turn up at this Alphabet City American, and if the grub seems like a "lukewarm" "potluck dinner" to some, at least it's "unbelievably cheap"; given poor decor and service, it may be best enjoyed "taken home."

Mandarin Court [S] — 20 | 9 | 12 | $20
61 Mott St. (bet. Bayard & Canal Sts.), 212-608-3838
■ "Solid dim sum" makes this Chinatown "great buy" "near the courts" an "excellent alternative" to larger, noisier competitors; though there's "no decor" and "no service", the food's just fine.

Manducatis (Queens) [S] — 21 | 14 | 19 | $36
13-27 Jackson Ave. (47th Ave.), 718-729-4602
■ "Give yourself plenty of time" at this LI City old-style Italian, as there may be "long waits between courses", but die-hard fans insist it "can't be beat" for "delicious", "family-style" cooking; though "off the beaten path", it's worth the trek to an earlier era.

F | D | S | C

Mangia 21 | 14 | 14 | $19
16 E. 48th St. (bet. 5th & Madison Aves.), 212-754-0637
50 W. 57th St. (bet. 5th & 6th Aves.), 212-582-5554
Trump Bldg., 40 Wall St. (bet. Broad & William Sts.), 212-425-4040
■ A "nice departure from the mundane", this "upscale" Med-Eclectic chainlet offers an "array of gastronomic treats" that's "hard to beat" for a "quick lunch" (some eat in, but most take out); despite "crowds" and serious prices, it "never disappoints."

Mangia e Bevi ◐[S] 17 | 14 | 16 | $27
800 Ninth Ave. (53rd St.), 212-956-3976
■ "Grab your tambourine" and plan to "dance on the tables" at this "hopping" Hell's Kitchen Southern Italian, a "constant party" where "everybody's celebrating something" and almost "anything goes"; if you like your just-"ok" dining "loud and cheap", look no further.

Manhattan Chili Co. ◐[S] 16 | 12 | 14 | $21
Ed Sullivan Theater, 1697 Broadway (bet. 53rd & 54th Sts.), 212-246-6555
1500 Broadway (entrance on 43rd St.), 212-730-8666
◪ "Cost-conscious feasts" of "delicious chiles" turn up at these Midtown Southwesterners that are "good Theater District standbys" "if you're in a hurry"; dissenters down the product as "merely average."

Manhattan Grille [S] 22 | 21 | 21 | $47
1161 First Ave. (bet. 63rd & 64th Sts.), 212-888-6556
■ "Attentive, accommodating service" sets the "country-club" tone at this "stately" East Side steakhouse, an "undiscovered gem" that's frequented by an "older" "carnivorous crowd"; expect "great steaks and great everything else", though it may seem "stuffy" to trendoids.

MANHATTAN OCEAN CLUB ◐[S] 25 | 22 | 23 | $56
57 W. 58th St. (bet. 5th & 6th Aves.), 212-371-7777
■ "Fish doesn't come any better" than at this Midtown seafooder that's "tops in its class" with "not a bad dish in the place" and a "quiet, understated beauty" in the "great NY tradition of power dining"; it's like flying first class – "you get what you pay for."

Maratti [S] ▽ 23 | 22 | 22 | $55
135 E. 62nd St. (bet. Lexington & Park Aves.), 212-826-6686
■ Seafood Italian-style is the specialty of this "fabulous", "imaginative" Eastsider in a "beautiful townhouse"; as its ratings show, everything is top-notch, including the price.

Marbella (Queens) ◐[S] ▽ 20 | 18 | 19 | $37
Ramada Inn, 220-33 Northern Blvd. (bet. 220th & 221st Sts.), 718-423-0100
■ "Who'd of thunk" they'd find this "excellent", "authentic" Spanish "tucked inside a dumpy hotel" in Queens?; yet this "lovely" spot not only offers a "romantic" ambiance, but "reasonable prices" too – so "relax and enjoy."

MARCH [S] 26 | 25 | 26 | $73
405 E. 58th St. (bet. 1st Ave. & Sutton Pl.), 212-754-6272
■ "Go in like a lion and come out like a lamb" at this "memorable" Sutton Place New American, an "ultraromantic" "charmer" in an "intimate townhouse" complete with a "lovely garden"; "ace" chef Wayne Nish creates a "phenomenal" small-dish, prix fixe menu ($68 dinner) with "a revelation in every mouthful", abetted by a "brilliant sommelier" and "flawless service"; "if you can afford it – go!"

Marchi's 19 | 18 | 20 | $46
251 E. 31st St. (bet. 2nd & 3rd Aves.), 212-679-2494
◪ There are "no decisions" to be made at this menu-less Kips Bay Italian "institution" (since 1930) as its $34.90 prix fixe dinner "never changes"; cranks complain it's "way too much food" and "ordinary" at that, but it's just the ticket for "large", hungry groups.

Marco Polo (Brooklyn) S | 19 | 17 | 19 | $36 |

345 Court St. (Union St.), 718-852-5015

■ When Brooklynites "don't want to cross the bridge", this "old-world" Carroll Gardens Italian delivers "delicious" "red-sauce" dishes in a somewhat "formal" setting; though "there are no surprises here", it's as comfortable as an old shoe.

Mardi Gras (Queens) S | 19 | 18 | 18 | $28 |

70-20 Austin St. (70th Rd.), 718-261-8555

■ "Authentic New Orleans flavors" spice up the menu of this "upbeat" Cajun-Creole in Forest Hills where revelers "always have fun" "while listening to down-home" live music that makes for a "party-like" scene.

Marichu S | 22 | 18 | 21 | $42 |

342 E. 46th St. (bet. 1st & 2nd Aves.), 212-370-1866

■ "If you're stuck by the UN", drop into this "Basque find" that's "better than Barcelona", with "exquisite food", "unusual Spanish wines" and a "wonderful garden"; diplomats say though "a bit cramped", it "never fails to please."

Marina Cafe (Staten Island) S | 17 | 20 | 18 | $35 |

154 Mansion Ave. (bet. Hillside Terr. & Hylan Blvd.), 718-967-3077

☑ The "beautiful harbor view" sets the "nautical" tone at this Staten Island fish palace, but that may be its "saving grace"; though "efforts have been made to improve" the midpriced food, you're really "paying for the atmosphere" here.

Marion's Continental ●S | 16 | 20 | 17 | $28 |

354 Bowery (bet. 4th & Great Jones Sts.), 212-475-7621

■ "Daffy decor" with a "thrift-shop twist" separates this tragically "hip", happily affordable, Bowery Continental-cum-cocktail lounge from the pack; barflies suggest you "stick with the martinis and use the food for absorption."

Mario's (Bronx) S | 19 | 14 | 18 | $34 |

2342 Arthur Ave. (bet. 184th & 186th Sts.), 718-584-1188

☑ "Generous portions" of "good, old-fashioned Italian" food draw nostalgists to this 1919 Bronx "prototype" that's especially handy "after a Yankee game"; but an "unimaginative" menu and "cheesy decor" lead some to say "there are better" choices nearby.

Mark's S | 24 | 25 | 24 | $57 |

The Mark, 25 E. 77th St. (Madison Ave.), 212-879-1864

■ "You feel so well taken care of" at this "fashionable" Eastsider whose "plush surroundings" conjure up "a private club in London"; "very satisfying" French-American food, a "knowledgeable sommelier" and "super service" make it "as good as a hotel restaurant can be"; P.S. their desserts "take the cake."

Markt ●S | 18 | 20 | 17 | $38 |

401 W. 14th St. (9th Ave.), 212-727-3314

☑ "Hot newcomer" in the Meatpacking District; this "dark-paneled" Belgian brasserie offers "plenty of beers", "more mussels than Stallone" and other good, easy, fast food; though its "long wood bar" and outside tables are "jammed with glamour-pusses", some scene-makers sneer: "Balthazar wanna-be."

Maroons ●S | – | – | – | M |

244 W. 16th St. (bet. 7th & 8th Aves.), 212-206-8640

A stone's throw from Chelsea's bustling Eighth Avenue drag, this newcomer is offering moderately priced Jamaican and Southern comfort food to an enamored, eclectic crowd in both a loungey cafe and comfy dining room; give it a try, mon.

Marquet Patisserie
| – | – | – | M |

15 E. 12th St. (bet. 5th Ave. & University Pl.), 212-229-9313
Villagers addicted to this very Parisian pastry shop's sweets are delighted that it now serves dinner; tablecloths and candles dress it up at night, and the changing bistro menu is made even more affordable by the BYO policy and prix fixe option.

Mars 2112 S
| 13 | 23 | 15 | $27 |

1633 Broadway (51st St.), 212-582-2112
☑ For a "far-out" time, "take the kids" to this cavernous Theater District theme restaurant that provides an ersatz "galactic experience", starting with a "spaceship ride" at the entry; the "novelty wears off quickly", though, after tasting the "not-so-great" 'global fusion' cooking.

Marumi S
| ▽ 22 | 15 | 16 | $26 |

546 La Guardia Pl. (bet. Bleecker & W. 3rd Sts.), 212-979-7055
■ "NYU students" cram this "small" Village Japanese for some of the "freshest-tasting sushi" around; since it "feels like home" and offers "reasonable prices", there's "always a wait."

Maruzzella ●S
| ▽ 19 | 16 | 18 | $30 |

1483 First Ave. (bet. 77th & 78th Sts.), 212-988-8877
■ Devotees of this "small, quiet" Upper Eastsider dub it an "Italian's Italian" due to its "really great pastas" that arrive in "good-sized portions"; add a "welcoming staff", "pleasant surroundings" and fair prices for a true "neighborhood find."

Mary Ann's S
| 16 | 12 | 14 | $22 |

1503 Second Ave. (bet. 78th & 79th Sts.), 212-249-6165
2452 Broadway (bet. 90th & 91st Sts.), 212-877-0132
116 Eighth Ave. (16th St.), 212-633-0877 ⊟
80 Second Ave. (5th St.), 212-475-5939 ⊟
☑ Its "tequila-soaked crowd" says this Tex-Mex minichain "does the job" when it comes to "economical", "no-surprises" grub that you can "eat like there's no *mañana*"; teetotalers scoff they're "predictable" "margarita mills" "for the masses."

Marylou's ●S
| 19 | 18 | 19 | $39 |

21 W. Ninth St. (bet. 5th & 6th Aves.), 212-533-0012
☑ "Pleasant Village ambiance" abounds at this "beautiful brownstone" Continental long known for its "fantastic fish" and "bargain brunch"; though some find it "a trifle dingy", most insist it's still a "treat."

Mary's ●S
| 18 | 19 | 19 | $34 |

42 Bedford St. (bet. Carmine & Leroy Sts.), 212-741-3387
■ You'll "feel like you're dining in someone's home" at this West Village New American that delivers "reasonably priced", "fantastic feeds"; upstairs, the "brilliant" Angie Dickinson Room is held for private parties, while the downstairs bar hosts a "spirited gay crowd."

Massimo Al Ponte Vecchio S
| ▽ 21 | 17 | 19 | $36 |

206 Thompson St. (bet. Bleecker & W. 3rd Sts.), 212-228-7701
■ "Thankfully undiscovered and unspoiled", this "outstanding" Village Italian offers game in season as well as "sidewalk seating"; an "owner who loves to pamper his customers" does just that at this "real find."

Master Grill International (Queens) S
| 18 | 14 | 16 | $29 |

34-09 College Point Blvd. (bet. 34th & 35th Aves.), 718-762-0300
☑ "Fast for three days" before you tackle this sprawling Brazilian churrascaria in Flushing, an "eating orgy" where you're served "enough meat for the year in one seating"; "it can't get any tackier", but it's "good for the price" and "fun for the kids."

Match ●🅢   18 | 17 | 15 | $36
160 Mercer St. (bet. Houston & Prince Sts.), 212-343-0020
☑ Perhaps "not as cool as it used to be", this "dark, brooding" SoHo American-Asian is still "reliable" for "stylish people-watching" and midpriced "sushi at 2 AM"; attitudinal service from "beautiful waitresses" makes some sigh "trendy can get tiring."

Match Uptown ●🅢   20 | 19 | 17 | $42
33 E. 60th St. (bet. Madison & Park Aves.), 212-906-9177
☑ "Lots of beautiful people" turn up at this American-Asian Eastsider that offers a "better after-work bar scene" than its Downtown sibling; sure, it can be "noisy as hell" and "a tad overpriced", but an "inventive menu" and "a good raw bar" compensate.

Matthew's 🅢   21 | 21 | 19 | $48
1030 Third Ave. (61st St.), 212-838-4343
■ "Hats off to Matthew Kenney", whose "classy", eponymous East Side Mediterranean remains nearly "perfect" thanks to an "ingenious" Moroccan-influenced menu set in a "breezy", ceiling fan–adorned white room; the consensus is this "breath of fresh air" is "sorely needed in the neighborhood."

Mavalli Palace 🅢   21 | 14 | 16 | $27
46 E. 29th St. (bet. Madison Ave. & Park Ave. S.), 212-679-5535
☑ "Surprisingly uncrowded", this Curry Hill Southern Indian features "100 percent vegetarian" dishes that earn cheers for being "tasty" and "inexpensive"; the "minimal decor" and "curious service" evoke a quieter response.

Max & Moritz (Brooklyn) 🅢   22 | 16 | 18 | $34
426A Seventh Ave. (14th St.), 718-499-5557
☑ For a taste of "Manhattan in Brooklyn", Park Slopers stay put at this "sweet" New American–French bistro, dining either in its "cozy" main room or "enchanting garden"; "bargain prices" blind locals to the somewhat "spotty service."

Maxx ●🅢   – | – | – | E
1803 Second Ave. (93rd St.), 212-426-8350
Way up on the East Side, this appealing French newcomer is a bit schizophrenic – downstairs it's young and casual with a long bar, street-side tables and a lounge area, while incongruously, in the mezzanine in back, it's a serious, somewhat formal restaurant with entree prices breaking the $20 barrier.

Maya 🅢   24 | 21 | 20 | $43
1191 First Ave. (bet. 64th & 65th Sts.), 212-585-1818
■ "Mexican food doesn't get any better" than at this Eastsider offering "imaginative", "authentic" dishes with "knockout cocktails"; though some complain about "the din" and warn "bring lots of money", most "want to splurge" as it's "far and away the best" of its kind.

Mayrose 🅢   14 | 12 | 13 | $19
920 Broadway (21st St.), 212-533-3663
■ "Breakfast is the best meal" at this "trendy" Flatiron diner with "enough funk" to attract a "hip local crowd"; despite an "unwavering menu", it often draws lines.

Maz Mezcal 🅢   20 | 16 | 19 | $31
316 E. 86th St. (bet. 1st & 2nd Aves.), 212-472-1599
■ "Not your typical soggy enchilada joint", this Yorkville "sleeper" is "the way Mexican should be", offering "tasty dishes" and "lots of TLC" from an "attentive" staff; reaction to its pricing, though, is split.

116

Mazzei Osteria S
22 | 18 | 21 | $47

1562 Second Ave. (81st St.), 212-628-3131
☑ This East Side Italian "has a good thing going" in its "delightful brick oven", which turns out some "excellent", "well-prepared" dishes; though it can be "noisy, crowded and expensive", initiates insist it's simply "terrific."

Mediterraneo ●S
18 | 15 | 15 | $33

1260 Second Ave. (66th St.), 212-734-7407
■ "Outdoor eating" ("just like in Rome") amuses the "cell-phone" set at this "cute little" Italian Eastsider; inside, "tasty pastas" and "delicious pizzas" keep the place "tightly packed."

Medusa ●S
17 | 19 | 17 | $34

239 Park Ave. S. (bet. 19th & 20th Sts.), 212-477-1500
☑ "Chic" and "sexy", this Flatiron Mediterranean seduces some with its "devil-red" interior; the nonseduced are "turned to stone" by the "only fair" food and feel it's "overshadowed by its neighbors."

Mekka S
19 | 15 | 15 | $28

14 Ave. A (bet. Houston & 2nd Sts.), 212-475-8500
☑ Those seeking "a taste of the South" should mosey over to this "friendly", "laid-back" Alphabet City Caribbean–Soul Fooder; its "hip" clientele calls it a "great change of pace", especially on the patio.

MeKong S
18 | 15 | 16 | $27

44 Prince St. (bet. Mott & Mulberry Sts.), 212-343-8169
☑ "Good, simple Vietnamese" cooking is yours at this "great little find" that's "not mainstream" and perhaps "not chic enough for SoHo", but at least can be had at a "fair price"; now if only they can fix the "puny portions" and "distracted staff."

Meltemi S
19 | 16 | 19 | $37

905 First Ave. (51st St.), 212-355-4040
☑ "Fresh grilled fish" supplies the uplift at this "pleasant" Sutton Place Greek taverna that's "consistently fine"; some protest the "high prices", but that just may be why it's so "easy to get a table" here.

Menchanko-tei
18 | 10 | 14 | $20

131 E. 45th St. (bet. Lexington & 3rd Aves.), 212-986-6805 ●S
43-45 W. 55th St. (bet. 5th & 6th Aves.), 212-247-1585 ●S
257 World Trade Ctr. Concourse (bet. Church & Vesey Sts.), 212-432-4210
■ "For noodles and only that", these Japanese slurp shops offer "quick, cheap sustenance" that's a "good value"; as there's "no decor", many go the takeout route to best enjoy the "simple but tasty" edibles.

Mercer Kitchen, The ●S
23 | 23 | 19 | $50

Mercer Hotel, 99 Prince St. (Mercer St.), 212-966-5454
☑ "Everything you've heard is true" about this "nearly perfect" American-Provençal in the Mercer Hotel basement that "outshines everything else in SoHo"; "Jean-Georges Vongerichten doesn't let up" with an "unbelievable, innovative" menu that's presented to a "very hot crowd" either at "communal tables" or in the "architecturally pleasing" main room; the only drawbacks: "no windows", "wild food-swings", "sticker shock."

Merchants, N.Y. ●S
15 | 17 | 14 | $28

1125 First Ave. (62nd St.), 212-832-1551
521 Columbus Ave. (bet. 85th & 86th Sts.), 212-721-3689
112 Seventh Ave. (bet. 16th & 17th Sts.), 212-366-7267
■ A "partying crowd" jams these New Americans where the "bar scene is the draw"; though it's "tough to be over 35" here, it's "dark enough to make anyone look good"; as for the food – "eat at home."

Meriken ◐ [S] — 18 | 14 | 16 | $29
189 Seventh Ave. (21st St.), 212-620-9684
◪ Though it's "been there forever" (since '82), some surveyors need "reminding" that this "offbeat" "Chelsea standout" still offers "good-quality sushi" and other "Japanese dishes with flair"; dissenters cite "lackluster service" and "sickly green lighting."

Merlot Bar & Grill ◐ [S] — 17 | 20 | 16 | $40
Radisson Empire Hotel, 48 W. 63rd St. (bet. B'way & Columbus Ave.), 212-363-7568
◪ The "jazzy", "Daliesque", "*Alice in Wonderland* on acid" decor "far surpasses the food and service" at this French-American, though fans tout the "amazing wine list" and "convenient" Lincoln Center location; P.S. "the Sunday brunch is a steal at $14.95."

MESA GRILL [S] — 24 | 21 | 21 | $45
102 Fifth Ave. (bet. 15th & 16th Sts.), 212-807-7400
■ It "always feels like a party" at this "theatrical" Union Square–area Southwestern where "cooking god" Bobby Flay "hits the bull's-eye" (when he's not on TV) with his "wonderful use of ingredients"; granted, the decibel level often reaches a "mild roar" and the haute-cafeteria decor is not to everyone's taste, but overall this "next best thing to New Mexico" "actually deserves all its positive hype."

Meskerem ◐ [S] — 21 | 9 | 15 | $20
468 W. 47th St. (bet. 9th & 10th Aves.), 212-664-0520
■ "Nonadventurous types need not apply" at this "dynamite", "bargain" Ethiopian "secret hangout" near the Theater District; be sure to "wash your hands" first (you'll be eating with them) and pay no mind to the "zero decor."

Mesopotamia ◐ [S] — 18 | 17 | 15 | $27
98 Ave. B (bet. 6th & 7th Sts.), 212-358-1166
◪ The "food saves the day" at this "funky" East Village Belgian-Turkish – yes, that's right – Eclectic; though "a little rough around the edges" and with "spacey service", it delivers some mighty "interesting combinations" at "inexpensive" tabs.

Métisse [S] — 21 | 17 | 20 | $36
239 W. 105th St. (bet. Amsterdam Ave. & B'way), 212-666-8825
■ Though mostly "undiscovered" due to its "out-of-the-way location" near Columbia, this Classic French is a "great find" in a dining "wasteland"; credit the "authentic bistro fare", "charming" ambiance and "caring owner" for making it "worth the trek."

Metro Grill [S] — ▽ 21 | 19 | 19 | $33
45 W. 35th St. (bet. 5th & 6th Aves.), 212-279-3535
■ Fashionistas call this Garment District New American a "savior in the area", as there's "nowhere else to take clients" nearby; most credit the "great chef" ("working in obscurity"), though a few fret it "needs help on the service" side.

Metronome ◐ — 18 | 21 | 18 | $37
915 Broadway (21st St.), 212-505-7400
■ "Fred and Ginger would feel at home" in this "huge", "high-ceilinged" art deco Mediterranean in the Flatiron District, where "better-than-you-would-think" food and "great jazz" lure time travelers; though postmodernists say it "needs an adrenaline shot", most find this "classy throwback" just fine as is.

Metropolitan Cafe ◐ [S] — 16 | 17 | 17 | $31
959 First Ave. (bet. 52nd & 53rd Sts.), 212-759-5600
■ A "charming garden" "redeems" this "casual", sprawling Sutton Place American that's otherwise "nothing amazing", though it does provide "decent salads and sandwiches", "modestly priced."

Mexicana Mama 🅂⊄
▽ 24 | 14 | 19 | $24

525 Hudson St. (bet. Charles & W. 10th Sts.), 212-924-4119
■ "Salsa extraordinaire" and other "deliciously authentic", "really cheap" items have made this "ab fab" West Village Mexican a hit with neighborhood types; but "cramped" conditions cause *compadres* to beg "make it bigger."

Mezzaluna ◑🅂
19 | 15 | 16 | $35

1295 Third Ave. (bet. 74th & 75th Sts.), 212-535-9600
☑ "If you want a quick meal" and don't mind being "cramped", this "pricey", "loud" East Side Italian offers a variety of "excellent pastas and pizzas"; even though the tables are thisclose, partisans insist it's "still good after all these years."

Mezzanine ◑🅂
▽ 18 | 21 | 16 | $36

Paramount Hotel, 235 W. 46th St. (bet. B'way & 8th Ave.), 212-827-4183
■ There's "terrific people-watching" to be had at this attractive Theater District New American "hideaway" and, big surprise, the food is "better than in most hotel dining" rooms.

Mezze
19 | 14 | 15 | $23

10 E. 44th St. (bet. 5th & Madison Aves.), 212-697-6644
■ For an "out-of-the-ordinary lunch", this Midtown Mediterranean-Moroccan courtesy of Matthew Kenney is a "great change of pace"; in exchange for "something different" that's "reasonably priced", fans suffer the "poor seating" in silence.

Mezzogiorno ◑🅂
19 | 17 | 16 | $38

195 Spring St. (Sullivan St.), 212-334-2112
☑ "Everything tastes straight from the garden" at this "consistently good" SoHo Italian that acolytes also find "very chic", with a "Victoria's Secret model at the next table"; the unimpressed cite "expensive" tabs and a "staff that would rather not be working."

Michael Jordan's The Steak House 🅂
21 | 22 | 19 | $53

Grand Central Terminal, 23 Vanderbilt Ave. (44th St.), 212-655-2300
■ "An extraordinary setting" above "the refurbished Grand Central Concourse" makes this steakhouse-cum-memorabilia boutique fronted by the legendary former Chicago Bulls star "special", and it follows through with "top-notch" meats and the "best sides"; yet spoilers say it's "a layup, not quite a dunk" and point to brand-name prices.

Michael's
22 | 21 | 21 | $50

24 W. 55th St. (bet. 5th & 6th Aves.), 212-767-0555
■ "NY-style LA food" reigns at this "civilized" Midtown Californian, an "old standby" that's just the ticket for "deal-making" and "occasional celebrity sightings"; a "serene setting" replete with "striking artwork" and "well-spaced tables" makes this a breath of "fresh air" "for a business breakfast or lunch."

Mickey Mantle's 🅂
13 | 17 | 15 | $31

42 Central Park S. (bet. 5th & 6th Aves.), 212-688-7777
☑ "Little boys of all ages" like this Central Park South "Yankee shrine" to the legendary No. 7 because it has "lots of TVs" and fun "sports memorabilia"; though it's a good "place for father-son bondings", the "stadium-quality" pub grub "only gets to first base."

Mi Cocina 🅂
22 | 15 | 17 | $32

57 Jane St. (Hudson St.), 212-627-8273
■ "Expect close quarters" at this "tiny" West Village Mexican "unsung hero" that's "worth all the elbowing" in return for "darn good" cooking that "keeps getting better"; kick off with "one of the best frozen margaritas in Manhattan."

F | D | S | C

Mignon (Brooklyn) [S]⇏ — | — | — | M
394 Court St. (bet. Carroll St. & 1st Pl.), 718-222-8383
Easing the pain of Carroll Gardens yups priced out of Manhattan is this new French-Mediterranean with attractive decor, a pleasant garden, poised staff and moderately priced bistro fare; with all these attributes, it's no wonder this spot is hot.

Mike & Tony's (Brooklyn) [S] 22 | 19 | 20 | $43
239 Fifth Ave. (Carroll St.), 718-857-2800
◪ "Big, juicy steaks" pull Park Slopers to this "pretty" palace of beef where "you can feel the effort put into every last detail"; though a "good complement to Cucina" (its across-the-street sibling), protesters pronounce it "overpriced for Brooklyn."

MILOS, ESTIATORIO ◐[S] 26 | 24 | 22 | $61
125 W. 55th St. (bet. 6th & 7th Aves.), 212-245-7400
■ "Sleek" surroundings set the "very chic" tone at this high-ceilinged Midtowner, the *Survey's* top-rated Greek and a "beautiful temple" to all things piscatory, with "fish so fresh they almost bite back at you" and "fantastic service"; but the "ouch" factor – "staggering" per-pound pricing – leads adherents to suggest you "stick to the wonderful appetizers to stay solvent."

Minetta Tavern ◐[S] 18 | 16 | 18 | $35
113 MacDougal St. (bet. Bleecker & W. 3rd Sts.), 212-475-3850
■ There's "lots of history" at this Village Italian, a "throwback to the '30s" where memory-laners "love the faded decor" even if cutting-edgers think it has "seen better days"; foodwise, it's "always reliable" and "just right after the theater."

Mingala Burmese [S] 17 | 12 | 16 | $21
1393 Second Ave. (bet. 72nd & 73rd Sts.), 212-744-8008
21-23 E. Seventh St. (bet. 2nd & 3rd Aves.), 212-529-3656
■ "Refreshingly different flavors" separate these "unpretentious" Burmese twins from the crowd; they may be as "plain as plain can be" and are "not known for good service", but they're a "real bargain" for something "tasty and unusual."

Mi Nidito ◐[S] 18 | 10 | 15 | $22
852 Eighth Ave. (bet. 51st & 52nd Sts.), 212-265-0022
■ "Gigantic margaritas" and "healthy" menu options coax crowds into this "casual" West Side Mexican that's "good for its price range"; those who say it's "not much to look at" might not have been by since its recent redo.

Miracle Grill ◐[S] 20 | 18 | 17 | $31
112 First Ave. (bet. 6th & 7th Sts.), 212-254-2353
415 Bleecker St. (bet. Bank & W. 11th Sts.), 212-924-1900
■ "Always mobbed" with a "youthful Downtown crowd", these "affordable" and consistently good Southwesterners are "downscale" versions of Mesa Grill, but at least you can "enjoy the bill"; a "gorgeous back garden" at the East Village outpost enchants fans, in spite of the "no-reservations" policy.

Mishima [S] ▽ 20 | 9 | 16 | $26
164 Lexington Ave. (bet. 30th & 31st Sts.), 212-532-9596
■ "A major sushi find in barren Murray Hill", this "reliable" Japanese slices up some of the "freshest" fish around; the only "drawback" – it's "so small" – leads claustrophobes to opt for delivery.

Miss Saigon [S] 19 | 13 | 16 | $25
1425 Third Ave. (bet. 80th & 81st Sts.), 212-988-8828
■ This low-budget "Yorkville favorite" turns out Vietnamese fare that's "always done right"; the "undistinguished" decor doesn't bother stay-at-homes who laud its "quick delivery."

Miss Williamsburg Diner (Bklyn) ◐[S]≠ — – | – | – | I

206 Kent Ave. (bet. Metropolitan Ave. & N. 3rd St.), 718-963-0802
Pilar Rigone, the charismatic former co-owner of highly rated Il Bagatto, has opened this new dinner-only Italian in a renovated Williamsburg diner; expect cheap, yummy Italian fare and hipsters modeling funky eyewear, but bear in mind that the industrial location is a schlep from the subway.

Mitali East/West ◐[S] — 20 | 14 | 17 | $25

296 Bleecker St. (7th Ave. S.), 212-989-1367
334 E. Sixth St. (bet. 1st & 2nd Aves.), 212-533-2508
■ You "can't go wrong" at these "surefire" Village "workhorses" offering "aromatic", "consistently scrumptious" Indian fare; aficionados say "East beats West" foodwise, while the reverse is true for decor, yet both are "a cut above" the competition.

Mme. Romaine de Lyon [S] — 17 | 14 | 17 | $31

132 E. 61st St. (bet. Lexington & Park Aves.), 212-758-2422
■ "Endless omelets" (over 500 varieties) comprise most of the menu at this East Side French "cholesterol heaven" that's been around since 1938 in varying locations; critics cluck it's "fussy" and "very, very expensive", while late risers crow about its omeletless dinner menu.

Mocca Restaurant [S]≠ — 18 | 10 | 16 | $23

1588 Second Ave. (bet. 82nd & 83rd Sts.), 212-734-6470
■ "One of the few places left to get Hungarian food", this "no-pretenses" Eastsider is "the real thing", with "down-home Magyar" meals at "*gemütlich* prices"; devotees defend its "prehistoric charm" and insist it "be kept alive" – as the "last of its kind."

MOLYVOS ◐[S] — 23 | 21 | 21 | $45

871 Seventh Ave. (bet. 55th & 56th Sts.), 212-582-7500
■ "Instead of a Hellenic holiday", fly over to this "high-class treat" "convenient to Carnegie Hall" that's "like dining in the Greek islands, only with shoes on"; fans wax ecstatic about its grilled fish, "impressive service" and "roomy", "earth-colored" digs, despite somewhat "over-the-top prices."

Monk ◐[S] — ▽ 20 | 16 | 16 | $34

309 E. Fifth St. (bet. 1st & 2nd Aves.), 212-228-2181
■ "Perfect and undiscovered", this East Village French-Armenian offers an "original menu" of "tasty" victuals; despite sometimes "inept" service, "the name fits – it's a meditative, uplifting dining experience."

Monkey Bar [S] — 21 | 23 | 20 | $49

Hotel Elysée, 60 E. 54th St. (bet. Madison & Park Aves.), 212-838-2600
■ "Step into another era" at this "glamorous nod to the past" that conjures up "Hollywood on 54th Street"; though its "exuberant" bar can be a "zoo", the "plush" burgundy dining room is a delight, with a "wonderful" New American menu that has diners "going ape"; P.S. new chef Andrew Chase (ex Sign of the Dove) has swung into action.

Mon Petit Cafe [S] — 17 | 14 | 16 | $29

801 Lexington Ave. (62nd St.), 212-355-2233
◪ "Simple, everyday" French bistro near Bloomie's with a "bygone ambiance" ("Edith Piaf recordings") and "dependable", if "not fancy", food; though it "could be more exciting", shop-till-you-drop types find this a "pleasant" enough stop "once in a while."

Montebello — 21 | 19 | 22 | $43

120 E. 56th St. (bet. Lexington & Park Aves.), 212-753-1447
■ The "same faces at lunchtime speak well" of the staying power of this "reliable" Midtown Northern Italian that's a "home away from home" to regulars; "high costs" give penny-pinchers pause, but "great food and a friendly staff" compensate.

Monte's Italian (Brooklyn) 🅂   20 | 15 | 18 | $34
451 Carroll St. (bet. Nevins St. & 3rd Ave.), 718-624-8984
■ "Roll back the clock and enjoy the atmosphere" at this vintage 1906 Carroll Gardens Italian "institution"; moms say it's so "homey" that "the waiter wouldn't serve my kids more soda until they cleared more off of their plates."

MONTRACHET   27 | 21 | 24 | $61
239 W. Broadway (bet. Walker & White Sts.), 212-219-2777
■ "Glorious eating", a "wine list to make your head spin" and "attentive but not intrusive service" make some wonder "does it get any better?" than Drew Nieporent's "essential" TriBeCa French bistro; though a few feel the "decor needs an overhaul", most tout this "masterpiece" as simply "the top" (especially Friday's "great buy" prix fixe lunch).

Moomba ◗🅂   19 | 18 | 15 | $50
133 Seventh Ave. S. (bet. Charles & W. 10th Sts.), 212-989-1414
☑ "Surprisingly good food" startles the swell patrons of this tri-level West Village New American better known for its "VIP room" and "celebrity-ridden" crowd; however, some critical surveyors find it a "ridiculously pretentious" "Eurotrash landfill" and shrug "don't bother" – "Leo can dine on his own."

Moran's Chelsea 🅂   18 | 19 | 20 | $37
146 10th Ave. (19th St.), 212-627-3030
☑ This "better-than-average Irish pub" is a Chelsea "neighborhood place" offering "solid, simple" surf 'n' turf in an "out-of-the-way" locale; it's particularly "cozy around the fireplace" in winter.

Moreno 🅂   17 | 16 | 17 | $41
65 Irving Pl. (18th St.), 212-673-3939
☑ A "lovely Gramercy setting", "outside tables" offering "fun people-watching" and a "very entertaining owner" make "you feel wanted and welcome" at this "engaging" neighborhood Italian; but critics – and food ratings – suggest it "may be slipping."

Morgan Court Cafe 🅂   15 | 25 | 16 | $24
Pierpont Morgan Library, 29 E. 36th St. (Madison Ave.), 212-685-0008
☑ "Hidden lunchtime treasure" in the skylit, "airy" atrium of Murray Hill's august Pierpont Morgan Library; though the "limited" salad-and-sandwich menu and "medium" service "aren't up to the wonderful setting", the setting is enough reason to go.

Mormando's Steakhouse 🅂   ▽ 18 | 17 | 17 | $39
73 W. 71st St. (bet. Columbus Ave. & CPW), 212-874-3474
☑ Look for "unbelievable entrees" at this Upper West Side chophouse where devotees also tout the "relaxing" ambiance and "nice" staff; however, others find it "disappointing" and suggest you "head to Midtown for a *real* steak."

Morton's of Chicago 🅂   23 | 19 | 21 | $55
551 Fifth Ave. (45th St.), 212-972-3315 ◗
90 West St. (bet. Albany & Cedar Sts.), 212-732-5665
☑ "Perfectly executed" steaks "fit for a king" reign at this "cow palace" duo whose "consistent excellence" causes the awed to utter it's "unbelievable that they're a chain"; though the "corny" menu recitation and "gross presentation of Saran-wrapped meats" "doesn't cut it in Gotham", ultimately the food's "so good that the bill hardly hurts."

Mosaico Food of the Americas   ▽ 18 | 9 | 13 | $13
175 Madison Ave. (bet. 33rd & 34th Sts.), 212-213-4700
■ "Inventive South American" cooking draws globe-trotters to this "undiscovered" Pan-Latino in Murray Hill; the undecided call it "hit-or-miss", but most agree this "cute but cramped" place can't be beat for "super value."

Moustache ●S⊅
90 Bedford St. (bet. Barrow & Grove Sts.), 212-229-2220
265 E. 10th St. (bet. Ave. A & 1st Ave.), 212-228-2022

21 | 12 | 16 | $19

Moustache Pitza S⊅
405 Atlantic Ave. (bet. Bond & Nevins Sts.), Brooklyn, 718-852-5555
■ "Be prepared to wait" at these "low-rent", "dirt cheap" Middle Easterns, but the lingering's "worth it" when "savory" eats, including "freshly made" pita-based pizzas, are the payoff; N.B. the Brooklyn outpost is separately owned.

Mr. Chow ●S
324 E. 57th St. (bet. 1st & 2nd Aves.), 212-751-9030

22 | 21 | 19 | $55

■ Some sniff it's "passé", others say it's "making a comeback", but all agree that this "chichi" black-and-white art deco Chinese Eastsider serves "superior" if "expensive" fare; dress to fit in with an "arty crowd", including "second-tier celebs", at this theatrically "pretty" place.

Mr. K's ●S
570 Lexington Ave. (51st St.), 212-583-1668

23 | 25 | 24 | $51

■ Finally catching on, this "spectacular" pink East Side Chinese yearling presents "fancy" dishes "worthy of the emperors", but it's better known for its "all-over-you" service (they "practically wipe your mouth between courses"); be advised that all this attention comes at "astronomical" prices.

Mugsy's Chow Chow ●S
31 Second Ave. (bet. 1st & 2nd Sts.), 212-460-9171

▽ 22 | 19 | 19 | $28

■ "Miracles emerge from the tiny kitchen" of this "funky", "cramped" East Village Italian "hideaway"; you may have to "wait for a table", but patient types say it's "worth it" for the "excellent pastas" alone.

Nadaman Hakubai S
Kitano Hotel, 66 Park Ave. (38th St.), 212-885-7111

▽ 22 | 21 | 24 | $68

■ A "first-class" import, this Murray Hill Japanese satisfies the yen for authenticity with its "outstanding" takes on the classics; "exquisite" presentation, "geisha-like service" and top tabs give it an "in-Japan" feel, but a three-point drop in food ratings spells trouble at these prices.

Nadine's ●S
99 Bank St. (Greenwich St.), 212-924-3165

16 | 16 | 17 | $29

■ This "dark", "funky" Villager gets "crowded" with "neighborhood" types lingering over its Southern-style "comfort food"; though not a pacesetter, it's "kid-friendly" and a "favorite for brunch."

Nam Phuong S
19 Sixth Ave. (bet. Walker & White Sts.), 212-431-7715

▽ 20 | 9 | 13 | $20

☑ "Just point" at the bargain menu and "you'll never go hungry" at this "truly original" yet "authentic" TriBeCa Vietnamese "dive"; fans insist that the "spotty service" and "charmless" decor are just "part of the scene" – a jump in food ratings supports their argument.

Nanni's
146 E. 46th St. (bet. Lexington & 3rd Aves.), 212-697-4161

22 | 16 | 21 | $48

■ "Nanni's sauce" and angel hair pasta are the hallmarks of this "old-fashioned Northern Italian" that serves the Grand Central–area "business set"; its "traditional" tastes and "wonderful" service ensure its status as a "consistent" "favorite."

Naples 45
MetLife Bldg., 200 Park Ave. (45th St., bet. Lexington & Vanderbilt Aves.), 212-972-7001

17 | 15 | 15 | $28

☑ "When a slice just won't do", this Southern Italian in a "cavernous, tiled space" supplies "real" "thin-crust" Neapolitan pizzas and basic "lite" bites; a "convenient" layover for the Grand Central–bound, it suffers from "so-so service" and "noise" at peak times.

Nation Restaurant & Bar
| 19 | 15 | 17 | $35 |

12 W. 45th St. (bet. 5th & 6th Aves.), 212-391-8053
☑ With a booming, "noisy barroom" on the ground floor and "intimate", "comfortable" dining upstairs, this tri-level Midtown yearling attracts all types; the "creative" Eclectic menu proves "interesting" too, though "high" prices cause consternation.

Neary's ◑S
| 17 | 14 | 20 | $35 |

358 E. 57th St. (1st Ave.), 212-751-1434
■ The "irresistible", "leprechaunish" Jimmy Neary hosts this "upscale Irish pub" near Sutton Place where Erin aristocrats mingle over "hearty" "meat-and-potatoes" fare; the "happy, hectic" scene fully absolves the "average" eating – 'tis an "institution."

Negril ◑S
| 18 | 16 | 15 | $27 |

362 W. 23rd St. (bet. 8th & 9th Aves.), 212-807-6411
☑ "Jamaican jerk at its best" spices up this "cozy" "taste of the Caribbean" in Chelsea, where the "funky and flavorful" island specialties are matched with "exciting drinks"; despite "crowded" conditions and service lapses, "genuine" flavors and reggae-infused "fun" win it many a 'yea-ah.'

Nello ◑S
| 18 | 16 | 17 | $47 |

696 Madison Ave. (bet. 62nd & 63rd Sts.), 212-980-9099
☑ An East Side "Euro magnet" with "great outside tables", Nello Balan's tony tratt is ground zero for "pretty people-watching" and "pretty good" Italian food; vocal foes balk at "break-the-bank" tabs and say it's been "spoiled by success."

New City Bar & Grill (Brooklyn) S
| – | – | – | E |

25 Lafayette Ave. (bet. Ashland Pl. & St. Felix St.), 718-875-7197
Relocated across from BAM but with the same chef who made it a destination, this New American seduces an eclectic crowd with its tony, comfy quarters and versatile menu (you can order any dish as either an appetizer or entree); less versatile is the expensive tab.

New Green Bo ◑S⊞⊄
| ▽ 21 | 9 | 15 | $22 |

66 Bayard St. (bet. Elizabeth & Mott Sts.), 212-625-2359
☑ It's breaking no new ground, but this "solid" Chinatown upstart offers some "fabulous" multiregional fare in an "antiseptic", "crowded" setting; even meeting the "good food, good value" Chinese formula, though, it has skeptics shrugging "same as the others."

New Pasteur S⊄
| 20 | 6 | 13 | $16 |

85 Baxter St. (bet. Bayard & Canal Sts.), 212-608-3656
■ "Bargain *pho*" fans gather at this "no-frills" C-town Vietnamese to sample "savory" soups and dumplings at "unbeatable prices"; sure, it's "down and dirty", but it's also a "good" "change from Chinese."

New Prospect Cafe (Brooklyn) S
| 20 | 13 | 17 | $25 |

393 Flatbush Ave. (bet. Plaza St. & Sterling Pl.), 718-638-2148
■ This "hippie/yuppie hybrid" caters to Prospect Heights types in search of a "casual meal" with Eclectic, "New Ageish" eats; the backdrop is "nondescript", but the "varied", "reasonable" menu makes it a local "standby" and a weekend brunch hub.

New World Grill S
| 18 | 15 | 17 | $28 |

Worldwide Plaza, 329 W. 49th St. (bet. 8th & 9th Aves.), 212-957-4745
■ An "intimate" "find" "tucked away" in West Midtown, this indoor/outdoor New American with a "funky little bar" offers "imaginative" Cal-style cooking in a "pleasant" plaza serving "after-work suits" and the "pre- or post-theater" crowd.

New York Noodle Town ●🇸🌱
28½ Bowery (Bayard St.), 212-349-0923

21 | 5 | 11 | $18

■ "Hectic" Chinatown joint that's known for big bowls of "superb noodles" and "phenomenal seafood" served in plain Formica-and-neon digs; its rep for "delicious", "dirt cheap" dining is "fully justified", so "be prepared to wait."

Nha Trang 🇸🌱
87 Baxter St. (bet. Bayard & Canal Sts.), 212-233-5948

22 | 6 | 14 | $17

■ "Who needs decor?" ask fans of this Chinatown Vietnamese "stalwart", a "real dive" where "fast, delicious", "amazingly cheap" Mekong meals offset the weak service and "simple" setting; it's a popular "lunch place for jurors."

Nice Restaurant 🇸
35 E. Broadway (bet. Catherine & Market Sts.), 212-406-9510

19 | 11 | 14 | $25

■ Living up to its name, this Chinatown "classic Cantonese" is a "consistent winner" thanks to its "delicious dim sum" and "Chinese banquets"; Hong Kong–"kitsch" decor signals it's "authentic", so bring an interpreter.

Nick & Toni's Cafe 🇸
100 W. 67th St. (bet. B'way & Columbus Ave.), 212-496-4000

18 | 15 | 17 | $41

☑ Lincoln Center–area Mediterranean that satisfies its "yuppie" clientele with "creative" fare and "accommodating" service; but holdouts insist this spin-off is "overpriced" and "doesn't come close" to the East Hampton original.

NICK'S PIZZA (Queens) 🇸🌱
108-26 Ascan Ave. (bet. Austin & Burns Sts.), 718-263-1126

25 | 14 | 17 | $19

■ Fah-rest Hills' own "pizza apogee" wins fierce loyalty with its "light, crusty" brick-oven pies, loaded with "fresh" toppings and "made just right"; the "world's best cannoli" sweeten the deal; P.S. "no slices, though."

Nicola Paone
207 E. 34th St. (bet. 2nd & 3rd Aves.), 212-889-3239

19 | 18 | 19 | $50

☑ This Murray Hill vet wins "bravos" for its "old-fashioned" haute price, haute Italian menu, fine wines and "pleasant" service; even so, a few critics argue it's a "stuffy" warhorse that "was tired years ago."

Nicola's ●
146 E. 84th St. (bet. Lexington & 3rd Aves.), 212-249-9850

21 | 17 | 20 | $48

☑ "Down-home Italian" meets "Upper East Side cool" at this "celebrity hangout", a "popular" "scene" for a "sumptuous dinner" that draws a "clubby", necessarily well-heeled clientele; P.S. the staff's "attitude" "improves drastically if you're a regular."

Nicole's 🇸
Nicole Farhi, 10 E. 60th St. (bet. 5th & Madison Aves.), 212-223-2288

– | – | – | E

Britain's answer to Donna Karan, Nicole Farhi, exports her eponymous emporium and on-site eatery to the East Side; while this subterranean Med-Eclectic may be starkly minimal and heftily priced, its ground-zero location for Madison Avenue power shoppers can't be beat.

Niederstein's (Queens) 🇸
69-16 Metropolitan Ave. (69th St.), 718-326-0717

18 | 16 | 17 | $31

■ Dating back to 1889, this midpriced Middle Village German supplies wurst and strudel in *sehr* "authentic" style, making for "heavy" eating in "lively", "old-country environs" – "bring on the Alka-Seltzer."

Niko's Mediterranean Grill ◐ [S] — 18 | 11 | 15 | $25

2161 Broadway (76th St.), 212-873-7000

◪ With a "menu longer than *War and Peace*", this West Side "Greek island" taverna provides an endless array of "tasty" standards in "huge portions" at bargain prices; expect "cheesy" Hellenic decor and "a lot of noise."

Nino's ◐ [S] — 23 | 20 | 21 | $48

1354 First Ave. (bet. 72nd & 73rd Sts.), 212-988-0002

■ "First-class" treatment from soup to nuts marks this East Side "shining star", where "terrific" Northern Italian cuisine and "charming" service unite to produce a "great dining experience"; a pianist adds to the "romantic" mood.

Nippon — 23 | 18 | 21 | $48

155 E. 52nd St. (bet. Lexington & 3rd Aves.), 212-758-0226

■ The "traditional" setup and "serene" style enhance the "excellent" sushi and other "authentic" fare at this East Midtown Japanese; it "feels like you're in Japan" – especially when the check arrives.

Nirvana ◐ [S] — 17 | 26 | 19 | $45

30 Central Park S. (bet. 5th & 6th Aves.), 212-486-5700

◪ "Winning views" of Central Park and an *Arabian Nights* interior "treat" the eyes at this rooftop Indian aerie, a "romantic" favorite for sunset dining; however, the merely "decent" food can't match the room's karma and lofty prices.

NOBU [S] — 28 | 24 | 24 | $63

105 Hudson St. (Franklin St.), 212-219-0500

■ Nobu Matsuhisa's TriBeCa Japanese, "like a shiatsu massage of the tongue", inspires "sheer bliss" among its bicoastal, "star-studded" clientele, offering "sushi at its finest" and other unique Japanese-Peruvian fare presented amid delightful David Rockwell–designed decor; however, this brand of "culinary perfection" "ain't cheap" and "you can make a career of getting a dinner reservation" – fortunately, it's easier to get a table for lunch.

NOBU, NEXT DOOR ◐ — 27 | 23 | 23 | $54

105 Hudson St. (Franklin St.), 212-334-4445

■ Rated as this year's No. 1 newcomer and more than just a replica of its renowned next-door neighbor, this TriBeCa standout delivers some of the "best Japanese in town", perfecting the "art of sushi" and soba in a bamboo-bedecked room; it's "less of a scene" and the "no-reservations policy" for parties under five promises access to "ordinary people" – "finally, a table!"

Nocello [S] — ▽ 20 | 19 | 20 | $37

257 W. 55th St. (bet. B'way & 8th Ave.), 212-713-0224

■ "Small and charming", this Northern Italian is a Midtown "oasis" for "delightful" dining, complete with "smart" decor and "accommodating" service; what's more, the package is "reasonably priced" – thus, its rep as a "sleeper" continues to grow.

NoHo Star ◐ [S] — 17 | 15 | 15 | $26

330 Lafayette St. (Bleecker St.), 212-925-0070

◪ This "lovable" NoHo "standby" offers "quick", "dependable dining" from an "inventive" Asian-American menu, not to mention a "relaxed" vibe; it's "still a favorite brunch spot", despite rumors of "so-so" food and "bad acoustics."

Noodle Pudding (Brooklyn) [S] $̸ — 21 | 17 | 20 | $30

38 Henry St. (bet. Cranberry & Middagh Sts.), 718-625-3737

■ Despite its "low profile" ("no sign out front"), this "homey", cash-only Brooklyn Heights Italian is a "booming neighborhood spot" with a "well-executed bistro" menu served by a "caring" staff; it's a true "find."

Noodles on 28 ◐[S] — 18 | 9 | 15 | $17
394 Third Ave. (28th St.), 212-679-2888
◪ "Amazing dumplings and noodle dishes" await at this "cheap and filling" Gramercy "standby" where an array of Chinese "standards" are tossed together "in plain view" and "served with a smile"; "zero atmosphere" keeps the focus on the food.

Norma's [S] — ▽ 26 | 21 | 23 | $33
Le Parker Meridien, 118 W. 57th St. (bet. 6th & 7th Aves.), 212-708-7460
■ Early and late risers alike can sit down to a "fantastic" "gourmet" breakfast at this hotel-based Midtowner, where "inventive" takes on morning fare are "served beautifully" in a "bright, cheerful room" until 3 PM; it's quite simply the "best breakfast" in town.

North West ◐[S] — – | – | – | E
392 Columbus Ave. (79th St.), 212-799-4530
Sleek, oak-paneled West Side newcomer with a limited New American menu featuring seafood plus frites that alone are worthy of the trip; upstairs, late-night revelers can sink into cushy chairs to puff and sip (and make noise).

Notaro [S] — 19 | 16 | 18 | $34
635 Second Ave. (bet. 34th & 35th Sts.), 212-686-3400
◪ The "quintessential" "local", this Murray Hill trattoria is a haven for "delicious" Northern Italian cooking, "pleasant" service and the "comfort" of home; even if some find it "ordinary", "every neighborhood should have one."

Novecento ◐[S] — 18 | 17 | 16 | $34
343 W. Broadway (bet. Broome & Grand Sts.), 212-925-4706
■ "Lots of Euros" congregate over "out-of-this-world" steaks at this SoHo Argentine, which rounds out its menu with empanadas, tapas and other Spanish-accented fare; it's one of the few hip hangouts that comes at a "reasonable" cost.

Novitá [S] — 23 | 20 | 21 | $44
102 E. 22nd St. (Park Ave. S.), 212-677-2222
■ An "elegant" "hideaway" for a "well-heeled" clientele, this "true" Italian in Gramercy inspires loyalty with a "classy, warm setting", "top-notch" food and "courteous service"; it's a prime place to "take visitors" or "begin an affair."

Ñ 33 Crosby ◐[S]≠ — 18 | 19 | 14 | $24
33 Crosby St. (bet. Broome & Grand Sts.), 212-219-8856
■ At this "too-cool-for-school" SoHo tapas bar, "aspiring models" squeeze into "sexy", "cramped quarters" to indulge in "bite-sized nibbles" and "terrific sangria"; if you "can find it", the flamenco-charged scene is a worthy reward.

Nyonya ◐[S]≠ — 22 | 13 | 15 | $21
194 Grand St. (bet. Mott & Mulberry Sts.), 212-334-3669
5323 Eighth Ave. (54th St.), Brooklyn, 718-633-0808
◪ "If you like spicy", consider this "interesting", "tasty" Malaysian duo in Little Italy and Sunset Park; the prices are "very reasonable", but plan on "coffee-shop digs" and "abrupt service."

Oak Room [S] — 19 | 24 | 20 | $51
Plaza Hotel, 768 Fifth Ave. (Central Park S.), 212-546-5330
◪ "Pretend you're in an Edith Wharton novel" at this "beautiful", "high-priced" Midtown hotel chophouse, an oak-clad ode to "early 20th-century" "opulence" and "old money"; the post-*Survey* arrival of new chef Marc Felix should help revitalize one of NY's "great rooms."

Obeca Li
19 | 22 | 17 | $41

62 Thomas St. (bet. Church St. & W. B'way), 212-393-9887
■ This "huge", "trendy" TriBeCan boasts a "gorgeous setup" on multiple levels and a "sophisticated" Asian menu of "innovative dishes" both "raw and cooked"; the "fantastic" space makes for a "great show", but doubters deem the service "disappointing."

OCEANA
27 | 24 | 25 | $61

55 E. 54th St. (bet. Madison & Park Aves.), 212-759-5941
■ "Exceptional", "fresh" seafood is "done to perfection" at this marvelous Midtowner, which follows through with "glitzy" "luxury-liner" decor and silky-smooth service; fish fanciers consider it "transcendent" eating that's "worth every penny" (prix fixe only, $42 lunch, $65 dinner).

Ocean Grill ●S
23 | 21 | 21 | $43

384 Columbus Ave. (bet. 78th & 79th Sts.), 212-579-2300
■ For "fresh", "tasty fish" with "no airs", Upper Westsiders surface at this "lively", "noisy" hot spot with a "dynamite" seafood menu and "great raw bar"; added draws are "bright service" and alfresco seating – "not bad at all."

Ocean Palace (Brooklyn) ●S
20 | 12 | 15 | $23

5423 Eighth Ave. (55th St.), 718-871-8080
1418 Ave. U (bet. 14th & 15th Sts.), 718-376-3838
■ Brooklynites praise this "good-to-the-last-egg-roll" Chinese pair for bringing "Chinatown authenticity" to them, with "tasty", "plentiful" fare led by "wonderful" dim sum; regulars report it's "just like Hong Kong – crowded and loud", with decor that's "yet to be invented."

Odeon, The ●S
20 | 18 | 18 | $37

145 W. Broadway (bet. Duane & Thomas Sts.), 212-233-0507
■ "Tried and true", this cafeteria-like "'80s" arbiter of "Downtown chic" is "still a stellar standby" serving moderately priced New American–cum–French bistro fare to a "bustling", "see-and-be-seen" crowd; and yes, the Cosmopolitans and "flattering lighting" still pull in the hip night owls.

Odessa ●S
16 | 9 | 14 | $16

119 Ave. A (bet. 7th St. & St. Marks Pl.), 212-253-1470
☑ E. Europe meets E. Village at this 24-hour pierogi specialist, a "cheap", "convenient" "dive" with a menu mixing Slavic fare with "greasy-spoon" standards; it's a perennial for a "quick fix" or "late-night nosh", but beware the "strung-out crowd" and slam-bam service.

Official All Star Cafe ●S
11 | 17 | 12 | $25

1540 Broadway (45th St.), 212-840-8326
☑ "Sports maniacs" can't resist the "memorabilia" at this "raucous" Times Square player, an arena-sized sports bar on steroids decked out with "all the TVs in the world"; but the "mediocre", "burgers-and-nachos" American food is "worse than at Yankee Stadium" and some insist you "must be young or deaf to enjoy" this place.

O.G. ●S
21 | 15 | 17 | $28

507 E. Sixth St. (bet. Aves. A & B), 212-477-4649
■ Notably "fun and cool", this "tiny East Village local" is favored for its "imaginative", "delicious" Pan-Asian cooking, "chummy" service and "dark", "romantic" feel; it's also a "terrific value", causing fans to dub it the "poor man's China Grill."

	F	D	S	C

Oggi ◐[S] – | – | – | M

211 Ave. A (13th St.), 212-979-7044

Transported, seemingly, from the Upper East Side to a corner of the East Village, this new midrange regional Italian boasts handsome decor (light walls and cool marble) and staffers who know their cues but are still settling in; locals report it's a good choice for a quiet date or after-work soothing.

Oikawa ◐ ▽ 20 | 18 | 19 | $38

805 Third Ave., 2nd fl. (50th St.), 212-980-1400

■ A second-floor sanctuary in Midtown, this midpriced Japanese is a haven for "beautifully presented" sushi and tempura from a "varied menu"; it's "dependable" for an "elegant", "unhurried" meal, offering "freshness", "quiet" and "no surprises."

Old Devil Moon [S] 17 | 16 | 16 | $20

511 E. 12th St. (bet. Aves. A & B), 212-475-4357

◪ "You won't need to eat for a week" after a trip to this "funky" East Village "pit stop" for some "Southern trailer-park fare"; the cheap "down-home" dinin' comes complete with "clueless" service and decor that "brings trash to an art form."

Old Homestead [S] 21 | 16 | 18 | $48

56 Ninth Ave. (bet. 14th & 15th Sts.), 212-242-9040

◪ Die-hard beef eaters turn to this "institution" for slabs of red meat "the size of Oklahoma" served in a "landmark" (circa 1868) Chelsea room with a "dark wood" interior that "looks a bit like the Munsters' house"; modernists yawn "ho-hum" and observe this "old-timer" is "showing its age."

Old San Juan [S] 17 | 12 | 16 | $24

765 Ninth Ave. (bet. 51st & 52nd Sts.), 212-262-6761
462 Second Ave. (26th St.), 212-779-9360

◪ This "crowded, boisterous" Westsider is home to an "unusual", "surprisingly good" combo of Puerto Rican and Argentine food; but though "the price is right", the "garish decor" and service "based on geologic time" need work; a Gramercy branch was scheduled to open at press time.

Old Town Bar ◐[S] 14 | 17 | 14 | $20

45 E. 18th St. (bet. B'way & Park Ave. S.), 212-529-6732

■ "Old NY" is alive and kicking underneath the "tin ceiling" of this "unpretentious" Flatiron "watering hole", a "classic" for "greasy" burgers chased with beer and "*Iceman Cometh*" atmosphere.

Ollie's ◐[S] 16 | 10 | 13 | $19

2957 Broadway (116th St.), 212-932-3300
2315 Broadway (84th St.), 212-362-3712
1991 Broadway (67th St.), 212-595-8181
200B W. 44th St. (bet. B'way & 8th Ave.), 212-921-5988

◪ Noodle nuts in need of a "quickie" rely on this Chinese chain for "consistent, simple" feeding at "wholesale" prices; it's popular "in a pinch", in spite of "Americanized", "assembly-line" fare, "cafeteria-like" digs and "brusque" servers who can "make Saddam Hussein look like Captain Kangaroo."

Omen [S] 23 | 19 | 20 | $42

113 Thompson St. (bet. Prince & Spring Sts.), 212-925-8923

■ For "delicious" Japanese food "prepared Kyoto-style", all signs point to this SoHo retreat; with "lovely" presentations to complement the "cool setting", the results are predictably "exquisite" – but "at a price."

Omonia Cafe ◐[S]

F	D	S	C
21	15	16	$21

7612 Third Ave. (bet. 76th & 77th Sts.), Brooklyn, 718-491-1435
32-20 Broadway (33rd St.), Queens, 718-274-6650

◪ "Regardless of where you have dinner, the place for dessert" is this team of Greek sweet specialists in Astoria and Bay Ridge; they're "dependable" local faves for "late-night coffee" with pastry "showcases to drool over."

Once Upon a Tart [S]

F	D	S	C
21	13	13	$14

135 Sullivan St. (bet. Houston & Prince Sts.), 212-387-8869

■ "Heavenly scones" compete with "sinful muffins" at this "cute, cute, cute" SoHo cafe, purveyor of pastries, "gourmet sandwiches" and other sweet and savory treats; a "quick-bite" mecca, it gets "mobbed on weekends", with best service allegedly reserved for those who "look like a tart."

O'Neals' ◐[S]

F	D	S	C
16	16	17	$33

49 W. 64th St. (bet. B'way & CPW), 212-787-4663

◪ A Lincoln Center "tradition", this "saloon/bistro" "gets you to the show on time" with its "tasty", casual (some say "forgettable") American menu and "fast but not rushed" service; the "handy" location and "pleasant" setting win applause before or after any performance.

One 51 [S]

F	D	S	C
–	–	–	M

151 E. 50th St. (bet. Lexington & 3rd Aves.), 212-753-1144

Just in time for millennium celebrations, this Midtown East supper club (formerly Tatou) has reopened as a softly lit, modern dining and dancing venue offering Eclectic fare and live music or a DJ nightly; the upstairs VIP lounge overlooks the dance floor, which swings into action at 10:30 PM.

147 ◐

F	D	S	C
19	20	16	$42

147 W. 15th St. (bet. 6th & 7th Aves.), 212-929-5000

◪ Set in a former firehouse, this Chelsea New American is a "cool space" where the "cell-phone crowd" comes to chill out; it features a "limited" but "well-prepared" menu, an often-hopping "bar scene" and "live music" to distract from the high-end prices and service that can be "indifferent" at times.

ONE IF BY LAND, TIBS ◐[S]

F	D	S	C
24	27	24	$60

17 Barrow St. (bet. 7th Ave. S. & W. 4th St.), 212-228-0822

■ For the "ultimate date", this "flawless" restored Village townhouse that once belonged to Aaron Burr exudes "sheer romance" as "gorgeous flowers", flickering firelight and a pianist set the mood for a "sure score"; the reliably good, if pricey, New American–Continental menu is matched with "impeccable service", and the "beef Wellington and chocolate soufflés" are reputed to win hearts on their own; $56 prix fixe dinner only.

101 (Brooklyn) ◐[S]

F	D	S	C
19	16	16	$29

10018 Fourth Ave. (101st St.), 718-833-1313

◪ The "Brooklyn scene" thrives at this Bay Ridge Italian, a "crowded joint" where "friends meet friends" over pizzas and "terrific pastas"; during peak hours, the "young" clientele keeps the place "very noisy."

O'Nieal's Grand St. [S]

F	D	S	C
20	22	20	$38

174 Grand St. (bet. Centre & Mulberry Sts.), 212-941-9119

■ "Dark mahogany" paneling and a "beautiful bar" set the tone for "fine food and wine" at this Little Italy New American, a "yuppie power scene" that's a "trendy but not pretentious" class act with "quite tasty" food; N.B. the lounge is stogie central ("holy smokes!").

Onigashima [S] — 20 | 14 | 17 | $31
43-45 W. 55th St. (bet. 5th & 6th Aves.), 212-541-7145
■ Sushi on a shoestring is the draw at this "Midtown secret" spot for "fast and fresh" Japanese; offering oodles of udon and a set-price "lunchtime sushi fix", it's "better than average" for less than average.

O Padeiro [S] — 19 | 16 | 15 | $21
641 Sixth Ave. (bet. 19th & 20th Sts.), 212-414-9661
■ "Inventive sandwiches" built on "delicious", "crusty breads" are the main appeal of this "tiny" Portuguese bakery/cafe in Chelsea; with tiled decor, "tippy tables" and Iberian wines, it offers a "touch of Lisbon on Ladies Mile."

Opaline ◐ — 18 | 20 | 17 | $35
85 Ave. A (bet. 5th & 6th Sts.), 212-475-5050
◪ The "opium-den ambiance" at this "sensual" East Village French draws in the "beautiful people" for "simple", "yummy" bistro fare followed by after-dinner mingling in the "cozy lounge"; but critics cite prices and portions respectively large and small.

Orienta ◐[S] — 19 | 16 | 17 | $39
205 E. 75th St. (bet. 2nd & 3rd Aves.), 212-517-7509
◪ "Charming and different", this "neighborhood" Asian fusion outlet offers a "creative menu" prepared with "flair"; staff "attitude" and "close quarters" tend to tarnish an otherwise bright rep.

Oriental Garden ◐[S] — ▽ 22 | 12 | 15 | $28
14 Elizabeth St. (bet. Bayard & Canal Sts.), 212-619-0085
■ "Outstanding fresh fish", shrimp and crab pulled straight from the tank and fixed "Cantonese style" is the big lure at this Chinatown seafood specialist; with "wonderful" steamed fresh vegetables rounding out the spread, most are able to overlook slack service, crowds and white Formica decor.

Oriont — – | – | – | E
431 W. 14th St. (bet. 9th & 10th Aves.), 212-645-1988
Energizing the old Meatpacking District, this hipper-than-thou new 'concept' offers sushi and raw bars along with a dance floor in its ground-floor cabaret, while the more formal upstairs (about to swing into action at press time) promises fine French fare with Asian accents; early positive reports are confirmed by a full house of Gen Next.

Oro Blu [S] — ▽ 20 | 19 | 19 | $34
333 Hudson St. (Charlton St.), 212-645-8004
■ Hailed as a "welcome addition" to West SoHo – almost anything would be – this Italian newcomer "feels like a bit of Midtown moved Downtown" given its upscale menu and "noisy atmosphere"; it adds growing evidence of life in this "out-of-the-way" nabe.

Orologio ◐[S]⊘ — 18 | 16 | 15 | $24
162 Ave. A (bet. 10th & 11th Sts.), 212-228-6900
■ Named for its "cute clock" decor, this "relaxed" East Village Italian is appreciated for supplying very good food at "bargain" prices; it's a "satisfying" "hangout", with sidewalk seating relieving the somewhat "cramped" conditions inside.

Orso ◐[S] — 22 | 18 | 20 | $44
322 W. 46th St. (bet. 8th & 9th Aves.), 212-489-7212
■ A long-running hit with the "theater crowd", this Restaurant Row "trip to Tuscany" is famed for serving "innovative pastas and pizzas" with plenty of "celeb-watching" on the side; the "clubby" ambiance and "superior service" keep insiders coming back, so it's notoriously "hard to get in."

Osaka (Brooklyn) 🆂 ▽ 21 | 19 | 18 | $27
272 Court St. (bet. DeGraw & Kane Sts.), 718-643-0044
■ Brooklyn's sushi-heads sigh over the "simply splendid" fish and "specialty rolls" at this "spartan, modern" Cobble Hill Japanese newcomer; area advocates claim it's a "rival to Gotham" – "at last!" – crowds and noise inclusive.

Oscar's ◐🆂 18 | 17 | 18 | $34
Waldorf-Astoria, 301 Park Ave. (enter at 50th St. & Lexington Ave.), 212-872-4920
☑ This old Waldorf "standby" has achieved "new life" thanks to a $3 million "face-lift"; the revised menu offers better-than-expected "modern updates" of American classics, conveniently at all hours.

Osteria al Doge ◐🆂 19 | 17 | 18 | $38
142 W. 44th St. (bet. B'way & 6th Ave.), 212-944-3643
■ It "feels like Venezia" at this rustic Theater District Northern Italian "favorite"; while the "dependable" pasta-based menu wins warm applause, regulars report it's less "noisy" and "rushed" post-show than before.

Osteria Laguna ◐🆂 20 | 19 | 18 | $36
209 E. 42nd St. (bet. 2nd & 3rd Aves.), 212-557-0001
■ This "great find" brings "excellent Tuscan" and "comfortable" dining to Midtown East; it's a boon for the "business" crowd, so "clients" and "corporate credit cards" abound.

Otabe 🆂 22 | 22 | 21 | $47
68 E. 56th St. (bet. Madison & Park Aves.), 212-223-7575
■ Amid "Zen-like" harmony, this "elegant" Midtown Japanese harbors a "serene" front dining room and a "teppan room" in back; "top sushi" and "inspired" chefs make it an "authentic" treat, best enjoyed when "someone else pays."

Our Place 🆂 21 | 16 | 21 | $30
1444 Third Ave. (82nd St.), 212-288-4888
141 E. 55th St. (bet. Lexington & 3rd Aves.), 212-753-3900
■ They "live to please" at this East Side Chinese duo and it shows in the "classy", "high-quality" cooking and "civilized" service; fans place them "a few notches above" the typical chopstick joint – and well "worth the extra cost."

Oyster Bar 22 | 17 | 16 | $40
Grand Central, lower level (42nd St. & Vanderbilt Ave.), 212-490-6650
■ An undisputed "NY classic", this "cavernous", "noisy" Grand Central seafooder serves "fine fish with flourish" from a menu with "more choices than at a Greek diner", but the serious shucking at the "top raw bar" is where the real action is; it's "never boring" and some say the "recent face-lift has sparked it to new heights."

Oyster Bar at the Plaza ◐🆂 20 | 20 | 19 | $45
Plaza Hotel, 768 Fifth Ave. (58th St., bet. 5th & 6th Aves.), 212-546-5340
☑ "An oasis with oysters", this seafooder is the Plaza Hotel's least known (and least formal) room, a "perfect place to have a few drinks" and a few bivalves in a dark wood English pub setting; but fin-icky types think it "could be better for the money."

Oznot's Dish (Brooklyn) ◐🆂 22 | 20 | 19 | $28
79 Berry St. (N. 9th St.), 718-599-6596
■ The "alternative set" gathers at this affordable, funky "Williamsburg treasure" for "excellent", "always surprising" French–Near Eastern cuisine served to an audience of artists and would-be clients; P.S. the "unique brunch" is a weekend winner, and locals marvel as "a wine list grows in Brooklyn."

Palacinka 🅂⇗ ▽ 20 | 17 | 15 | $19
28 Grand St. (bet. 6th Ave. & Thompson St.), 212-625-0362
■ "Escape from the West Broadway" throngs and "step into Budapest" at this SoHo crêperie, a "mellow" "little cafe" offering an "unusual" variety of "mouthwatering" crêpes, sweet or savory; the name is Czech for pancake, though they come "small"-scale here.

Palette ●🅂 — | — | — | E
1375 Sixth Ave. (bet. 55th & 56th Sts.), 212-957-2727
Its soothing ambiance, elegant dark wood decor and gracious service make this Midtown Mediterranean newcomer an inviting – if not cheap – option, as does its wine bar with 65 choices by the glass; crowded with business-lunching suits, it's quieter at night.

Palio 23 | 25 | 22 | $58
151 W. 51st St. (bet. 6th & 7th Aves.), 212-245-4850
☑ "Top-notch" Midtown Northern Italian duplex that charms with a "beautiful setting" (featuring a four-wall Sandro Chia mural in the "handsome" downstairs bar) and "delicious" cooking in the elegant, blond wood–paneled upstairs dining room; its "expense-account" tabs point up the perils of "*alta cucina* – small portions, high prices."

Palladin 🅂 22 | 19 | 18 | $56
Time Hotel, 224 W. 49th St. (bet. B'way & 8th Ave.), 212-320-2929
☑ Celebrated chef Jean-Louis Palladin's new, "very modern" French bistro in the Time Hotel is favored to be a Theater District "hit" on the strength of his name alone; however, low-budget mod decor at high-budget prices and the chef's absences are causes for concern.

PALM ●🅂 25 | 16 | 19 | $54
837 Second Ave. (bet. 44th & 45th Sts.), 212-687-2953
Palm Too 🅂
840 Second Ave. (bet. 44th & 45th Sts.), 212-697-5198
Palm West 🅂
250 W. 50th St. (bet. B'way & 8th Ave.), 212-333-7256
☑ Now a trio, these Midtown cow palaces are "nothing fancy", but their fab "football-sized filets" and marvelous "monster" lobsters keep the he-men coming; caricature-covered walls, "curmudgeonly waiters" and "NY attitude" please the regulars, but a few outsiders find the "sawdust-caked" look and "macho" mentality "very dated."

Palm Court, The ●🅂 21 | 25 | 21 | $47
Plaza Hotel, 768 Fifth Ave. (59th St.), 212-546-5350
■ With its "waltz music", "Victorian" polish and "legendary Plaza atmosphere", this courtyard Continental is a "regal" retreat for a "lovely cup of tea" or a "buffet brunch extraordinaire"; cynics sniff it's "for tourists and grandmas" or for "young ladies to learn manners", but it's tough to criticize "a legend."

Palmetta Plantation House 19 | 20 | 18 | $36
265 E. 78th St. (bet. 2nd & 3rd Aves.), 212-327-2012
■ An "interior by Laura Ashley and Fidel Castro" sets the upscale "colonial" tone at this "teeny" Upper East Side Caribbean; the "memorably spicy" cooking smacks of "high soul" and the "sexy" setup makes it easy to "savor every mouthful."

Pamir 🅂 20 | 16 | 19 | $31
1437 Second Ave. (bet. 74th & 75th Sts.), 212-734-3791
1065 First Ave. (58th St.), 212-644-9258
■ Experience Kabul minus the shooting at these "atmospheric" Afghan Eastsiders, "reliable" "rarities" known for their "succulent kebabs" and "great stews"; with "polite service" and "modest" prices, the two branches are "equals", so "try the one you're near."

133

Pampa ◐🅂≠
21 | 16 | 16 | $28

768 Amsterdam Ave. (bet. 97th & 98th Sts.), 212-865-2929

■ "Vegans stay home" warn denizens of this "hot", cash-only "bargain" Upper West Side Argentine grill showcasing "superb, imported" beef "charred" and "seasoned to near-perfection"; some nights the only action on this "barren stretch of Amsterdam" is the "line outside."

Pangea ◐🅂
▽ 19 | 19 | 18 | $29

178 Second Ave. (bet. 11th & 12th Sts.), 212-995-0900

■ Though not as scene-y as many of its East Village neighbors, this Med-Eclectic is valued by locals for its "good food", "reasonable prices" and "relaxing, pretty" setting; the staff may be a bit "flaky", but at least they're "attentive."

Pão! 🅂
22 | 16 | 19 | $35

322 Spring St. (Greenwich St.), 212-334-5464

■ "Order anything in a copper pot" say regulars at this "cozy", "convivial", "authentic" Portuguese "sleeper" "in nowhere land" at SoHo's edge, where a "feast" is always in progress; it "goes the extra mile to please."

Paola's 🅂
23 | 19 | 21 | $43

245 E. 84th St. (bet. 2nd & 3rd Aves.), 212-794-1890

■ Eastsiders in "need of pampering" rely on this "romantic", "family-run" Italian for "exquisite" "homemade pastas", "heavenly desserts" and "solicitous service"; "pretty" quarters and Paola's always pleasing presence guarantee a high comfort quotient.

Papaya King ◐🅂≠
19 | 5 | 10 | I

179 E. 86th St. (3rd Ave.), 212-369-0648
121 W. 125th St. (bet. Lenox & 7th Aves.), 212-665-5732

☑ "Decor be damned", this Yorkville "landmark" stand and its new Harlem branch strive to supply "the world's best bargain" hot dog chased with a "tropical drink"; though "tacky", for a "walking lunch" the king "reigns supreme."

Paper Moon Express
18 | 14 | 15 | $24

54 E. 59th St. (bet. Madison & Park Aves.), 212-688-5500

☑ Maxed-out shoppers turn to this East Side Italian to fill up on "quick" "yuppie food" (sandwiches, pasta, pizza) at "moderate prices"; citing the "stuck-up staff" and "cattle-car" lunch scene, critics contend it hops the track.

Paper Moon Milano
19 | 17 | 18 | $42

39 E. 58th St. (bet. Madison & Park Aves.), 212-758-8600

☑ A "popular business lunch hangout" that segues into a "young scene" by night, this East Side Northern Italian offers "easy" access to some "very tasty" eating, even if "high noise levels" (and prices) are cited as irritants.

Pappardella ◐🅂
17 | 15 | 16 | $32

316 Columbus Ave. (75th St.), 212-595-7996

☑ Long a "favorite" "Upper West Side haunt", this recently revamped Northern Italian now presents a menu of Ligurian specialties; the "decent" food and "pleasant service" make it "fun with friends", but some rate the overall results too "bland" for this "spicy neighborhood."

Paris Commune 🅂
19 | 18 | 18 | $30

411 Bleecker St. (bet. Bank & W. 11th Sts.), 212-929-0509

■ Champions claim you "can't beat the atmosphere" of this Eclectic Village bistro that's popular for a "cozy" brunch; its "intimate pleasure" peaks "in winter by the open fire", but spoilers warn of weekend waits and smokers.

Park Avalon ●S
20 | 20 | 18 | $36

225 Park Ave. S. (bet. 18th & 19th Sts.), 212-533-2500

■ "Still going strong", this "airy" New American in a "dramatic, candlelit setting" near Union Square is a "loud", "hip" "scene for twenty- and thirtysomethings", serving "a darn good meal" to a consistently "good-looking" crowd; the "hot" bar and "amazing brunch" have their own followings.

PARK AVENUE CAFE S
24 | 23 | 22 | $55

100 E. 63rd St. (bet. Lexington & Park Aves.), 212-644-1900

■ Chef "David Burke is a magician" who conjures up an "incredible" "blend of tradition and modernism" at this East Side New American whose "delicious" cooking is matched by "first-rate" service and an attractive "Americana"-oriented setting; from the "yummy bread basket" to the "stunning desserts", the "svelte patrons dive in" "with zest"; P.S. a "special table in the kitchen" offers a unique perspective.

Park Bistro S
21 | 17 | 19 | $45

414 Park Ave. S. (bet. 28th & 29th Sts.), 212-689-1360

■ The new regime of chef Philippe Roussel (ex Chelsea Bistro) is winning early praise for its "authentic" Gallic style; partisans pray this "warm", "crowded" Gramercy-area "Paris redux" will remain "a step above the standard."

Park Side (Queens) ●S
23 | 19 | 21 | $38

107-01 Corona Ave. (51st Ave.), 718-271-9276

☑ At this decidedly "non-Manhattan" Italian "staple" "in the heart of Corona's Little Italy", "the Sopranos" and lots of decent folks gather for first-rate "classic" cooking and "old-world" service; good "value" for good food keeps it "crowded", so "reserve early."

Park View at the Boathouse S
18 | 26 | 17 | $43

Central Park Lake (East Park Dr. & 72nd St.), 212-517-2233

☑ As advertised, this American overlooks the "romantic" Central Park Lake ("pretend you're in a movie"), and "on a beautiful day" the encounter with "nature" in mid-city strikes some as "surreal"; if the food is still "secondary", chef John Villa is "trying hard" and getting increasingly "good" results at what seems like "a mini-vacation."

Parma ●S
21 | 15 | 20 | $45

1404 Third Ave. (bet. 79th & 80th Sts.), 212-535-3520

☑ Loyal Eastsiders continue to make this Northern Italian standby their "home away from home"; it's "more expensive than average" and in "need of a little spruce-up", but the good old-style food is "hearty to a fault" and the staff is so "friendly" that it's reported "they even kiss the men goodbye."

Parsonage, The (Staten Island) S ▽
23 | 24 | 23 | $43

74 Arthur Kill Rd. (Clarke Ave.), 718-351-7879

■ "Escape to a simpler time" at this "manor-like" Continental in a "romantic" Historic Richmondtown locale; it offers "delicious" "fine dining" in "Victorian" comfort away from the "hustle and bustle" of that other island.

Pascalou S
21 | 15 | 18 | $36

1308 Madison Ave. (bet. 92nd & 93rd Sts.), 212-534-7522

■ Locals in pursuit of "unpretentious" bistro fare pack this "minute" French-Eclectic "Carnegie Hill favorite" that's a "prix fixe bargain"; it's a "tight squeeze", but even claustrophobes say it's "worth it."

Pasha S
22 | 20 | 20 | $37

70 W. 71st St. (bet. Columbus Ave. & CPW), 212-579-8751
■ Take a "magic carpet ride" to "'20s Istanbul" at this "beautifully decorated" "taste of Turkey near Lincoln Center"; it's an "eye-catching" bazaar of "fresh", "flavorful" fare delivered by a "polite", "knowledgeable" staff; a "real find."

Passage to India ⦿S
17 | 13 | 15 | $21

306-308 E. Sixth St. (2nd Ave.), 212-529-5770
◪ This cheap "Sixth Street joint" has made its name as a "reliable" supplier of "rich-flavored" Indian fare, though antis argue that indifferent service and a "narrow interior" in need of a "paint job" make it a "passage in steerage class" where "E.M. Forster would hide under the tablecloth."

Pasticcio S
▽ 19 | 16 | 19 | $32

447 Third Ave. (bet. 30th & 31st Sts.), 212-679-2551
■ Like a Murray Hill social club, this "friendly neighborhood Italian" provides a "comfortable" setting for residents to congregate over "quality" eats from a "big menu"; though the "candlelit" room can grow "noisy", it's "surprisingly undiscovered."

Pastrami Queen S
18 | 8 | 13 | $20

1269 Lexington Ave. (bet. 85th & 86th Sts.), 212-828-0007
◪ Although the decor and service are as plain as ever, this relocated and transgendered Upper Eastsider is "not quite" the old Queens-based Pastrami King; but loyal subjects still pay homage to the "best, leanest pastrami ever" and other inexpensive kosher staples, especially now that it's closer.

Patois (Brooklyn) S
23 | 17 | 19 | $33

255 Smith St. (bet. DeGraw & Douglass Sts.), 718-855-1535
■ "Believe the hype" – this very "happening" "piece of Paris" in a "charming" Carroll Gardens space-cum-garden is home to chef-owner Alan Harding's "innovative, flavorful" French bistro fare; "the secret is out" with a natural downside – it's "packed."

Patoug Manhattan S≠
– | – | – | I

11 E. 30th St. (bet. 5th & Madison Aves.), 212-696-0300
One cuisine that Manhattan isn't saturated with is Persian, which is reason enough to welcome this entry on the Gramercy/Murray Hill border; other reasons are low prices (BYO) and a simple but pleasant setting with big open-to-the-street windows.

PATRIA S
25 | 23 | 22 | $53

250 Park Ave. S. (20th St.), 212-777-6211
■ Chef Douglas Rodriguez, aka "the king of Nuevo Latino", orchestrates a "symphony" of "incredible flavors" at this ever-popular Flatiron phenom where every "jazzy" dish is "one of a kind"; even the "fiesta" feel fueled by "exotic drinks" can't compete with food so "exciting" that people want to "lick the plate"; $54 dinner, $30 lunch prix fixe.

Patrissy's ⦿S
19 | 15 | 18 | $40

98 Kenmare St. (bet. Lafayette & Mulberry Sts.), 212-226-8509
■ Yesteryear's Little Italy is alive and well at this "solid" centenarian, a "subdued" trattoria off the main tourist drag that serves "typical Neapolitan" fare; it's always a "pleasant" repast with "no big fuss."

Patroon
23 | 21 | 22 | $61

160 E. 46th St. (bet. Lexington & 3rd Aves.), 212-883-7373
◪ Catering to all types ("business types, tycoon types and movie types"), Ken Aretsky's "clubby" Midtown American pulls the "power" crowd in with chef Geoffrey Zakarian's "excellent" meat-and-potatoes fare followed by a spell in the "cigar lounge"; if you have to ask how much, you're not the type.

Patsy's 🅂
20 | 15 | 19 | $39

236 W. 56th St. (bet B'way & 8th Ave.), 212-247-3491
☑ There's a trove of "history on the walls" at this "comforting relic of the '40s", a midpriced Midtown "haven for Sinatra fans" and devotees of "solid", "grandma"-style Italian; in spite of recent spiffing up, the ambiance is a tad "too Rat Pack" for some.

Patsy's Pizza 🅂⊽
21 | 13 | 15 | $21

2287-91 First Ave. (bet. 117th & 118th Sts.), 212-534-9783 ◗
1312 Second Ave. (69th St.), 212-639-1000
61 W. 74th St. (bet. Columbus Ave. & CPW), 212-579-3000
509 Third Ave. (bet. 34th & 35th Sts.), 212-689-7500
67 University Pl. (bet. 10th & 11th Sts.), 212-533-3500
■ A "solid contender" in the ultracompetitive "thin-crust pizza" stakes, this chain weighs in with a "crisp" "brick-oven" pie loaded with "very fresh" toppings; one quibble: "'cash only' is a pain."

Paul & Jimmy's 🅂
18 | 16 | 18 | $37

123 E. 18th St. (bet. Irving Pl. & Park Ave. S.), 212-475-9540
■ "Bring an extra stomach" to this "easygoing" Gramercy Italian, a 50-year-old "favorite" frequented by an "over-40 crowd"; it's a "comfortable" area "standby" that offers a "dependable", moderately priced menu and "no surprises."

Payard Pâtisserie
24 | 21 | 19 | $42

1032 Lexington Ave. (bet. 73rd & 74th Sts.), 212-717-5252
■ The ultimate reward after a "trip to the gym", François Payard's East Side cafe (what Longchamp's should have been) showcases his "poetry in pastry" as the finale to chef Philippe Bertineau's "delightful" savory French menu; it's a bit of "overindulgence", complete with "attitude" at a "Prada-esque level"; P.S. "it's hard to go back to Krispy Kreme" after this.

Peacock Alley 🅂
23 | 24 | 22 | $62

Waldorf-Astoria, 301 Park Ave. (bet. 49th & 50th Sts.), 212-872-4895
■ These days the "pride of the Waldorf" is chef Laurent Gras' stylish French "class act" offering "superb" cuisine in a "most elegant" room; from the "power breakfast scene" through lunch and dinner to the "exquisite Sunday brunch" (complete with harpist), this is true "luxury dining"; P.S. a new menu format eliminates the appetizer/entree distinction in favor of midsized dishes priced according to the number you order.

Peanut Butter & Co. 🅂
20 | 14 | 18 | $13

240 Sullivan St. (bet. Bleecker & W. 3rd Sts.), 212-677-3995
■ "PBJ fanatics" and budget-balancers say this Village outlet is a "unique idea" gone right, serving 14 "yummy, gooey" incarnations of its namesake; certified nut cases who find the fare "better than mom used to make" volunteer the inside dope: "get the Elvis."

PEARL OYSTER BAR
25 | 14 | 18 | $32

18 Cornelia St. (bet. Bleecker & W. 4th Sts.), 212-691-8211
■ Hook up with a stool at this affordable, "cramped" Village storefront and it's smooth sailing, with some of the "freshest", most "amazing" New England–style seafood to be found "south of Maine"; seafarers plead "find bigger quarters" but are resigned to "waiting outside" to get to the "treasure."

Peking Duck House 🅂
21 | 9 | 14 | $26

22 Mott St. (bet. Chatham Sq. & Pell St.), 212-227-1810
☑ The "phenomenal" "crispy duck" is a "must" at this "authentic Chinatown" vet since there's little else to recommend it; hopefully, its move to 28 Mott Street in fall '99 will involve a decorator.

	F	D	S	C
Peking Park [S]	17	13	15	$28

100 Park Ave. (40th St.), 212-725-5570
◪ With "such a great location for business lunch", this sprawling Midtown "alternative to Chinatown" should do better than serving merely "ordinary" Chinese; however, regulars tout its "dependable" inexpensive chow and "fast service"; busy at noon, it's light at night.

	F	D	S	C
Pellegrino's ◐[S]	21	17	21	$34

138 Mulberry St. (bet. Grand & Hester Sts.), 212-226-3177
◪ "Classier than the usual" in "touristy Little Italy", this trattoria features "noteworthy" "fresh pastas" and "friendly staff"; it's a "pleasant surprise" in rubberneck territory, even if the "bordello" decor is "kind of tacky."

	F	D	S	C
Penang ◐[S]	19	18	16	$28

1596 Second Ave. (83rd St.), 212-585-3838
240 Columbus Ave. (71st St.), 212-769-3988
109 Spring St. (bet. Greene & Mercer Sts.), 212-274-8883
38-04 Prince St. (Main St.), Queens, 718-321-2078
Penang Bar & Grill ◐[S]
64 Third Ave. (11th St.), 212-228-7888
■ These "kitschy" "bamboo-paradise" Malaysians "make Trader Vic's look like Lespinasse", but are "hugely popular" for their "tasty", easily affordable "American-style" eats and "change of pace" ambiance; N.B. the B&G is separately owned.

	F	D	S	C
Pepe Giallo To Go ◐[S]🚫	21	10	13	$17

253 10th Ave. (25th St.), 212-242-6055
Pepe Rosso To Go [S]🚫
110 St. Marks Pl. (bet. Ave. A & 1st Ave.), 212-677-6563 ◐
149 Sullivan St. (bet. Houston & Prince Sts.), 212-677-4555
Pepe Verde To Go [S]🚫
559 Hudson St. (bet. Perry & W. 11th Sts.), 212-255-2221
■ "Honest", "no-frills" Italians that sling "awesome pastas and panini" at you for "dirt cheap" prices; their "authentic homemade" style qualifies them as "walk-in" or "take-out favorites."

	F	D	S	C
PERIYALI	25	21	23	$49

35 W. 20th St. (bet. 5th & 6th Aves.), 212-463-7890
■ "What Odysseus was surely looking for", this "chic Greek" "pacesetter" offers an "elegant and delicious" "taste of Athens" in the Flatiron area; it wins a chorus of kudos for its "spectacular seafood", "attentive service" and "understated" room, but be advised this is not the place to start breaking plates.

	F	D	S	C
Persepolis [S]	19	14	17	$29

1423 Second Ave. (bet. 74th & 75th Sts.), 212-535-1100
■ "Tehran meets Second Avenue" at this East Side "escape to Persia", where the "authentic shish kebab" and "delectable" sour cherry rice shine in a "rather ordinary space"; most find the modestly priced menu "limited" but usually a "delight."

	F	D	S	C
Pershing Square ◐[S]	–	–	–	E

90 E. 42nd St. (Park Ave.), 212-286-9600
Given his track record (River Cafe, Water Club), any restaurant from Buzzy O'Keeffe has to be a good bet; this newcomer is a commuter's dream: a handsome space across from Grand Central offering good, straightforward American fare and a boisterous, 10-deep bar scene; though totally new, it already looks like a vintage NY landmark.

Pescatore ◐[S] 18 15 16 $33

955 Second Ave. (bet. 50th & 51st Sts.), 212-752-7151

■ A "reliable" source of "Italian staples", this "affordable" East Midtowner keeps its *amici* loyal with "traditional" takes on "fish-house" favorites; even with "three sections" it gets "very crowded", but the alfresco patio provides "pleasant seating."

Petaluma ◐[S] 18 17 18 $38

1356 First Ave. (73rd St.), 212-772-8800

■ "Cell phones and baby strollers" are staples on the scene at this casual, "upmarket", "very Upper East Side" trattoria where the Sotheby's crew and other neighbors can be found happily munching on "good" salads, pizzas and grilled items delivered by a "loyal" staff; a handful hold the food is "edible, but forgettable."

PETER LUGER STEAK HOUSE 28 15 19 $55

(Brooklyn) [S]≠

178 Broadway (Driggs Ave.), 718-387-7400

■ For the 16th year running, surveyors have voted this Williamsburg heavyweight NY's No. 1 steakhouse – we may have to retire the title – praising its "porterhouse perfection"; beef-eaters brave the "not-so-great" macho service, German "beer-hall atmosphere" and "cash-only" policy in exchange for "amazing meat" "sizzling in butter" and the full pantheon of sides and rich desserts, fully expecting "paramedics to bring the check."

Pete's Downtown (Brooklyn) [S] 19 16 18 $32

2 Water St. (Cadman Plaza W.), 718-858-3510

◪ Ok, it's "not the River Cafe", but this "underrated" Brooklyn Heights Italian "shares the same view" of the NY harbor and is "a good alternative" because it's so "reasonably priced."

Pete's Tavern ◐[S] 14 16 15 $27

129 E. 18th St. (Irving Pl.), 212-473-7676

◪ A Gramercy "landmark" since 1864, this "loud and crowded", "quintessential tavern" personifies "grunge with character"; though author "O. Henry hung out here", the pub-priced Italian-American fare is "nothing to write home about."

Petite Abeille [S] 20 13 16 $20

107 W. 18th St. (bet. 6th & 7th Aves.), 212-604-9350
466 Hudson St. (Barrow St.), 212-741-6479
400 W. 14th St. (9th Ave.), 212-727-1505 ◐
134 W. Broadway (bet. Duane & Reade Sts.), 212-791-1360

■ The name translates as 'little bee', and this Belgian quartet has a solid buzz due to "magic waffles", "fries that make you swoon" and "charming Tintin posters"; but they're so petite it's like eating in a hive.

Petite Crevette (Brooklyn) [S]≠ 19 8 16 $22

127 Atlantic Ave. (bet. Clinton & Henry Sts.), 718-858-6660

◪ "Unassuming" BYO Brooklyn Heights French seafooder with a brisk trade owing to its great "value on the plate"; the positively "no-frills" decor makes fidgeters feel it's "not a place to linger."

Petrossian ◐[S] 25 24 23 $63

182 W. 58th St. (7th Ave.), 212-245-2214

■ You "feel like royalty for a night" at this Russo-Continental "caviar and champagne paradise" near Carnegie Hall that's all the more memorable for its "art deco elegance" and "smooth" service; for maximum "indulgence" bring "lots of rubles"; however, there's a surprisingly "inexpensive prix fixe lunch" for proles.

Philip Marie ●S
19	18	20	$35

569 Hudson St. (W. 11th St.), 212-242-6200
■ "Charming, midpriced" West Village newcomer that "celebrates American" cooking with very good, "homey" fare (try the parsley salad); early visitors find it a "great addition to the neighborhood."

Pho Bang S
19	7	12	$17

6 Chatham Sq. (Mott St.), 212-587-0870
157 Mott St. (bet. Broome & Grand Sts.), 212-966-3797 ⊅
3 Pike St. (bet. Canal & Division Sts.), 212-233-3947 ⊅
82-90 Broadway (Elmhurst Ave.), Queens, 718-205-1500 ⊅
41-07 Kissena Blvd. (Main St.), Queens, 718-939-5520 ⊅
■ "Authentic" cooking ("the best noodle soup") at "rock-bottom" tabs draws fans to these Chinatown and Queens Vietnamese vets; the pho-bic fret about "zero decor" and middling service.

Phoenix Garden S⊅
22	10	15	$27

242 E. 40th St. (bet. 2nd & 3rd Aves.), 212-983-6666
■ "If you love Cantonese", this brick-walled Tudor City standby offers "all your traditional favorites", "reasonably priced"; it may "need a face-lift" (and a jolt in the service end), yet fans report you're "never disappointed" here.

Pho Viet Huong S
21	10	13	$19

73 Mulberry St. (bet. Bayard & Canal Sts.), 212-233-8988
■ "Delicious adventures" await intrepid wayfarers at this Chinatown Vietnamese that's a grand "jury duty stop" – so long as you focus on the "low prices" and ignore the "divey" digs and barely "ok service."

Piadina ●S⊅
19	17	16	$29

57 W. 10th St. (bet. 5th & 6th Aves.), 212-460-8017
■ Offering "disfiguringly delicious" dishes, refreshingly "low-key" ambiance and "light on the wallet" tabs, this "popular" Village "Tuscan treasure" has "great date place" potential.

Piccola Venezia (Queens) S
25	17	22	$46

42-01 28th Ave. (42nd St.), 718-721-8470
■ "Astoria's contribution to fine dining", this Northern Italian standby continues to delight with "solid", "old-fashioned" fare, a "fine wine list" and "attentive service"; now if only they could work on the "retro funeral-parlor decor" and Manhattan prices; "the menu means nothing – they make anything you want" – and do it very well.

Piccolo Angolo S
23	14	21	$29

621 Hudson St. (Jane St.), 212-229-9177
■ "Expect a wait", "crowds" and "noise galore" at this justly "popular" low-budget Italian Villager where a "hoot" of an owner, Renato Migliorini, "rattles off the daily specials like an auctioneer" in "broken English"; it's an only in NY "experience."

PICHOLINE ●S
26	23	24	$61

35 W. 64th St. (bet. B'way & CPW), 212-724-8585
■ Proving that "there is life on the West Side", this "inspired" "showstopper" courtesy of chef-owner Terrance Brennan is the city's top-rated Mediterranean and "far and away the best near Lincoln Center"; besides Brennan's sensational cooking, which inches up in our ratings each year, highlights include NYC's best cheese cart, "unobtrusive" service and a "bargain" prix fixe lunch.

Pierre au Tunnel S
20	16	20	$41

250 W. 47th St. (bet. B'way & 8th Ave.), 212-575-1220
■ One of the Theater District's longest-running hits (since 1950), this "not fancy", "no-airs" bistro remains "a pleasant retreat for fine French cuisine"; maybe it "never changes" and is a bit expensive, but it "never fails" to "get you to the play well fed and on time."

Pierrot Bistro ●🅂
▽ 20 | 17 | 21 | $28

28 Ave. B (bet. 2nd & 3rd Sts.), 212-673-1999

■ "Have a seat at the bar" and check out the "lively" scene at this Alphabet City Eclectic, a "real find" with a "friendly", casual feel; among the "well-priced" eats is a hard-to-beat $14.95 prix fixe.

Pier 25A (Queens) 🅂
17 | 15 | 17 | $33

215-16 Northern Blvd. (215th St.), 718-423-6395

☑ "No-nonsense", family-friendly Bayside seafooder that's "just a step above a diner" offering "hearty", modestly priced "simple dishes"; though the setting is definitely "uninspired", "crowds" of "locals" aver there's "something for everyone" here.

Pietrasanta 🅂
20 | 15 | 18 | $30

683 Ninth Ave. (47th St.), 212-265-9471

■ "Delicioso" Hell's Kitchen Italian that's "an affordable alternative" to pricier pre-theater places and worth a visit "for the homemade breads alone"; you "must make a reservation" as it's always "crowded."

Pietro's
22 | 14 | 20 | $51

232 E. 43rd St. (bet. 2nd & 3rd Aves.), 212-682-9760

■ "The '50s are alive" at this Italian steakhouse veteran near Grand Central with a "devoted following" that touts its beef and finds its "down-to-earth" atmosphere like "eating at home with lots of friends"; trendoids yawn it's "tired" and "overpriced."

Pig Heaven ●🅂
16 | 11 | 15 | $28

1540 Second Ave. (bet. 80th & 81st Sts.), 212-744-4333

☑ "If you like pork", you'll be in "hog heaven" at this Chinese Eastsider known for its "piggy decor" and "great ribs"; longtimers say it's "not like the old days", but a sleek post-*Survey* renovation seems to have revitalized the kitchen as well; stay tuned.

Ping's Seafood ●🅂
▽ 21 | 12 | 17 | $27

20 E. Broadway (bet. Catherine & Market Sts.), 212-965-0808
83-09 Queens Blvd. (Goldsmith St.), Queens, 718-396-1238

■ "Worth a trip to Queens" or Chinatown, this much-improved Chinese seafooder specializes in Hong Kong–style fin fare, featuring fish tanks full of exotic shrimp, cod and crab; credit chef Chuen Ping Hui for the "simply delicious" delicacies, which come at relatively affordable prices with efficient service.

Pink Tea Cup ●🅂☞
18 | 13 | 15 | $20

42 Grove St. (bet. Bedford & Bleecker Sts.), 212-807-6755

■ Come "satisfy your Soul Food cravings" at this longtime Villager where the "cheap", "damn good" "comfort food" is almost "fried to the point of breakage"; provided you're not "claustrophobic" ("it's tiny") or overly fastidious ("grungy"), this will be your cup of tea.

Pintaile's Pizza 🅂
19 | 7 | 12 | $13

26 E. 91st St. (bet. 5th & Madison Aves.), 212-722-1967
1577 York Ave. (bet. 83rd & 84th Sts.), 212-396-3479
1443 York Ave. (bet. 76th & 77th Sts.), 212-717-4990
1237 Second Ave. (bet. 64th & 65th Sts.), 212-752-6222
124 Fourth Ave. (bet. 12th & 13th Sts.), 212-475-4977

☑ Converts to this minichain's "wafer-thin-crust" pizzas applaud their "healthy", "gourmet" approach and "creative toppings", yet nonbelievers put down the pies as more "like Triscuits" with "ketchup" that may be "light on the tummy" but are "heavy on the wallet."

Pintxos
▽ 20 | 15 | 18 | $28

510 Greenwich St. (bet. Canal & Spring Sts.), 212-343-9923

■ Its name means 'pinch of food', and this SoHo entry puts a unique Basque spin on "Manhattan's tapas bar madness"; there's also a variety of Spanish dishes and wine at this "fairly priced" spot.

Pisces ◐[S] 21 | 16 | 17 | $32

95 Ave. A (6th St.), 212-260-6660

■ "Fish is the star" at this Tompkins Square bi-level "seafood heaven" with "clever cuisine" at "honest prices"; it's "no longer Avenue A's hot spot", but fin-atics feel "if it's fresh fish you're after, you've got the right place."

Pitchoune [S] 20 | 14 | 16 | $37

226 Third Ave. (19th St.), 212-614-8641

◪ "Great bistro cooking" by way of Provence pleases Gramercy Parkers who tout this midpriced "neighborhood" place as worth trying "for its molten chocolate cake" alone; however, tables "too close for comfort" and "disorganized" service may be turnoffs.

Pizza Borgo [S]≠ – | – | – | I

30 E. 13th St. (bet. 5th Ave. & University Pl.), 212-242-8333

The brick oven at this new Village pizza offshoot of nearby Borgo Antico not only produces tasty thin-crust pies, roasted calamari and the like, but also emits heady aromas that add to the rustic warmth of the small, beamed-ceiling room; it's a bargain too.

Pizzeria Uno Chicago ◐[S] 13 | 11 | 12 | $19

220 E. 86th St. (bet. 2nd & 3rd Aves.), 212-472-5656
432 Columbus Ave. (81st St.), 212-595-4700
391 Sixth Ave. (bet. 8th St. & Waverly Pl.), 212-242-5230
55 Third Ave. (bet. 10th & 11th Sts.), 212-995-9668
South St. Seaport, 89 South St. (Pier 17), 212-791-7999
9201 Fourth Ave. (92nd St.), Brooklyn, 718-748-8667
39-10 Bell Blvd. (bet. 39th & 40th Sts.), Queens, 718-279-4900
107-16 70th Rd. (bet. Austin St. & Queens Blvd.), Queens, 718-793-6700

◪ "When you've had enough thin-crust", doughty doughboys dig this deep-dish Chicago chain for its "basic" meal-in-a-slice pies; but crusty thin-crust types say this "mediocre" "McDonald's of pizza" (with "incompetent service") is only good "when you miss the suburbs."

P.J. Bernstein Deli [S] 16 | 8 | 13 | $21

1215 Third Ave. (bet. 70th & 71st Sts.), 212-879-0914

◪ "Reliable" Upper East Side deli that fails to evoke much enthusiasm ("decent", "so-so", "not bad"); most customers show up "because it's in the neighborhood" – and then "mainly for takeout" since the digs really "need perking up."

Place, The [S] ▽ 22 | 21 | 20 | $36

310 W. Fourth St. (bet. Bank & W. 12th Sts.), 212-924-2711

◪ "Understated little" West Village Mediterranean yearling with an "inventive kitchen" and a "quaint", "cozy" air complemented by caring service; however, its "stylish" crowd would prefer a better name and lower prices.

Planet Hollywood ◐[S] 11 | 17 | 13 | $26

140 W. 57th St. (bet. 6th & 7th Aves.), 212-333-7827

◪ The Eclectic-American "food is not the point" of this memorabilia-laden movie shrine near Carnegie Hall that's "fine if you're under 12" or "obsessed by *Titanic*"; however, crestfallen cineasts consider this "dining equivalent of *Ishtar*" "nothing but a tourist attraction"; luckily, Arnold, Bruce and Sly kept their day jobs.

Planet Sushi ◐[S] 19 | 14 | 16 | $28

380 Amsterdam Ave. (78th St.), 212-496-1279

◪ "Open late", this "welcome" new Westsider slices up quite "decent sushi" at modest prices; "varying quality" and "hit-or-miss service" detract, but "no lines" and "alfresco" seating are pluses.

Planet Thailand (Brooklyn) ●S⊅   23 | 11 | 14 | $18
141 N. 7th St. (bet. Bedford Ave. & Berry St.), 718-599-5758
■ Arguably offering the "best Thai in all five boroughs", this "out-of-control delicious" "bargain" spot is seemingly "single-handedly feeding Williamsburg's artists"; N.B. its new, improved (i.e. larger and more stylish) location is not reflected in our ratings.

PÓ S   24 | 17 | 20 | $42
31 Cornelia St. (bet. Bleecker & W. 4th Sts.), 212-645-2189
■ "You'll be in heaven" at chef/TV star "Mario Batali's starter place" (Babbo's parent), a "tiny" Village Italian "powerhouse" where "the tasting menu is the way to go"; there's been so much "hoopla" that "reservations are a problem."

Polistina's S   18 | 12 | 15 | $20
2275 Broadway (bet. 81st & 82nd Sts.), 212-579-2828
■ "Popular with families with kids" ("weekends can get like *Romper Room*"), this Upper West Side pie palace from the folks behind Carmine's is lauded for its "excellent thin-crust pizza"; "being close to Zabar's draws crowds" despite the slices' high prices.

Pomaire S   17 | 15 | 18 | $28
371 W. 46th St. (bet. 8th & 9th Aves.), 212-956-3056
■ "Homemade Chilean" specialties that make you "think you're in Santiago" keep this South American a "pre-theater" "favorite on Restaurant Row"; count on an "authentic" experience, backed by "competent, friendly service" in a bland could-be-anywhere setting.

Pomodoro Rosso S   19 | 15 | 18 | $30
229 Columbus Ave. (bet. 70th & 71st Sts.), 212-721-3009
■ Locals say this "midpriced" Upper West Side "neighborhood place" is "like stumbling into a family-run trattoria in Italy"; its "wonderful staff" "really tries to keep customers happy" and succeeds with very good, "reliable" cooking.

Pongal S   21 | 14 | 14 | $22
110 Lexington Ave. (bet. 27th & 28th Sts.), 212-696-9458
■ Probably the "best on Curry Hill", this Southern Indian Vegetarian is not only "original" and "authentic", but kosher too; cynics say until they "hire professional waiters", "make sure to ask for everything at least twice" – there's no such easy answer to the decor problem.

Pongsri Thai ●S   21 | 13 | 17 | $23
244 W. 48th St. (bet. B'way & 8th Ave.), 212-582-3392
311 Second Ave. (18th St.), 212-477-4100
■ "Consistent" quality at "prices that can't be beat" draws devotees to this Thai duo with Theater District and Gramercy locations; maybe "sad atmosphere" detracts, but the lunch specials compensate.

Ponticello (Queens) S   ▽ 25 | 17 | 23 | $40
46-11 Broadway (bet. 46th & 47th Sts.), 718-278-4514
■ "Sensational pastas" spark the menu of this Astoria Italian that amici call "the best Queens has to offer"; "unpretentious" and "nice all-around", it's "worth the trip."

Pop ●   17 | 20 | 16 | $48
127 Fourth Ave. (bet. 12th & 13th Sts.), 212-767-1800
☑ "Oh so fab" New French–American Central Villager whose snappy looks – a primary-colored homage to Eero Saarinen's TWA terminal at JFK – garner more buzz than its "ok but expensive" nibbles; hipsters say this "NY scene" will "only get more pop-ular."

Popover Cafe [S] 18 | 15 | 15 | $22
551 Amsterdam Ave. (bet. 86th & 87th Sts.), 212-595-8555
◪ Famed for "lighter-than-air popovers with strawberry butter" and "ridiculous" weekend lines, this one-of-a-kind Westsider is best known as a breakfast/brunch place; cynics find its "charming teddy bear decor" "terminally cute" ("bring insulin").

Porta Rossa [S] ▽ 20 | 14 | 23 | $32
176 Lexington Ave. (31st St.), 212-889-2939
◪ Believers call this "authentic" Murray Hill Italian "a cut above" the neighborhood competition, yet a few disbelievers say the food "barely cuts it"; service is "friendly" and "dignified rather than obsequious" according to regulars.

Porto Bello [S] 21 | 15 | 18 | $31
208 Thompson St. (bet. Bleecker & W. 3rd Sts.), 212-473-7794
■ "Aptly named" Italian Villager that comes across with some of the "best grilled portobellos in NY", along with "reliable pastas"; "reasonable prices" compensate for its "tight squeeze" layout.

Post House [S] 24 | 21 | 22 | $56
Lowell Hotel, 28 E. 63rd St. (bet. Madison & Park Aves.), 212-935-2888
■ "Suspendered" "expense-accounters" and their ladies take their "favorite steak break" at this handsome East Side "carnivore's paradise" in the Lowell Hotel; "clubby" but surprisingly "woman-friendly", it's "always consistent" and you can "always get in."

Pravda ◐[S] 16 | 21 | 14 | $37
281 Lafayette St. (bet. Houston & Prince Sts.), 212-226-4944
◪ For "socialistic socializing", "überchic" "Prada" wearers invade this SoHo "basement" Russian for its "excellent martinis" and "the scene, not the food"; trendoids think it's "fallen out of favor", but surveyors say it's still "hanging on" despite neo-communist service.

Primavera ◐[S] 24 | 21 | 23 | $57
1578 First Ave. (82nd St.), 212-861-8608
■ "Excellent" "classic Italian" cuisine arrives in a "wood-paneled" setting that epitomizes "old-world charm" at this "enduring" Upper Eastsider; "owner Nicola Civetta is as good as they come" and his "wonderful" black-tie staff assures a "thoroughly enjoyable" high-end "dining experience."

Primola ◐[S] 22 | 17 | 20 | $48
1226 Second Ave. (bet. 64th & 65th Sts.), 212-758-1775
■ "Celeb sightings" make for entertaining eating at this "popular" East Side Italian standby that's "keeping its edge" thanks to "great pasta", "delish fish" and a "relaxing" ambiance; the "service is better if they know you", yet those who "eat early" also "get a lot of attention."

Privé [S] 19 | 17 | 18 | $41
39 E. 19th St. (bet. B'way & Park Ave. S.), 212-253-5522
◪ Promoters of this New American "on a hidden block" in the Flatiron District call it a "real find" owing to its "good food and ambiance"; contrarians find it "unremarkable" and "overpriced", perhaps explaining why it's "often empty" enough to feel privé.

Provence ◐[S] 22 | 22 | 19 | $46
38 MacDougal St. (Prince St.), 212-475-7500
■ "Oh so Gallic" right down to the bill, this taste of "Paris in SoHo" "remains true to its bistro origins" while staying "old-fashioned in all the right ways"; "imaginative dishes", a "friendly, hip" staff and a "pretty garden" space explain why it's "still going strong."

Provi Provi S
18 | 17 | 17 | $33

228 W. 72nd St. (bet. B'way & West End Ave.), 212-875-9020

☑ "Giving new meaning to kosher dining", this West Side Italian is a "blessing" to believers who insist it's "so delicious you'll forget it's kosher"; still, a few heretics put down the "so-so menu" and tabs that would only be considered high on this block.

Puccini ●S
18 | 15 | 17 | $27

475 Columbus Ave. (83rd St.), 212-875-9532

■ "Mix-and-match pastas and sauces" make beautiful music together at this "small, romantic" Italian Westsider that's a favorite of the budget-minded; no wonder "it's always crowded."

Punch ●S
20 | 19 | 18 | $32

913 Broadway (bet. 20th & 21st Sts.), 212-673-6333

■ "Imaginatively decorated" Flatiron New American that "aspires to be a scene" and often is; if the droll menu's "outrageous descriptions" need "decoding", that's just part of its "fun approach."

Puttanesca ●S
19 | 16 | 17 | $30

859 Ninth Ave. (56th St.), 212-581-4177

☑ "Way off the beaten track", this Hell's Kitchen Italian still manages to be both "noisy" and "bustling", no doubt because it's both very good and "unbelievably cheap"; expansion has made the room "airy", but may have also slowed down service.

Q, a Thai Bistro (Queens) S
23 | 20 | 21 | $32

108-25 Ascan Ave. (bet. Austin & Burns Sts.), 718-261-6599

■ Forest Hills hosts this "affordable, adventurous" Thai that's "tiny" yet "comfortable"; "well-prepared", "top-quality" dishes and a "pleasant bistro" feel make for a "very Manhattan" experience.

Quake S
– | – | – | M

785 Broadway (10th St.), 212-505-7175

This roomy new Village Pan-Asian has lots going for it: an interesting, midpriced menu, sweet service and colorful contemporary decor; what it doesn't yet have is many patrons, but that makes it refreshingly quiet.

Quantum Leap S
17 | 10 | 16 | $18

88 W. Third St. (bet. Sullivan & Thompson Sts.), 212-677-8050
65-64 Fresh Meadow Ln. (67th Ave.), Queens, 718-461-1307

☑ Greens eaters ascend to "macrobiotic heaven" at these "cheap" Village and Queens "healthy living" Vegetarians; predictably, meat eaters dub them "pretty boring."

Quatorze Bis ●S
20 | 19 | 19 | $46

323 E. 79th St. (bet. 1st & 2nd Aves.), 212-535-1414

☑ "Very Parisian" "neighborhood bistro" catering to East Side "blue bloods" in search of "tasty French cooking"; ok, it's "pricey" ("but still cheaper than round-trip airfare") and service may be "snooty", but locals insist there's "none better" of its kind.

Quattro Gatti S
19 | 16 | 18 | $38

205 E. 81st St. (bet. 2nd & 3rd Aves.), 212-570-1073

☑ "Another reliable Italian" on the Upper East Side with roughly equal numbers of fans ("can't say enough") and foes ("the same as so many others"); the bottom line seems to be "fine if you're in the neighborhood", but not worth a "special trip."

Queen (Brooklyn) S
22 | 14 | 19 | $35

84 Court St. (bet. Livingston & Schermerhorn Sts.), 718-596-5955

■ "Homemade everything" makes up the moderately priced menu of this perennial Brooklyn Italian that's been a "courthouse crowd hangout" since 1958; though the "so-so" decor needs work, it won't deter anyone who enjoys "good, old-fashioned" cooking.

Quilty's [S] 24 | 20 | 21 | $49

177 Prince St. (bet. Sullivan & Thompson Sts.), 212-254-1260

■ Celebrated chef Katy Sparks' "lovely and imaginative" SoHo New American sets "high standards" in a "small, sparsely decorated" space where "serenity and good taste preside"; despite plenty of accolades, many feel this "strong performer" is still "underrated."

Rachel's American Bistro ◐[S] 19 | 15 | 18 | $31

608 Ninth Ave. (bet. 43rd & 44th Sts.), 212-957-9050

■ "Charming" and relatively "cheap", this Theater District American "cozy cottage" (aka "sardine city") is ultrapopular due to its "creative" food; "uncomfortable" at busy times, it's better for brunch when it's less crowded and there's light "to see what you're eating."

Radio Perfecto ◐[S]⊄ 20 | 18 | 18 | $24

190 Ave. B (bet. 11th & 12th Sts.), 212-477-3366

■ "Perfecto" chicken, fries and "special sauce" in a "whimsical" room using "old radios" for decor plus a "wonderful" garden are the reasons this "wallet-friendly" rotisserie "casts a glow in Alphabet City", but where's the "volume control knob?"

Rafaella Ristorante [S] 20 | 20 | 19 | $34

381 Bleecker St. (bet. Charles & Perry Sts.), 212-229-9885

■ "Ultraromantic" with "old Village feeling", this Italian stalwart's "well-done" pastas and "warm" vibes add up to "one of the city's best dining atmospheres", and it's surprisingly reasonably priced too.

Raffaele ◐ 21 | 14 | 20 | $43

1055 First Ave. (bet. 57th & 58th Sts.), 212-750-3232

◪ "A Sutton Place sleeper for great Italian food", "especially the specials", or a meal orchestrated by its "extremely friendly" owner; however, the "decor isn't so great" compared to its upscale prices.

Rafina [S] 20 | 14 | 19 | $35

1481 York Ave. (bet. 78th & 79th Sts.), 212-327-0950

■ For "a fresh taste of the Mediterranean" on the East Side, this Greek taverna's grilled whole fish at "fair prices" certainly suit; as its ratings indicate, the decor, despite renovations, lags.

Raga [S] 21 | 18 | 19 | $34

433 E. Sixth St. (bet. Ave. A & 1st Ave.), 212-388-0957

◪ "Inventive Indian fusion in an elegant-funky room" with "friendly" service sums up this young, modestly priced East Villager where "dessert can be a religious experience"; even critics are kind: "good concept: execution could improve."

Rain [S] 21 | 21 | 19 | $35

1059 Third Ave. (bet. 62nd & 63rd Sts.), 212-223-3669

100 W. 82nd St. (bet. Amsterdam & Columbus Aves.), 212-501-0776

■ Outstanding Pan-Asian menus, "great" bars, "knockout" Sadie Thompson settings and "attentive service" draw a "trendy" "young crowd" to this moderately tabbed crosstown pair; ergo, there's often a line but somehow they even "make it fun to wait for a table."

Rao's ⊄ 24 | 17 | 22 | $53

455 E. 114th St. (Pleasant Ave.), 212-722-6709

■ "A unique ambiance" (think "*Goodfellas* video"), "guaranteed" celebrity sightings and "lots" of very good Southern Italian food await at this amazing "East Harlem landmark" – that is, "if you can get a reservation" before the year 3000 (if you know owner Frank Pellegrino, maybe he can do something for you); parking is no problem, the bodyguards out front will watch your car.

Raoul's ●S
23 | 19 | 19 | $45
180 Prince St. (bet. Sullivan & Thompson Sts.), 212-966-3518
■ Long a hip fixture in the SoHo scene, this "archetypal French bistro", with its classic "dark" bar, "lovely" back garden, "great cooking" (e.g. "steak and snails") and "helpful" waitresses "with tatoos" has "aged beautifully" – très bien."

Rasputin (Brooklyn) S
▽ 17 | 20 | 17 | $56
2670 Coney Island Ave. (Ave. X), 718-332-8111
☑ "What a party" this Brighton Beach Russian puts on, with a "wonderful floor show" ($55 cover), "unusual" food "that never stops coming", "surly waiters" and "vodka, vodka, vodka"; still, some say the experience is more "like a bad family wedding."

Ratners S
18 | 9 | 12 | $23
138 Delancey St. (bet. Norfolk & Suffolk Sts.), 212-677-5588
☑ "For a real taste of Jewish NY", visit this "tacky" Lower East Side relic where "crotchety old waiters" are "part of the show" and the dairy menu (blintzes, matzoh brei) evokes "nostalgia" (and heartburn).

Raymond's Cafe S
▽ 18 | 15 | 19 | $29
88 Seventh Ave. (bet. 15th & 16th Sts.), 212-929-1778
☑ This "glorified" Chelsea luncheonette is one of those "friendly" neighborhood spots where the Continental food is nothing special "but the people are so nice, one likes to go there" anyway.

Red Cat ●S
▽ 23 | 21 | 21 | $39
227 10th Ave. (bet. 23rd & 24th Sts.), 212-242-1122
■ "Refreshingly unmodernist", this young Chelsea Mediterranean is "catnip to those who want creative food for not much 'scratch'", "a cozy room", "great service" and a lively scene; early visitors have made it their pet.

Redeye Grill ●S
21 | 20 | 18 | $42
890 Seventh Ave. (56th St.), 212-541-9000
■ A "big", "dramatic" "eyeful" with "tall ceilings", "great" food and "sleek" dining areas that are a "power scene" at lunch, Shelly Fireman's "happening" American brasserie opposite Carnegie Hall runs like a "smooth", well-oiled machine.

Red Garlic ●S
▽ 19 | 15 | 17 | $27
916 Eighth Ave. (bet. 54th & 55th Sts.), 212-489-5237
☑ Fka Siam Inn, this pre-theater "Thai standby" earns plaudits for "wonderfully fresh food" and a "helpful" crew; yet service (too little) and seasoning problems (too much garlic) make others "see red."

Regency S
20 | 22 | 21 | $53
(aka 540 Park)
Regency Hotel, 540 Park Ave. (61st St.), 212-339-4050
■ Everyone knows the "ultimate power breakfast" is served in this Tisch-family, East Side hotel dining room, but there's less buzz about the fact that it can also make you "feel like one of the big shots" at a "quiet lunch" or dinner with its "first-class" American food and service.

Regional Thai Sa-Woy S
▽ 22 | 25 | 22 | $36
1479 First Ave. (77th St.), 212-744-6374
■ "Sa-Wow" say those who've tried this Thai in a "gorgeous" East Side space and its "unusual" dishes (most "a delight"); though expensive for Asian food, it's more than fair in light of all it offers.

Regional Thai Taste S
19 | 14 | 16 | $25
208 Seventh Ave. (22nd St.), 212-807-9872
☑ A "funky" setting "belies the attention given to the food preparation and presentation" at this cheap Chelsea Thai; now they should work on improving the service.

F | D | S | C

Remi ◐[S] 23 | 22 | 21 | $49

145 W. 53rd St. (bet. 6th & 7th Aves.), 212-581-4242

■ "Beautiful" and "sophisticated", with "elegant" Venetian food, solid service and a lovely Adam Tihany–designed setting featuring a huge mural of the Grand Canal, this "expense-account" Midtowner is sure to "impress"; even its flaws – "tables too close together" – can be a plus given who your fellow diners are.

René Pujol 22 | 20 | 22 | $46

321 W. 51st St. (bet. 8th & 9th Aves.), 212-246-3023

■ "France without pretension" in a "tasteful, spacious dining room", this "theater country" mainstay offers "excellent" bourgeois cuisine and "cordial", timely service, all for a "reasonable" prix fixe.

Republic [S] 16 | 14 | 14 | $20

37 Union Sq. W. (bet. 16th & 17th Sts.), 212-627-7172

◪ Despite complaints about its "refectory" ambiance, picnic-bench seating and "absurd" decibel levels, sated surveyors slurp down the "tasty noodles" and Pan-Asian fast food at this Union Square teflon; even with so-so food, it's popular for being "hip" and "affordable."

Rialto ◐[S] 18 | 17 | 14 | $35

265 Elizabeth St. (bet. Houston & Prince Sts.), 212-334-7900

◪ "Dark, sexy, with red leather booths" and a "lovely" garden, this surprisingly good SoHo American attracts a "relaxed" young crowd whose top priority is more who they see than what they eat.

Ribollita ◐[S] 18 | 15 | 16 | $32

260 Park Ave. S. (bet. 20th & 21st Sts.), 212-982-0975

◪ A "rustic" setting and "hearty" Italian dishes like its "namesake" soup bring a taste of Florence to the Flatiron District; despite dissing for "uneven" food and "unpolished service", locals "feel at home."

Rice ◐[S]≠ 18 | 14 | 13 | $17

227 Mott St. (bet. Prince & Spring Sts.), 212-226-5775

■ "Healthy and hip", the fast food "alternative" dining at this "tiny" NoLita spot consists of rice with a variety of "A+" Eclectic toppings and "mellow" vibes; given "cramped quarters", some prefer takeout.

Rice 'n' Beans [S] 20 | 9 | 15 | $19

744 Ninth Ave. (bet. 50th & 51st Sts.), 212-265-4444
120 W. Third St. (bet. MacDougal St. & 6th Ave.), 212-375-1800

◪ "Chicken that falls off the bone" is one example of the "cheap", "fattening and delicious" Brazilian "homestyle" cooking dished up in this "tiny", "no-frills" Hell's Kitchen storefront and its Village kin.

Rinconcito Peruano [S] ▽ 21 | 7 | 16 | $20

803 Ninth Ave. (bet. 53rd & 54th Sts.), 212-333-5685

◪ This Hell's Kitchen hole-in-the-wall is "a great place" – and a cheap place – to try "homemade Peruvian cooking" prepared "with pride"; but don't look for any other amenities.

Rinçon de España [S] 20 | 13 | 18 | $32

226 Thompson St. (bet. Bleecker & W. 3rd Sts.), 212-260-4950

■ "Great paella" and "sangria that goes straight to your head", "hilarious mariachi" and "waiters with personality" add up to a perpetual weekend party at this "homey" ("maybe it's good that it's so dark") West Village Spaniard; ratings suggest the food's improving.

Rino Trattoria [S] ▽ 23 | 12 | 22 | $20

877 Eighth Ave. (bet. 52nd & 53rd Sts.), 212-307-0666

◪ In Midtown West, this small but "cute new Italian" is a "surprisingly good place for a business lunch", with "consistent" cooking and a "try-hard" crew – because its "owner is almost always there."

Rio de Janeiro's ◐⧈
19 | 16 | 18 | $35
127 W. 43rd St. (bet. B'way & 6th Ave.), 212-575-0808
■ Maybe your "big-eating cousin" from Texas can handle this AYCE "pig-out" Theater District churrascaria, but it makes ordinary mortals moan "the food comes out of your pores" – yet it's all good "fun."

Riodizio ⧈
18 | 16 | 17 | $36
417 Lafayette St. (bet. Astor Pl. & 4th St.), 212-529-1313
☑ An "endless parade" of grilled meat and pitchers of "powerful" drinks make this AYCE South American "burpfest" near Astor Place "festive", especially "for big groups" who have the next day free.

Rio Mar ◐⧈
19 | 12 | 15 | $27
7 Ninth Ave. (Little W. 12th St.), 212-242-1623
☑ "Inexpensive", "good" "garlicky food", a "low-key" tapas bar and "killer" sangria make this "low-rent" West Village standby feel "so Spanish, you forget you're in NY"; a few are not transported: "no atmosphere, food just ok."

Rive Gauche ⧈
17 | 16 | 15 | $35
560 Third Ave. (37th St.), 212-949-5400
☑ Murray Hill locals enjoy having this "authentic-feeling" French bistro with outdoor seating nearby; but some wish for "better" food and less "spotty service" from owners who know how to do better.

River ⧈
19 | 17 | 17 | $27
345 Amsterdam Ave. (bet. 76th & 77th Sts.), 212-579-1888
☑ "Tasty" versions of familiar Viet-Thai dishes, "friendly" manners and "good prices" type this West Side Asian; the unimpressed prefer to wait in Rain (though it's harder to get in).

RIVER CAFE (Brooklyn) ◐⧈
24 | 27 | 23 | VE
1 Water St. (Brooklyn Bridge), 718-522-5200
■ The "breathtaking" Downtown NYC skyline view from this "romantic" East River barge restaurant lures the most jaded Manhattanites to Brooklyn, where a "star-studded" ambiance, "excellent" American food and a "soft", gilt-edged "formality" enhance the "magical" setting; "I fell in love that night – with NY"; dinner is $70 prix fixe only.

Roberto's (Bronx) ⧈
24 | 13 | 19 | $35
632 E. 186th St. (Belmont Ave.), 718-733-9503
■ At the "best" Arthur Avenue–area Italian, owner "Roberto and his sister Anna [Paciulto] bring [you] back to the Amalfi Coast with every bite" of their "hearty" fare and "treat you like family"; despite dated decor, The Bronx never had it so good.

Rocco
∇ 20 | 14 | 19 | $33
181 Thompson St. (bet. Bleecker & Houston Sts.), 212-677-0590
☑ Offering some of NYC's "best" Italian pastries, this "old-fashioned" Village fixture also serves Italian comfort food in a "stuck in time" setting to mixed reviews: some say it's "like eating at your best friend's house", others shrug "routine."

Rocking Horse Cafe Mexicano ⧈
21 | 16 | 17 | $30
182 Eighth Ave. (bet. 19th & 20th Sts.), 212-463-9511
■ Though it "looks like a million other Mexican joints", this Chelsea cafe's food is "quite creative and surprisingly good" and it has a "friendly staff"; any problems? it's "too small and crowded."

Rodeo Bar & Grill ◐⧈
– | – | – | I
375 Third Ave. (27th St.), 212-683-6500
For BBQ, Tex-Mex and Texas-size steaks at reasonable prices, this Gramercy pub would be popular anyway, but the real draws here are the super country western setting (e.g. a stuffed full-size buffalo over the bar), nightly bands and free-flowing brew.

Roettele A.G. 🖪

18 | 16 | 17 | $31

126 E. Seventh St. (bet. Ave. A & 1st Ave.), 212-674-4140

☑ At its best "in warm weather" in its "hidden" garden, this East Village Swiss-German is a bit of a "rabbit warren" inside; still, it "satisfies winter cravings" for fondue or sauerbraten, but "order half of what they suggest" and you'll be stuffed.

Rolf's 🖪

17 | 18 | 15 | $32

281 Third Ave. (22nd St.), 212-477-4750

■ They still "do Christmas" with "wonderful", "over-the-top decor" and "special" goose, but this "festive" Gramercy German is a year-round excuse for overdosing on "substantial food" and beer.

Roppongi ●🖪

▽ 21 | 17 | 19 | $31

434 Amsterdam Ave. (81st St.), 212-362-8182

■ There's always room on the Upper West Side for another Japanese, especially when it has a "surprisingly fresh" approach to familiar dishes ("try the eel"), "reasonable prices" and "friendly service."

Rosa Mexicano ●🖪

23 | 19 | 20 | $41

1063 First Ave. (58th St.), 212-753-7407

■ "World-famous", "tableside-made guacamole and pomegranate margaritas" keep this "high-end" East Side Mexican "always packed" and "noisy" at night; still, "patience" is rewarded by "great authentic" food, pretty "people-watching" and "Baja kitsch."

Rosa's Place ●🖪

18 | 14 | 18 | $30

303 W. 48th St. (bet. 8th & 9th Aves.), 212-586-4853

☑ Handy to the theater, this Mexican dishes up "quality food" and keeps "refilling the pitcher of margaritas", all for a modest price; "you can pay less for better Mexican", but not with this location.

Rosehill

– | – | – | M

2 Park Ave. (32nd St., bet. Madison & Park Aves.), 212-684-2122

Larry Forgione has gently revamped the Murray Hill site of his An American Place (which decamped for Midtown) into a roomy, moderately priced seafooder enhanced by caring service and an impressively flexible wine list.

Rosemarie's

24 | 20 | 22 | $45

145 Duane St. (bet. Church St. & W. B'way), 212-285-2610

■ "Consistently excellent" food, "caring service" and a "civilized" environment explain why "one hates to leave" this TriBeCa Italian "treasure"; surveyors find it equally rewarding for a "quiet intimate dinner" or "business lunch."

Rose of India ●🖪

18 | 14 | 15 | $18

308 E. Sixth St. (bet. 1st & 2nd Aves.), 212-533-5011

☑ "Cramped, kitschy" and "cheap"; at one of Indian Row's "finest", plan on "cheesy dime-store Christmas decorations", "wacky birthday tributes" and lots of "spicy", "ok" food.

Rossini's ●🖪

20 | 18 | 21 | $44

108 E. 38th St. (bet. Lexington & Park Aves.), 212-683-0135

☑ Everything about this "comforting" Murray Hill "time warp", from the old-fashioned setting to the "good, traditional" Italian food and service to the Saturday night opera, strikes chords for its "over-50 crowd"; others sing another tune: "dated", "so-so."

Route 66 Cafe ●🖪

17 | 14 | 15 | $18

858 Ninth Ave. (bet. 55th & 56th Sts.), 212-977-7600

■ A "great cheap take on healthy diner food" typifies this coffee shop–style Hell's Kitchen Eclectic; its "amazing burgers", smoothies and "crowded brunch" scene keep the "nice staff" hopping.

Royal Siam 🖫
20 | 13 | 18 | $24

240 Eighth Ave. (bet. 22nd & 23rd Sts.), 212-741-1732

■ The Thai food is "reliable" and "tasty", service is "accommodating" and the lack of decor doesn't faze Chelsea neighbors who swear by it for "unpretentious" "after-movie" meals.

Roy's New York 🖫
24 | 22 | 24 | $46

Marriott Financial Ctr., 130 Washington St. (bet. Albany & Carlisle Sts.), 212-266-6262

■ A Hawaiian "sea breeze" wafts through this "light, bright", open-feeling Downtown venue for showman-chef Roy Yamaguchi's "very original", "tailored to fit NY", seafood-strong Asian-Euro fusion cuisine; delighted fans (saves a "12 hour flight") willingly forgive early glitches.

Ruby Foo's Dim Sum & Sushi Palace ●🖫
21 | 25 | 19 | $38

2182 Broadway (77th St.), 212-724-6700

■ "More fun with chopsticks can't be had" than at this 400-seat duplex West Side party-going "hot spot", a David Rockwell–designed "theatrical space" with "surprisingly good" Asian food ranging from "sushi to woks" and dim sum to Thai; it's "a bit chaotic" ("to put it kindly") and predictably "hard to get reservations."

Rungsit Thai 🖫
18 | 8 | 13 | $19

161 E. 23rd St. (bet. Lexington & 3rd Aves.), 212-260-0704

■ This "Tuesday night" fallback dishes up "generous helpings" of cheap, "down-home" Thai food in "grubby" Gramercy digs that scream "order the food and eat at home."

Russian Samovar ●🖫
19 | 18 | 18 | $41

256 W. 52nd St. (bet. B'way & 8th Ave.), 212-757-0168

■ Spend a "Russian evening" ("after the theater", preferred) at this handy Theater District location, where it's "all about the vodka and mood lighting", live music and almost too "authentic" food.

Russian Tea Room ●🖫
– | – | – | E

150 W. 57th St. (bet. 6th & 7th Aves.), 212-974-2111

With Tavern on the Green's showman owner Warner LeRoy at the helm, it's safe to predict that the newly rebuilt four-level Russian Tea Room – opened in 1927 by Russian émigré ballet stars and for decades a glittering nexus for NY's theatrical and literary sets – will be an eye-popping extravaganza, with such touches as the old Maxwell's Plum ceiling and a 16-foot-high crystal bear filled with live sturgeon; due to open as we go to press, RTR has just about everyone in NY, not just foodies, waiting to partake of its vodka, caviar and blini.

Ruth's Chris Steak House ●🖫
22 | 19 | 20 | $50

148 W. 51st St. (bet. 6th & 7th Aves.), 212-245-9600

☑ "Surprisingly competent", this franchise's "delicious", "sizzling", butter-drenched beef and "attractive", "library"-like Midtown setting are comforting to customers who find it "not as haughty" as its competition; critics say it "can't shake the out-of-town feel."

Sachi 🖫
∇ 20 | 12 | 16 | $34

1350 Madison Ave. (bet. 94th & 95th Sts.), 212-534-5600

■ The "Upper Madison crowd" descends on this "simple" Carnegie Hill Japanese for "big portions" of "fresh sushi" and "lunch box specials"; by area standards, it's a real deal.

Saffron 🖫
– | – | – | I

81 Lexington Ave. (26th St.), 212-696-5130

For bargain-priced Indian Vegetarian cuisine that's kosher to boot, you can't go wrong at this bright, clean Curry Hill newcomer; first-timers should try the house specialty saffron *khas,* a tasting of five dishes.

S'Agapo (Queens) ●S
∇ | 24 | 18 | 21 | $32

34-21 34th Ave. (35th St.), 718-626-0303

■ "Not your typical Astoria Greek" say partisans of this "first-rate" taverna (plus terrace) offering "outstanding" food and "friendly service"; enthusiasts line up for the experience.

Sahara (Brooklyn) ●S
∇ | 19 | 11 | 15 | $21

2337 Coney Island Ave. (bet. Aves. T & U), 718-376-8594

☑ "Dress down" and head to Gravesend for gyros, shish kebab and other "great", "cheap" Med-Mideast eats at this recently expanded restaurant; it's now Sahara-sized (600 seats) and there's a garden too.

Saigon Grill ●S
| 22 | 8 | 16 | $20

1700 Second Ave. (88th St.), 212-996-4600
2381 Broadway (87th St.), 212-875-9072

■ "Fresh, flavorful", bargain Vietnamese fare draws "overflow" crowds to these cross-the-park siblings; the decor is "the reverse of elegance" and service "brusque", but thankfully, they "deliver in a flash."

Sala ●S
| – | – | – | I

344 Bowery (Great Jones St.), 212-979-6606

It's tough to spot on a bleak Bowery block, but find this newcomer and you're in a low-lit, rustically sexy Spanish scene, with hip young things sipping sangria and sampling a menu ranging from *pinchos* (tastes) to full *platos,* all affordably priced.

Salaam Bombay S
| 22 | 18 | 18 | $32

317 Greenwich St. (bet. Duane & Reade Sts.), 212-226-9400

■ "Classy" decor and "attentive staff" can "make you feel like a rajah" at this TriBeCa Indian "oasis of calm"; "check out the sitar player" weekend nights and the "terrific" AYCE lunch/brunch buffet.

Salam Cafe & Restaurant S
| 21 | 16 | 16 | $28

104 W. 13th St. (bet. 6th & 7th Aves.), 212-741-0277

☑ "Quality" Med-Mideastern fare at "reasonable prices" (for wine too) makes this "hidden" West Villager worth seeking out; "friendly", if "haphazard", service and a "relaxed" vibe negate the "basement feel."

Sal Anthony's S
| 17 | 16 | 18 | $35

55 Irving Pl. (bet. 17th & 18th Sts.), 212-982-9030

☑ It's "somewhat past its prime", but this "comfortable", "old-style" Gramercy Italian remains a local "standby" thanks to "prix fixe bargains", a Caesar that's "still made right" and sidewalk tables.

Sal Anthony's S.P.Q.R. S
| 18 | 18 | 18 | $34

133 Mulberry St. (bet. Grand & Hester Sts.), 212-925-3120

☑ The "hearty", "better-than-average" Italian fare "pleases most" at this "big", "attractive" Little Italy stop with "quick service" and prix fixe "deals"; some rate it "standard", but it's a good bet to "impress" out-of-town guests.

Sala Thai S
| 20 | 14 | 17 | $27

1718 Second Ave. (bet. 89th & 90th Sts.), 212-410-5557

■ An "unpretentious" East Side "neighborhood standard" for "varied", "well-executed" Thai food at low prices; its "sweet service" offsets decor that's "a bit tattered."

Saloon, The ●S
| 14 | 13 | 14 | $29

1920 Broadway (64th St.), 212-874-1500

☑ Lincoln Center proximity, painless prices and "people-watching" from sidewalk seats keep this "huge", high-ceilinged American hopping despite "routine, pub-type" food, "noise" and "indifferent service."

Salt 🅂
19 | 19 | 17 | $37

507 Columbus Ave. (bet. 84th & 85th Sts.), 212-875-1993
■ "Surprisingly good" – "as it should be, since it's not cheap" is the impression given by this "trendy" Westsider's "skillfully prepared" Eclectic food and "dramatic" modern decor; what's more, service is "finally starting to catch up."

Salute! ◑🅂
17 | 17 | 15 | $33

270 Madison Ave. (39th St.), 212-213-3440
⚫ A lunch and happy hour "must" for Murray Hill office types, this "sunny", "open-kitchen" Tuscan earns salutes for its "good" pasta and pizza, but less-genteel gestures for "noise", service lapses and being "consistently underwhelming."

Sambuca, Trattoria 🅂
18 | 16 | 18 | $29

20 W. 72nd St. (bet. Columbus Ave. & CPW), 212-787-5656
■ It's not Carmine's, but this West Side "family-style" Southern Italian's fans tout its "huge portions" of "solid", fairly priced food and the fact that it's "quieter" than you-know-who; you can reserve too.

Sammy's Noodle Shop ◑🅂
18 | 9 | 13 | $17

453 Sixth Ave. (11th St.), 212-924-6688
⚫ "Huge, steaming bowls" of soup and "fat noodles" plus other "incredibly cheap" Chinese chow explain this Villager's appeal; it's certainly not the borderline "rude" service or "plain" room.

Sammy's Roumanian 🅂
18 | 11 | 15 | $43

157 Chrystie St. (Delancey St.), 212-673-0330
⚫ It's a nightly "bar mitzvah" party at this Lower East Side "Yiddish theme park" that's "so tacky, it's wonderful"; you'll imbibe frozen vodka along with "huge platters of cholesterol disguised as food", but it's "the most fun you can have legally in NY", so "bring Tums" and go.

Sam's Noodle Shop ◑🅂
19 | 8 | 15 | $17

411 Third Ave. (29th St.), 212-213-2288
■ "Chinatown without the trek" say Gramercy bargain-hunters who praise the "amazing noodle dishes" at this "efficient", "reliable" standby; C-town–caliber decor and "cramped" seats are minuses.

San Domenico 🅂
23 | 22 | 22 | $60

240 Central Park S. (bet. B'way & 7th Ave.), 212-265-5959
■ Tony May's "elegant", "refined" Central Park South celeb stomping ground serves chef Odette Fada's "inventive" Contemporary Italian fare at haute evening prices, but at a bargain for prix fixe lunch; at any hour, it's "a class act."

Sandoval 🅂
18 | 16 | 18 | $32

270 Columbus Ave. (bet. 72nd & 73rd Sts.), 212-362-3939
⚫ A "welcome" West Side addition with "above-average" SW fare and "eager" service in a "cool", "informal" setting; at "a few bucks less" and without the "rough edges", it could be a "hit."

San Giusto
20 | 19 | 21 | $47

935 Second Ave. (bet. 49th & 50th Sts.), 212-319-0900
■ "Old-fashioned" Midtown Northern Italian that's "a notch above" the norm in quality and price, with "excellent food", a "congenial host", comfortable quarters and graciousness "that never wavers."

San Pietro ◑
24 | 20 | 22 | $53

18 E. 54th St. (bet. 5th & Madison Aves.), 212-753-9015
■ A "stylish" Midtown Italian "place to be seen" catering to a "beautiful power crowd" with "extravagant" pasta, "fab fish" and "off-menu favorites"; it's pricey, "busy" and "a bit loud", but they sure "know what they're doing."

F	D	S	C

Santa Fe ◐[S] | 19 | 19 | 18 | $35

72 W. 69th St. (bet. Columbus Ave. & CPW), 212-724-0822

■ The fireplace and "peach-colored walls are sooo soothing", ditto the "great margaritas", at this West Side "SW staple"; its "tasty" cooking "with a twist" draws a loyal crowd ("look for TV stars").

Sant Ambroeus [S] | 21 | 17 | 18 | $41

1000 Madison Ave. (bet. 77th & 78th Sts.), 212-570-2211

◪ "Milan on Madison" sums up this "pricey" Northern Italian cafe; only Italy has "comparable cappuccino", pastries and pastas, but its tented back room is likened to "being gift-wrapped" or "eating in a coffin."

Sapore [S]🚫 ▽ | 19 | 13 | 18 | $21

55 Greenwich Ave. (Perry St.), 212-229-0551

■ It's "worth the wait" to score a table at this "tiny", "rustic" Village Italian given its "satisfying" "good pasta at the right price" served by an "adorable staff."

Sapphire Indian Cuisine [S] | – | – | – | M

1845 Broadway (bet. 60th & 61st Sts.), 212-245-4444

A sibling of Salaam Bombay, this Indian newcomer just north of Columbus Circle serves multiregional fare in an airy, serene space; though prices are slightly higher than the Indian norm, by any other standard it's a fair deal, and the $11.95 prix fixe lunch is a fantastic buy.

Sapporo East ◐[S] | 19 | 11 | 15 | $22

245 E. 10th St. (1st Ave.), 212-260-1330

■ Forget the "Japanese coffee shop" decor because this East Village "deal" serves "well-priced", "huge slabs" of "dependable sushi"; no reserving often means a "wait."

Sarabeth's [S] | 20 | 18 | 17 | $30

Hotel Wales, 1295 Madison Ave. (bet. 92nd & 93rd Sts.), 212-410-7335
Whitney Museum, 945 Madison Ave. (75th St.), 212-570-3670
423 Amsterdam Ave. (bet. 80th & 81st Sts.), 212-496-6280

■ To enter "brunch heaven" can require waiting in hellish lines at these "feminine" Americans best known for their baked goods and breakfasts but also offering "above-average" "comfort food"; critics ("cutesy-poo", "goyish", "dullsville") are easily outvoted.

Sardi's ◐[S] | 15 | 19 | 17 | $42

234 W. 44th St. (bet. B'way & 8th Ave.), 212-221-8440

◪ If this Theater District "institution" with "uninspired" Continental cooking "ain't what it used to be", it's still an "actors' hangout" and a "must-see" for its caricature-lined walls that conjure up "B'way magic."

Sarge's Deli ◐[S] | 18 | 9 | 13 | $21

548 Third Ave. (bet. 36th & 37th Sts.), 212-679-0442

◪ Though not the Carnegie, at "3 AM" in Murray Hill this "no-frills" deli is "close enough"; expect "open-wide" sandwiches and other "guilt"-producers, but no TLC from the "cranky" staff.

Saul (Brooklyn) **[S]** | – | – | – | M

140 Smith St. (Bergen St.), 718-935-9844

Don't blink or you'll walk right by the signless, brick exterior of chef Saul Bolton's (ex Bouley) Boerum Hill New American, an instant hit on the sizzling Smith Street dining scene thanks to appealing seasonal cuisine, polished low-key ambiance and modest prices given the quality.

Savann [S] | 20 | 15 | 17 | $37

414 Amsterdam Ave. (bet. 79th & 80th Sts.), 212-580-0202

◪ Plan on "creative", "well-priced" French food at this "dark", "much too cozy" West Side "sleeper"; a few foes claim it "used to be" better.

F	D	S	C

Savore ◐[S] 21 | 18 | 21 | $41
200 Spring St. (Sullivan St.), 212-431-1212
■ "Low-key" SoHo Northern Italian favored for its "lovely" food, "charming", "Tuscan yellow" setting and "solicitous", "friendly" staff; in sum, "a find."

Savoy [S] 23 | 22 | 22 | $46
70 Prince St. (Crosby St.), 212-219-8570
■ This small, "snob-free" "SoHo standout" serves "well-executed" Mediterranean fare in a setting exuding "country inn" warmth; though no bargain, most find it "delightful in every way", especially the chef's tasting menu.

Scaletta [S] 21 | 20 | 22 | $44
50 W. 77th St. (bet. Columbus Ave. & CPW), 212-769-9191
■ A "crowd-pleaser", this "not too glitzy", "spacious" West Side Northern Italian is "always good" if "never exciting", with a "comfy", conversation-friendly setting and "warm", "attentive service."

Scalinatella ◐[S] 24 | 17 | 20 | $55
201 E. 61st St. (3rd Ave.), 212-207-8280
■ "You're in another world" at this East Side Italian "basement grotto" offering "fantastic food" and what seems like "100 specials a night" in a setting that's "warm" and "charming" to most, but "claustrophobic" to a few; "if you have to ask, you can't afford it."

Scalini Fedeli – | – | – | VE
165 Duane St. (bet. Greenwich & Hudson Sts.), 212-528-0400
Occupying the gorgeous vaulted TriBeCa space that originally housed Bouley is this respected Italian import from Chatham, NJ (that state's No. 1 Italian); while it's too soon to predict the tastes from the kitchen with certainty, the owners sure have good taste in locations.

Scarabée [S] 22 | 20 | 21 | $50
230 E. 51st St. (bet. 2nd & 3rd Aves.), 212-758-6633
■ Behind the "buzz", this East Midtown Med-French yearling affords "well-executed", "interesting" food in a "peaceful, elegant" room with "attentive" service; still, a small faction feels it "misses, expensively."

Scopa – | – | – | E
27 E. 28th St. (bet. Madison Ave. & Park Ave. S.), 212-686-8787
Gramercy Italian "up-and-comer" from Vincent Scotto of Fresco fame; comprising a takeout shop, cafe and dining room, it has a "Euro atmo" (Venetian chandeliers) and fine food including grilled pizza.

Screening Room, The ●[S] 20 | 20 | 19 | $36
54 Varick St. (bet. Canal & Laight Sts.), 212-334-2100
■ "Dinner and a movie" dates were "never easier or better" than at this "trendy" TriBeCa American with its own "mini" cinema; its "clever" concept is backed up with "surprisingly good food", "swank" decor, "respectful service" and a good prix fixe deal.

S. Dynasty [S] ▽ 22 | 19 | 20 | $33
Hotel Lexington, 511 Lexington Ave. (48th St.), 212-355-1200
■ Midtown hotel-based Chinese that's a "great business lunch spot" thanks to "excellent" food and service, "reasonable" prices and "posh" (some say "Las Vegas Chinese") decor.

Sea Horse Grill [S] 18 | 17 | 16 | $36
787 Eighth Ave. (48th St.), 212-307-9449
■ "Good new Theater District option" offering "fresh", "eclectic seafood choices" in a "sunny" setting at "affordable prices"; service could "use improvement" though.

Seaport Soup Company S
∇ 20 | 9 | 15 | $12

76 Fulton St. (Gold St.), 212-693-1371
■ "Slurp it up" at what zealots dub the Seaport's "Le Cirque of soups", ladling out "delicious", "creative" concoctions plus sandwiches and salads; if "a little pricey", that comes with the location.

Seasons (Brooklyn) S
∇ 20 | 14 | 19 | $33

556 Driggs Ave. (N. 7th St.), 718-384-9695
✓ Now serving "comforting" Italian-French fare, this simple-looking Williamsburg "sleeper" with outside seats is a "find" for "good food" and "attentive" service at a "low price."

Second Avenue Deli ●S
22 | 10 | 15 | $22

156 Second Ave. (10th St.), 212-677-0606
■ For many NYers, this East Village "classic" sets "the standard" for kosher Jewish delis, from its "fabulous" pastrami, corned beef and matzoh ball soup to its "noisy, crowded", "free-for-all" ambiance; for noshing or "nostalgia", it's "the real thing."

Seeda Thai S
19 | 14 | 17 | $24

309 W. 50th St. (bet. 8th & 9th Aves.), 212-586-4040
■ A Theater District "bang for the buck" with "reliable", "tasty" Thai-Vietnamese fare, "pleasant service" and "inexpensive" prices that make up for its "lacking ambiance."

Seppi's ●S
∇ 22 | 21 | 20 | $45

Le Parker Meridien, 123 W. 56th St. (bet. 6th & 7th Aves.), 212-708-7444
■ If this "lovely" French bistro newcomer's "Downtown feel" seems "contrived" given its Midtown hotel setting and "Uptown prices", its "young, beautiful crowd" doesn't mind; a sibling to SoHo's Raoul's, it comes by its Downtown vibes naturally.

Serafina Fabulous Grill ●S
19 | 17 | 16 | $37

29 E. 61st St. (bet. Madison & Park Aves.), 212-702-9898
✓ Despite a name change (from Sofia), "pretty people" still "jam into" this East Side Italian for its "happening" scene and "surprisingly good" pizzas and grilled items, plus a pleasant choice of seating areas.

Serafina Fabulous Pizza ●S
20 | 17 | 15 | $34

1022 Madison Ave. (79th St.), 212-734-2676
■ "Go for the rooftop" terrace and "delicious, fresh-ingredient" pizzas and salads at this "superchic" East Side Italian "scene"; it's "affordable" for this zip code, hence "crowded" and "noisy."

Serafina on the Run ⊘
∇ 20 | 15 | 16 | $22

38 E. 58th St. (bet. Madison & Park Aves.), 212-832-8888
■ "Cute" East Side take-out/eat-in arm of the Serafina group that's a new "Euro" "lunch favorite" thanks to "great" salads and pastas; it does breakfast too – before its normal clientele is probably awake.

Serendipity 3 ●S
18 | 20 | 15 | $24

225 E. 60th St. (bet. 2nd & 3rd Aves.), 212-838-3531
✓ The "last of the great ice cream parlors" (don't miss the frozen hot chocolate) is this kitschy East Side toy store where "dessert counts more than dinner", but you can warm up on foot-long hot dogs and odd sandwiches ("BLT on challah – talk about an oxymoron"); despite "long lines", it's sure "fun for kids" and your "inner child"; even one's "cellulite dimples [leave] smiling."

Seryna
24 | 21 | 22 | $54

11 E. 53rd St. (bet. 5th & Madison Aves.), 212-980-9393
■ "Fork"-tender steak "cooked on a heated rock" is a standout at this "serene" Midtown Japanese "hideout" that also serves "serious sushi" and other "exceptional" fare; prices may seem high, but its "expense-account" clients aren't complaining.

Sesso 🅂
18 | 14 | 18 | $30

285 Columbus Ave. (bet. 73rd & 74th Sts.), 212-501-0607
■ "Nothing exceptional, but easy to like" West Side Italian with "affordable", "creative" food in a "relaxed", "intimate" upstairs dining room; there's also "good people-watching" from sidewalk seats.

Sesumi 🅂
▽ 19 | 16 | 18 | $28

1649 Second Ave. (bet. 85th & 86th Sts.), 212-879-1024
■ Look for "the usual Japanese" suspects (sushi, combo boxes, etc.), which are "well prepared" and well priced at this East Side "neighbor" that's also liked for its "quiet" ambiance and "at-home hospitality."

Settanta Sette ◐🅂
− | − | − | M

77 St. Marks Pl. (bet. 1st & 2nd Aves.), 212-777-2537
Early visitors to this elegant, new East Village contemporary Italian report "excellent food" and a crew that "obviously thinks service is an honorable profession"; there's a pleasant garden too.

Sette Mezzo ◐🅂⇚
21 | 16 | 18 | $45

969 Lexington Ave. (bet. 70th & 71st Sts.), 212-472-0400
🆉 Chic East Side regulars "run into everyone they know" at this "clubby" Italian with equally "excellent" "people-watching" and pastas; the downsides: "all-cash", too many tables "per square inch" and "dollops of arrogance" for unknowns.

Sette MoMA 🅂
17 | 20 | 17 | $39

Museum of Modern Art, 11 W. 53rd St. (bet. 5th & 6th Aves.), 212-708-9710; after 5 PM, enter at 12 W. 54th St.
🆉 Though the "pricey" Italian food is no masterwork, this Midtowner is helped by its "artistic" location, "sublime" terrace and view of MoMA's sculpture garden; active at lunch, it's "not crowded" at night.

Sevilla ◐🅂
21 | 14 | 17 | $32

62 Charles St. (W. 4th St.), 212-929-3189
■ The quality "never wavers" and the crowds never flag at this "friendly", sangria-fueled Spanish "garlic heaven" with "old-time Village atmosphere" and "delicious food" at "fair prices"; it's a "tight squeeze" and "needs a face-lift", but "there's no place like it – olé!"

Shaan 🅂
22 | 21 | 20 | $36

Rockefeller Ctr., 57 W. 48th St. (bet. 5th & 6th Aves.), 212-977-8400
■ Rock Center "Indian refuge" that should be "more popular" given its "first-rate" food and "opulent" space (which a few find "as warm as Grant's Tomb"); it all comes at "a decent price" via buffet lunch and pre-theater deals.

Shabu-Shabu 70 🅂
19 | 13 | 18 | $32

314 E. 70th St. (bet. 1st & 2nd Aves.), 212-861-5635
■ "Steady" East Side "neighborhood Japanese" that is packed in winter when you can "cook it yourself" on tabletop grills or opt for "fresh sushi"; expect "no pretensions" in looks, attitude or price.

Shabu-Tatsu 🅂
20 | 14 | 17 | $30

1414 York Ave. (75th St.), 212-472-3322
216 E. 10th St. (bet. 1st & 2nd Aves.), 212-477-2972 ◐
■ BBQ lovers "bring friends" to this "bright" Japanese duo and grill (or simmer) to their heart's content; it's "a good value" and helpful if dating someone "you have nothing in common with."

Shaffer City Oyster Bar & Grill
20 | 17 | 19 | $40

5 W. 21st St. (bet. 5th & 6th Aves.), 212-255-9827
■ "The owner is on-site and it shows" at this "witty, well-done" Flatiron fish house serving "excellent" seafood in a "cozy" "old tavern" space; though "pricey", it deserves "more recognition."

Shanghai Cuisine 🅂⇗   20 | 12 | 14 | $23
89 Bayard St. (Mulberry St.), 212-732-8988
☑ Soup dumplings and other "authentic" Shanghai eats make this a "class A" Chinatown choice; though typically "no-frills", it's "more comfortable" than most, albeit with the usual "rushed" service.

Shanghai Gourmet ◑🅂⇗   ▽ 20 | 8 | 13 | $16
57 Mott St. (bet. Bayard & Canal Sts.), 212-732-5533
☑ "A less-crazed" Chinatown "alternative for soup dumplings" and other "fresh" Shanghai-style fare; it may be a "sparse" storefront with sparse service, but it's the "place to be" for "cheap, good" eats.

Shanghai Tang 🅂   ▽ 20 | 14 | 16 | $26
77 W. Houston St., 2nd fl. (bet. W. B'way & Wooster St.), 212-614-9550 ◑
135-20 40th Rd. (Main St.), Queens, 718-661-4234
■ The "spacious" Flushing original has been joined by a new SoHo sibling, both serving "very good soup dumplings" and other bargain Shanghai fare (plus Japanese dishes in SoHo); go "with a group."

Shark Bar ◑🅂   20 | 16 | 17 | $32
307 Amsterdam Ave. (bet. 74th & 75th Sts.), 212-874-8500
■ Elbow "past the bar scene" and "feed your soul" on the "sumptuous" "Southern home cooking" at this West Side buppie "in crowd" fave; it has "good celeb-spotting" and the "best brunch nobody's heard of."

Sharz Cafe & Wine Bar 🅂   21 | 15 | 19 | $33
177 E. 90th St. (bet. Lexington & 3rd Aves.), 212-876-7282
■ "Pasta lovers and wine aficionados" both tout this "sweet", "good value" East Side "hole-in-the-wall" for its "ambitious" Med-Eclectic kitchen and "friendly" staff; sure it's a "tight squeeze."

Shinbashi   23 | 19 | 21 | $48
280 Park Ave. (48th St.), 212-661-3915
■ "High-end minimalist" Midtown Japanese touted for its "fine" sushi, sashimi and shabu-shabu as well as its "serene" ambiance; it's "a good place to talk", but talk ain't cheap here.

Shopsin's General Store   ▽ 21 | 15 | 15 | $22
63 Bedford St. (Morton St.), 212-924-5160
■ With a menu covering "as many cuisines as countries in the UN" and old general store ambiance, Kenny Shopsin's Village Eclectic is a "total trip"; plan on "good", "homey" grub, but "follow the rules" since the place is "not without attitude."

Short Ribs (Brooklyn) 🅂   18 | 15 | 16 | $27
9101 Third Ave. (91st St.), 718-745-0614
☑ "Bring your bib" and "wallow" in "monster portions" of "good ribs, burgers", chicken and the like at this Bay Ridge BBQ joint; it's "fun for kids" and there's "bar action" for adults, but plan to "leave deaf and very full", toting a doggy bag.

Shun Lee ◑🅂   24 | 21 | 21 | $43
43 W. 65th St. (bet. Columbus Ave. & CPW), 212-595-8895
■ "Any performance at Lincoln Center is improved" by a visit to Michael Tong's "upscale" West Side Chinese offering "scrumptious" food, "glamorous", black-and-white "'80s" decor and "celeb-spotting potential"; for Chinese, it's "the best in the West" (Side).

Shun Lee Cafe ◑🅂   21 | 17 | 18 | $33
43 W. 65th St. (bet. Columbus Ave. & CPW), 212-769-3888
■ "Who needs Chinatown" when you have this "fast, fun and tasty" Lincoln Center dim sum dazzler with "attractive" prices and mod decor; it's perfect pre-performance or as a "hangover buster."

Shun Lee Palace ◐[S] 24 | 22 | 22 | $46
155 E. 55th St. (bet. Lexington & 3rd Aves.), 212-371-8844
■ "Chinese reaches a new level" at Michael Tong's "classy" East Midtown flagship; it costs more than the norm, but is "fit for an emperor" with "superb" food, "elegant" Adam Tihany decor and "formal" service from waiters who "know what you like" better than you do – so take their advice and enjoy NY's "best luxe Chinese."

Siam Inn ◐[S] 21 | 14 | 18 | $26
854 Eighth Ave. (bet. 51st & 52nd Sts.), 212-757-4006
■ "Crisp, fresh, light" Thai fare featuring "spicy flavor combos" mark this "quiet" Theater District "good value"; the decor is a bit "droopy" but "courteous" service makes amends.

Sichuan Palace [S] ▽ 21 | 16 | 19 | $33
310 E. 44th St. (bet. 1st & 2nd Aves.), 212-972-7377
■ "The food rarely misses" at this "spacious, unhurried" UN-area Chinese with service that goes the extra mile; still, some feel it's "stuffy" with diplomat-geared prices.

Siena [S] 21 | 17 | 19 | $40
200 Ninth Ave. (bet. 22nd & 23rd Sts.), 212-633-8033
■ "Gino [Diaferia] and Scott [Bryan] have another winner" in this Northern Italian Chelsea yearling offering "simple", "well-prepared food"; it can be "relaxing" or "jungle"-like depending on the hour, and, though "no bargain", it's a "decent value."

Silk Road Palace [S]🚫 18 | 9 | 16 | $19
447B Amsterdam Ave. (bet. 81st & 82nd Sts.), 212-580-6294
■ "Big portions" of "good food" at "bargain prices" explains the line at this "basic" West Side Chinese; the "torturous waits" and lack of ambiance are offset by "hardworking staff" and "free wine" with dinner.

Silver Pond (Queens) ◐[S] 20 | 11 | 13 | $24
56-50 Main St. (bet. Booth Memorial & 56th Aves.), 718-463-2888
■ A "converted diner" in Flushing is the setting for "dim sum like in Chinatown" and "good Cantonese seafood" that was swimming around just minutes before being cooked; it won't win any decor prizes, but the price is right and "their English has improved."

Silver Swan ◐[S] 17 | 14 | 17 | $33
41 E. 20th St. (bet. B'way & Park Ave. S.), 212-254-3611
■ "If your cholesterol is ok", head to this "gut-busting" Flatiron German with *wunderbar* wursts, schnitzel, etc. plus "divine" beers in a "dark", "kitschy" setting; it's an "oasis when you're Italian-ed or French-ed" out.

Simply Caviar [S] ▽ 21 | 18 | 19 | $59
350 Park Ave. (51st St.), 212-838-3900
◪ Tendering a taste of "a gilded age" with its "superb sampler", this Midtown caviar house also offers "good", if pricey, French-Continental fare; despite solid ratings, critics say it has "untrained service" and "little charm" apart from its "view of St. Bartholomew's."

Sirabella's [S] 22 | 15 | 21 | $35
72 East End Ave. (bet. 82nd & 83rd Sts.), 212-988-6557
■ Locals would like to keep this "cramped but cozy" far East Side Italian "a secret", but that's not easy to do given its "bountiful" portions of "excellent" food, "warm service" and "good prices."

Sistina ◐[S] 22 | 18 | 20 | $51
1555 Second Ave. (bet. 80th & 81st Sts.), 212-861-7660
■ "Often forgotten", this "elegant" East Side "sleeper" "should be remembered" for its "fine" Northern Italian food and service; that it's "pricey" may explain the memory block.

	F	D	S	C

Smith & Wollensky ◐ [S] — 23 | 17 | 20 | $53

797 Third Ave. (49th St.), 212-753-1530

■ In just over 20 years, this East Midtown duplex has become entrenched as a "classic NY steakhouse" with all the genre's best attributes – "melt-in-your-mouth" steaks, "sublime" wines, a "manly" ambiance and "Armani suit" crowd, plus "deafening" noise and studiously "tough waiters"; now it's branched out to other cities with equal success.

Sobaya [S] — 20 | 19 | 17 | $25

229 E. Ninth St. (bet. 2nd & 3rd Aves.), 212-533-6966

■ "Your wallet won't complain" at this East Village Japanese noodle house and neither will your palate, given "fresh, healthy", "authentic" fare; its "tranquil" aura may make you "want to kick off your shoes and stay a while."

Soho Kitchen & Bar ◐ [S] — 16 | 16 | 15 | $28

103 Greene St. (bet. Prince & Spring Sts.), 212-925-1866

◪ "Airplane hangar"–size, brick-walled SoHo "staple" whose "basic" American food is just a layover between "wine flights"; "loud" as a runway, its "twentysomething" bar crowd seems oblivious to the fact that it "could be confused with Houlihan's or T.G.I. Friday's."

Soho Steak [S] ≠ — 20 | 15 | 15 | $33

90 Thompson St. (bet. Prince & Spring Sts.), 212-226-0602

■ You'll "get to know your neighbor" at this "impossibly noisy and crowded" SoHo French-American steakhouse, but since the crowd is "cool" that's not so bad and the food is a "tremendous value" – how often do you hear the words "underpriced steak"?

Sol (Brooklyn) [S] — ▽ 18 | 20 | 17 | $28

229 DeKalb Ave. (bet. Adelphi & Clermont Aves.), 718-222-1510

◪ "Interesting fusion in a funky 'hood" describes this little Fort Greene newcomer serving "creative" Caribbean-Asian fare at "Brooklyn prices" in a softly lit setting with a corrugated metal ceiling; doubters say "style only goes so far."

Solera — 21 | 20 | 20 | $46

216 E. 53rd St. (bet. 2nd & 3rd Aves.), 212-644-1166

■ Visit "Barcelona" in Midtown at this Spanish "oasis" offering "irresistible tapas" and other "authentic" fare in a "posh", "tiled townhouse" with helpful staff; it's "pricey" but "worth the visit."

Soma Park — ▽ 21 | 20 | 17 | $52

Lombardy Hotel, 109 E. 56th St. (bet. Lexington & Park Aves.), 212-750-5656

◪ There's "very interesting" New American food to be had in the "wonderful" Midtown space that once housed the renowned Laurent restaurant, but "high prices" and a rather "cold" feel dampen the mood for some; it's "quiet", thus good for private conversation.

Sonia Rose [S] — 22 | 20 | 21 | $49

150 E. 34th St. (bet. Lexington & 3rd Aves.), 212-545-1777

◪ "Everything about" this Murray Hill French-Eclectic "should bring crowds", but it's simply "not the same" and often empty since moving from its original site; still, by most accounts, it continues to produce an "excellent" meal.

Sono [S] — – | – | – | VE

106 E. 57th St. (bet. Lexington Ave. & Park Ave. S.), 212-752-4411

Foodies are salivating over this soon-to-open Eastsider, which brings Tadashi Ono's unique American-Japanese cuisine to the lavishly revamped former home of Le Chantilly; Ono is partnered with André and Rita Jammet (La Caravelle) and Larry Goldenberg (Gramercy Tavern, Union Square Cafe), so a pro operation is assured.

Sonora [S] ▽ 21 | 18 | 18 | $36

Eastgate Tower Hotel, 222 E. 39th St. (bet. 2nd & 3rd Aves.), 212-297-0280

■ Though "little known", this new, midpriced Murray Hill Nuevo Latino is "a keeper" thanks to its "seriously wonderful" fare and "great patio"; "save room for dessert" – the "dulche de leche rules."

Sosa Borella [S] ▽ 19 | 16 | 17 | $25

460 Greenwich St. (bet. Desbrosses & Watts Sts.), 212-431-5093

■ "What a find" say those who've uncovered this TriBeCa "diamond in the rough", a "quaint" Italian-Argentine cafe with sandwiches at lunch, meatier fare for dinner and "bang for your buck" anytime.

Soul Cafe ◐[S] 19 | 18 | 17 | $32

444 W. 42nd St. (bet. 9th & 10th Aves.), 212-244-7685

■ West Midtowner serving "upscale Soul Food" in a slickly "funky" setting with live music some nights; it's a "cool place to hang out", fill up "pre-theater" or "ring in a mellow Sunday afternoon" over brunch.

Soul Fixins' 20 | 7 | 15 | $12

371 W. 34th St. (bet. 8th & 9th Aves.), 212-736-1345

◪ The Soul Food is "addictive" and there's "great blues on the sound system" at this elemental storefront slice of "Harlem, or Georgia", near Penn Station; an "amazing bargain", it has "long lunch lines."

Souperman 20 | 6 | 12 | $12

77 Pearl St. (Stone St.), 212-269-5777

■ "The best lunch in lower Manhattan for the money" say devotees of Johannes Sanzin's "creative", "haute" soups and stews at this take-out favorite; it can be the highlight "of the work day."

SOUP KITCHEN INTERNATIONAL, AL'S ⊄ 26 | 4 | 8 | $12

259-A W. 55th St. (bet. B'way & 8th Ave.), 212-757-7730

■ "Don't be fooled by imitations", this Midtown hole-in-the-wall started the soup craze (with Seinfeld's help) and "has no competition"; "tourists make the line worse", but it moves fast if everyone "follows the rules" – if not, Al will "shake his dripping ladle" and it's "no soup for you!"; closed summers.

South Shore Country Club (S.I.) ▽ 21 | 23 | 20 | $40

200 Huguenot Ave. (W. Shore Expy., exit 4), 718-356-7017

◪ "They aim to please" at this Staten Island French-Continental with a "lovely" golf course view and "fine food"; a few critics say it's "uneven" and trying "to be NYC", at least price-wise.

SouthWest NY [S] – | – | – | M

2 World Financial Ctr. (Liberty St.), 212-945-0528

About to go into full swing at press time, this 300-seat WFC effort by Abraham Merchant (Merchants, La Fourchette) will offer affordable SW fare and, not unimportantly for the after-work crowd, 50-plus kinds of margaritas in an indoor/outdoor space with an alfresco lounge.

SPARKS STEAK HOUSE 25 | 19 | 21 | $57

210 E. 46th St. (bet. 2nd & 3rd Aves.), 212-687-4855

■ "What a steakhouse should be" say the myriad clients of this "huge", "packed with suits" Midtown "classic" offering prime beef that "cuts like butter" and an "unbelievable" wine list; some claim it "lost character" since expanding, but with the Cettas treating all customers as kings, it's still "awesome, baby!"

Spartina ◐[S] 21 | 19 | 19 | $43

355 Greenwich St. (Harrison St.), 212-274-9310

■ TriBeCa "Mediterranean delight" serving Stephen Kalt's "esoteric" food (including "divine" pizzas) in an "attractive" setting with "great outdoor tables"; it's a bit "pricey", but usually bats a "home run."

F	D	S	C

Spazzia S
19 | 15 | 17 | $37

366 Columbus Ave. (77th St.), 212-799-0150
☑ Spartina's new West Side sibling strikes most as a "welcome"
option for a "casual" Mediterranean meal, but "given its pedigree",
some "expected more", knocking "uneven food and service" in a
"cramped", "bland" space; time will tell.

Spencer S
– | – | – | E

119 E. 18th St. (bet. Irving Pl. & Park Ave. S.), 212-260-0100
Spencer Hugh Levy (ex Monkey Bar) has jumped into the Gramercy
Park fray with this new solo effort, attracting diners by blending
his homey, though not inexpensive, New American menu with an
understated yet refined and intimate dining room.

Spice S
19 | 13 | 16 | $24

1411 Second Ave. (bet. 73rd & 74th Sts.), 212-988-5348
199 Eighth Ave. (bet. 20th & 21st Sts.), 212-989-1116 ◐
☑ You can "tickle your Thai palate" cheaply at these "reliable" local
spots; given their decor or lack of it, "quick delivery" is a plus.

Spirit Cruises S
12 | 20 | 15 | $51

Pier 62, W. 23rd St. (Hudson River), 212-727-2789
☑ "Forget" the American buffet fare because "the skyline" is the main
course on these "floating party" harbor cruises with live entertainment;
it's "totally touristy" and not cheap, but it's a "nice ride."

Spring Street Natural ◐S
17 | 14 | 15 | $25

62 Spring St. (Lafayette St.), 212-966-0290
■ A "fixed point in a changing world", this SoHo Health Food mainstay
offers "wholesome" fare (veggie and non) plus "space to breathe" in
a comfy, "relaxed" setting; now "where's that waitress?"

Stage Deli ◐S
19 | 10 | 13 | $24

834 Seventh Ave. (bet. 53rd & 54th Sts.), 212-245-7850
☑ Tourists pack this Midtown deli for "unhinge your jaw" sandwiches
and theatrically "gruff" service; however, deli cognoscenti say it
can't compare "with the Carnegie or Second Avenue Deli."

Starbucks S
14 | 12 | 12 | $9

120 E. 87th St. (Lexington Ave.), 212-426-2580
1445 First Ave. (75th St.), 212-472-7784
Sony Plaza, 550 Madison Ave. (bet. 55th & 56th Sts.), 212-833-6102
280 Park Ave. (48th St.), 212-573-9869
330 Madison Ave. (42nd St.), 212-682-1880
77 W. 125th St. (Lenox Ave.), 917-492-2454
2379 Broadway (87th St.), 212-875-8470 ◐
1841 Broadway (60th St.), 212-307-0162
322 W. 57th St. (bet. 8th & 9th Aves.), 212-399-0714
682 Ninth Ave. (47th St.), 212-397-2288
600 Eighth Ave. (39th St.), 212-997-7337
494 Eighth Ave. (35th St.), 212-947-3860
462 Seventh Ave. (35th St.), 212-279-6432
684 Sixth Ave. (22nd St.), 212-691-1948
21 Astor Pl. (Lafayette St.), 212-982-3563 ◐
78 Spring St. (Crosby St.), 212-219-2961
55 Broad St. (Beaver St.), 212-742-2488
45 Wall St. (bet. Pearl & William Sts.), 212-269-8717
Battery Park, 24 State St. (Pearl St.), 212-482-1180
314 E. Fordham Rd. (Elm Pl.), Bronx, 718-329-9026
Plus other locations throughout the NY area.
☑ "Ubiquitous, but much maligned" coffee bar chain providing addicts
a "welcoming place" to "wait, meet, drink and pee" while griping
about "Stepford" servers and paying "too much" for a daily "high
octane" fix; critics say "kill it before it spreads."

St. Dymphnas ◐[S] 16 | 15 | 16 | $19

118 St. Marks Pl. (bet. Ave. A & 1st Ave.), 212-254-6636

■ "The patron saint of Mental Health shines" on this East Village Irish pub with its "good Guinness", fish 'n' chips, real Irish breakfast and the chance to "feel" what it's like "in Donegal" – "join the locals" on Sunday afternoon in the garden.

Steak au Poivre ◐[S] 18 | 16 | 16 | $36

1162 First Ave. (bet. 63rd & 64th Sts.), 212-758-3518

◩ "He's baack" – irrepressible chef David Ruggerio returns to the kitchen in (what some term) "a small-scale triumph" for this French-accented East Side steakhouse; while praised for its "pre-theater deal" and ambiance, "so-so steaks" and "touch-and-go" service are serious drawbacks.

Steak Frites ◐[S] 18 | 16 | 16 | $36

9 E. 16th St. (bet. 5th Ave. & Union Sq. W.), 212-463-7101

◩ "French fries are unhealthy, but who can resist?", especially when paired with a "juicy steak" or mussels in this "noisy", atmospheric French bistro near Union Square; service is its weak point.

Stella del Mare 20 | 18 | 20 | $44

346 Lexington Ave. (bet. 39th & 40th Sts.), 212-687-4425

■ With a "charming piano bar downstairs" and an "attentive" dining room above, this Murray Hill Italian with "very fresh fish dishes" plays an "old-fashioned", but pleasing, tune for a "houseful of locals."

Stingy Lulu's ◐[S]≠ 14 | 17 | 14 | $19

129 St. Marks Pl. (bet. Ave. A & 1st Ave.), 212-674-3545

◩ An East Village "romp" with drag queen waitresses, dark '50s "retro decor", "zany" pin-cushion patrons and "bargain" American eats, but "Lulu's too stingy with cooking ability" to please everyone.

St. Maggie's Cafe 18 | 17 | 18 | $33

120 Wall St. (bet. Front & South Sts.), 212-943-9050

◩ With "not much on Wall Street" by way of a "conservative setting for a work lunch", most rate this Victorian's American food and service "decent" to "good"; its "great bar" is one of the area's "best hangouts."

St. Michel (Brooklyn) [S] 24 | 19 | 22 | $42

7518 Third Ave. (bet. 75th & 76th Sts.), 718-748-4411

■ "Terrific all-around", this "intimate" and "romantic French bistro" in Bay Ridge is the "next best thing to going to Paris" – and this "gem" definitely beats paying "Manhattan prices."

Sud ◐[S] ▽ 18 | 14 | 18 | $32

210 W. 10th St. (bet. Bleecker & W. 4th Sts.), 212-255-3805

■ "Tremendous food with tremendous waits" – the latter are hardly surprising since this Village French-Mediterranean has about 20 seats, "varied", "unusual" fare and is "very polite" and "inviting."

Sugar Bar ◐[S] 19 | 22 | 18 | $40

254 W. 72nd St. (bet. B'way & West End Ave.), 212-579-0222

■ Don't be surprised if Nick Ashford or Valerie Simpson greets you "at the door" of their "lovely" Afro-Asian-Mediterranean Westsider – it's a hands-on operation whose "wonderful" African ambiance, secret garden and "exotic" flavors captivate.

Sugiyama ▽ 28 | 21 | 25 | $72

251 W. 55th St. (bet. B'way & 8th Ave.), 212-956-0670

■ A "Tokyo"-level kaiseki dinner at this Midtown Japanese is an "incredible" "dining adventure" capturing the essence of its genre with "exotic" ingredients, "lovely presentation" and a serene setting; chef-owner Nao Sugiyama (ex Katana) is seemingly everywhere; in short, "a treat!", albeit an expensive one.

Sultan, The 🄂   ▽ 21 | 15 | 21 | $29
1435 Second Ave. (bet. 74th & 75th Sts.), 212-861-0200
■ Turkish food, with its "intricate" flavors, is "made easy" at this "fresh", "well-priced" (most entrees below $12) Upper Eastsider whose staff is "enthusiastic and helpful" – besides, "who doesn't like eating meat on sticks?"

Sung Chu Mei 🄂   ▽ 20 | 12 | 21 | $19
615 Hudson St. (bet. Jane & 12th Sts.), 212-675-0016
■ "No [place] is friendlier" or more obliging ("custom-make anything") than this "bright" West Village Chinese whose "reliable" (if "not very original") food is good enough to keep this place "clubby."

Sunny East 🄂   ▽ 19 | 15 | 18 | $30
21 W. 39th St. (bet. 5th & 6th Aves.), 212-764-3232
🄄 "Good Chinese food" and "nice decor" in a Garment District location ("where you least expect it") explains why this "pro" spot is "busy for lunch", yet "quiet" at night; but a few warn it's "slipping a little."

Supper Club, The   16 | 22 | 17 | $48
240 W. 47th St. (bet. B'way & 8th Ave.), 212-921-1940
■ Dress up for an "adult prom date" in this "elegant, retro" big band ballroom just off Broadway, with "decent" French-Continental food and service, as if you cared – "you're there to dance" and to "watch the hard-core", "glad rag–clad pros."

Sur (Brooklyn) ◑🄂   21 | 18 | 17 | $32
232 Smith St. (bet. Butler & Douglass Sts.), 718-875-1716
■ "Chic" comes to Carroll Gardens at this "accommodating" brick-walled Argentine steakhouse with beef "flown in from the pampas", "sumptuous desserts", "good prices" and a hip crowd – resulting in the "tightest seating" imaginable.

Surya 🄂   21 | 19 | 16 | $38
302 Bleecker St. (bet. Grove St. & 7th Ave. S.), 212-807-7770
🄄 Besides serving "sophisticated" modern Indian food in a "stylish" setting, this West Villager hosts a major scene with "model sightings"; one critic quips "service may be outpaced by glaciers."

Sushiden   23 | 18 | 20 | $45
19 E. 49th St. (bet. 5th & Madison Aves.), 212-758-2700
123 W. 49th St. (bet. 6th & 7th Aves.), 212-398-2800
■ Corporate types "bring clients and a credit card" to these "spartan" Midtown Japanese for "some of the best fresh sushi in the city"; they're often "noisy and cramped, but the food is worth it."

Sushi Hana ◑🄂   22 | 15 | 17 | $30
1501 Second Ave. (78th St.), 212-327-0582
■ "Unfortunately, the entire East Side is onto" this modest Japanese "sushi steal", so expect to "wait" for the "freshest and biggest pieces of fish anywhere"; there are also "delicious" dumplings and tempura and takeout to avoid being "rushed."

Sushihatsu ◑🄂   23 | 14 | 18 | $51
1143 First Ave. (bet. 62nd & 63rd Sts.), 212-371-0238
■ "Amazing sushi" at "Tokyo prices", but it's "worth the cost" since you're paying for "excellent quality and technique" at this East Side Japanese; presumably you're not paying for the "nonexistent decor."

SUSHI OF GARI 🄂   26 | 13 | 18 | $47
402 E. 78th St. (1st Ave.), 212-517-5340
■ Eastsiders lament that others know about their 35-seat "secret sushi heaven" where you "sit at the sushi bar", "put your trust in [chef-owner] Gari" and are rewarded by his "extraordinary" preparations; just "don't plan on lingering."

Sushi Rose

23	17	17	$38

248 E. 52nd St., 2nd fl. (bet. 2nd & 3rd Aves.), 212-813-1800
■ At this "intriguing" East Midtown sushi yearling, the "freshest ingredients" are handled almost as if "sacred"; customers feel "comfortable" and the Japanese food is "inexpensive" and "good" – all in all, a "great neighborhood stop."

SUSHISAY

26	18	21	$48

38 E. 51st St. (bet. Madison & Park Aves.), 212-755-1780
■ "Clean, spare, traditional" in appearance and "incredibly well-run", this "very authentic" Nipponese's "fresh, perfectly seasoned and prepared" sushi and sashimi bring "Ginza taste, and also prices", to Midtown's "best" Japanese business lunch; "you're in capable hands", so go ahead and "indulge."

Sushi Sen-nin

▽ 26	18	21	$38

49 E. 34th St. (bet. Madison & Park Aves.), 212-889-2208
■ In Murray Hill, this little-known Japanese slices top "quality sushi" and lobster sashimi that's so fresh it may blink at you from the plate; as "one of the best", it's priced accordingly.

Sushiya 🅂

20	14	17	$29

28 W. 56th St. (bet. 5th & 6th Aves.), 212-247-5760
■ "No-nonsense" Midtown Japanese that is "cheaper than the high-end places, but very, very good", with "big slices of fresh fish" and "relaxing", if minimal, decor – even the service is "not too bad."

Sushi Zen

23	17	20	$43

57 W. 46th St. (bet. 5th & 6th Aves.), 212-302-0707
■ "Intricate and beautiful" is how acolytes describe the "unique" sushi at this "peaceful" Theater District Japanese, adding that its "cooked food is wonderful" too; apart from "cramped seating" and "expense-account" pricing, its karma is "good."

Sweet Mamas (Brooklyn) 🅂⊄

–	–	–	M

168 Seventh Ave. (bet. 1st St. & Garfield Pl.), 718-768-8766
Southern comfort in Park Slope comes with Formica tabletops, mismatched chairs and C&W on the jukebox serenading locals who saunter in for finger-lickin' good catfish, chicken-fried steak and Coca-Cola baked ham, all at down-home prices; can I get you some hush puppies with that, hon?

Sweet Melissa Pâtisserie (Brooklyn) 🅂⊄

▽ 23	18	18	$15

276 Court St. (bet. Butler & Douglass Sts.), 718-855-3410
■ "Melissa (Murphy) really exists", and her bargain "sophisticated sweets", "delicious" salads and light French fare plus "delightful" backyard and "sweet small space" have Cobble Hillers crowing: "heaven", "a Saturday morning must."

Sweet-n-Tart Cafe ⦿🅂⊄

20	9	12	$14

20 Mott St. (bet. Chatham Sq. & Pell St.), 212-964-0380
76 Mott St. (Canal St.), 212-334-8088
136-11 38th Ave. (Main St.), Queens, 718-661-3380
■ These "unique little joints" specialize in *tong shui* (Chinese health tonics), Hong Kong cafe snacks, noodles and "amazing" fruit shakes; given their "low prices", you can "experiment freely."

Swifty's ⦿🅂

–	–	–	M

1007 Lexington Ave. (bet. 72nd & 73rd Sts.), 212-535-6000
Upper East Side socialites who've had nowhere to lunch since the demise of Mortimer's look forward to the opening of this midpriced clone boasting the same chef, maître d' and straightforward American fare as the original; hopefully, the old attitude has not been transplanted.

Sylvia's [S] 19 | 13 | 17 | $28

328 Lenox Ave. (bet. 126th & 127th Sts.), 212-996-0660

■ A justly celebrated Harlem institution whose "sink to the bottom of your belly Soul Food", rich desserts, "warm energy" and live music, all at low tabs, keep it "mobbed with tourists", "famous people" and jazz buffs; the "gospel choir" brunch is a real experience.

Syrah [S] 18 | 16 | 19 | $36

1400 Second Ave. (bet. 72nd & 73rd Sts.), 212-327-1780

◪ "Uncork and unwind" could be the mantra of this Upper East Side Mediterranean with its "interesting pairing of wine and food" and its "enthusiastic" owner and "caring" staff; still, in the face of "tough local competition", some find it "ordinary."

TABLA [S] 26 | 26 | 25 | $58

11 Madison Ave. (25th St.), 212-889-0667

■ Another Meyer "grand slam", this new Indian-spiced American on Madison Square Park became an instant hit thanks to chef Floyd Cardoz's "exciting" food, an "exotic", stylish duplex setting and "super" service; if a few cite "weird" combos, the vast majority says "everything works" and "the hype", and cost ($52 prix fixe dinner, except at the Bread Bar downstairs), are "justified."

Table d'Hôte [S] 22 | 18 | 21 | $43

44 E. 92nd St. (bet. Madison & Park Aves.), 212-348-8125

■ While this Carnegie Hill Franco-American is *très petit*, it's "worth squeezing into" for "unfailingly superior" food, "formidable" service and "calm" "rustic charm"; check out the "bargain" prix fixe.

Tai Hong Lau [S] ▽ 20 | 8 | 11 | $25

70 Mott St. (bet. Bayard & Canal Sts.), 212-219-1431

◪ You feel like you "crashed a Chinese wedding banquet" at this big, "noisy" C-town Cantonese with a wide range of cheap fare plus fine dim sum; expect the usual "no atmosphere" and harried service.

Taka [S] 25 | 14 | 19 | $34

61 Grove St. (bet. Bleecker St. & 7th Ave. S.), 212-242-3699

■ At this "tiny" Village Japanese, "masterful" chef-owner Takako Yonzyama offers platters of "unique rolls" and sushi that's "up there with the best"; two reasons to go early: it gets very "crowded quickly" and "the early bird is a steal."

Takahachi ◐[S] 21 | 14 | 16 | $27

85 Ave. A (bet. 5th & 6th Sts.), 212-505-6524

■ "Large pieces" of "succulent sushi" at "East Village prices" are why this underdecorated, dinner-only Japanese is "always crowded"; there are plenty of other "consistent" dishes plus "great sake."

Tang Pavilion [S] 22 | 17 | 20 | $32

65 W. 55th St. (bet. 5th & 6th Aves.), 212-956-6888

■ "Good Shanghai cooking" is the highlight at this "upscale" Midtown Chinese "find" for "authentic", modestly priced food (try "the unusual dishes"); the staff is "helpful", if sometimes "hurried."

Tanti Baci Caffé [S] 20 | 16 | 18 | $24

163 W. 10th St. (bet. 7th Ave. S. & Waverly Pl.), 212-647-9651

■ Some of NY's "most affordable homemade Italian" food draws crowds to this "cramped" but "cute" Village "basement bargain" with "warm service"; though "difficult to find", it's "worth the effort."

Taormina ◐[S] 22 | 17 | 20 | $37

147 Mulberry St. (bet. Grand & Hester Sts.), 212-219-1007

■ "One of the nicer-looking restaurants in Little Italy" is also "a cut above" in terms of its "very good" Italian fare and "gracious" staff; a former John Gotti hangout, it still offers "good people-watching."

F | D | S | C

Taperia Madrid ◑[S] — – | – | – | M

1471 Second Ave. (bet. 76th & 77th Sts.), 212-794-2923

Compadres of this East Side tapas house perch on benches at long wooden communal tables or on stools in the wine cellar–like downstairs sampling midpriced mini dishes; come early if you want to snag a seat for the 9:30 PM Monday flamenco show.

Tapika [S] — 21 | 21 | 19 | $43

950 Eighth Ave. (56th St.), 212-397-3737

■ "Cowboy-size portions" of "fiery, creative" SW fare including "excellent steaks" are the focus at this roomy, attractive Midtowner; it's "not for wimpy palates" or wallets, but the $28 pre-theater prix fixe is a "saving grace."

Taqueria de Mexico [S]⊄ — 19 | 12 | 15 | $21

93 Greenwich Ave. (bet. Bank & W. 12th Sts.), 212-255-5212

■ "The real enchilada" say fans of the "authentic" Mexican food at Mi Cocina's "cute" Village sister; it's "inexpensive" and "cozy" to the point of being "uncomfortable", but luckily there's always takeout.

Tartine [S]⊄ — 22 | 15 | 15 | $24

253 W. 11th St. (W. 4th St.), 212-229-2611

■ "Almost Paris" sums up this "tiny", "tippy-tabled" West Village bistro with "earthy, hearty" fare, brunch and desserts to "drool" over and "attitude city" service; "go at off-hours" as the low prices and BYO policy draw "crazy" lines of "young" patrons.

Tatany [S] — 22 | 14 | 17 | $30

380 Third Ave. (bet. 27th & 28th Sts.), 212-686-1871

Tatany 52 ◑[S]

250 E. 52nd St. (bet. 2nd & 3rd Aves.), 212-593-0203

■ Japanese neighbors that "rarely let you down", offering "big pieces of fresh sushi" at "very good prices"; "decor and service could be better" but they're still "popular", i.e. "cramped", "crowded."

Taverna Kyclades (Queens) ◑[S] ▽ — 22 | 15 | 18 | $30

33-07 Ditmars Blvd. (bet. 33rd & 35th Sts.), 718-545-8666

■ All one expects of an Astoria taverna can be found here: "good grilled fish", lamb dishes and other Greek fare in "big portions" at modest prices plus lots of locals having "noisy" "fun"; there's not much decor but that comes with the territory.

Taverna Vraka (Queens) ◑[S] ▽ — 20 | 15 | 18 | $36

23-15 31st St. (bet. 23rd & 24th Aves.), 718-721-3007

■ "You're in Greece", especially on live music nights, at this Astoria taverna serving appealing food at moderate prices; however, it's "quiet" when the musicians have the night off.

Tavern on Jane ◑[S] — 18 | 15 | 17 | $27

31 Eighth Ave. (Jane St.), 212-675-2526

■ "Cozy", "tavern"-like "hangout" that's a second "living room" for West Villagers; the "affordable" American menu goes beyond "good pub grub" and a "lively spirit" makes this a place to "unwind."

TAVERN ON THE GREEN [S] — 17 | 25 | 18 | $51

Central Park West (bet. 66th & 67th Sts.), 212-873-3200

◪ A "must-see" "NYC extravaganza", Warner LeRoy's world-famous Central Park "fairyland" with its "glitz and glitter" decor is "magical" at any time, but even more so "when snow falls" or outdoors in summer; its American food can be quite good if kept simple and has never stopped it from drawing tourists and not a few Gothamites who admit it's "a hell of a show" and one of NYC's best party sites; P.S. check out the early-bird prix fixe.

F | D | S | C

Tazza [S] 20 | 16 | 20 | $30
196 Eighth Ave. (20th St.), 212-633-6735
■ "Solid" Chelsea Mediterranean that's "good" pre-Joyce and fine anytime for tasty "comfort food" served by "cooperative", "campy" staff; it's "cute", "quiet" and low cost, especially the early bird.

Tea Box, The [S] 22 | 22 | 19 | $26
Takashimaya, 693 Fifth Ave. (bet. 54th & 55th Sts.), 212-350-0180
■ So "serene and soothing" it "beats therapy", this "oasis" in the Takashimaya store offers elegant Midtown "escapism"; besides a "potpourri of teas", there's "light" Japanese-American fare and "delightful" bento box lunches.

Tello's Ristorante [S] – | – | – | M
263 W. 19th St. (bet. 7th & 8th Aves.), 212-691-8696
Looking like the set of a Martin Scorsese film, this midpriced Chelsea Italian fills a void in this red sauce–barren area, with chef Alonso Tello promising Italian cooking 'the way it was meant to be' – time will tell.

Telly's Taverna (Queens) ◐[S]⌀ 23 | 12 | 19 | $31
28-13 23rd Ave. (bet. 28th & 29th Sts.), 718-728-9056
■ "Welcome to the Adriatic" in Astoria; grilled fish at its "juiciest" stars at this "friendly" storefront, but there are also "excellent" appetizers and grilled meats, all at modest prices; "sit in the garden" for ambiance.

Temple Bar ◐[S] 15 | 24 | 16 | $29
332 Lafayette St. (bet. Bleecker & E. Houston Sts.), 212-925-4242
■ People allude more to adultery and martinis than the nibbles at this "swanky" NoHo bar; some find the crowd "hatefully hip", but in a place this "seductive", it behooves you to focus on just one person.

Ten Kai [S] 19 | 13 | 17 | $32
20 W. 56th St. (bet. 5th & 6th Aves.), 212-956-0127
■ A boon to Midtown office workers, this "consistent, basic Japanese" has "fab sushi and sashimi", "good value" lunch specials and "caring" service; if "rushed" at noon, it's "quiet at night."

Tennessee Mountain [S] 16 | 12 | 14 | $26
121 W. 45th St. (bet. B'way & 6th Ave.), 212-869-4545
143 Spring St. (Wooster St.), 212-431-3993
◪ You "need two bibs to eat the ribs" and fried chicken at this SoHo (original) and Times Square (bigger) BBQ duo serving "mountains" of "messy" chow; some call it "delicious", others sneer "down-home it ain't", but low prices make them ideal for pig outs.

Teodora [S] 21 | 17 | 19 | $39
141 E. 57th St. (bet. Lexington & 3rd Aves.), 212-826-7101
■ Though "easily overlooked", this "unpretentious" East Side Northern Italian provides "surprisingly good" food in a "small, attractive" space; the staff "tries hard" and the "price is right" too.

Teresa's [S]⌀ 18 | 10 | 15 | $18
103 First Ave. (bet. 6th & 7th Sts.), 212-228-0604
80 Montague St. (Hicks St.), Brooklyn, 718-797-3996
■ You can "fill up" on "budget" blintzes, borscht and other "Polish peasant fare" at these plain-Jane coffee shops; they "feel like family" dining right down to staffers who don't hide their bad moods.

Terrace, The 24 | 26 | 23 | $58
400 W. 119th St. (Amsterdam Ave. & Morningside Dr.), 212-666-9490
■ For "elevated dining", "take a lover" to this "romantic" Morningside Heights rooftop French-Eclectic that proves "you can have both outstanding views and fabulous food"; about to reopen at press time after a renovation and chef change, it may seem "as expensive as tuition" at Columbia, but it's a summa cum laude experience.

Tevere 84 S
22 19 19 $46
155 E. 84th St. (bet. Lexington & 3rd Aves.), 212-744-0210
■ "You don't have to be kosher" or well-heeled to love this Upper East Side Northern Italian, but it sure helps; plan on "terrific" food and service in an "elegant", "cozy" setting.

T.G.I. Friday's
10 11 11 $22
604 Fifth Ave. (bet. 48th & 49th Sts.) 212-767-8335 S
47 E. 42nd St. (bet. Madison & Vanderbilt Aves.), 212-922-5671 S
1680 Broadway (52nd St.), 212-767-8326 ●S
21 W. 51st St. (bet. 5th & 6th Aves.), 212-767-8352 S
761 Seventh Ave. (50th St.), 212-767-8350 ●S
484 Eighth Ave. (34th St.), 212-630-0307 S
47 Broadway (Exchange Pl.), 212-483-8322
☑ If the staff can "remember what you ordered", this American beer and burger "mall food" chain will do for a "quick bite" or "with kids" in tow; critics ask "who let them in?"

Thady Con's S
15 19 18 $24
915 Second Ave. (bet. 48th & 49th Sts.), 212-688-9700
■ To enjoy "Galway without the dampness", try this "convivial" East Midtown Irish pub stoked by four working fireplaces and an open tap; the "plain" but hearty food goes well with "a proper pint."

Thai Cafe (Brooklyn) S⊘
▽ 22 12 17 $20
923-925 Manhattan Ave. (Kent St.), 718-383-3562
☑ "Williamsburg artists" aren't starving thanks to this "excellent value" Greenpoint Thai and its "well-served", "good and spicy" food; but they may wince at the "questionable decor."

Thai House Cafe ⊘
22 11 19 $20
151 Hudson St. (Hubert St.), 212-334-1085
■ "Let the owner order for you and you won't be disappointed" at this better-than-ever TriBeCa Thai that's "delicious", "consistent", "fast" and "cheap"; even given "cafeteria-like" digs, it's "worth a detour."

Thailand Restaurant S
23 10 16 $20
106 Bayard St. (bet. Baxter & Mulberry Sts.), 212-349-3132
■ The "courthouse" types who frequent this Chinatown Thai say it's guilty of serving "some of the best" "spicy, authentic, cheap" eats in town, thus it's cleared for its "complete lack of atmosphere."

Thali Vegetarian S⊘
▽ 20 11 16 $16
28 Greenwich Ave. (bet. Charles & W. 10th Sts.), 212-367-7411
☑ "A bowling alley is wider", but this "peaceful", "minimalist" Village BYO Indian-Vegetarian is "an amazing bang for the buck" given its no-choice set menus ($6 lunch, $10 dinner); despite "some off nights", it's "worth a gamble."

Thé Adoré ⊘
19 17 15 $16
17 E. 13th St., 2nd fl. (bet. 5th Ave. & University Pl.), 212-243-8742
■ "Sweet little" Village tea shop serving pleasing pastries, salads and sandwiches in an upstairs room mixing "stark Japanese simplicity" with "French country" warmth; it's a "Zen-like" breather.

Tibet on Houston S⊘
– – – I
136 W. Houston St. (bet. MacDougal & Sullivan Sts.), 212-995-5884
Step down into another world at this Village Tibetan newcomer, a small, smartly decorated room that opens onto a tiny front patio in summer; the menu ranges from *momos* (dumplings) to hearty beef dishes, all at soothing prices.

Tierras Colombianas
(Queens) S⇗   ▽ 22 | 12 | 18 | $21

33-01 Broadway (33rd St.), 718-956-3012
82-18 Roosevelt Ave. (83rd St.), 718-426-8868
■ This Queens Colombian duo lures "gringos as well as natives" with "hearty", "delicious", "authentic" food that's good and getting better; though lacking ambiance, the "helpful English-speaking staff" and low prices are also *"que bueno."*

Tiffin
▽ 21 | 17 | 16 | $24

18 Murray St. (bet. B'way & Church St.), 212-791-3510
■ The first scouting reports on this new Downtown Indian-Vegetarian are all good: "excellent" food, "pretty" room and low prices.

Time Cafe ◐S
15 | 15 | 14 | $28

2330 Broadway (85th St.), 212-579-5100
380 Lafayette St. (Great Jones St.), 212-533-7000
☒ Critics say "it's about time they did something about" the New American food and not so timely service at this sorta "hip" duo, but they're liked anyway for "cost-effective" meals, "good people-watching", outdoor seats and brunch.

Tino's ◐
▽ 20 | 19 | 20 | $41

40 W. 56th St. (bet. 5th & 6th Aves.), 212-262-9300
■ Fans of Tino Scarpa are happy he's back at this Midtown Continental–Northern Italian that's "up to his high standards", serving "excellent food" in a "warm setting" with "gracious service."

Tin Room Cafe (Brooklyn) S
18 | 17 | 17 | $32

Ferry Bank, 1 Front St. (Old Fulton St.), 718-246-0310
☒ Now in "lovely new rooms" in a historic bank a few doors from its old home under the Brooklyn Bridge (ratings may not reflect the move), this moderately tabbed and immoderately good Italian still serves "opera with your pasta" (Saturdays) and has a "good garden."

Tio Pepe ◐S
19 | 18 | 19 | $30

168 W. Fourth St. (bet. 6th & 7th Aves.), 212-242-9338
☒ Village Spanish-Mexican that's been around "for years" (30) and is still "reliable" for very good food and "value" plus an "adorable" garden room; still, a few shrug "nothing to write home about."

Tir Na Nóg S
▽ 21 | 20 | 21 | $29

5 Penn Plaza (8th Ave., bet. 33rd & 34th Sts.), 212-630-0249
■ "Up-and-coming" newcomer near Penn Station with "tasty" Celtic-American food (who'd have believed it?), "excellent service" and a stylish setting with Irish ambiance – in short, 'tis a "happy place."

Titou S
20 | 17 | 17 | $32

259 W. Fourth St. (bet. Charles & Perry Sts.), 212-691-9359
■ The West Village "*cousine* of Tartine" serves "inexpensive" but "sophisticated" French fare in a "cozy" brick-walled setting; it "feels like France, but without the attitude."

Tivoli S
– | – | – | I

515 Third Ave. (bet. 34th & 35th Sts.), 212-532-3300
Despite the TVs over the up-front bar, this neighborly newcomer delivers quite respectable American food and drink in a warm, old-fashioned, brick-walled, tin-ceilinged Murray Hill setting; better yet, it all comes at modest pub prices.

Toledo
22 | 21 | 22 | $45

6 E. 36th St. (bet. 5th & Madison Aves.), 212-696-5036
■ "Murray Hill's Spanish star" is a "grown-up place" with "excellent food", "lovely", if dated, decor and "attentive" staff; if prices are a notch above the norm, so is the quality.

Tommaso's (Brooklyn) S
22 | 18 | 19 | $40

1464 86th St. (bet. 14th & 15th Aves.), 718-236-9883
■ "Old-world Italian at its best", this "institution" is "what Bensonhurst is about"; you'll "love the [opera] singing" plus the "wonderful" (if "heavy") food and "entertaining" owner Tommaso – he and the wine list are the real "stars."

TOMOE SUSHI
27 | 9 | 15 | $32

172 Thompson St. (bet. Bleecker & Houston Sts.), 212-777-9346
☑ "Heaven on rice", "an orgasm in your mouth" are how surveyors describe the sensational sushi that draws "masses" to this "zero" ambiance Village Japanese; it would be "a bargain at twice the price."

Tomo Sushi & Sake Bar ●S
19 | 17 | 17 | $23

2850 Broadway (bet. 110th & 111th Sts.), 212-665-2916
☑ "Solid sushi" and "student prices" make this "stylish" new Japanese a "super addition to the Columbia area"; "good" noodles and teriyaki also get nods; still, ratings for decor and service are less than stellar.

Tom's (Brooklyn) ⇗
∇ 21 | 17 | 21 | $16

782 Washington Ave. (bet. Sterling & St. John's Pls.), 718-636-9738
■ At this "classic, family-run" 1936 coffee shop in Prospect Heights, super breakfast and lunch staples come at "the right price", served by the "nicest" people – they "adopt you when you get there."

Tonic, The ●S
23 | 23 | 22 | $50

108 W. 18th St. (bet. 6th & 7th Aves.), 212-929-9755
■ This "hot" Chelsea newcomer has a "dual personality": first, a "beautiful", "pricey" dining room with "inventive" New American fare from Chris Gesualdi (ex Montrachet), "good wines" and "sharp service", and second, a handsome tavern with a "lively bar scene" and simpler pub eats; either way, it's "a winner."

Tony's Di Napoli ●S
18 | 13 | 16 | $28

1606 Second Ave. (bet. 83rd & 84th Sts.), 212-861-8686
☑ "Come hungry" to this "kid-friendly" Italian Upper East Side Carmine's-comparable "concept" catering to cacophonous crowds craving "consistent", cost-conscious "comfort" classics; contributors concur: for copious "quantities", it's colossal.

Toons
18 | 15 | 16 | $26

417 Bleecker St. (Bank St.), 212-924-6420 ●S
363 Greenwich St. (bet. Franklin & Harrison Sts.), 212-925-7440
☑ Whether in the Village original or more atmospheric TriBeCa branch, expect "reliable" Thai food at good prices in an "unhurried" ambiance.

Topaz Thai S
21 | 14 | 17 | $25

127 W. 56th St. (bet. 6th & 7th Aves.), 212-957-8020
■ Handy to Carnegie Hall and City Center, this Midtown Thai has "delicious dishes, both unique and typical", at heat levels ranging "from mild to flamethrower"; it's a "bargain", thus a "tight squeeze."

Top of the Tower ●S
18 | 26 | 19 | $44

Beekman Tower, 3 Mitchell Pl. (1st Ave. & 49th St.), 212-980-4796
☑ "Go for romance" and "some of the best NYC views" at this "serene", art deco Beekman American-Continental penthouse; the "food can never match" the scenery "but they try", so "take someone special" and see if you can catch some stardust.

Toraya
21 | 22 | 21 | $27

17 E. 71st St. (bet. 5th & Madison Aves.), 212-861-1700
■ "Otherworldly" Upper East Side Japanese tearoom that's an "oasis" of "perfect peace" and a "truly aesthetic experience", serving "jewel box desserts" and light lunches; it's a "very different", "relaxing" place in which to "undo" the NY mindset.

F	D	S	C

Torch ◐ [S] 19 | 23 | 18 | $39

137 Ludlow St. (bet. Rivington & Stanton Sts.), 212-228-5151

■ Given its "sexy-as-it-comes" decor, "good-looking" crowd and "cool" "crooners", this "edgy" Lower Eastsider's "mostly very good" French–South American fare comes as a pleasant "surprise"; still, some say the staff "needs to act less famous."

Torre di Pisa 19 | 22 | 17 | $45

19 W. 44th St. (bet. 5th & 6th Aves.), 212-398-4400

◩ If this "pricey" Midtown Tuscan's "off-kilter" "*Alice in Wonderland*" goes to Pisa look "doesn't make you dizzy, you'll enjoy your meal"; though some find it uneven, it's handy for "theaters and shopping" and good for business lunches.

Tortilla Flats ◐ [S] 15 | 17 | 15 | $22

767 Washington St. (W. 12th St.), 212-243-1053

◩ "Kitsch to compete with Graceland", "hula hoop contests", bingo nights, shots and margaritas make this "raucous" West Village Tex-Mex fun house a hit with young "dudes" and dudettes; "oh yeah, there's also food" and they "practically give it away"; 'nuff said.

Toscana 19 | 18 | 18 | $42

843 Lexington Ave. (bet. 64th & 65th Sts.), 212-517-2288

◩ "Reliable and conservative", this Tuscan Eastsider offers "solid" fare in a "quiet", "small" space; maybe it's a bit expensive, but "they try hard to please" and it's "lovely" post-Bloomie's.

Tossed [S] 20 | 10 | 13 | $15

295 Park Ave. S. (bet. 22nd & 23rd Sts.), 212-674-6700

◩ A Flatiron chlorophyll cruncher's dream with "mix 'n' match" makings for "creative" salads; some say you "toss out too much money" and end up "hungry", but this yearling is big with the fashionably famished: "all models all the time."

Totonno Pizzeria Napolitano [S] 21 | 11 | 14 | $20

1544 Second Ave. (bet. 80th & 81st Sts.), 212-327-2800

1524 Neptune Ave. (bet. 15th & 16th Sts.), Brooklyn, 718-372-8606 ⊘

◩ Maybe it's "the sea air", but purists say the brick-oven pizzas at the 1924 Coney Island original are "better" than those at the spiffier East Side offshoot; still, both serve "delish" thin-crust pies that earn votes as "NY's best", but they also get dissed as "overrated."

Tout Va Bien ◐ [S] 19 | 14 | 18 | $35

311 W. 51st St. (bet. 8th & 9th Aves.), 212-974-9051

◩ Just as the name says, "all goes well" at this Theater District bistro that's been serving "dependably decent" food for half a century; it's "a bit dowdy, but likable enough", with "fair" prices, a "Left Bank" feel and "welcoming" staff.

Townhouse, The [S] 17 | 18 | 19 | $34

206 E. 58th St. (bet. 2nd & 3rd Aves.), 212-826-6241

■ Popular with "great-looking" confirmed bachelors, this "gay-but-everyone-feels-welcome" East Side Continental comes through with "good", though not extraordinary, food, decor and service; bargain-hunters say "the prix fixe dinner is a best buy."

Trastevere [S] 21 | 17 | 21 | $42

347 E. 85th St. (bet. 1st & 2nd Aves.), 212-517-3118

■ Like "dining in the old quarter of Rome", this little-known Upper East Side "gem" serves "superior" Southern Italian food in a "tiny, dark, romantic" setting; "willing staff" and "fair prices" add to its charm.

Trata [S] — 22 | 16 | 17 | $45

1331 Second Ave. (bet. 70th & 71st Sts.), 212-535-3800

■ The "East Side in-crowd" streams into this "authentic" new Greek (à la Milos) for "delicious grilled fish" and "delectable" sides in a "cheery, airy" room with "fish on display"; despite gripes about high tabs and service glitches, it's "very popular", so book ahead.

Trattoria Alba — 20 | 18 | 19 | $34

233 E. 34th St. (bet. 2nd & 3rd Aves.), 212-689-3200

■ "Not much action" here, but that's just fine with the Murray Hill set for whom this "attractive", midpriced Northern Italian is a "comfy" "old standby" that's "always good and homey"; "everyone is eager to please, and they do."

Trattoria Dell'Arte ◐[S] — 23 | 21 | 20 | $44

900 Seventh Ave. (57th St.), 212-245-9800

■ With its "awesome" antipasto bar, "stylish" "body parts decor" and "celeb"/"power" "people-watching", this first-rate Midtown Italian is always a "happening" scene; it couldn't be more "convenient to Carnegie Hall", but the "noise", crowds and cost may give some pause.

Trattoria Dopo Teatro ◐[S] — 17 | 16 | 16 | $36

125 W. 44th St. (bet. B'way & 6th Ave.), 212-869-2849

◪ "A reasonably good Theater District choice" tendering "tasty" Northern Italian fare in a "spacious" setting with a new downstairs garden room ("a plus"); critics say "acceptable, not memorable."

Trattoria I Pagliacci ◐[S]≠ — 18 | 12 | 16 | $24

240 Park Ave. S. (bet. 19th & 20th Sts.), 212-505-3072

◪ Though overshadowed by "hipper" Flatiron neighbors, this "little" Italian is "a local favorite" for a cheap "quick fix" of pastas and the like; but some wish they'd "ditch" the "clown paintings."

Trattoria L'incontro (Queens) [S] — – | – | – | M

21-76 31st St. (Ditmars Blvd.), 718-721-3532

It's a pleasant surprise to find this good-looking, high-ceilinged new Italian on a busy Astoria boulevard; full-house weekend crowds attest to the appeal of its food (including pizzas from the on-view brick oven) and moderate prices.

Trattoria Pesce & Pasta ◐[S] — 20 | 13 | 18 | $28

1562 Third Ave. (bet. 87th & 88th Sts.), 212-987-4696
1079 First Ave. (59th St.), 212-888-7884
262 Bleecker St. (bet. 6th Ave. & 7th Ave. S.), 212-645-2993

■ "Lines and crowded tables are a problem", but also proof of the popularity of these "homey", "bustling" Italians whose "cheap", "reliable and sometimes very, very good" fish and pasta please locals; "cross your fingers" and you may also get good service.

Trattoria Romana (S.I.) [S] — ▽ 25 | 15 | 22 | $33

1476 Hylan Blvd. (Benton Ave.), 718-980-3113

■ "Standing room only" most nights, this Staten Island Italian packs 'em in for "generous portions" of "well-prepared" pastas and brick-oven pizzas at fair prices; sure it's "noisy" and "cramped", but the "owner oversees all" and superior "service makes the meal."

Trattoria Rustica [S] — 20 | 15 | 19 | $31

343 E. 85th St. (bet. 1st & 2nd Aves.), 212-744-1227

■ Its "larger space" has made this "homey" local Italian even more of an Upper East Side "favorite"; "wonderful food combined with reasonable prices" and "accommodating service" make it "a find."

Treehouse, The ●S   19 | 22 | 20 | $32
436 Hudson St. (Morton St.), 212-989-1363
■ "As kid-friendly as they come", this rustically "quaint" (some say "a bit precious") West Village French-American bistro also does well by adults with "good food", "personal service" and fair prices; it's a "roomier-than-most" brunch option.

Triangolo ●S⌿   21 | 16 | 19 | $32
345 E. 83rd St. (bet. 1st & 2nd Aves.), 212-472-4488
■ "A cut above the usual" East Side pasta place, this "intimate", affordable Italian on a "quiet side street" offers "food that will make you smile" served "with a smile"; ergo, it's often "crowded."

Tribeca Grill S   22 | 20 | 20 | $47
375 Greenwich St. (Franklin St.), 212-941-3900
☑ After 10 "trendy" years, Drew Nieporent and Robert De Niro's "classy" TriBeCa warehouse New American retains its "fresh, distinctive character" thanks to "always interesting" food and a celeb-laden crowd; the main quibbles are with prices, noise ("you talkin' to me?") and a few "actor wanna-be" staffers who put too much "attitude" into the role of The Waiter.

Trionfo ●S   21 | 18 | 20 | $42
224 W. 51st St. (bet. B'way & 8th Ave.), 212-262-6660
■ "One of the better" Theater District options, this "attractive, classic" Italian is "a bit pricey" but offers "superior food" and "eager service" in a "soothing" setting; if "nothing exciting", "this place tries hard" and by most accounts "succeeds."

Triple Eight Palace S   18 | 11 | 11 | $23
88 E. Broadway (bet. Division & Market Sts.), 212-941-8886
☑ "Cacophonous", "cavernous, chaotic" Chinatown dim sum palace where an "astonishing variety" of low-cost dumplings comes via the "fairly medieval point and eat" system; though "it used to be better", it's "fun for large" groups that can laugh off "zero" decor and service.

Triplets Old NY Steak House S   19 | 16 | 19 | $43
11-17 Grand St. (6th Ave.), 212-925-9303
☑ "A total gas!", so "BYO Alka-Seltzer" and "taste the fat" at this "party all the time" SoHo Jewish steakhouse where you dig into huge plates of "artery-clogging" fare as waiters "dance and sing around you"; it's a "nostalgic" "hoot", except for the "terminal heartburn."

Trois Canards S   19 | 17 | 18 | $36
184 Eighth Ave. (bet. 19th & 20th Sts.), 212-929-4320
☑ A "good choice near the Joyce", this "quaint", "relaxing" Chelsea French bistro is ducky for its "bargain" early-bird and brunch prix fixes; still, a few shrug "ok, but unmemorable" and feel it needs goosing up.

Trois Jean S   20 | 18 | 18 | $48
154 E. 79th St. (bet. Lexington & 3rd Aves.), 212-988-4858
☑ "Very chic" and "grown-up", this attractive East Side duplex bistro with street-side seats is praised for its "excellent" French fare highlighted by *plats du jour* (keeping every day interesting), truffle dishes and "delectable desserts"; but it's also knocked for crowding, high tabs and "spotty" service with occasional "attitude", if you're not a Bass or de la Renta.

Tropica Bar & Seafood House   22 | 19 | 19 | $46
MetLife Bldg., 200 Park Ave. (45th St. & Lexington Ave.), 212-867-6767
■ A restaurant near Grand Central with a chef named Deletrain suggests a happy kismet, and this Caribbean seafooder certainly brightens Midtown with its "creative" fare and "Key West"–style setting; for the "corporate" types who pack into this often "hectic" space, it's a transporting experience.

T Salon & T Emporium 🅂
$17 \mid 20 \mid 15 \mid \$24$

11 E. 20th St. (bet. B'way & 5th Ave.), 212-358-0506

■ A "sweet" Flatiron "retreat" for an "amazing variety" of teas plus "good" soups, salads, etc. in a "feminine" setting; dissenters say they "take themselves too seriously", but it's a "civilized" place to "slow down" and sip.

Tsampa ●🅂
$18 \mid 21 \mid 19 \mid \$23$

212 E. Ninth St. (bet. 2nd & 3rd Aves.), 212-614-3226

■ Wound-up East Villagers seeking "serenity now!" would do well to head to this "dark", "mellow" East Village Tibetan; while most praise "atypical" "food cooked with care", a few feel it's "redefined tasteless", but no matter, the place "exudes good karma."

Tse Yang 🅂
$24 \mid 23 \mid 23 \mid \$51$

34 E. 51st St. (bet. Madison & Park Aves.), 212-688-5447

■ "Outstanding Peking duck" and other "high-quality", "delicately cooked" Chinese fare is "beautifully presented" at this "elegant", "formal" Midtowner; prices are as "top-notch" as the food, but for "glamorous Chinese dining" the "old school" way, you can't do better.

T.S. Ma 🅂
$17 \mid 14 \mid 18 \mid \$26$

5 Penn Plaza (8th Ave. & 33rd St.), 212-971-0050

☒ An "unexpected treat", this "pleasant", decent if undistinguished Chinese in the "dining-challenged" Madison Square Garden area is a "reliable", low-risk pre-game bet; it may even be the evening's highlight if you go to see the Rangers.

Tudor Grill 🅂
$\triangledown \ 18 \mid 17 \mid 18 \mid \$39$

45 Tudor City Pl. (43rd St., bet. 1st & 2nd Aves.), 212-922-0002

☒ "A much-needed refuge" in Tudor City, this New American "sleeper" may also be kind of sleepy ("needs more traffic"); while most laud its "good" food, "pleasant" service and "quiet, relaxing" mien, a few demur: "uneven", "ho-hum."

Tupelo Grill 🅂
$19 \mid 17 \mid 18 \mid \$42$

1 Penn Plaza (33rd St., bet. 7th & 8th Aves.), 212-760-2700

■ For a "testosterone fix" pre-Knicks, try this roomy, high-ceilinged steakhouse across from Madison Square Garden; "needed in the area", it offers "huge portions" of "good" meat and seafood.

Turkish Kitchen 🅂
$21 \mid 18 \mid 19 \mid \$34$

386 Third Ave. (bet. 27th & 28th Sts.), 212-679-1810

■ The "terrific appetizer platter" is a fine intro to the "authentic" fare at this dependably "tasty" Gramercy Turk; with "red walls", "exotic" decor and friendly service, it makes for a "transporting" meal.

Tuscan Square 🅂
$19 \mid 20 \mid 18 \mid \$39$

16 W. 51st St. (bet. 5th & 6th Aves.), 212-977-7777

☒ "Pottery Barn"-esque Rock Center Tuscan-cum-boutique that strikes many as a "great concept" in a "unique setting", but critics clout "too much attention on concept", not enough on execution.

Tuscany Grill (Brooklyn) 🅂
$24 \mid 18 \mid 20 \mid \$38$

8620 Third Ave. (bet. 86th & 87th Sts.), 718-921-5633

■ If this "small", "crowded" Tuscan is any indication, "Bay Ridge knows how to eat", and how to treat diners; its "consistently good", even "exciting", food comes at "fair prices" in a "warm" ambiance, making it worth the "squeeze."

12th St. Bar & Grill (Brooklyn) 🅂
$20 \mid 18 \mid 19 \mid \$30$

1123 Eighth Ave. (12th St.), 718-965-9526

■ Park Slopers call this American bistro the "perfect neighborhood" place: "casual, cozy and consistent", it offers "nouvelle comfort food" plus a "bit of sophistication without pretension"; brunch is a highlight.

'21' CLUB

21 W. 52nd St. (bet. 5th & 6th Aves.), 212-582-7200

■ "As old school as you can get" and proud of it, this Midtown "icon" remains a "total power place", offering "class, style and history" plus American fare that's "excellent" and still "getting better" under chef Erik Blauberg; even the likes of burgers and chicken hash come at "high-end prices" here, but that also buys you some of the world's most expert "coddling" and most intriguing surroundings, including the extraordinary wine cellar and handsome rooms for private parties.

27 Standard S

116 E. 27th St. (bet. Lexington & Park Aves.), 212-447-7733

■ Eat to the beat at this "beautiful", "loft"-like Gramercy New American with a "creative" menu that's way "better than average, especially as jazz clubs go"; a few rate it just "standard" since changing chefs, but even they can't argue with those "great sounds."

26 Seats S⊄

168 Ave. B (bet. 10th & 11th Sts.), 212-677-4787

The '26 seats' are all different at this dinner-only New American tucked into a cupboard of space in the East Village; early reports indicate that the modestly priced menu, service with a comfortable cadence and funkily glamorous decor have led locals to welcome this new addition.

Two Boots S

37 Ave. A (bet. 2nd & 3rd Sts.), 212-505-2276 ●
42 Ave. A (3rd St.), 212-254-1919 ●
74 Bleecker St. (B'way), 212-777-1033 ●
201 W. 11th St. (7th Ave. S.), 212-633-9096 ●
514 Second St. (bet. 7th & 8th Aves.), Brooklyn, 718-499-3253

☑ For just a few bucks you can "stuff yourself silly" at these "funky" pizzerias whose "inventive" Cajun-style pies are "spicier than Rita Moreno and Charo put together"; they're "kid-friendly", i.e. "noisy."

212 Restaurant & Bar ●S

133 E. 65th St. (bet. Lexington & Park Aves.), 212-249-6565

Tucked away in an East Side brownstone, this American newcomer in a minimalist setting has quickly become a hot spot; martinis and vodkas fuel such a clamoring bar scene that you wonder if the neighbors will complain.

Two Toms (Brooklyn) ⊄

255 Third Ave. (bet. President & Union Sts.), 718-875-8689

☑ Don't expect menus or decor at this Boerum Hill "mom-and-pop" "throwback to the '40s", just "huge portions" of "excellent cheap Italian eats" including the "biggest pork chops on the planet"; "bring cash" and your loudest friends.

Two Two Two S

222 W. 79th St. (bet. Amsterdam Ave. & B'way), 212-799-0400

■ Fans give three cheers for this West Side townhouse Continental–New American that's ideal for "special occasions or romance", with "creative" food, "elegant" decor and "superb" service; though many call it "too, too, too pricey", there are "good buy" prix fixe menus.

Typhoon Restaurant & Brewery

22 E. 54th St. (bet. 5th & Madison Aves.), 212-754-9006

☑ "Spicy Thai" food, "thirst-quenching" housemade suds and typhoon-level noise are what to expect at this "hot" bi-level Midtowner; though the food "could be better for the price", the "booming happy hour crowd" of "recent grads" doesn't mind.

Ubol's Kitchen (Queens) [S] ▽ 22 | 11 | 19 | $23
24-42 Steinway St. (25th Ave.), 718-545-2874
■ As this "authentic Thai" "hole-in-the-wall" proves, there's more to Astoria than souvlaki; it's "worth the subway ride" for "consistently good", low-cost "fiery food" and "cordial service."

Uguale [S] – | – | – | M
396 West St. (W. 10th St.), 212-229-0606
The far West Village gets a high-quality, affordable Italian with this comfy new corner boîte and adjoining bar; besides boasting attractive yellow-toned decor and two fireplaces, it has a Hudson view.

Ukrainian East Village [S]⊄ 18 | 9 | 14 | $20
140 Second Ave. (bet. 9th St. & St. Marks Pl.), 212-529-5024
◪ "On a bleak, wintry day", you can warm up with "pierogi galore", "heavenly" borscht and other "cheap, solid" eats at this Ukrainian East Villager; at these prices, "who needs ambiance?"

Ulrika's [S] ▽ 23 | 19 | 21 | $40
115 E. 60th St. (bet. Lexington & Park Aves.), 212-355-7069
■ "At last, affordable Swedish cuisine" is the astonished reaction to this East Side rookie offering "delicious" food in a crisp, rustic setting; among its other assets are a good buy prix fixe lunch and service "so friendly, you know they're out-of-towners."

Uncle George's (Queens) ◐[S]⊄ 20 | 9 | 14 | $21
33-19 Broadway (34th St.), 718-626-0593
◪ A "*real* Greek diner", this 24-hour "Astoria favorite" has "great lamb anytime" and lots of other "fresh, cheap food", but "zero" decor and "sloppy service"; it's as "bustling" as "Athens at rush hour."

Uncle Jack's Steakhouse (Queens) [S] ▽ 22 | 18 | 21 | $51
39-40 Bell Blvd. (40th Ave.), 718-229-1100
■ Some of the "best steaks in Queens" (including Kobe beef) plus good seafood and sides are served at this "comfortable" Bayside steakhouse; some find it "expensive" and "too smoky", if "not a cigar person."

Uncle Nick's [S] 20 | 12 | 16 | $27
747 Ninth Ave. (bet. 50th & 51st Sts.), 212-245-7992
◪ Upbeat but decidedly "not fancy" Hell's Kitchen Greek where the "appetizers are a must", seafood "yummy" and the "price is right"; though "noisy and crowded", it's "easier than a trip to Astoria."

Uncle Pho (Brooklyn) [S] – | – | – | M
263 Smith St. (DeGraw St.), 718-855-8737
Shellacked Saigon newspapers adorn the facade of this Carroll Gardens French-influenced Vietnamese sibling to the nearby Patois; look for a lively bar filled with Manhattan expats, a colorful collage-like interior and food that may be slightly faux, but is still worth a go.

UNION PACIFIC 25 | 25 | 24 | $65
111 E. 22nd St. (bet. Lexington Ave. & Park Ave. S.), 212-995-8500
■ In a "gorgeous", "serene" Gramercy setting with a "mesmerizing waterfall", Rocco DiSpirito's "supremely creative" and "beautifully presented" New American cuisine "takes risks and delivers", backed up by "excellent service" and "extraordinary wines"; if a few find the food and prices "a little far out", far more say "all aboard" for a "truly exciting" dining "adventure"; dinner is $65 prix fixe only.

F | D | S | C

UNION SQUARE CAFE [S] 27 | 24 | 26 | $55
21 E. 16th St. (bet. 5th Ave. & Union Sq. W.), 212-243-4020
■ "Danny Meyer's masterpiece" and NY's Most Popular Restaurant for four years running, this New American remains "unsurpassed" as a "fully satisfying dining experience" because its "formula works": offer "fabulous food" (from Michael Romano) in a "relaxed" yet "classy" space with "gold standard" service for less than your competition; "if you can get in", odds are it will "steal your heart."

Üsküdar [S] 20 | 11 | 19 | $30
1405 Second Ave. (bet. 73rd & 74th Sts.), 212-988-2641
◪ "Tiny" East Side Turk that "does lots with little", making up for "tight quarters" with affordable, "tasty" fare and "family-like" warmth and service; you must be "size 4 or less to use the bathroom."

Va Bene [S] 20 | 17 | 17 | $41
1589 Second Ave. (bet. 82nd & 83rd Sts.), 212-517-4448
■ "Kosher Italian is done right" at this "elegant" Upper Eastsider that earns special praise for its pasta and fish; it's "a little pricey" but worth it for "well-made, well-seasoned" fare.

Vandam ◐ ▽ 19 | 19 | 17 | $44
150 Varick St. (Vandam St.), 212-352-9090
◪ It's a "model scene" with "attitude", but this West SoHo newcomer has "potential" thanks to "imaginative" French–South American fusion fare in a "funky"/"beautiful" setting; on the downside, you may wait an "eternity" even with a reservation.

V&T Pizzeria ◐[S] 19 | 8 | 12 | $16
1024 Amsterdam Ave. (bet. 110th & 111th Sts.), 212-663-1708
◪ The "best pizza near Columbia" is found at this "old favorite" "relic", where trying to "make a waiter smile" is as tough as avoiding grease spots while eating the gloriously "gloppy, gooey" pies; if you want decor, "bring it home."

Vatan [S] 21 | 22 | 21 | $29
409 Third Ave. (29th St.), 212-689-5666
■ Make "no decisions", wear "no shoes", just "lean back" and enjoy an "excellent" fixed-price Indian-Vegetarian feast in a Gramercy space resembling a "South Indian village"; it's a relaxing, "transporting" "bang for the buck."

Va Tutto! [S] – | – | – | M
23 Cleveland Pl. (bet. Kenmare & Spring Sts.), 212-941-0286
Alumna of Gotham Bar & Grill in the kitchen and front of the house lend a sure hand to this midpriced SoHo Italian newcomer that has improved upon one of the better gardens in the area; it's worth checking out even in indoor dining weather.

Vegetarian Paradise [S] 19 | 10 | 14 | $18
144 W. Fourth St. (bet. MacDougal St. & 6th Ave.), 212-260-7130
33 Mott St. (Pell St.), 212-406-6988
◪ "If not paradise", these separately owned Chinese Vegetarians satisfy most with a "huge selection" of "fake meat" and other "fresh", "cheap, tasty" fare; cynics say it all "tastes the same."

Velli Ristorante [S]⊘ 19 | 16 | 16 | $31
132 W. Houston St. (bet. MacDougal & Sullivan Sts.), 212-777-8437
■ Velli equals Village "value" according to fans of this "cute" trattoria's "consistent", velli good food and "warm", "relaxed atmosphere"; no plastic, but "the prices won't faze you."

Velvet Restaurant & Lounge ◑ ▽   19 | 18 | 17 | $33
223 Mulberry St. (bet. Prince & Spring Sts.), 212-965-0439
☑ Dark, sexy SoHo Eclectic that fans call a real "sleeper", with good food and decor, a "best deal" early bird and an upstairs lounge for private parties; others shrug "not bad, not exciting."

Veniero's ◑S   23 | 13 | 13 | $14
342 E. 11th St. (bet. 1st & 2nd Aves.), 212-674-7070
☑ At this vintage 1894 East Village Italian "dessert heaven", "banish thoughts of calories" and hit the "killer cannoli" and other "gym be damned" sweets; it's "overpopular" with "insane lines" and "slow service", but "worth the wait and the weight."

Vera Cruz (Brooklyn) ◑S   ▽ 19 | 18 | 16 | $21
195 Bedford Ave. (bet. N. 6th & 7th Sts.), 718-599-7914
■ Williamsburg's "favorite Mexican" is an upbeat place with "good food", "super" decor and a "hip crowd"; even those who fault sometimes "slow" service can't argue with the back garden.

Verbena S   24 | 23 | 22 | $53
54 Irving Pl. (bet. 17th & 18th Sts.), 212-260-5454
■ Diane Forley's "inspired" and "soulful" Med–New American food, a "serene" room that "looks like smooth scotch tastes" and a "lovely garden" make for "highly civilized" first-class dining at this Gramercy standout; high prices make sense since most people call it a "jewel."

VERITAS S   25 | 23 | 25 | $67
43 E. 20th St. (bet. B'way & Park Ave. S.), 212-353-3700
■ "In truth, a stunner": Scott Bryan and Gino Diaferia's Flatiron New American is certainly a contender for rookie of the year; it's not only an oenophile's "paradise" with a "phenomenal" cellar ("not a list, it's a novel"), but the food also "dazzles" and is "graciously served" in an "intimate", "elegant" room; however, with dinner at a prix fixe $62 sans wine, this "wow" can easily turn into an "ouch!"

Vermicelli S   20 | 18 | 19 | $27
1492 Second Ave. (bet. 77th & 78th Sts.), 212-288-8868
■ With "yummy" noodle dishes, "savory soups" and other "tasty" Vietnamese fare, this Upper Eastsider is an "excellent value", especially when you tack on "attractive" decor, "helpful staff" and sidewalk seats; no wonder it's "getting busier" all the time.

Veronica ⊭   ▽ 22 | 7 | 16 | $18
240 W. 38th St. (bet. 7th & 8th Aves.), 212-764-4770
■ It "looks like a soup kitchen", but this "cafeteria-style" Garment District Italian "meta-diner" dishes up a "fantastic", "gourmet" lunch; "wait in line – it's worth it."

Veselka ◑S   18 | 11 | 13 | $16
144 Second Ave. (9th St.), 212-228-9682
☑ For "boffo borscht", "perfect pierogi" and other "hearty" (maybe "too hearty") Eastern European eats, this "homey" East Village Ukrainian "is the place"; it's "super cheap", open 24/7 and often "annoyingly crowded" with "curt" service.

Vespa Cibobuono S   21 | 17 | 19 | $32
1625 Second Ave. (bet. 84th & 85th Sts.), 212-472-2050
■ "Cozy", "comfortable", "oh so cute" poster-adorned Upper East Side Italian with "consistently good", affordable food, a "vivacious" host and charming patio; the "sometimes slow" service is also "authentic Italian."

Via Brasil 🟥

20 | 15 | 19 | $31

34 W. 46th St. (bet. 5th & 6th Aves.), 212-997-1158
■ You can "gorge on beef" and other "huge portions" of "excellent" Brazilian food at this modestly priced Midtowner; "delicious tropical drinks" and "good music" give it a "noisy but fun" "nightclub" feel.

Viand 🟥

16 | 7 | 14 | $17

300 E. 86th St. (2nd Ave.), 212-879-9425 ◑
1011 Madison Ave. (78th St.), 212-249-8250
673 Madison Ave. (bet. 61st & 62nd Sts.), 212-751-6622 ⌷
☑ A boon for "budget-conscious" diners, these separately owned "quintessential NY coffee shops" are "always there" for "a real breakfast", "the best turkey sandwich" and other "basics"; they're "noisy, cramped and rushed", but what did you expect?

Via Oreto 🟥

22 | 14 | 20 | $37

1121 First Ave. (bet. 61st & 62nd Sts.), 212-308-0828
■ "Mama's cooking has never been better, and there's a real mama" who treats you "like one of the family" at this "homey" East Side Southern Italian serving "solid", "reasonably priced" fare; the "small" interior makes it just that much more "cozy."

Viceroy, The ◑🟥

14 | 17 | 14 | $28

160 Eighth Ave. (18th St.), 212-633-8484
☑ "Very glam-gay" but "accommodating" to all, this Chelsea New American bistro has "deco-smart decor", "kick-ass martinis" and "gorgeous" waiters "practicing their runway" moves; whether the food's "good" or they work harder "at being cool" is debatable.

ViceVersa 🟥

– | – | – | E

325 W. 51st St. (bet. 8th & 9th Aves.), 212-399-9291
With a talented chef from Bergamo, Italy and co-owners/managers hailing from NY's San Domenico, this West Side Contemporary Italian, new from the ground up on a block full of vintage restaurants, is off to a fast start; well-priced food along with a pretty room and back garden have made it an instant hit.

Vico ◑🟥⌷

20 | 14 | 18 | $46

1302 Madison Ave. (bet. 92nd & 93rd Sts.), 212-876-2222
☑ "Excellent" pasta and veal plus an "attentive" staff that "recognizes neighborhood regulars" make this clubby Carnegie Hill Italian popular with those who can handle "high", "cash-only" prices.

Victor's Cafe ◑🟥

20 | 18 | 18 | $40

236 W. 52nd St. (bet. B'way & 8th Ave.), 212-586-7714
☑ "Ricky Ricardo would love" this Theater District standby that transports you to "old Havana" with Cuban food that "tingles the tongue", "sensual" drinks and piano music; critics may say it's "getting old", but most tout it for pre- or post-curtain "Latino fun."

Vietnam 🟥

23 | 7 | 15 | $18

11-13 Doyers St. (bet. Bowery & Pell St.), 212-693-0725
■ For under $20, "you get stuffed and happy" at this Chinatown Vietnamese "hole-in-the-wall" whose "cheap, delicious" food and "courteous", "no-rush" service negate its "dreary" digs; ratings support those who call it "NY's best Vietnamese."

View, The 🟥

19 | 26 | 20 | $48

Marriott Marquis Hotel, 1535 Broadway (bet. 45th & 46th Sts.), 212-704-8900
☑ Times Square really seems like the center of the universe at this hotel "rotating rooftop" Continental where the city appears to orbit around you; it's "touristy", natch, but the food is "better than expected", though some feel you pay a lot to "spin."

Villa Berulia 22 | 19 | 22 | $42

107 E. 34th St. (bet. Lexington & Park Aves.), 212-689-1970

■ Owner "John is a charming host" and insures "everyone is taken care of" at this Murray Hill Italian with "steady", "no-surprises" cooking and a fairly "classy" setting; its "accommodating" ways make locals "want to return."

Villa Mosconi 18 | 15 | 18 | $37

69 MacDougal St. (bet. Bleecker & W. Houston Sts.), 212-673-0390

■ "Old-world" flavors and ambiance mark this "longtime" Village Italian, a "reliable, comfortable standby" where "big, happy family groups" enjoy "good food" at "fair prices" served by "caring" staff; in sum, an oldie but goody.

Vince and Eddie's ◐[S] 19 | 16 | 18 | $41

70 W. 68th St. (bet. Columbus Ave. & CPW), 212-721-0068

◪ "Filling" American "comfort food" and "country inn" decor make this a "charming" Lincoln Center pick; but "cozy" can turn into a "tight", "noisy" "submarine" scene before 8 PM and critics say it "used to be better."

Vinnie's Pizza ◐[S]⊄ 21 | 6 | 14 | $14

285 Amsterdam Ave. (bet. 73rd & 74th Sts.), 212-874-4382

◪ "Yeah, it's a dump", but picky pie partisans insist that when it comes to "huge slices" of "cheesy", "thick-crust" pizza, Vinnie's is the "best in the West" Side; thankfully, they deliver.

Virgil's Real BBQ [S] 20 | 14 | 16 | $27

152 W. 44th St. (bet. B'way & 6th Ave.), 212-921-9494

◪ You dine with "tourists", not "rednecks", but even so many say this "loud", "mildly chaotic" Times Square Southerner is "the real deal" for the "best danged" BBQ around; it's "cheap", so "bring the kids", "lots of Wet-Naps" and go hog wild, though some warn "it's a heart attack waiting to happen."

Vittorio Cucina [S] 20 | 18 | 19 | $35

308-310 Bleecker St. (bet. Grove St. & 7th Ave. S.), 212-463-0730

■ "Fine regional Italian" fare, "sweet waiters" and a "lovely garden" distinguish this Village "sleeper" – all this plus moderate prices leave admirers wondering why it's "never crowded."

Viva Brasil ◐[S] – | – | – | M

473 Columbus Ave. (bet. 82nd & 83rd Sts.), 212-877-0170

Exposed brick, well-spaced tables and piano music (Wednesday–Saturday) add to the relaxed feel of this new West Side Brazilian from the Churrascaria Plataforma team; while it doesn't follow its sib's rodizio-style format, it offers plenty of dishes unfamiliar to most NYers.

Vivolo ◐ 20 | 18 | 19 | $41

140 E. 74th St. (bet. Lexington & Park Aves.), 212-737-3533

■ "Consistent", "civilized" and "above all, comfortable" sums up this atmospheric old East Side duplex townhouse Italian favored by a "mature" crowd for its "gracious" service, fireplaces and "realistic prices" (especially the early bird); it also works for romance, if you don't mind being scrutinized by "blue-haired ladies."

Volare 22 | 20 | 24 | $41

147 W. Fourth St. (bet. MacDougal St. & 6th Ave.), 212-777-2849

■ "Even if you're not Italian, you're family" at this "Village standby" where the "warm staff" feeds you "very good" food and "make you so comfy you never want to leave"; "no surprises, but who needs them?"

VONG 🅂 | 25 | 25 | 23 | $55 |

200 E. 54th St. (3rd Ave.), 212-486-9592

☑ "Exuberant", "exotic" and "exciting", Jean-Georges Vongerichten's East Midtown French-Thai tongue tingler remains a "wower" with "explosive flavors", "dramatically beautiful" decor and a "look at me" crowd; some knock "noise", "small portions" and high prices, but you "can't go Vong" with the prix fixe lunch or early bird – unless you don't like coconut milk, cilantro and lemongrass.

Vox ◐🅂 | – | – | – | E |

165 Eighth Ave. (bet. 18th & 19th Sts.), 646-486-3188

A breath of fresh air in Chelsea, this newcomer near the Joyce offers a global menu (accenting Asian and Latino fare) in a cool, creamy space; late hours, experienced owners (Cara Mia, Zuccherino) and a chef with a good pedigree, Brady Duhame (Bouley, Picholine), are all promising.

Walker's ◐🅂 | 17 | 15 | 16 | $25 |

16 N. Moore St. (Varick St.), 212-941-0142

■ An "anomaly" in trendy TriBeCa, this "down-to-earth", vintage 1890 "hangout" is "what a NY watering hole should be": "friendly", "inexpensive and unpretentious", with "steady" pub food and a "neat old bar"; "what more can one ask for?"

Wally's and Joseph's ◐ | 21 | 17 | 20 | $47 |

249 W. 49th St. (bet. B'way & 8th Ave.), 212-582-0460

■ For some, a B'way evening "wouldn't be complete without a visit" to this Theater District Italian steakhouse, a "'50s throwback" that's pricey but "worthwhile" for "good" food in a comfy setting.

Water Club, The 🅂 | 22 | 25 | 22 | $54 |

500 E. 30th St. (East River), 212-683-3333

■ The view alone would make this East River barge a "nautical nirvana", but it also has "good" American fare, "yacht club" looks and an "unbelievable" brunch; it works for anything from "romance" to "a deck drink", with prix fixe deals to avoid the financial bends.

Waterfront Ale House 🅂 | 18 | 12 | 16 | $23 |

540 Second Ave. (30th St.), 212-696-4104
155 Atlantic Ave. (bet. Clinton & Henry Sts.), Brooklyn, 718-522-3794

■ Though most popular as "relaxed" neighborhood "joints" in which to "have a beer or six", these "friendly" saloons also come up with "surprisingly original" Eclectic food; as you'd expect, they can be "loud and smoky."

Waterloo Brasserie ◐🅂 | 21 | 19 | 17 | $39 |

145 Charles St. (Washington St.), 212-352-1119

☑ If "long waits" and "so hip it hurts" ambiance aren't your waterloo, try this "airy", "minimalist" West Village Belgian for "tasty" *moules frites* and brews; since it's full of "babes in black" and "men in tight pants", many find the "crowd more exciting than the food."

Water's Edge (Queens) | 23 | 26 | 23 | $55 |

44th Dr. & East River (Vernon Blvd.), 718-482-0033

■ "Begin the night with a fabulous [free] boat ride" to this Long Island City American, then enjoy "surprisingly good" food and service as "Manhattan glitters before you"; it's costly but worth it if you want to impress a date, "pop the question" or simply "celebrate."

Well's ◐🅂 | ▽ 19 | 14 | 16 | $28 |

2247-49 Seventh Ave. (bet. 132nd & 133rd Sts.), 212-234-0700

■ The few who have plumbed this wells report that this modestly priced, 60-year-old Harlem Soul Food institution still provides "a good meal" served by pros; you can also "swing all night" to a live band on Mondays or catch some cool jazz on weekends.

West Bank Cafe ●S
18 | 16 | 18 | $31

Manhattan Plaza, 407 W. 42nd St. (bet. 9th & 10th Aves.), 212-695-6909
■ A "lively", "congenial" Theater District American that "works well before", after or during a show thanks to "consistently good" food, a "comfortable" setting and "fair prices"; you may even "spot celebs."

West 63rd St. Steakhouse ●S
21 | 22 | 20 | $54

Radisson Empire Hotel, 44 W. 63rd St., mezzanine level (bet. B'way & Columbus Ave.), 212-246-6363
■ Maybe there are "better" steakhouses, but none are closer to Lincoln Center and few are as "spacious" and "quiet" as this "clubby" carnivore's lair; though it costs a pretty penny, it pays back with "excellent food", "fine service" and "extreme comfort."

White Horse Tavern ●S≠
13 | 15 | 13 | $21

567 Hudson St. (11th St.), 212-989-3956
☑ In business since 1880, this West Village landmark pub has an interior that looks the part, however, it boasts summer sidewalk seating and can provide "decent" burgers and the like; still, many prefer to follow Dylan Thomas' lead and "drink, not eat."

Wild Blue
▽ 25 | 26 | 25 | $57

1 World Trade Ctr., 107th fl. (West St., bet. Liberty & Vesey Sts.), 212-524-7107
■ Early visitors to the WTC's "new kid" in the clouds rate it "A-1", from Michael Lomonaco's New American 'chophouse' fare to the "tremendous wine list", "intimate", "upscale" setting and, of course, the wondrous views; prices are suitably lofty.

Wilkinson's Seafood S
22 | 17 | 20 | $48

1573 York Ave. (bet. 83rd & 84th Sts.), 212-535-5454
☑ Low on "fanfare" but high on fin fare, this Yorkville seafood standby is known for "well-prepared", "graciously" served food in a "quiet, dignified" setting; however, apart from the prix fixe, it's "pricey" "for a neighborhood place."

Willow S
19 | 20 | 19 | $42

1022 Lexington Ave. (73rd St.), 212-717-0703
☑ "Charming" is how most view this "pretty" French-American duplex townhouse with "inventive" food, "attentive" service and a "romantic" aura; a few say "nothing special", but the prix fixe "deal", "primo brunch" and sidewalk seats are quite convincing.

Windows on India ●S
18 | 15 | 16 | $22

344 E. Sixth St. (1st Ave.), 212-477-5956
☑ This East Village Indian's "pretty" setting "rises above the 6th Street" norm, but while the food is also "a cut above", some feel it subscribes to the "let's make the place look nice and raise prices" philosophy.

WINDOWS ON THE WORLD S
21 | 27 | 22 | $57

1 World Trade Ctr., 107th fl. (West St., bet. Liberty & Vesey Sts.), 212-524-7000
☑ "Just looking out the window" makes this huge, 107th-floor New American a "wow"; maybe it won't "take your breath away" like the view, but Michael Lomonaco's cooking has "really made a difference" with "much-improved" food that "rounds out a great evening" including fine wines and "gracious" service; N.B. the pre-theater prix fixe helps keep costs earthbound at this must for out-of-town visitors.

Wolf & Lamb Steakhouse S
▽ 19 | 15 | 15 | $33

10 E. 48th St. (bet. 5th & Madison Aves.), 212-317-1950
☑ Midtown kosher deli/steakhouse newcomer that earns mostly good reviews for its modestly priced, "tasty" food, but "slow service" causes some to say "fine-tune the staff, please" and nobody's asking the decorator to make an encore.

Wollensky's Grill ◑ [S] — 22 | 17 | 19 | $42

205 E. 49th St. (3rd Ave.), 212-753-0444

◪ "Suits" seeking Smith & Wollensky "quality at gentler prices" head to its more "casual" next-door annex, a "crowded", "noisy" East Side grill serving "very good" burgers and steaks "without the fancy wrapping"; late hours are a plus.

Wondee Siam [S] ≠ — – | – | – | I

792 Ninth Ave. (bet. 52nd & 53rd Sts.), 212-459-9057

Odds are you'd walk right by this Hell's Kitchen Thai hole-in-the-wall, but its fresh, well-prepared and very affordable fare (check out the lunch specials) is worth a stop; given less than wondee-ful decor, however, takeout may be your best bet.

Wong Kee [S] ≠ — 22 | 7 | 12 | $17

113 Mott St. (bet. Canal & Hester Sts.), 212-966-1160

◪ It's "not pretty", but for Cantonese food "at its cheapest" and "best", this "Chinatown reliable" is the way to go; even with "spotty service" it's a "favorite" of many.

Won Jo ◑ [S] — 21 | 11 | 14 | $25

23 W. 32nd St. (bet. B'way & 5th Ave.), 212-695-5815

◪ Go "very hungry", preferably with a group, to this 24-hour "mainstay" in Midtown's Little Korea; the "decor is not so great", but it's "fun to BBQ at your table" and the rest of the menu is reliable and well priced.

Woo Chon ◑ [S] — 21 | 13 | 15 | $29

8-10 W. 36th St. (bet. 5th & 6th Aves.), 212-695-0676

41-19 Kissena Blvd. (Main St.), Queens, 718-463-0803

■ "Damn good Korean BBQ", "100 side dishes" and "warmer than expected service" win fans for this low-budget 24-hour duo; just "point to pictures" on the "huge menu" and you "can't go wrong."

Woo Lae Oak [S] — – | – | – | E

148 Mercer St. (Prince St.), 212-925-8200

Several years after its Midtown branch went up in flames (literally), this Seoul-based, high-end Korean has found a new home in SoHo, serving the likes of *kal-bi* and kimchi in a fashionable setting, with tabs befitting the ever-trendy nabe.

World Yacht [S] — 14 | 22 | 16 | $61

Pier 81, W. 41st St. & Hudson River (12th Ave.), 212-630-8100

◪ With the skyline as scenery and "the Statue of Liberty as a dining companion", it seems harsh to complain about the Continental fare on these dinner cruises, yet critics compare it to a "NJ bar mitzvah"; however, they might change their tune given the line's new 'Best of NY' menu featuring dishes based on recipes from such top chefs as David Burke, François Payard and Marcus Samuelsson.

Wu Liang Ye [S] — 20 | 12 | 15 | $25

215 E. 86th St. (bet. 2nd & 3rd Aves.), 212-534-8899

36 W. 48th St. (bet. 5th & 6th Aves.), 212-398-2308

338 Lexington Ave. (bet. 39th & 40th Sts.), 212-370-9647

■ "Not just the same old, same old" Chinese, this trio serves authentic, "spiceee!" Szechuan that's a "distinct cut above" the norm in quarters that are a cut below; still, they're cheap and save you the fare to C-town.

Xunta [S] — 19 | 14 | 14 | $23

174 First Ave. (bet. 10th & 11th Sts.), 212-614-0620

■ "A barrel of fun, especially on flamenco nights", this "*divertido*" East Village Spaniard serves "authentic" tapas plus lots of potent sangria; it's "tiny, dark, noisy", jammed and "cheap" – "let's fiesta!"

Yaffa's ◐S
18 | 19 | 14 | $21
353 Greenwich St. (Harrison St.), 212-274-9403

Yaffa's Tea Room ◐S
19 Harrison St. (Greenwich St.), 212-966-0577

■ The "kooky" decor at this TriBeCa duo appeals to many, but reminds others of a "'60s hash fantasy" ("where did they get all that weird stuff?"); still, beyond the "velvet and beads" there's some "good", reasonable Eclectic food – try brunch or tea and give yourself plenty of time, as the staff isn't too swift.

YAMA
25 | 12 | 15 | $33
122 E. 17th St. (Irving Pl.), 212-475-0969
38-40 Carmine St. (bet. Bedford & Bleecker Sts.), 212-989-9330 S
92 W. Houston St. (bet. La Guardia Pl. & Thompson St.), 212-674-0935 ◐S

■ "Orca-sized" sushi generates "insane" waits at the "closet"-sized, no-reserving Gramercy original; the pretty new Carmine Street site "accepts reservations!", but at all three, the "waiters are too busy."

Yamaguchi S
18 | 16 | 17 | $34
35 W. 45th St. (bet. 5th & 6th Aves.), 212-840-8185

■ Though "nothing outstanding food-wise", this "reasonable" Midtown Japanese can be counted on for "always good, fresh sushi", "attentive service" and a "relaxing" setting; it's handy to theaters too.

Ye Waverly Inn S
17 | 21 | 18 | $31
16 Bank St. (Waverly Pl.), 212-929-4377

☑ "Charm, not chow", is the draw at this "rustic" Village American, a "cozy" hideout with "fireplaces, beamed ceilings" and a garden; that said, the "comfy" food can be "good" and comfy prices help.

York Grill S
20 | 19 | 20 | $37
1690 York Ave. (bet. 88th & 89th Sts.), 212-772-0261

■ In the "middle of nowhere" (East Yorkville), this New American stands out with "good food" and a "jazzy" setting with occasional live jazz; even those who find it "uneven" admit it's a "pleasant" "haunt."

Yura & Co. S
19 | 12 | 14 | $23
1645 Third Ave. (92nd St.), 212-860-8060
1292 Madison Ave. (92nd St.), 212-860-8060

■ A "fancy stroller crowd" fancies this Upper East Side BYO Eclectic (and its "airy" Carnegie Hill take-out offshoot) for "good" breakfast/ lunch fare and "light bites"; it "needs atmosphere", so some get it to go.

Zarela S
22 | 17 | 17 | $37
953 Second Ave. (bet. 50th & 51st Sts.), 212-644-6740

■ "Still jumping", this "colorful" East Midtown Mexican led by vivacious owner Zarela Martinez draws crowds with its "delicious" food and strong margaritas; given the "boisterous" downstairs "bar scene", you may want to sit in the quieter upstairs room.

Zenith Vegetarian Cuisine S
18 | 15 | 17 | $24
888 Eighth Ave. (52nd St.), 212-489-8263

☑ The "ersatz meat" at this Midtown "poor man's Zen Palate" "looks and tastes" so real it "scares" sprout eaters; there's also other "tasty", cheap Asian-Vegetarian fare, but foes say it doesn't live up to its name.

Zen Palate S
19 | 18 | 17 | $25
2170 Broadway (bet. 76th & 77th Sts.), 212-501-7768
663 Ninth Ave. (46th St.), 212-582-1669
34 Union Sq. E. (16th St.), 212-614-9291

■ At these "upscale" yet "economical" Vegetarian "havens", "they make gluten taste good, and that takes talent" – so did the "beautifully designed" spaces; however, "slow service" promotes meditation on the virtues of patience and unappreciative diners would rather "suck bark instead" of eating here.

Zócalo 🄢   22 | 19 | 19 | $38
174 E. 82nd St. (bet. Lexington & 3rd Aves.), 212-717-7772
Grand Central Terminal, Dining Concourse (42nd St. & Vanderbilt Ave.),
212-687-5666
■ "Always happening", "upscale" East Side Mexican (with a new Grand Central branch) where a "young, hip crowd" heads for "imaginative" food, "pretty decor" and "killer" drinks.

Zoë 🄢   23 | 20 | 20 | $44
90 Prince St. (bet. B'way & Mercer St.), 212-966-6722
■ It "started as a trendsetter" but has settled in as one of SoHo's most "solid" citizens, offering "distinctive" New American fare, "lovely wines" and pro service in an "attractive" (if noisy), airy space with an open kitchen; in an ever-changing area, it seems "they're here to stay."

Zuccherino ●🄢   – | – | – | M
1484 Second Ave. (bet. 77th & 78th Sts.), 212-249-2556
The latest branch of the ever-growing Pomodoro chain has the good looks and moderate prices that have won its siblings success; even in the over-Italianized Upper East Side, it should be a good neighbor.

Zucchero e Pomodori 🄢   18 | 15 | 16 | $28
1431 Second Ave. (bet. 74th & 75th Sts.), 212-517-2541
▨ "Even better together" say those who feel that a merger has "improved" these Eastsiders – there may be "better Italian" around, "but not for so little" money; however, it can be "jam-packed" with service needing "smoothing out."

Zula ●🄢   ▽ 23 | 11 | 16 | $22
1260 Amsterdam Ave. (122nd St.), 212-663-1670
■ "Not fancy" is an understatement, but this Ethiopian is "worth the trek" to the Columbia area for "good, cheap, interesting" food that you scoop up with spongy native bread; you go through a lot of napkins this way, but at least you avoid "dropping silverware."

Zum Stammtisch (Queens) 🄢   22 | 19 | 19 | $31
69-46 Myrtle Ave. (Cooper Ave.), 718-386-3014
■ A rarity in NYC: some of the "best German food this side of Munich" can be found at this "friendly", often "crowded" Glendale "neighborhood landmark" with "real Bavarian atmosphere"; in contrast to the wursts and brews, the bill is fairly light.

Zuni ●🄢   19 | 15 | 17 | $30
598 Ninth Ave. (43rd St.), 212-765-7626
■ "Zippy, tasty" New American eats at a "fine price" make this "cheerful" Theater District performer a "solid" pre-curtain choice, though it could benefit from fewer tables and "a little sprucing up."

Zutto 🄢   21 | 18 | 18 | $33
62 Greenwich Ave. (bet. 6th & 7th Aves.), 212-229-1796
77 Hudson St. (bet. Harrison & Jay Sts.), 212-233-3287
■ "You relax the moment" you enter this "serene" TriBeCa Japanese (with a new Village branch) tendering "excellent sushi" and other "creative" items ("try the viper or vampire" roll); fair prices are another reason it's been a local "favorite" for years.

186

Indexes to Restaurants

Special Features and Appeals

CUISINES

Restaurant name followed by Food Rating* and Neighborhood.

Afghan
Afghan Kebab Hse./*17/Multi. Loc*
Kabul Cafe/*18/W 50s*
Khyber Pass/*18/E Vil*
Pamir/*20/Multi. Loc*

African
Sugar Bar/*19/W 70s*

American (New)
ABC Parlour Cafe/*15/Flatiron*
Abigael's/*18/Multi. Loc*
Aesop's Tables/*21/Staten Is.*
Alaia/*19/Central Vil*
Alex & Max's/*17/Garment*
Alley's End/*19/Chelsea*
Alva/*19/Flatiron*
Ambassador Grill/*19/E 40s*
An American Place/*23/E 50s*
Aquagrill/*25/SoHo*
Atlas/*–/W 50s*
Aureole/*28/E 60s*
Bagatelle/*18/E Vil*
Bateaux NY/*19/Chelsea*
Beacon/*–/W 50s*
Bellew/*23/Murray Hill*
Berkeley B&G/*20/E 50s*
Blackbird/*20/E 40s*
Blue Water Grill/*23/Union Sq.*
Boughalem/*21/Village*
Brasserie Americaine/*17/W 60s*
Bridge Cafe/*21/Dtown*
Broome St. Bar/*15/SoHo*
Bryant Park Cafe/*16/W 40s*
Bryant Park Grill/*18/W 40s*
Butterfield 81/*21/E 80s*
Cafe Colonial/*19/SoHo*
Cafe Luxembourg/*20/W 70s*
Cafe S.F.A./*18/E 40s*
Cafeteria/*17/Chelsea*
CamaJe Bistro/*19/Village*
Candela/*20/Union Sq.*
Celadon/*20/E 80s*
Chadwick's/*19/Bay Ridge*
Charlotte/*20/W 40s*
Cibo/*21/E 40s*
City Crab/*18/Flatiron*
Clementine/*21/Central Vil*
Coconut Grill/*16/E 70s*
Cornelia St. Cafe/*18/Village*
Coup/*20/E Vil*
C3/*21/Village*
Cub Room/*21/SoHo*
Cub Room Cafe/*19/SoHo*

Della Femina/*–/E 50s*
Demi/*19/E 90s*
Dojo/*15/Multi. Loc*
Duane Park/*24/TriBeCa*
Eleven Mad. Pk./*25/Gramercy*
Eli's Vinegar Factory/*20/E 90s*
EQ/*25/Village*
Etats-Unis/*23/E 80s*
57 57/*23/E 50s*
First/*22/E Vil*
Five Points/*–/NoHo*
44/*21/W 40s*
Fressen/*20/Village*
Friend of Farmer/*17/Gramercy*
Garage/*16/Village*
Garden Cafe/*23/Prospect Hts.*
Giorgio's/*21/Flatiron*
Globe/*18/Gramercy*
Gotham B&G/*27/Central Vil*
Gramercy Tavern/*27/Flatiron*
Grove/*19/Village*
Halcyon/*22/W 50s*
Harbour Lights/*17/Dtown*
Heartbeat/*20/E 40s*
Heartland Brewery/*13/Multi. Loc*
Henry's End/*23/Bklyn Hts.*
Herban Kitchen/*20/SoHo*
Hush/*–/Flatiron*
Indigo/*22/Village*
Island/*17/E 90s*
JB/*–/Chelsea*
Jekyll & Hyde/*11/W 50s*
Josephina/*19/W 60s*
JUdson Grill/*22/W 50s*
Juniper Café/*19/TriBeCa*
Kalio/*20/Cobble Hill*
Knickerbocker B&G/*20/Central Vil*
Lenox Room/*22/E 70s*
Le Train Bleu/*15/E 50s*
Levana/*21/W 60s*
Lobster Club/*22/E 80s*
Local/*–/W 40s*
Lola/*20/Flatiron*
London Lennie's/*21/Rego Pk.*
Louie's Westside/*16/W 80s*
Lucian Blue/*21/Ft. Greene*
Maison/*22/E 70s*
March/*26/E 50s*
Mark's/*24/E 70s*
Mary's/*18/Village*
Match/*18/SoHo*
Match Uptown/*20/E 60s*
Max & Moritz/*22/Park Slope*

---

* Dash denotes restaurant is unrated.

188

Mercer Kitchen/23/SoHo
Merchants/15/Multi. Loc
Merlot B&G/17/W 60s
Metro Grill/21/Garment
Mezzanine/18/W 40s
Mike & Tony's/22/Park Slope
Monkey Bar/21/E 50s
Moomba/19/Village
New City B&G/–/Dtown Bklyn.
New World Grill/18/W 40s
NoHo Star/17/NoHo
Norma's/26/W 50s
North West/–/W 70s
Oceana/27/E 50s
Odeon/20/TriBeCa
O'Neals/16/W 60s
147/19/Chelsea
One if by Land/24/Village
O'Nieal's Grand/20/SoHo
Oscar's/18/E 40s
Park Avalon/20/Flatiron
Park Ave. Cafe/24/E 60s
Park View/Boathse./18/E 70s
Philip Marie/19/Village
Planet Hollywood/11/W 50s
Pop/17/Central Vil
Privé/19/Flatiron
Punch/20/Flatiron
Quilty's/24/SoHo
Rachel's/19/W 40s
Raga/21/E Vil
Redeye Grill/21/W 50s
Regency/20/E 60s
Rialto/18/SoHo
River Cafe/24/Bklyn Hts.
Sarabeth's/20/Multi. Loc
Saul/–/Boerum Hill
Screening Room/20/TriBeCa
Shaffer City/20/Flatiron
Soho Steak/20/SoHo
Soma Park/21/E 50s
Sono/–/E 50s
Spencer/–/Gramercy
Stingy Lulu's/14/E Vil
Tabla/26/Gramercy
Table d'Hôte/22/E 90s
Tavern on Green/17/W 60s
Tea Box/22/E 50s
Temple Bar/15/NoHo
Time Cafe/15/Multi. Loc
Tonic/23/Chelsea
Top of the Tower/18/E 40s
Tossed/20/Flatiron
Treehouse/19/Village
Tribeca Grill/22/TriBeCa
Tropica/22/E 40s
Tudor Grill/18/E 40s
12th St. B&G/20/Park Slope
27 Standard/21/Gramercy

26 Seats/–/E Vil
212/–/E 60s
Two Two Two/23/W 70s
Union Pacific/25/Gramercy
Union Sq. Cafe/27/Union Sq.
Verbena/24/Gramercy
Veritas/25/Flatiron
Viceroy/14/Chelsea
Walker's/17/TriBeCa
Water Club/22/Murray Hill
Water's Edge/23/LIC
West Bank Cafe/18/W 40s
Wild Blue/25/Dtown
Willow/19/E 70s
Windows on World/21/Dtown
York Grill/20/E 80s
Zoë/23/SoHo
Zuni/19/W 40s

American (Regional)
America/13/Flatiron
An American Place/23/E 50s
Brother Jimmy's/15/Multi. Loc
Canal House/19/SoHo
Citrus B&G/18/W 70s
Coach House/24/Murray Hill
Cooking w/Jazz/24/Whitestone
Delta Grill/18/W 40s
Drovers/19/Village
Grange Hall/20/Village
Harvest/17/Cobble Hill
Home/21/Village
Hudson Riv. Club/23/Dtown
Independent/18/TriBeCa
Joe Allen/17/W 40s
Laight Street/–/TriBeCa
Mesa Grill/24/Union Sq.
Michael's/22/W 50s
Nadine's/16/Village
Old Devil Moon/17/E Vil
Pearl Oyster Bar/25/Village
Pink Tea Cup/18/Village
Radio Perfecto/20/E Vil
Rodeo B&G/–/Gramercy
St. Maggie's/18/Dtown
Sweet Mamas/–/Park Slope
Tennessee Mtn./16/Multi. Loc
Tropica/22/E 40s
Vince & Eddie's/19/W 60s

American (Traditional)
Adrienne/22/E 50s
Algonquin/16/W 40s
America/13/Flatiron
American Park/20/Dtown
Amy's Bread/23/Multi. Loc
Anglers & Writers/17/Village
Annie's/16/E 70s
Astray Café/19/Village
Avenue/20/W 80s

Barking Dog/16/E 90s
Ben Benson's/22/W 50s
Billy's/17/E 50s
Black & White/–/Central Vil
Brooklyn Diner/15/W 50s
Brown's/16/E 60s
Bubby's/19/TriBeCa
Cafe Nosidam/18/E 60s
Campo/20/Village
Charley O's/–/W 40s
Chat 'n Chew/16/Flatiron
Chelsea Grill/19/Chelsea
Christina's Kitchen/19/Garment
Christine's/16/E Vil
Cité/22/W 50s
Cité Grill/21/W 50s
City Grill/15/W 70s
City Hall/21/TriBeCa
Clarke's, P.J./15/E 50s
Coffee Shop/15/Union Sq.
Comfort Diner/15/Multi. Loc
Corner Bistro/22/Village
Dan Maxwell's/18/E 80s
Diner/19/Williamsburg
E.A.T./20/E 80s
Edison Cafe/15/W 40s
Eighteenth & Eighth/18/Chelsea
EJ's Lunch./16/Multi. Loc
Eli's Manhattan/20/E 80s
Ellen's Stardust/12/W 50s
Empire Diner/15/Chelsea
ESPN Zone/–/W 40s
Fanelli's Cafe/14/SoHo
Fireman's of B'klyn/–/E 60s
Fraunces Tavern/15/Dtown
Fred's/18/W 80s
Gallagher's/21/W 50s
Good Enough to Eat/20/W 80s
Grill Room/20/Dtown
Hard Rock/12/W 50s
Harley Davidson/11/W 50s
Houston's/19/Multi. Loc
Island Burgers/21/W 50s
Jackson Hole/15/Multi. Loc
Jerry's/17/SoHo
J.G. Melon/17/E 70s
Johnny Rockets/–/Central Vil
Junior's/17/Dtown Bklyn.
Keens Steakhse./21/Garment
King Cole Bar/19/E 50s
Kitchenette/20/TriBeCa
Kokachin/21/E 50s
Landmark Tavern/16/W 40s
Le Bar Bat/13/W 50s
London Lennie's/21/Rego Pk.
Lucky Strike/17/SoHo
Maloney & Porcelli/22/E 50s
Mama's Food/20/E Vil
Manhattan Grille/22/E 60s

Mayrose/14/Flatiron
Metropolitan Cafe/16/E 50s
Mickey Mantle's/13/W 50s
Moran's/18/Chelsea
Morgan Ct./15/Murray Hill
Neary's/17/E 50s
Official All Star/11/W 40s
Old Homestead/21/Chelsea
Old Town Bar/14/Flatiron
Oyster Bar (Gr. Cent.)/22/E 40s
Palm/25/Multi. Loc
Patroon/23/E 40s
Peanut Butter/20/Village
Pershing Sq./–/E 40s
Pete's Tavern/14/Gramercy
Popover Cafe/18/W 80s
Post House/24/E 60s
Rosehill/–/Murray Hill
Ruth's Chris/22/W 50s
Saloon/14/W 60s
Screening Room/20/TriBeCa
Serendipity 3/18/E 60s
Soho Kitchen/16/SoHo
Spirit Cruises/12/Chelsea
Swifty's/–/E 70s
Tavern on Jane/18/Village
T.G.I. Friday's/10/Multi. Loc
Tir Na Nóg/21/Garment
Tivoli/–/Murray Hill
Tom's/21/Prospect Hts.
Tupelo Grill/19/Garment
12th St. B&G/20/Park Slope
'21' Club/22/W 50s
Viand/16/Multi. Loc
Vince & Eddie's/19/W 60s
Walker's/17/TriBeCa
White Horse/13/Village
Wollensky's Grill/22/E 40s
Ye Waverly Inn/17/Village

Argentinean
Chimichurri Grill/21/W 40s
El Ombú/–/E 70s
Lx/–/E 60s
Novecento/18/SoHo
Old San Juan/17/Multi. Loc
Pampa/21/W 90s
Sosa Borella/19/TriBeCa
Sur/21/Carroll Gdns.

Armenian
Monk/20/E Vil

Asian
Asia de Cuba/22/Murray Hill
Bright Food Shop/19/Chelsea
Cafe Asean/19/Village
Celadon/20/E 80s
Cendrillon/20/SoHo
Cool Hse. of Loo/–/E 70s
Helianthus/18/SoHo

Kelley & Ping/*18/SoHo*
Lucky Cheng's/*12/E Vil*
Match/*18/SoHo*
Match Uptown/*20/E 60s*
NoHo Star/*17/NoHo*
Obeca Li/*19/TriBeCa*
O.G./*21/E Vil*
Orienta/*19/E 70s*
Quake/*–/Central Vil*
Rain/*21/Multi. Loc*
Republic/*16/Union Sq.*
River/*19/W 70s*
Roy's NY/*24/Dtown*
Ruby Foo's/*21/W 70s*
Sol/*18/Ft. Greene*
Sugar Bar/*19/W 70s*
Vox/*–/Chelsea*
Zenith Vegetarian/*18/W 50s*

Austrian
Danube/*–/TriBeCa*

Bakeries
Amy's Bread/*23/Multi. Loc*
Blue Ribbon Bakery/*22/Village*
Bouley Bakery/*26/TriBeCa*
City Bakery/*22/Union Sq.*
Columbus Bakery/*19/Multi. Loc*
Cupcake Cafe/*22/Garment*
Le Pain Quotidien/*20/Multi. Loc*
Marquet Patisserie/*–/Central Vil*
Once Upon a Tart/*21/SoHo*
O Padeiro/*19/Chelsea*
Payard Pâtisserie/*24/E 70s*

Bar-B-Q
Brother Jimmy's/*15/Multi. Loc*
Brothers BBQ/*15/Village*
Cowgirl Hall/*14/Village*
Dallas BBQ/*14/Multi. Loc*
Emily's/*20/E 90s*
Green Field/*18/Corona*
Hog Pit/*17/Village*
Rodeo B&G/*–/Gramercy*
Short Ribs/*18/Bay Ridge*
Tennessee Mtn./*16/Multi. Loc*
Virgil's BBQ/*20/W 40s*

Belgian
Belgo/*17/Central Vil*
Café de Bruxelles/*20/Village*
Le Pain Quotidien/*20/Multi. Loc*
Markt/*18/Chelsea*
Mesopotamia/*18/E Vil*
Petite Abeille/*20/Multi. Loc*
Waterloo Brass./*21/Village*

Brazilian
Brasilia/*18/W 40s*
Cabana Carioca/*17/W 40s*
Cafe Colonial/*19/SoHo*
Casa/*19/Village*

Churr. Plantation/*20/W 50s*
Churr. Plataforma/*21/W 40s*
Circus/*21/E 60s*
Coffee Shop/*15/Union Sq.*
Delícia/*18/Village*
Green Field/*18/Corona*
Ipanema/*20/W 40s*
Master Grill Int'l/*18/Flushing*
Rice 'n' Beans/*20/Multi. Loc*
Via Brasil/*20/W 40s*
Viva Brasil/*–/W 80s*

Burmese
Mingala Burmese/*17/Multi. Loc*

Cajun/Creole
Acadia Parish/*18/Bklyn Hts.*
Cooking w/Jazz/*24/Whitestone*
Delta Grill/*18/W 40s*
Great Jones Cafe/*19/NoHo*
La Belle Epoque/*16/Central Vil*
La Gould Finch/*–/E Vil*
L-Ray/*18/Village*
Mardi Gras/*19/Forest Hills*
Two Boots/*19/Multi. Loc*

Californian
Berkeley B&G/*20/E 50s*
California Pizza/*15/E 60s*
Michael's/*22/W 50s*

Cambodian
Cambodian Cuisine/*21/Ft. Greene*

Caribbean
Bambou/*21/E Vil*
Brawta Carib./*19/Boerum Hill*
Cabana/*20/Multi. Loc*
Calle Ocho/*23/W 80s*
Caribe/*17/Village*
Ideya/*19/SoHo*
Island Spice/*20/W 40s*
Justin's/*17/Flatiron*
Les Deux Lapins/*19/Village*
Mekka/*19/E Vil*
Negril/*18/Chelsea*
Palmetta/*19/E 70s*
Sol/*18/Ft. Greene*
Tropica/*22/E 40s*

Central European
Andrusha/*17/E 90s*

Chilean
Pomaire/*17/W 40s*

Chinese
Au Mandarin/*19/Dtown*
Big Wong/*21/Ctown*
Canton/*25/Ctown*
Chiam/*22/E 40s*
China Fun/*15/Multi. Loc*
Chin Chin/*23/E 40s*
Cho-Sen Garden/*21/Forest Hills*

Dish of Salt/20/W 40s
East Lake/20/Flushing
Empire Szechuan/15/Multi. Loc
Evergreen Shanghai/19/Multi. Loc
Excellent Dumpling/18/Ctown
Flor de Mayo/20/Multi. Loc
Flower Drum/19/E 40s
Golden Monkey/20/Flushing
Golden Unicorn/20/Ctown
Goody's/21/Multi. Loc
Grand Sichuan/22/Multi. Loc
Great Shanghai/21/Ctown
Henry's Evergreen/18/E 60s
HSF/19/Ctown
Hunan Park/18/Multi. Loc
Jade Palace/22/Flushing
Jade Plaza/21/Sunset Pk.
Jing Fong/19/Ctown
Joe's Shanghai/22/Multi. Loc
Kam Chueh/23/Ctown
K.B. Garden/22/Flushing
Keewah Yen/19/W 50s
La Caridad 78/17/W 70s
Lili's Noodle Shop/–/E 80s
Little Szechuan/19/Ctown
Mandarin Court/20/Ctown
Mr. Chow/22/E 50s
Mr. K's/23/E 50s
New Green Bo/21/Ctown
New York Noodle/21/Ctown
Nice Rest./19/Ctown
Noodles on 28/18/Gramercy
Ocean Palace/20/Multi. Loc
Ollie's/16/Multi. Loc
Oriental Garden/22/Ctown
Our Place/21/Multi. Loc
Peking Duck/21/Ctown
Peking Park/17/E 40s
Phoenix Garden/22/E 40s
Pig Heaven/16/E 80s
Ping's Seafood/21/Multi. Loc
Sammy's Noodle/18/Village
Sam's Noodle/19/Gramercy
S. Dynasty/22/E 40s
Shanghai Cuisine/20/Ctown
Shanghai Gourmet/20/Ctown
Shanghai Tang/20/Multi. Loc
Shun Lee/24/W 60s
Shun Lee Cafe/21/W 60s
Shun Lee Palace/24/E 50s
Sichuan Palace/21/E 40s
Silk Rd. Palace/18/W 80s
Silver Pond/20/Flushing
Sung Chu Mei/20/Village
Sunny East/19/Garment
Sweet-n-Tart/20/Multi. Loc
Tai Hong Lau/20/Ctown
Tang Pavilion/22/W 50s
Triple 8 Palace/18/Ctown

Tse Yang/24/E 50s
T.S. Ma/17/Garment
Veg. Paradise/19/Multi. Loc
Wong Kee/22/Ctown
Wu Liang Ye/20/Multi. Loc

Coffeehouses/Desserts
Cafe Lalo/20/W 80s
Cafe Mozart/15/W 70s
Caffe Rafaella/17/Village
Columbus Bakery/19/Multi. Loc
Cupcake Cafe/22/Garment
DT•UT/17/E 80s
Edgar's Cafe/18/W 80s
Emack & Bolio's/23/Multi. Loc
Grey Dog's/19/Village
Krispy Kreme/22/Multi. Loc
La Lanterna/Vittorio/19/Village
Le Pain Quotidien/20/Multi. Loc
Omonia Cafe/21/Multi. Loc
Once Upon a Tart/21/SoHo
Sant Ambroeus/21/E 70s
Serendipity 3/18/E 60s
Starbucks/14/Multi. Loc
Veniero's/23/E Vil

Coffee Shops/Diners
Bendix Diner/14/Multi. Loc
Broadway Diner/13/Multi. Loc
Brooklyn Diner/15/W 50s
Burger Heaven/14/Multi. Loc
Chat 'n Chew/Union Sq.
Christina's Kitchen/19/Garment
Christine's/16/E Vil
Comfort Diner/15/Multi. Loc
Diner/19/Williamsburg
Edison Cafe/15/W 40s
Eisenberg/18/Flatiron
EJ's Lunch./16/Multi. Loc
Ellen's Stardust/12/W 50s
Empire Diner/15/Chelsea
Ferrara/19/Multi. Loc
Florent/18/Village
Jerry's/17/SoHo
Junior's/17/Dtown Bklyn.
Mayrose/14/Flatiron
Norma's/26/W 50s
Odessa/16/E Vil
Stingy Lulu's/14/E Vil
Tom's/21/Prospect Hts.
Uncle George's/20/Astoria
Viand/16/Multi. Loc

Colombian
Tierras Colombianas/22/Multi. Loc

Continental
Cafe du Pont/20/E 50s
Carlyle/23/E 70s
Delmonico's/20/Dtown
Four Seasons/26/E 50s

Harry's/Hanover Sq./*17/Dtown*
Historic Bermuda Inn/*18/Staten Is.*
Kings' Carriage Hse./*22/E 80s*
Kitchen Club/*20/SoHo*
Leopard/*22/E 50s*
Londel's/*21/W 130s*
Marion's/*16/E Vil*
Marylou's/*19/Village*
One if by Land/*24/Village*
Palm Court/*21/W 50s*
Parsonage/*23/Staten Is.*
Petrossian/*25/W 50s*
Raymond's/*18/Chelsea*
Sardi's/*15/W 40s*
Simply Caviar/*21/E 50s*
South Shore/*21/Staten Is.*
Supper Club/*16/W 40s*
Tino's/*20/W 50s*
Top of the Tower/*18/E 40s*
Townhouse/*17/E 50s*
Two Two Two/*23/W 70s*
View/*19/W 40s*
World Yacht/*14/W 40s*

Cuban

Asia de Cuba/*22/Murray Hill*
Cabana/*20/Multi. Loc*
Cafe Con Leche/*16/Multi. Loc*
Café Habana/*18/SoHo*
Calle Ocho/*23/W 80s*
Havana Chelsea/*20/Chelsea*
La Caridad 78/*17/W 70s*
Little Havana/*17/Village*
L-Ray/*18/Village*
Victor's Cafe/*20/W 50s*

Delis/Sandwich Shops

Amy's Bread/*23/Multi. Loc*
Barney Greengrass/*23/W 80s*
Ben's Kosher Deli/*18/Multi. Loc*
Carnegie Deli/*20/W 50s*
Cosi Sandwich/*20/Multi. Loc*
E.A.T./*20/E 80s*
Eisenberg/*18/Flatiron*
Ess-a-Bagel/*22/Multi. Loc*
Kaplan's/*16/E 50s*
Katz's Deli/*20/Low E Side*
Liebman's/*18/Bronx*
Pastrami Queen/*18/E 80s*
P.J. Bernstein Deli/*16/E 70s*
Ratners/*17/Low E Side*
Sarge's Deli/*18/Murray Hill*
Second Ave. Deli/*22/E Vil*
Stage Deli/*19/W 50s*
Wolf & Lamb/*19/E 40s*

Dim Sum

Chiam/*22/E 40s*
China Fun/*15/Multi. Loc*
East Lake/*20/Flushing*
Golden Unicorn/*20/Ctown*

Henry's Evergreen/*18/E 60s*
HSF/*19/Ctown*
Jade Palace/*22/Flushing*
Jade Plaza/*21/Sunset Pk.*
Jing Fong/*19/Ctown*
K.B. Garden/*22/Flushing*
Mandarin Court/*20/Ctown*
Nice Rest./*19/Ctown*
Ocean Palace/*20/Multi. Loc*
Ruby Foo's/*21/W 70s*
Shun Lee/*24/W 60s*
Shun Lee Cafe/*21/W 60s*
Shun Lee Palace/*24/E 50s*
Silver Pond/*20/Flushing*
Sunny East/*19/Garment*
Tai Hong Lau/*20/Ctown*
Triple 8 Palace/*18/Ctown*

Dominican

Cafe Con Leche/*16/Multi. Loc*

Eastern European

Odessa/*16/E Vil*
Ukrainian/*18/E Vil*
Veselka/*18/E Vil*

Eclectic/International

Archives/*20/Dtown Bklyn.*
Bendix Diner/*14/Multi. Loc*
Bleu Evolution/*16/W 180s*
Blue Ribbon/*25/SoHo*
Blue Ribbon Bakery/*22/Village*
Boom/*16/SoHo*
B. Smith's/*18/W 40s*
Café Boulud/*27/E 70s*
Cafe Margaux/*19/E Vil*
Cafe Mozart/*15/W 70s*
Café Word/Mouth/*18/E 70s*
Cal's/*19/Flatiron*
Carol's Cafe/*25/Staten Is.*
Chelsea Grill/*19/Chelsea*
China Grill/*23/W 50s*
Club Macanudo/*13/E 60s*
Cupping Room/*17/SoHo*
Delegates' Din. Rm./*20/E 40s*
Dining Room/Columbus/*19/W 70s*
Dishes/*21/E 40s*
Divine Bar/*17/Multi. Loc*
Druids/*21/W 50s*
East of Eighth/*17/Chelsea*
Eli's Vinegar Factory/*20/E 90s*
Emerald Planet/*16/NoHo*
Empire Diner/*15/Chelsea*
Gamut/*20/Gramercy*
Garden Cafe/*19/Murray Hill*
Global 33/*17/E Vil*
Heights Cafe/*16/Bklyn Hts.*
Indigo/*22/Village*
i Rest./*21/TriBeCa*
Josie's/*21/W 70s*
Lemon/*14/Flatiron*

Lola/20/Flatiron
Lot 61/16/Chelsea
Lucky Cheng's/12/E Vil
Luxia/19/W 40s
Mangia/21/Multi. Loc
Mars 2112/13/W 50s
Mesopotamia/18/E Vil
Nation/19/W 40s
New Prospect/20/Prospect Hts.
Nicole's/–/E 60s
One 51/–/E 50s
Palacinka/20/SoHo
Pangea/19/E Vil
Paris Commune/19/Village
Pascalou/21/E 90s
Pierrot Bistro/20/E Vil
Planet Hollywood/11/W 50s
Popover Cafe/18/W 80s
Rice/18/SoHo
Route 66/17/W 50s
Roy's NY/24/Dtown
Salt/19/W 80s
Sharz Cafe/21/E 90s
Shopsin's/21/Village
Sonia Rose/22/Murray Hill
Spring St. Nat./17/SoHo
Terrace/24/W 110s
Thé Adoré/19/Central Vil
T Salon/17/Flatiron
Velvet/19/SoHo
Vox/–/Chelsea
Waterfront Ale/18/Multi. Loc
Yaffa's/18/Multi. Loc
Yura & Co./19/Multi. Loc

Egyptian
Casa La Femme/17/SoHo

English
Lady Mendl's/21/Gramercy
Landmark Tavern/16/W 40s

Ethiopian
Ghenet/20/SoHo
Meskerem/21/W 40s
Zula/23/W 120s

Filipino
Cendrillon/20/SoHo

French
Adrienne/22/W 50s
Bayard's/24/Dtown
Bouley Bakery/26/TriBeCa
Bouterin/23/E 50s
Box Tree/23/E 40s
Café Botanica/21/W 50s
Café Boulud/27/E 70s
Café des Artistes/24/W 60s
Cafe Margaux/19/E Vil
Café Pierre/23/E 60s
Can/19/SoHo

Carlyle/23/E 70s
Casimir/21/E Vil
Cello/–/E 70s
Chanterelle/28/TriBeCa
Chez Es Saada/18/E Vil
Chez Napoléon/19/W 50s
Chez Oskar/18/Ft. Greene
Cool Hse. of Loo/–/E 70s
Daniel/28/E 60s
Destinée/24/E 60s
Eq/25/Village
14 Wall St./20/Dtown
Indochine/21/Central Vil
Jean Georges/28/W 60s
Joanie's/22/Gramercy
Kitchen Club/20/SoHo
La Baraka/22/Little Neck
La Belle Epoque/16/Central Vil
La Bergamote/22/Chelsea
La Boheme/18/Village
La Caravelle/26/W 50s
La Côte Basque/27/W 50s
La Forêt/22/E 80s
La Fourchette/23/E 80s
La Grenouille/27/E 50s
La Réserve/24/W 40s
Le Bernardin/28/W 50s
Le Biarritz/19/W 50s
Le Cirque 2000/26/E 50s
L'Ecole/22/SoHo
Le Gamin/18/Multi. Loc
Leopard/22/E 50s
Le Perigord/25/E 50s
Le Refuge/22/E 80s
Le Refuge Inn/23/Bronx
Le Régence/24/E 60s
Lespinasse/27/E 50s
Les Pyrénées/19/W 50s
Levana/21/W 60s
Lucien/20/E Vil
Lutèce/26/E 50s
Maison/22/E 70s
Mark's/24/E 70s
Maxx/–/E 90s
Mercer Kitchen/23/SoHo
Merlot B&G/17/W 60s
Métisse/21/W 90s
Monk/20/E Vil
Oriont/–/Chelsea
Oznot's Dish/22/Williamsburg
Pascalou/21/E 90s
Peacock Alley/23/E 50s
Petite Crevette/19/Bklyn Hts.
Pop/17/Central Vil
René Pujol/22/W 50s
Savann/20/W 70s
Scarabée/22/E 50s
Simply Caviar/21/E 50s
Soho Steak/20/SoHo

Sonia Rose/*22/Murray Hill*
South Shore/*21/Staten Is.*
Steak au Poivre/*18/E 60s*
Sud/*18/Village*
Supper Club/*16/W 40s*
Table d'Hôte/*22/E 90s*
Terrace/*24/W 110s*
Torch/*19/Low E Side*
Vandam/*19/SoHo*
Vong/*25/E 50s*
Willow/*19/E 70s*

French Bistro
Acacia/*–/E 50s*
Alison on Dominick/*24/SoHo*
Alouette/*21/W 90s*
André/*–/W 50s*
Au Troquet/*20/Village*
Avenue/*20/W 80s*
Balthazar/*22/SoHo*
Bar Six/*17/Village*
Bienvenue/*20/Murray Hill*
Bistro du Nord/*19/E 90s*
Bistro Les Amis/*19/SoHo*
Bistro Le Steak/*18/E 70s*
Bistro Metro/*20/Forest Hills*
Bistrot Margot/*18/SoHo*
Brasserie Americaine/*17/W 60s*
Brasserie Julien/*19/E 80s*
Cafe Centro/*19/E 40s*
Café Crocodile/*21/E 70s*
Café de Bruxelles/*20/Village*
Café de Paris/*18/E 40s*
Cafe du Pont/*20/E 50s*
Café Guy Pascal/*19/E 80s*
Café Loup/*20/Village*
Cafe Luxembourg/*20/W 70s*
Cafe Milou/ */Village*
Cafe St. John/*17/W 110s*
Cafe 1 2 3/*16/W 40s*
CamaJe Bistro/*19/Village*
Capsouto Frères/*23/TriBeCa*
Casimir/*21/E Vil*
Chelsea Bistro/*22/Chelsea*
Chez Brigitte/*17/Village*
Chez Jacqueline/*21/Village*
Chez Josephine/*20/W 40s*
Chez Louis/*22/W 50s*
Chez Michallet/*24/Village*
Chez Suzette/*17/W 40s*
Cloister Cafe/*11/E Vil*
Cornelia St. Cafe/*18/Village*
Coté Sud/*18/E 70s*
Country Cafe/*21/SoHo*
Danal/*21/Central Vil*
Demarchelier/*17/E 80s*
Denizen/*19/SoHo*
Diner/*19/Williamsburg*
Elephant/*22/E Vil*

Félix/*17/SoHo*
Ferrier/*18/E 60s*
Flea Market/*19/E Vil*
Florent/*18/Village*
Franklin Station/*18/TriBeCa*
French Roast/*14/Multi. Loc*
Frontière/*21/SoHo*
Garrick Bistro/*20/W 40s*
Gascogne/*22/Chelsea*
Grove/*19/Village*
Jacques' Bistro/*20/E 80s*
Jean Claude/*22/SoHo*
Jo Jo/*25/E 60s*
Jubilee/*22/E 50s*
Jules/*19/E Vil*
La Boite en Bois/*21/W 60s*
La Bonne Soupe/*16/W 50s*
La Bouillabaisse/*23/Bklyn Hts.*
L'Absinthe/*22/E 60s*
L'Acajou/*20/Flatiron*
La Goulue/*19/E 60s*
La Jumelle/*19/SoHo*
La Lunchonette/*21/Chelsea*
La Mangeoire/*19/E 50s*
La Mediterranée/*19/E 50s*
La Metairie/*21/Village*
La Mirabelle/*21/W 80s*
La Petite Auberge/*20/Gramercy*
L'Ardoise/*19/E 60s*
La Ripaille/*20/Village*
La Tour/*–/E 70s*
L'Attitude/*–/Village*
Le Beaujolais/*19/W 40s*
Le Bilboquet/*19/E 60s*
Le Bistrot de Maxim/*18/E 60s*
Le Boeuf à la Mode/*20/E 80s*
Le Bouchon/*20/W 50s*
Le Charlot/*21/E 60s*
Le Gans/*19/Village*
Le Gigot/*22/Village*
Le Jardin Bistro/*21/SoHo*
Le Madeleine/*19/W 40s*
Le Marais/*20/W 40s*
Le Monde/*17/W 90s*
L'Entrecote/*19/E 50s*
Léon, Resto/*–/E Vil*
Le Pescadou/*21/SoHo*
Le Petit Hulot/*18/E 70s*
Le Quercy/*20/W 50s*
Le Rivage/*19/W 40s*
Les Deux Gamins/*19/Village*
Les Deux Lapins/*19/Village*
Les Halles/*21/Gramercy*
Le Singe Vert/*17/Chelsea*
Les Pyrénées/*19/W 50s*
Les Routiers/*20/W 80s*
Les Sans Culottes/*16/Multi. Loc*
Le Tableau/*21/E Vil*
Le Taxi/*17/E 60s*

Le Veau D'Or/18/E 60s
L'Express/16/Flatiron
Le Zoo/21/Village
L'Orange Bleue/18/SoHo
Lucky Strike/17/SoHo
Marquet Patisserie/–/Central Vil
Max & Moritz/22/Park Slope
Métisse/21/W 100s
Mignon/–/Carroll Gdns.
Mme. Romaine/17/E 60s
Mon Petit Cafe/17/E 60s
Montrachet/27/TriBeCa
Odeon/20/TriBeCa
Opaline/18/E Vil
Palladin/22/W 40s
Paris Commune/19/Village
Park Bistro/21/Gramercy
Patois/23/Carroll Gdns.
Payard Pâtisserie/24/E 70s
Pierre au Tunnel/20/W 40s
Pitchoune/20/Gramercy
Provence/22/SoHo
Quatorze Bis/20/E 70s
Raoul's/23/SoHo
Rive Gauche/17/Murray Hill
Seasons/20/Williamsburg
Seppi's/22/W 50s
Steak Frites/18/Flatiron
St. Michel/24/Bay Ridge
Sweet Melissa/23/Cobble Hill
Tartine/22/Village
Titou/20/Village
Tout Va Bien/19/W 50s
Treehouse/19/Village
Trois Canards/19/Chelsea
Trois Jean/20/E 70s

German
Gebhardt's/19/Glendale
Heidelberg/17/E 80s
Killmeyer's/21/Staten Is.
Niederstein's/18/Middle Village, Qns
Roettele/18/E Vil
Rolf's/17/Gramercy
Silver Swan/17/Flatiron
Zum Stammtisch/22/Glendale

Greek
Artos/20/E 50s
Briam/–/E Vil
Cafe Greco/17/E 70s
Christos Hasapo/21/Astoria
Eliá/27/Bay Ridge
Elias Corner/24/Astoria
Eros/17/E 50s
Esperides/22/Astoria
Gus' Place/20/Village
Ithaka/23/Village
Karyatis/22/Astoria
Meltemi/19/E 50s

Milos/26/W 50s
Molyvos/23/W 50s
Niko's/18/W 70s
Omonia Cafe/21/Multi. Loc
Periyali/25/Flatiron
Rafina/20/E 70s
S'Agapo/24/Astoria
Taverna Kyclades/22/Astoria
Taverna Vraka/20/Astoria
Telly's Taverna/23/Astoria
Trata/22/E 70s
Uncle George's/20/Astoria
Uncle Nick's/20/W 50s

Hamburgers
Broome St. Bar/15/SoHo
Burger Heaven/14/Multi. Loc
Cals/19/Flatiron
Charley O's/–/W 40s
Chelsea Grill/19/Chelsea
Cité Grill/21/W 50s
City Hall/21/TriBeCa
Clarke's, P.J./15/E 50s
Corner Bistro/21/Village
Cub Room Cafe/19/SoHo
Dallas BBQ/14/Multi. Loc
Diner/19/Williamsburg
Fanelli's Cafe/14/SoHo
Hard Rock/12/W 50s
Harley Davidson/11/W 50s
Heartland Brewery/13/Multi. Loc
Houston's/19/Multi. Loc
Island Burgers/21/W 50s
Jackson Hole/15/Multi. Loc
J.G. Melon/17/E 70s
Johnny Rockets/–/Central Vil
Official All Star/11/W 40s
Old Town Bar/14/Flatiron
Planet Hollywood/11/W 50s
Short Ribs/18/Bay Ridge
'21' Club/22/W 50s
Viand/16/Multi. Loc
Waterfront Ale/18/Multi. Loc
White Horse/13/Village
Wollensky's Grill/22/E 40s

Health Food
(Most restaurants will cook to
health specifications; see also
Vegetarian)
Dojo/15/Multi. Loc
Herban Kitchen/20/SoHo
Josie's/21/W 70s
Quantum Leap/17/Multi. Loc
Spring St. Nat./17/SoHo
Sweet-n-Tart/20/Multi. Loc

Hot Dogs
Gray's Papaya/18/Multi. Loc
Papaya King/19/Multi. Loc
Serendipity 3/18/E 60s

Hungarian
Mocca/18/E 80s

Indian
Baluchi's/19/Multi. Loc
Bay Leaf/20/W 50s
Bombay City/19/Village
Bombay Palace/19/W 50s
Bukhara Grill/–/E 40s
Cafe Spice/20/Central Vil
Chola/21/E 50s
Dakshin Indian/18/W 50s
Dawat/23/E 50s
Delhi Palace/20/Jackson Hts.
Diwan Grill/20/E 40s
Haveli/21/E Vil
India Grill/20/E 80s
Jackson Diner/22/Jackson Hts.
Jewel of India/20/W 40s
Kismat/19/W 180s
Mavalli Palace/21/Gramercy
Mitali E/W/20/Multi. Loc
Nirvana/17/W 50s
Passage to India/17/E Vil
Pongal/21/Gramercy
Raga/21/E Vil
Rose of India/18/E Vil
Saffron/–/Gramercy
Salaam Bombay/22/TriBeCa
Sapphire/–/W 60s
Shaan/22/W 40s
Surya/21/Village
Thali Vegetarian/20/Village
Tiffin/21/Dtown
Vatan/21/Gramercy
Windows on India/18/E Vil

Indonesian
Bali Nusa Indah/18/W 40s

Irish
Landmark Tavern/16/W 40s
Moran's/18/Chelsea
Neary's/17/E 50s
St. Dymphnas/16/E Vil
Thady Con's/15/E 40s
Tir Na Nóg/21/Garment

Italian
(N=Northern; S=Southern;
N&S=Includes both)
Acappella (N)/24/TriBeCa
Al Di La Trattoria (N)/–/Park Slope
Amarone (N&S)/20/W 40s
Anche Vivolo (N)/18/E 50s
Angelina's (N&S)/21/Staten Is.
Angelo's Coal Oven (N&S)/20/W 50s
Angelo's Mulberry (S)/19/SoHo
Antonio (N&S)/19/Village
Areo (N&S)/23/Bay Ridge
Arqua (N)/22/TriBeCa

Arté (N&S)/19/Central Vil
Arturo's Pizzeria (S)/19/Village
Artusi (N&S)/20/W 50s
Asti (N&S)/–/Central Vil
Babbo (N&S)/26/Village
Bacco (N)/19/SoHo
Baci Italian (N&S)/21/Bay Ridge
Bamonte's (S)/21/Williamsburg
Baraonda (N)/18/E 70s
Barbetta (N)/19/W 40s
Bar Cichetti (N)/18/Village
Bardolino (N&S)/19/E 70s
Barolo (N)/19/SoHo
Bar Pitti (N)/20/Village
Basta Pasta (N&S)/17/Flatiron
Becco (N)/20/W 40s
Bella Blu (N)/18/E 70s
Bella Donna (N&S)/18/Multi. Loc
Bella Luna (N)/18/W 80s
Bellavista (N&S)/20/Bronx
Bellini (N&S)/22/E 50s
Bello (N)/21/W 50s
Belluno (N)/23/Murray Hill
Bel Villagio (N&S)/17/Village
Bice Rist. (N)/20/E 50s
Biricchino (N)/19/Garment
Bondí (S)/20/Flatiron
Borgo Antico (N)/18/Central Vil
Bottino (N)/20/Chelsea
Bravo Gianni (N&S)/22/E 60s
Bricco (S)/19/Multi. Loc
Brio (N&S)/18/E 60s
Bruculino (S)/16/W 70s
Brunelli (N&S)/19/E 70s
Bruno (N&S)/21/E 50s
Cafe Fiorello (N&S)/19/W 60s
Cafe Milou (N)/–/Village
Cafe Nosidam (N&S)/18/E 60s
Cafe Trevi (N)/22/E 80s
Caffe Buon Gusto (N&S)/17/Multi.
Caffe Cielo (N)/18/W 50s
Caffe Grazie (N&S)/17/E 80s
Caffé on Green (N&S)/21/Bayside
Caffe Rafaella (N)/17/Village
Caffe Rosso (N)/20/Village
Campagna (N)/24/Flatiron
Campagnola (N&S)/23/E 70s
Canaletto (N&S)/22/E 60s
Candido Pizza (N&S)/19/E 80s
Cara Mia (N&S)/20/W 40s
Carino (N)/19/E 80s
Carmine's (S)/19/Multi. Loc
Casa Di Meglio (N&S)/17/W 40s
Casa Mia (N&S)/20/Gramercy
Castellano (N)/21/W 50s
Cavaliere (N)/18/Gramercy
Cellini (N&S)/21/E 50s
Cent'Anni (N)/22/Village
Chelsea Rist. (N)/21/Chelsea

Chianti (N)/20/E 50s
Chianti (Bklyn.) (N&S)/21/Bay Ridge
Ciao Europa (N&S)/19/W 50s
Cibi Cibi (N&S)/16/E 60s
Cibo (N&S)/21/E 40s
Cinquanta (N&S)/18/E 50s
Cinque Terre (N)/20/Murray Hill
Circo (N)/23/W 50s
Ci Vediamo (N)/18/E 80s
Cloister Cafe (N&S)/11/E Vil
Coco Marina (N)/–/Dtown
Coco Opera (N)/16/W 60s
Coco Pazzo (N&S)/22/E 70s
Coco Pazzo Café (N)/20/E 50s
Coco Pazzo Teatro (N&S)/19/W 40s
Colina (N&S)/19/Flatiron
Col Legno (N)/20/E Vil
Coppola's (N&S)/18/Multi. Loc
Cucina (N&S)/24/Park Slope
Cucina Fontana (N)/15/Village
Cucina Pesce (N&S)/19/E Vil
Cucina Stagionale (N&S)/18/Village
Cucina Vivolo (N&S)/20/E 70s
Da Andrea (N&S)/20/Village
Da Antonio (N)/21/E 50s
Da Beco (N)/21/Gramercy
Da Ciro (N&S)/21/Murray Hill
da Mario (N&S)/19/E 40s
Da Nico (N&S)/21/Little Italy
Daniella (N&S)/22/Chelsea
Da Silvano (N)/21/Village
Da Tommaso (N)/21/W 50s
Da Umberto (N)/25/Chelsea
Dazies (N&S)/20/Sunnyside
DeGrezia (N)/22/E 50s
Denino's Pizzeria (N&S)/23/Staten Is.
Denizen (S)/19/SoHo
Diva (N)/17/SoHo
Divino (N)/18/E 80s
Domani (N&S)/21/E 80s
Dominick's (S)/23/Bronx
Don Giovanni (N&S)/17/Multi. Loc
Don Peppe (N)/25/Ozone Park
Downtown (N)/19/SoHo
Due (N)/20/E 70s
East River Cafe (N)/19/E 60s
Ecco (N&S)/22/TriBeCa
Ecco-la (N&S)/17/E 90s
Elaine's (N&S)/13/E 80s
Elio's (N)/23/E 80s
Emilio Ballato (S)/18/SoHo
Ennio & Michael (N&S)/21/Central Vil
Enoteca I Trulli (N&S)/23/Gramercy
Erminia (N)/24/E 80s
Ernie's (N&S)/16/W 70s
Felidia (N)/26/E 50s
Ferdinando's (S)/22/Carroll Gdns.
Ferrara (N&S)/19/Multi. Loc
F.illi Ponte (N&S)/22/Dtown

Fino (N)/20/Murray Hill
Fiorentino's (S)/20/Gravesend
Firenze (N)/21/E 80s
Focacceria (N&S)/19/Village
Focaccia Fiorentina (N)/18/E 60s
Follonico (N&S)/23/Flatiron
Fontana di Trevi (N)/19/W 50s
Frank (N&S)/22/E Vil
Frankie & Johnnie's (N&S)/21/Multi.
Frank's Rest. (N&S)/20/Chelsea
Freddie & Pepper's (S)/19/W 70s
Fred's at Barneys (N&S)/19/E 60s
Fresco by Scotto (N)/23/E 50s
Fresco on the Go (N)/21/E 50s
Frico Bar (N)/20/W 40s
Frontière (N)/21/SoHo
Frutti di Mare (N)/18/E Vil
Gabriel's (N)/22/W 60s
Gargiulo's (N&S)/20/Coney
Gemelli (S)/16/Dtown
Gene's (N)/17/Village
Gennaro (N&S)/25/W 90s
Giambelli (N)/21/E 50s
Gigino Trattoria (N&S)/21/TriBeCa
Gino (S)/20/E 60s
Giovanni (N)/21/W 50s
Giovanni's Atrium (N&S)/19/Dtown
Girasole (N&S)/21/E 80s
Goodfella's (N&S)/19/Multi. Loc
Grace's (N&S)/16/E 70s
Grande Mela (N)/–/E 70s
Grand Ticino (N)/18/Village
Grano Trattoria (N&S)/20/Village
Grifone (N)/23/E 40s
Harry Cipriani (N&S)/21/E 50s
Il Coppi (N)/22/E Vil
Il Bagatto (N&S)/24/E Vil
Il Cantinori (N)/23/Central Vil
Il Corallo (N&S)/20/SoHo
Il Cortile (N&S)/23/Little Italy
Il Fornaio (N&S)/20/Little Italy
Il Gatto/La Volpe (N&S)/20/E 60s
Il Giglio (S)/25/Dtown
Il Menestrello (N)/22/E 50s
Il Monello (N)/23/E 70s
Il Mulino (N)/27/Village
Il Nido (N)/24/E 50s
Il Palazzo (N&S)/23/Little Italy
Il Pellicano (S)/18/E 60s
Il Postino (N&S)/22/E 40s
Il Riccio (S)/–/E 70s
Il Tinello (N)/24/W 50s
Il Vagabondo (N)/17/E 60s
Il Valentino (N)/20/E 50s
Il Valletto, Sofia (N&S)/20/E 60s
'ino (N&S)/22/Village
Isle of Capri (N&S)/17/E 60s
I Tre Merli (N)/17/SoHo
I Trulli (S)/23/Gramercy

Joanna's (N&S)/*19/E 90s*
Joe's Pizza (S)/*20/Village*
John's of 12th St. (N&S)/*20/E Vil*
Juniper Café (N&S)/*19/TriBeCa*
La Focaccia (N)/*20/Village*
La Giara (N&S)/*19/Murray Hill*
La Gioconda (N&S)/*22/E 50s*
La Gondola (N)/*–/E 70s*
La Griglia (N)/*–/Flatiron*
La Grolla (N&S)/*23/W 70s*
La Lanterna (N&S)/*19/Village*
Lamarca (S)/*19/Gramercy*
La Mela (N&S)/*18/Little Italy*
La Nonna (N)/*–/Village*
Lanza (N&S)/*17/E Vil*
La Pizza Fresca (N&S)/*21/Flatiron*
La Primavera (N)/*19/W 40s*
La Rivista (N)/*19/W 40s*
La Rocchetta (N)/*21/W 80s*
Lattanzi (N&S)/*21/W 40s*
Lavagna (N)/*22/E Vil*
La Vela (N&S)/*18/W 70s*
La Vineria (N&S)/*18/W 50s*
Le Madri (N&S)/*22/Chelsea*
Lento's (N&S)/*19/Multi. Loc*
Le Zie (N)/*–/Chelsea*
Limoncello (N&S)/*20/W 50s*
Little Italy Pizza (N&S)/*21/Multi. Loc*
Loui Loui (N)/*16/E 70s*
Luca (N)/*21/E 80s*
Luca Lounge (N&S)/*20/E Vil*
L'Ulivo Focacceria (N)/*21/SoHo*
Lumi (N&S)/*19/E 70s*
Luna Blu (N&S)/*19/E 40s*
Luna Piena (N)/*20/E 50s*
Lupa (N&S)/*–/Village*
Lusardi's (N)/*23/E 70s*
Luxia (N&S)/*19/W 40s*
Mad 28 (N&S)/*17/Gramercy*
Malatesta (N)/*20/Village*
Manducatis (N&S)/*21/LIC*
Mangia e Bevi (S)/*17/W 50s*
Maratti (N&S)/*23/E 60s*
Marchi's (N)/*19/Murray Hill*
Marco Polo (N&S)/*19/Carroll Gdns.*
Mario's (N&S)/*19/Bronx*
Maruzzella (N)/*19/E 70s*
Massimo (N&S)/*21/Village*
Mazzei Osteria (N&S)/*22/E 80s*
Mediterraneo (N)/*18/E 60s*
Mezzaluna (N&S)/*19/E 70s*
Mezzogiorno (N&S)/*19/SoHo*
Minetta Tavern (N&S)/*18/Village*
Miss Wmsburg (N&S)/*–/Wmsburg*
Montebello (N)/*21/E 50s*
Monte's Italian (S)/*20/Carroll Gdns.*
Moreno (N&S)/*17/Gramercy*
Mugsy's Chow (N&S)/*22/E Vil*
Nanni's (N)/*22/E 40s*

Naples 45 (S)/*17/E 40s*
Nello (N)/*18/E 60s*
Nicola Paone (N)/*19/Murray Hill*
Nicola's (N)/*21/E 80s*
Nino's (N)/*23/E 70s*
Nocello (N)/*20/W 50s*
Noodle Pudding (N&S)/*21/Bklyn Hts.*
Notaro (N)/*19/Murray Hill*
Novitá (N&S)/*23/Gramercy*
Oggi (S)/*–/E Vil*
101 (N&S)/*19/Bay Ridge*
Oro Blu (N)/*20/SoHo*
Orologio (N)/*18/E Vil*
Orso (N)/*22/W 40s*
Osteria al Doge (N)/*19/W 40s*
Osteria Laguna (N)/*20/E 40s*
Palio (N)/*23/W 50s*
Paola's (N&S)/*23/E 80s*
Paper Moon Exp. (N)/*18/E 50s*
Paper Moon Mil. (N)/*19/E 50s*
Pappardella (N&S)/*17/W 70s*
Park Side (N&S)/*23/Corona*
Parma (N)/*21/E 70s*
Pasticcio (N&S)/*19/Murray Hill*
Patrissy's (N&S)/*19/Little Italy*
Patsy's (S)/*20/W 50s*
Patsy's Pizza (N)/*21/Multi. Loc*
Paul & Jimmy's (N&S)/*18/Gramercy*
Pellegrino's (N&S)/*21/Little Italy*
Pepe Giallo (N&S)/*21/Chelsea*
Pepe Rosso (N&S)/*21/Multi. Loc*
Pepe Verde (N&S)/*21/Village*
Pescatore (N&S)/*18/E 50s*
Petaluma (N&S)/*18/E 70s*
Pete's Dtwn. (N&S)/*19/Bklyn Hts.*
Pete's Tavern (N&S)/*14/Gramercy*
Piadina (N)/*19/Village*
Piccola Venezia (N)/*25/Astoria*
Piccolo Angolo (N)/*23/Village*
Pietrasanta (N)/*20/W 40s*
Pietro's (N)/*22/E 40s*
Pó (N&S)/*24/Village*
Polistina's (S)/*18/W 80s*
Pomodoro Rosso (N&S)/*19/W 70s*
Ponticello (N&S)/*25/Astoria*
Porta Rossa (N&S)/*20/Murray Hill*
Porto Bello (N&S)/*21/Village*
Primavera (N&S)/*24/E 80s*
Primola (N&S)/*22/E 60s*
Provi Provi (N)/*18/W 70s*
Puccini (N&S)/*18/W 80s*
Puttanesca (N&S)/*19/W 50s*
Quattro Gatti (S)/*19/E 80s*
Queen (N&S)/*22/Bklyn Hts.*
Rafaella (N)/*20/Village*
Raffaele (S)/*21/E 50s*
Rao's (S)/*24/E 110s*
Remi (N)/*23/W 50s*
Ribollita (N)/*18/Flatiron*

Rino Trattoria (N&S)/*23/W 50s*
Roberto's (N&S)/*24/Bronx*
Rocco (N&S)/*20/Village*
Rosemarie's (N)/*24/TriBeCa*
Rossini's (N)/*20/Murray Hill*
Sal Anthony's (N&S)/*17/Gramercy*
Sal A's S.P.Q.R. (N&S)/*18/Little Italy*
Salute! (N)/*17/Murray Hill*
Sambuca (S)/*18/W 70s*
San Domenico (N&S)/*23/W 50s*
San Giusto (N)/*20/E 40s*
San Pietro (S)/*24/E 50s*
Sant Ambroeus (N)/*21/E 70s*
Sapore (N)/*19/Village*
Savore (N)/*21/SoHo*
Scaletta (N)/*21/W 70s*
Scalinatella (N&S)/*24/E 60s*
Scalini Fedeli (N)/*--/TriBeCa*
Scopa (N&S)/*--/Gramercy*
Seasons (N&S)/*20/Williamsburg*
Serafina Fab. Grill (N)/*19/E 60s*
Serafina Fab. Pizza (N)/*20/E 70s*
Serafina on Run (N&S)/*20/E 50s*
Sesso (N&S)/*18/W 70s*
Settanta Sette (N&S)/*--/E Vil*
Sette Mezzo (N&S)/*21/E 70s*
Sette MoMA (N&S)/*17/W 50s*
Siena (N)/*21/Chelsea*
Sirabella's (N)/*22/E 80s*
Sistina (N)/*22/E 80s*
Sosa Borella (N&S)/*19/TriBeCa*
Stella del Mare (N)/*20/Murray Hill*
Tanti Baci (N&S)/*20/Village*
Taormina (N&S)/*22/Little Italy*
Tello's Rist. (N&S)/*--/Chelsea*
Teodora (N)/*21/E 50s*
Tevere 84 (N&S)/*22/E 80s*
Tino's (N)/*20/W 50s*
Tin Room Cafe (N)/*18/Bklyn Hts.*
Tommaso's (N&S)/*22/Bensonhurst*
Tony's Di Napoli (S)/*18/E 80s*
Torre di Pisa (N)/*19/W 40s*
Toscana (N)/*19/E 60s*
Totonno Pizzeria (S)/*21/Multi. Loc*
Trastevere (S)/*21/E 80s*
Tratt. Alba (N)/*20/Murray Hill*
Tratt. Doll'Arte (N&S)/*23/W 50s*
Tratt. Dopo Teatro (N)/*17/W 40s*
Tratt. I Pagliacci (N)/*18/Flatiron*
Tratt. L'incontro (N&S)/*--/Astoria*
Tratt. Pesce/Pasta (N&S)/*20/Multi.*
Tratt. Romana (N&S)/*25/Staten Is.*
Tratt. Rustica (N)/*20/E 80s*
Triangolo (N)/*21/E 80s*
Trionfo (N&S)/*21/W 50s*
Tuscan Square (N)/*19/W 50s*
Tuscany Grill (N)/*24/Bay Ridge*
Two Boots (N&S)/*19/Multi. Loc*
Two Toms (S)/*21/Boerum Hill*

Uguale (N&S)/*--/Village*
Va Bene (S)/*20/E 80s*
V&T Pizzeria (N)/*19/W 110s*
Va Tutto! (N)/*--/SoHo*
Velli (N&S)/*19/Village*
Veniero's (N&S)/*23/E Vil*
Veronica (N&S)/*22/Garment*
Vespa (N)/*21/E 80s*
Via Oreto (S)/*22/E 60s*
ViceVersa (N)/*--/W 50s*
Vico (N&S)/*20/E 90s*
Villa Berulia (N)/*22/Murray Hill*
Villa Mosconi (N&S)/*18/Village*
Vittorio Cucina (N&S)/*20/Village*
Vivolo (N&S)/*20/E 70s*
Volare (N)/*22/Village*
Wally's & Joseph's (N)/*21/W 40s*
Zuccherino (N&S)/*--/E 70s*
Zucchero e Pomo. (N&S)/*18/E 70s*

Jamaican
Maroons/*--/Chelsea*
Negril/*18/Chelsea*

Japanese
Avenue A/*18/E Vil*
Benihana/*16/Multi. Loc*
Blue Ribbon Sushi/*26/SoHo*
Bond Street/*24/NoHo*
Chikubu/*21/E 40s*
Choga/*18/Village*
Cho-Sen Garden/*21/Forest Hills*
Choshi/*18/Gramercy*
Donguri/*25/E 80s*
Fujiyama Mama/*20/W 80s*
Garden Cafe/*19/Murray Hill*
Haikara Grill/*21/E 50s*
Hamachi/*21/Flatiron*
Haru/*23/Multi. Loc*
Hasaki/*23/E Vil*
Hatsuhana/*24/Multi. Loc*
Honmura An/*25/SoHo*
Ikeno Hana/*21/E 70s*
Inagiku/*23/E 40s*
Iso/*24/E Vil*
Japonica/*23/Central Vil*
Jeollado/*20/E Vil*
Junno's/*23/Village*
Katen/*21/W 40s*
Katsuhama/*20/E 40s*
Kiiroi-Hana/*20/W 50s*
Kitaro/*21/Multi. Loc*
Kitchen Club/*20/SoHo*
Korea Palace/*18/E 50s*
Kuruma Zushi/*25/E 40s*
Lan/*20/Central Vil*
Marumi/*22/Central Vil*
Menchanko-tei/*18/Multi. Loc*
Meriken/*18/Chelsea*
Mishima/*20/Murray Hill*

Nadaman Hakubai/22/*Murray Hill*
Nippon/23/*E 50s*
Nobu/28/*TriBeCa*
Nobu, Next Door/27/*TriBeCa*
Oikawa/20/*E 50s*
Omen/23/*SoHo*
Onigashima/20/*W 50s*
Oriont/–/*Chelsea*
Osaka/21/*Cobble Hill*
Otabe/22/*E 50s*
Planet Sushi/19/*W 70s*
Roppongi/21/*W 80s*
Ruby Foo's/21/*W 70s*
Sachi/20/*E 90s*
Sapporo East/19/*E Vil*
Seryna/24/*E 50s*
Sesumi/19/*E 80s*
Shabu-Shabu 70/19/*E 70s*
Shabu-Tatsu/20/*Multi. Loc*
Shanghai Tang/20/*Multi. Loc*
Shinbashi/23/*E 40s*
Sobaya/20/*E Vil*
Sono/–/*E 50s*
Sugiyama/28/*W 50s*
Sushiden/23/*Multi. Loc*
Sushi Hana/22/*E 70s*
Sushihatsu/23/*E 60s*
Sushi of Gari/26/*E 70s*
Sushi Rose/23/*E 50s*
Sushisay/26/*E 50s*
Sushi Sen-nin/26/*Murray Hill*
Sushiya/20/*W 50s*
Sushi Zen/23/*W 40s*
Taka/25/*Village*
Takahachi/21/*E Vil*
Tatany/22/*Multi. Loc*
Tea Box/22/*E 50s*
Ten Kai/19/*W 50s*
Tomoe Sushi/27/*Village*
Tomo Sushi/Sake/19/*W 90s*
Toraya/21/*E 70s*
Yama/25/*Multi. Loc*
Yamaguchi/18/*W 40s*
Zutto/21/*Multi. Loc*

Jewish
(See also Kosher)
Barney Greengrass/23/*W 80s*
Ben's Kosher Deli/18/*Multi. Loc*
E.A.T./20/*E 80s*
Ess-a-Bagel/22/*Multi. Loc*
Kaplan's/16/*E 50s*
Lattanzi/21/*W 40s*
Liebman's/18/*Bronx*
Ratners/18/*Low E Side*
Sammy's Roumanian/18/*Low E Side*
Sarge's Deli/18/*Murray Hill*
Second Ave. Deli/22/*E Vil*
Stage Deli/19/*W 50s*

Triplets Old NY/19/*SoHo*
Wolf & Lamb/19/*E 40s*

Korean
Bop/17/*NoHo*
Cho Dang Gol/22/*Garment*
Choga/18/*Village*
Clay/19/*SoHo*
Dok Suni's/20/*E Vil*
Hangawi/23/*Murray Hill*
Jeollado/20/*E Vil*
Kang Suh/20/*Garment*
Korea Palace/18/*E 50s*
Kori/–/*Dtown*
Kum Gang San/24/*Multi. Loc*
Won Jo/21/*Garment*
Woo Chon/21/*Multi. Loc*
Woo Lae Oak/–/*SoHo*

Kosher
Abigael's/18/*Multi. Loc*
Ben's Kosher Deli/18/*Multi. Loc*
Cho-Sen Garden/21/*Forest Hills*
Domani/21/*E 80s*
Haikara Grill/21/*E 50s*
Kaplan's/16/*E 50s*
Le Marais/20/*W 40s*
Levana/21/*W 60s*
Liebman's/18/*Bronx*
Pastrami Queen/18/*E 80s*
Pongal/21/*Gramercy*
Provi Provi/18/*W 70s*
Ratners/18/*Low E Side*
Saffron/–/*Gramercy*
Second Ave. Deli/22/*E Vil*
Tevere 84/22/*E 80s*
Va Bene/20/*E 80s*
Wolf & Lamb/19/*E 40s*

Lebanese
Al Bustan/19/*E 50s*

Malaysian
Ba Ba Malaysian/19/*Ctown*
Coco Reef/–/*Park Slope*
Franklin Station/18/*TriBeCa*
Nyonya/22/*Multi. Loc*
Penang/19/*Multi. Loc*

Mediterranean
Acquario/21/*NoHo*
Aesop's Tables/21/*Staten Is.*
Alaia/19/*Central Vil*
Amaranth/14/*E 60s*
Artos/20/*E 50s*
Bari/–/*SoHo*
Bouterin/23/*E 50s*
Briam/–/*E Vil*
Café Botanica/21/*W 50s*
Cafe Centro/19/*E 40s*
Café Crocodile/21/*E 70s*
Cafe Greco/17/*E 70s*

Café M/17/E 80s
Cafe Noir/16/SoHo
Cal's/19/Flatiron
Casa La Femme/17/SoHo
Circa/20/E Vil
Coté Sud/18/E 70s
Delphini/20/W 80s
Epices du Traitour/18/W 70s
Europa B&G/–/E 50s
Five Points/–/NoHo
Gus' Figs Bistro/21/Chelsea
Gus' Place/20/Village
Hourglass Tavern/17/W 40s
Il Buco/22/NoHo
Isabella's/20/W 70s
Istana/23/E 50s
Julian's/19/W 50s
La Mangeoire/19/E 50s
Lavagna/22/E Vil
Layla/20/TriBeCa
L'Orange Bleue/18/SoHo
Mangia/21/Multi. Loc
Matthew's/21/E 60s
Medusa/17/Flatiron
Metronome/18/Flatiron
Mezze/19/E 40s
Mignon/–/Carroll Gdns.
Nick & Toni's/18/W 60s
Nicole's/–/E 60s
Palette/–/W 50s
Pangea/19/E Vil
Picholine/26/W 60s
Place/22/Village
Provence/22/SoHo
Red Cat/23/Chelsea
Sahara/19/Gravesend
Salam Cafe/21/Village
Savoy/23/SoHo
Scarabée/22/E 50s
Sharz Cafe/21/E 90s
Spartina/21/TriBeCa
Spazzia/19/W 70s
Sud/18/Village
Sugar Bar/19/W 70s
Syrah/18/E 70s
Tazza/20/Chelsea
Verbena/24/Gramercy

Mexican/Tex-Mex
Benny's Burritos/17/Multi. Loc
Bright Food Shop/19/Chelsea
Burritoville/15/Multi. Loc
Café Frida/17/W 70s
Canyon Road/20/E 70s
El Parador/19/Murray Hill
El Teddy's/17/TriBeCa
Gabriela's/20/W 90s
Iguana/19/W 50s
La Cocina/18/Multi. Loc

L-Ray/18/Village
Lupe's East L.A./17/SoHo
Mamá Mexico/20/W 90s
Mary Ann's/16/Multi. Loc
Maya/24/E 60s
Maz Mezcal/20/E 80s
Mexicana Mama/24/Village
Mi Cocina/22/Village
Mi Nidito/18/W 50s
Rocking Horse/21/Chelsea
Rodeo B&G/–/Gramercy
Rosa Mexicano/23/E 50s
Rosa's Place/18/W 40s
Santa Fe/19/W 60s
Taqueria Mexico/19/Village
Tio Pepe/19/Village
Tortilla Flats/15/Village
Vera Cruz/19/Williamsburg
Zarela/22/E 50s
Zócalo/22/Multi. Loc

Middle Eastern
Al Bustan/19/E 50s
Azuri Cafe/21/W 50s
Black Betty/–/Williamsburg
Capital/19/E 70s
Casa La Femme/17/SoHo
Layla/20/TriBeCa
Moustache/21/Multi. Loc
Oznot's Dish/22/Williamsburg
Persepolis/19/E 70s
Sahara/19/Gravesend
Salam Cafe/21/Village

Moroccan
Bar Six/17/Village
Café Fès/17/Village
Cafe Noir/16/SoHo
Chez Es Saada/18/E Vil
Country Cafe/21/SoHo
L'Orange Bleue/18/SoHo
Lotfi's/19/W 40s
Mezze/19/E 40s

Noodle Shops
Big Wong/21/Ctown
Bo-Ky/19/Ctown
China Fun/15/Multi. Loc
Honmura An/25/SoHo
Kelley & Ping/18/SoHo
Lili's Noodle Shop/–/E 80s
Little Szechuan/19/Ctown
Menchanko-tei/18/Multi. Loc
New York Noodle/21/Ctown
Noodles on 28/18/Gramercy
Ollie's/16/Multi. Loc
Onigashima/20/W 50s
Republic/16/Union Sq.
Sammy's Noodle/18/Village
Sam's Noodle/19/Gramercy
Sobaya/20/E Vil
Sweet-n-Tart/20/Multi. Loc

Nuevo Latino

Cabana/*20/Multi. Loc*
Mosaico/*18/Murray Hill*
Patria/*25/Flatiron*
Sonora/*21/Murray Hill*
Vox/*–/Chelsea*

Persian

Patoug Manhattan/*–/Murray Hill*
Persepolis/*19/E 70s*

Peruvian

Coco Roco/*21/Park Slope*
El Pollo/*19/E 90s*
Flor de Mayo/*20/Multi. Loc*
Rinconcito Peru/*21/W 50s*

Pizza

Angelo's Coal Oven/*20/W 50s*
Arturo's Pizzeria/*19/Village*
Bella Blu/*18/E 70s*
Bella Donna/*18/Multi. Loc*
Bellavista/*20/Bronx*
Bricco/*19/Multi. Loc*
Brio/*18/E 60s*
Cafe Fiorello/*19/W 60s*
California Pizza/*15/E 60s*
Candido Pizza/*19/E 80s*
Chelsea Rist./*21/Chelsea*
Col Legno/*20/E Vil*
Da Ciro/*21/Murray Hill*
Da Nico/*21/Little Italy*
Denino's Pizzeria/*23/Staten Is.*
Don Giovanni/*17/Multi. Loc*
Europa B&G/*–/E 50s*
Freddie & Pepper's/*19/W 70s*
Fresco by Scotto/*23/E 50s*
Gigino Trattoria/*21/TriBeCa*
Goodfella's/*19/Multi. Loc*
Grimaldi's/*26/Bklyn Hts.*
Joe's Pizza/*20/Village*
John's Pizzeria/*21/Multi. Loc*
La Pizza Fresca/*21/Flatiron*
La Vineria/*18/W 50s*
Lento's/*19/Multi. Loc*
Little Italy Pizza/*21/Multi. Loc*
Lombardi's/*25/SoHo*
Luca Lounge/*20/E Vil*
L'Ulivo Focacceria/*21/SoHo*
Mad 28/*17/Gramercy*
Mediterraneo/*18/E 60s*
Mezzaluna/*19/E 70s*
Moustache Pitza/*21/Multi. Loc*
Naples 45/*17/E 40s*
Nick's Pizza/*25/Forest Hills*
101/*19/Bay Ridge*
Orso/*22/W 40s*
Paper Moon Exp./*18/E 50s*
Patsy's Pizza/*21/Multi. Loc*
Petaluma/*18/E 70s*
Pintaile's Pizza/*19/Multi. Loc*

Pizza Borgo/*–/Central Vil*
Pizzeria Uno/*13/Multi. Loc*
Polistina's/*18/W 80s*
Salute!/*17/Murray Hill*
Scopa/*–/Gramercy*
Serafina Fab. Grill/*19/E 60s*
Serafina Fab. Pizza/*20/E 70s*
Spartina/*21/TriBeCa*
Totonno Pizzeria/*21/Multi. Loc*
Tratt. L'incontro/*–/Astoria*
Tratt. Romana/*25/Staten Is.*
Two Boots/*19/Multi. Loc*
V&T Pizzeria/*19/W 110s*
Vinnie's Pizza/*21/W 70s*

Polish

Christine's/*16/E Vil*
Teresa's/*18/Multi. Loc*

Portuguese

Luzia's/*17/W 80s*
O Padeiro/*19/Chelsea*
Pão!/*22/SoHo*

Puerto Rican

Jimmy's Bronx/*19/Bronx*
La Taza de Oro/*18/Chelsea*
Old San Juan/*17/Multi. Loc*

Russian

Andrusha/*17/E 90s*
Caviar Russe/*24/E 50s*
Caviarteria/*23/Multi. Loc*
FireBird/*21/W 40s*
Kiev/*17/E Vil*
Petrossian/*25/W 50s*
Pravda/*16/SoHo*
Rasputin/*17/Brighton Bch.*
Russian Samovar/*19/W 50s*
Russian Tea Room/*–/W 50s*
Simply Caviar/*21/E 50s*

Scandinavian

Aquavit/*25/W 50s*
Christer's/*21/W 50s*
Ulrika's/*23/E 60s*

Seafood

Acadia Parish/*18/Bklyn Hts.*
Alex & Max's/*17/Garment*
American Park/*20/Dtown*
Aquagrill/*25/SoHo*
Atlantic Grill/*22/E 70s*
Blue Water Grill/*23/Union Sq.*
Bongo/*–/Chelsea*
Captain's Table/*19/E 40s*
Cello/*–/E 70s*
Chelsea Lobster/*–/Chelsea*
Christer's/*21/W 50s*
City Crab/*18/Flatiron*
City Hall/*21/TriBeCa*
Cucina Pesce/*19/E Vil*
Docks/*21/Multi. Loc*

Dolphins/*21/Central Vil*
Elias Corner/*24/Astoria*
Esperides/*22/Astoria*
Fish/*21/Village*
Fish Rest./*18/W 90s*
Foley's Fish/*20/W 40s*
Francisco's Centro/*21/Chelsea*
Frutti di Mare/*18/E Vil*
Gage & Tollner/*21/Bklyn Hts.*
Galapagos/*–/E Vil*
Go Fish/*17/E 90s*
Hurricane Island/*17/E 70s*
Jade Plaza/*21/Sunset Pk.*
Joanie's/*22/Gramercy*
Laight Street/*–/TriBeCa*
Le Bernardin/*28/W 50s*
Lobster Box/*17/Bronx*
London Lennie's/*21/Rego Pk.*
Lundy Bros./*15/Sheepshead Bay*
Manhattan Grille/*22/E 60s*
Manhattan Ocean/*25/W 50s*
Maratti/*23/E 60s*
Marina Cafe/*17/Staten Is.*
Marylou's/*19/Village*
Milos/*26/W 50s*
Moran's/*18/Chelsea*
Oceana/*27/E 50s*
Ocean Grill/*23/W 70s*
Oriental Garden/*22/Ctown*
Oyster Bar (Gr. Cent.)/*22/E 40s*
Oyster Bar/Plaza/*20/W 50s*
Pearl Oyster Bar/*25/Village*
Petite Crevette/*19/Bklyn Hts.*
Pier 25A/*17/Bayside*
Ping's Seafood/*21/Multi. Loc*
Pisces/*21/E Vil*
Rafina/*20/E 70s*
Rosehill/*–/Murray Hill*
Roy's NY/*24/Dtown*
Sea Horse Grill/*18/W 40s*
Shaffer City/*20/Flatiron*
Stella del Mare/*20/Murray Hill*
Taverna Kyclades/*22/Astoria*
Trata/*22/E 70s*
Tropica/*22/E 40s*
Tupelo Grill/*19/Garment*
Uncle Jack's/*22/Bayside*
Wilkinson's/*22/E 80s*

Senegalese
Chez Gnagna Koty's/*23/Garment*

Singaporean
Coco Reef/*–/Park Slope*

Soups
Daily Soup/*19/Multi. Loc*
Hale & Hearty/*20/Multi. Loc*
Seaport Soup/*20/Dtown*
Souperman/*20/Dtown*
Soup Kitchen, Al's/*26/W 50s*

South American
Bistro Latino/*18/W 50s*
Boca Chica/*19/E Vil*
Bolivar/*19/E 60s*
Cabana/*20/Multi. Loc*
Café Habana/*18/SoHo*
Calle Ocho/*23/W 80s*
Campo/*20/Village*
Chimichurri Grill/*21/W 40s*
Churr. Plantation/*20/W 50s*
Churr. Plataforma/*21/W 40s*
El Pollo/*19/E 90s*
Galapagos/*–/E Vil*
Ideya/*19/SoHo*
Mosaico/*18/Murray Hill*
Pampa/*21/W 90s*
Patria/*25/Flatiron*
Pomaire/*17/W 40s*
Rio de Janeiro's/*19/W 40s*
Riodizio/*18/Central Vil*
Sonora/*21/Murray Hill*
Torch/*19/Low E Side*
Vandam/*19/SoHo*
Via Brasil/*20/W 40s*
Viva Brasil/*–/W 80s*

Southern/Soul
Brother Jimmy's/*15/Multi. Loc*
Brothers BBQ/*15/Village*
B. Smith's/*18/W 40s*
Bubby's/*19/TriBeCa*
Copeland's/*19/W 90s*
Cowgirl Hall/*14/Village*
Emily's/*20/E 110s*
Harvest/*17/Cobble Hill*
Jezebel/*20/W 40s*
Justin's/*17/Flatiron*
Little Jezebel/*18/W 80s*
Live Bait/*14/Flatiron*
Lola/*20/Flatiron*
Londel's/*21/W 90s*
Mardi Gras/*19/Forest Hills*
Maroons/*–/Chelsea*
Mekka/*19/E Vil*
Nadine's/*16/Village*
Old Devil Moon/*17/E Vil*
Pink Tea Cup/*18/Village*
Shark Bar/*20/W 70s*
Soul Cafe/*19/W 40s*
Soul Fixins'/*20/Garment*
Sweet Mamas/*–/Park Slope*
Sylvia's/*19/W 120s*
Virgil's BBQ/*20/W 40s*
Well's/*19/W 90s*

Southwestern
Canyon Road/*20/E 70s*
Cilantro/*18/E 80s*
Citrus B&G/*18/W 70s*
Cowgirl Hall/*14/Village*

Manhattan Chili/16/Multi. Loc
Mesa Grill/24/Union Sq.
Miracle Grill/20/Multi. Loc
Sandoval/18/W 70s
Santa Fe/19/W 60s
SouthWest NY/–/Dtown
Tapika/21/W 50s

Spanish
Bolo/23/Flatiron
Cafe Español/20/Village
Domingo/18/E 40s
El Charro/22/Village
El Cid/22/Chelsea
El Faro/21/Village
El Pote/20/Murray Hill
El Quijote/19/Chelsea
Flor de Sol/18/TriBeCa
Francisco's Centro/21/Chelsea
Jimmy's Bronx/19/Bronx
La Paella/19/E Vil
Malaga/20/E 70s
Marbella/20/Bayside
Marichu/22/E 40s
Ñ 33 Crosby/18/SoHo
Pintxos/20/SoHo
Rinçon España/20/Village
Rio Mar/19/Village
Sala/–/NoHo
Sevilla/21/Village
Solera/21/E 50s
Taperia Madrid/–/E 70s
Tio Pepe/19/Village
Toledo/22/Murray Hill
Xunta/19/E Vil

Sri Lankan
Lakruwana/17/W 40s

Steakhouses
Angelo & Maxie's/20/Flatiron
Ben Benson's/22/W 50s
Benihana/16/Multi. Loc
Billy's/17/E 50s
Bobby Van's/21/E 40s
Bull & Bear/18/E 40s
Christos Hasapo/21/Astoria
Churr. Plantation/20/W 50s
Churr. Plataforma/21/W 40s
Cité/22/W 50s
City Hall/21/TriBeCa
Dan Maxwell's/18/E 80s
Delmonico's/20/Dtown
Embers/21/Bay Ridge
Frankie & Johnnie's/21/Multi. Loc
Frank's Rest./20/Chelsea
Gage & Tollner/21/Bklyn Hts.
Gallagher's/21/W 50s
Keens Steakhse./21/Garment
Knickerbocker B&G/20/Central Vil
Le Marais/20/W 40s

Les Halles/21/Gramercy
Maloney & Porcelli/22/E 50s
Manhattan Grille/22/E 60s
Michael Jordan's/21/E 40s
Mike & Tony's/22/Park Slope
Moran's/18/Chelsea
Mormando's/18/W 70s
Morton's/23/Multi. Loc
Oak Room/19/W 50s
Old Homestead/21/Chelsea
Palm/25/Multi. Loc
Peter Luger/28/Williamsburg
Pietro's/22/E 40s
Post House/24/E 60s
Ruth's Chris/22/W 50s
Smith & Wollensky/23/E 40s
Soho Steak/20/SoHo
Sparks/25/E 40s
Steak au Poivre/18/E 60s
Sur/21/Carroll Gdns.
Tapika/21/W 50s
Triplets Old NY/19/SoHo
Tupelo Grill/19/Garment
Uncle Jack's/22/Bayside
Wally's & Joseph's/21/W 40s
West 63rd Steak/21/W 60s
Wild Blue/25/Dtown
Wolf & Lamb/19/E 40s
Wollensky's Grill/22/E 40s

Swiss
Roettele/18/E Vil

Tapas
Cafe Español/20/Multi. Loc
Cafe Noir/16/SoHo
Divine Bar/17/Multi. Loc
El Cid/22/Chelsea
Flor de Sol/18/TriBeCa
Global 33/17/E Vil
La Paella/19/E Vil
Ñ 33 Crosby/18/SoHo
Pintxos/20/SoHo
Rio Mar/19/Village
Solera/21/E 50s
Taperia Madrid/–/E 70s
Xunta/19/E Vil

Thai
Bangkok Cuisine/17/W 50s
Chanpen Thai/20/W 50s
Elephant/22/E Vil
Holy Basil/22/E Vil
Jai Ya Thai/20/Multi. Loc
Jasmine/21/E 80s
Kin Khao/21/SoHo
Lemongrass Grill/17/Multi. Loc
Little Basil/–/Village
Planet Thailand/23/Williamsburg
Pongsri Thai/21/Multi. Loc
Q, a Thai Bistro/23/Forest Hills

Rain/*21/Multi. Loc*
Red Garlic/*19/W 50s*
Reg'l Thai Sa-Woy/*22/E 70s*
Reg'l Thai Taste/*19/Chelsea*
River/*19/W 70s*
Royal Siam/*20/Chelsea*
Ruby Foo's/*21/W 70s*
Rungsit Thai/*18/Gramercy*
Sala Thai/*20/E 80s*
Seeda Thai/*19/W 50s*
Siam Inn/*21/W 50s*
Spice/*19/Multi. Loc*
Thai Cafe/*22/Greenpt.*
Thai House/*22/TriBeCa*
Thailand/*23/Ctown*
Toons/*18/Multi. Loc*
Topaz Thai/*21/W 50s*
Typhoon/*17/E 50s*
Ubol's Kitchen/*22/Astoria*
Vong/*25/E 50s*
Wondee Siam/*–/W 50s*

Tibetan
Lhasa/*17/E Vil*
Tibet on Houston/*–/Village*
Tsampa/*18/E Vil*

Tunisian
Epices du Traiteur/*18/W 70s*
La Baraka/*22/Little Neck*

Turkish
Agora/*17/E 80s*
Deniz/*20/E 50s*
Mesopotamia/*18/E Vil*
Pasha/*22/W 70s*
Sahara/*19/Gravesend*
Sultan/*21/E 70s*
Turkish Kitchen/*21/Gramercy*
Üsküdar/*20/E 70s*

Ukrainian
Ukrainian/*18/E Vil*
Veselka/*18/E Vil*

Vegetarian
Angelica Kitchen/*19/E Vil*
Café Boulud/*27/E 70s*

Candle Cafe/*19/E 70s*
Hangawi/*23/Murray Hill*
Helianthus/*18/SoHo*
Herban Kitchen/*20/SoHo*
Josie's/*21/W 70s*
Mavalli Palace/*21/Gramercy*
Pongal/*21/Gramercy*
Quantum Leap/*17/Multi. Loc*
Saffron/*–/Gramercy*
Spring St. Nat./*17/SoHo*
Thali Vegetarian/*20/Village*
Tiffin/*21/Dtown*
Vatan/*21/Gramercy*
Veg. Paradise/*19/Multi. Loc*
Zenith Vegetarian/*18/W 50s*
Zen Palate/*19/Multi. Loc*

Venezuelan
Flor's Kitchen/*19/E Vil*

Vietnamese
Bo-Ky/*19/Ctown*
Can/*19/SoHo*
Cuisine de Saigon/*18/Village*
Cyclo/*21/E Vil*
Indochine/*21/Central Vil*
L'Annam/*19/Gramercy*
La Soirée d'Asie/*21/E 60s*
Le Colonial/*22/E 50s*
MeKong/*18/SoHo*
Miss Saigon/*19/E 80s*
Nam Phuong/*20/TriBeCa*
New Pasteur/*20/Ctown*
Nha Trang/*22/Ctown*
Pho Bang/*19/Multi. Loc*
Pho Viet Huong/*21/Ctown*
Rain/*21/Multi. Loc*
River/*19/W 70s*
Saigon Grill/*22/Multi. Loc*
Seeda Thai/*19/W 50s*
Uncle Pho/*–/Carroll Gdns.*
Vermicelli/*20/E 70s*
Vietnam/*23/Ctown*

LOCATIONS

Restaurant name followed by its street location.
(A = Avenue; s = Street, e.g. 1A/116s = First Ave. at 116th St.,
3A/82-3s = Third Ave. between 82nd & 83rd Sts.)

East 90s & Up
(East of Fifth Avenue)
Andrusha *Lex/90-1s*
Barking Dog *3A/94s*
Bistro du Nord *Mad/93s*
Brother Jimmy's *3A/92s*
Burritoville *3A/90-1s*
Demi *Mad/93s*
Ecco-la *3A/93s*
Eli's Vinegar Factory *91s/York-1A*
El Pollo *1A/90-1s*
Emily's *5A/111-2s*
Go Fish *3A/93-4s*
Island *Mad/92-3s*
Jackson Hole *Mad/91s*
Joanna's *92s/5A-Mad*
Maxx *2A/93s*
Pascalou *Mad/92-3s*
Patsy's Pizza *1A/117-8s*
Pintaile's Pizza *91s/5A-Mad*
Rao's *114s/Pleasant*
Sachi *Mad/94-5s*
Sarabeth's *Mad/92-3s*
Sharz Cafe *90s/3A-Lex*
Table d'Hôte *92s/Mad-Park*
Vico *Mad/92-3s*
Yura & Co. *Mad/92s; 3A/92s*

East 80s
(East of Fifth Avenue)
Agora *1A/82-3s*
Baluchi's *2A/81-2s*
Bella Donna *1A/86-7s*
Brasserie Julien *3A/80-1s*
Butterfield 81 *81s/Lex-3A*
Café Guy Pascal *Mad/89s*
Café M *5A/81s*
Cafe Trevi *1A/81-2s*
Caffe Grazie *84s/Mad-5A*
Candido Pizza *1A/83-4s*
Carino *2A/88-9s*
Celadon *Mad/85-6s*
Cilantro *2A/88-9s*
Ci Vediamo *3A/81s*
Comfort Diner *86s/Lex*
Dan Maxwell's *2A/88-9s*
Demarchelier *86s/Mad-Park*
Divino *2A/80-1s*
Domani *1A/82-3s*
Donguri *83s/1-2A*
Dt•UT *2A/84-5s*
E.A.T. *Mad/80-1s*
Elaine's *2A/88-9s*
Elio's *2A/84-5s*

Eli's Manhattan *3A/80s*
Erminia *83s/2-3A*
Etats-Unis *81s/2-3A*
Firenze *2A/82-3s*
Girasole *82s/Lex-3A*
Heidelberg *2A/85-6s*
India Grill *81s/2-3A*
Jackson Hole *2A/83-4s*
Jacques' Bistro *85s/2-3A*
Jasmine *2A/84s*
Kings' Carriage Hse. *82s/2-3A*
Krispy Kreme *3A/84-5s*
La Forêt *1A/88-9s*
La Fourchette *84s/1A*
Le Boeuf à la Mode *81s/York-E. End*
Le Pain Quotidien *Mad/84-5s*
Le Refuge *82s/Lex-3A*
Lili's Noodle Shop *3A/84-5s*
Lobster Club *80s/Mad-5A*
Luca *1A/88-9s*
Maz Mezcal *86s/1-2A*
Mazzei Osteria *2A/81s*
Miss Saigon *3A/80-1s*
Mocca *2A/82-3s*
Nicola's *84s/Lex-3A*
Our Place *3A/82s*
Paola's *84s/2-3A*
Papaya King *86s/3A*
Pastrami Queen *Lex/85-6s*
Penang *83s/2A*
Pig Heaven *2A/80-1s*
Pintaile's Pizza *York/83-4s*
Pizzeria Uno *86s/2-3A*
Primavera *1A/82s*
Quattro Gatti *81s/2-3A*
Saigon Grill *2A/88s*
Sala Thai *2A/89-90s*
Sesumi *2A/85-6s*
Sirabella's *E. End/82-3s*
Sistina *2A/80-1s*
Starbucks *87s/Lex*
Tevere 84 *84s/Lex-3A*
Tony's Di Napoli *2A/83-4s*
Totonno Pizzeria *2A/80-1s*
Trastevere *85s/1-2A*
Tratt. Pesce/Pasta *3A/87-8s*
Tratt. Rustica *85s/1-2A*
Triangolo *83s/1-2A*
Va Bene *2A/82-3s*
Vespa *2A/84-5s*
Viand *86s/2A*
Wilkinson's *York/83-4s*
Wu Liang Ye *86s/2-3A*

York Grill *York/88-9s*
Zócalo *82s/Lex-3A*

East 70s
(East of Fifth Avenue)
Afghan Kebab Hse. *2A/70-1s*
Annie's *3A/78-9s*
Atlantic Grill *3A/76-7s*
Baraonda *2A/75s*
Bardolino *2A/77-8s*
Bella Blu *Lex/70-1s*
Bella Donna *77s/1-2A*
Bistro Le Steak *3A/75s*
Brother Jimmy's *1A/76s*
Brunelli *York/75s*
Burritoville *1A/77-8s*
Café Boulud *76s/5A-Mad*
Café Crocodile *74s/1-2A*
Cafe Greco *2A/71-2s*
Café Word/Mouth *Lex/72-3s*
Caffe Buon Gusto *77s/2-3A*
Campagnola *1A/73-4s*
Candle Cafe *3A/74-5s*
Canyon Road *1A/76-7s*
Capital *2A/74-5s*
Carlyle *76s/Mad*
Cello *77s/Mad-Park*
Coconut Grill *2A/77s*
Coco Pazzo *74s/Mad-5A*
Cool Hse. of Loo *3A/78-9s*
Coté Sud *78s/Lex-3A*
Cucina Vivolo *74s/Lex-Park*
Dallas BBQ *3A/72-3s*
Due *3A/79-80s*
EJ's Lunch. *3A/73s*
El Ombú *1A/73-4s*
Grace's *71s/3A*
Grande Mela *2A/73-4s*
Haru *3A/76s*
Hurricane Island *3A/74-5s*
Ikeno Hana *Lex/72-3s*
Il Monello *2A/76-7s*
Il Riccio *79s/Lex-3A*
J.G. Melon *3A/74s*
La Gondola *2A/74-5s*
La Tour *3A/75-6s*
Lenox Room *3A/73-4s*
Le Petit Hulot *Lex/70-1s*
Loui Loui *3A/75s*
Lumi *Lex/70s*
Lusardi's *2A/77-8s*
Maison *2A/77s*
Malaga *73s/1A-York*
Mark's *77s/Mad*
Maruzzella *1A/77-8s*
Mary Ann's *2A/78-9s*
Mezzaluna *3A/74-5s*
Mingala Burmese *2A/72-3s*
Nino's *1A/72-3s*
Orienta *75s/2-3A*

Palmetta *78s/2-3A*
Pamir *2A/74-5s*
Park View/Boathse. *E. Park Dr./72s*
Parma *3A/79-80s*
Payard Pâtisserie *Lex/73-4s*
Persepolis *2A/74-5s*
Petaluma *1A/73s*
Pintaile's Pizza *York/76-7s*
P.J. Bernstein Deli *3A/70-1s*
Quatorze Bis *79s/1-2A*
Rafina *York/78-9s*
Reg'l Thai Sa-Woy *1A/77s*
Sant Ambroeus *Mad/77-8s*
Sarabeth's *Mad/75s*
Serafina Fab. Pizza *Mad/79s*
Sette Mezzo *Lex/70-1s*
Shabu-Shabu 70 *70s/1-2A*
Shabu-Tatsu *York/75s*
Spice *2A/73-4s*
Starbucks *1A/75s*
Sultan *2A/74-5s*
Sushi Hana *2A/78s*
Sushi of Gari *78s/1A*
Swifty's *Lex/72-3s*
Syrah *2A/72-3s*
Taperia Madrid *2A/76-7s*
Toraya *71s/5A-Mad*
Trata *2A/70-1s*
Trois Jean *79s/Lex-3A*
Üsküdar *2A/73-4s*
Vermicelli *2A/77-8s*
Viand *Mad/78s*
Vivolo *74s/Lex-Park*
Willow *Lex/73s*
Zuccherino *2A/77-8s*
Zucchero e Pomodori *2A/74-5s*

East 60s
(East of Fifth Avenue)
Amaranth *62s/5A-Mad*
Aureole *61s/Mad-Park*
Baluchi's *1A/63s*
Bolivar *60s/2-3A*
Bravo Gianni *63s/2-3A*
Brio *Lex/61-2s*
Brown's *61s/Mad-Park*
Cabana *3A/60-1s*
Cafe Nosidam *Mad/66s*
Café Pierre *61s/5A-Mad*
California Pizza *60s/2-3A*
Canaletto *60s/2-3A*
China Fun *2A/65s*
Cibi Cibi *60s/3A*
Circus *Lex/62-3s*
Club Macanudo *63s/Mad-Park*
Daniel *65s/Mad-Park*
Destinée *61s/Lex-Park*
East River Cafe *1A/61s*
Ferrier *65s/Mad-Park*
Fireman's of B'klyn *3A/63-4s*

Focaccia Fiorentina *1A/64s*
Fred's at Barneys *61s/5A-Mad*
Gino *Lex/60-1s*
Hale & Hearty *Lex/64-5s*
Henry's Evergreen *1A/69-70s*
Il Gatto/La Volpe *1A/63-4s*
Il Pellicano *62s/1A-York*
Il Vagabondo *62s/1-2A*
Il Valletto, Sofia *61s/Lex-Park*
Isle of Capri *3A/61s*
Jackson Hole *64s/2-3A*
John's Pizzeria *64s/1A-York*
Jo Jo *64s/Lex-3A*
Kitaro *1A/63-4s*
L'Absinthe *67s/2-3A*
La Goulue *Mad/64-5s*
L'Ardoise *1A/65-6s*
La Soirée d'Asie *64s/Lex-3A*
Le Bilboquet *63s/Mad-Park*
Le Bistrot de Maxim *Mad/61s*
Le Charlot *69s/Mad-Park*
Le Régence *64s/Mad-Park*
Le Taxi *60s/Mad-Park*
Le Veau D'Or *60s/Lex-Park*
Lx *60s/Mad-Park*
Manhattan Grille *1A/63-4s*
Maratti *62s/Lex-Park*
Match Uptown *60s/Mad-Park*
Matthew's *3A/61s*
Maya *1A/64-5s*
Mediterraneo *2A/66s*
Merchants *1A/62s*
Mme. Romaine *61s/Lex-Park*
Mon Petit Cafe *Lex/62s*
Nello *Mad/62-3s*
Nicole's *60s/5A-Mad*
Park Ave. Cafe *63s/Lex-Park*
Patsy's Pizza *2A/69s*
Pintaile's Pizza *2A/64-5s*
Post House *63s/Mad-Park*
Primola *2A/64-5s*
Rain *3A/62-3s*
Regency *Park/61s*
Scalinatella *61s/3A*
Serafina Fab. Grill *61s/Mad-Park*
Serendipity 3 *60s/2-3A*
Steak au Poivre *1A/63-4s*
Sushihatsu *1A/62-3s*
Toscana *Lex/64-5s*
212 *65s/Lex-Park*
Ulrika's *60s/Lex-Park*
Viand *Mad/61-2s*
Via Oreto *1A/61-2s*

East 50s
(East of Fifth Avenue)
Acacia *59s/2-3A*
Al Bustan *3A/50-1s*
An American Place *Lex/50-1s*
Anche Vivolo *58s/2-3A*

Artos *53s/1-2A*
Bellini *52s/2-3A*
Benihana *56s/Lex-Park*
Berkeley B&G *Mad/55-6s*
Bice Rist. *54s/5A-Mad*
Billy's *1A/52-3s*
Bouterin *59s/1A-Sutton Pl.*
Broadway Diner *Bway/55s*
Bruno *58s/2-3A*
Burger Heaven *Mad/54-5s; 53s/5A-Mad*
Cafe du Pont *1A/56-7s*
Caffe Buon Gusto *2A/53-4s*
Caviar Russe *Mad/54-5s*
Caviarteria *Park/59s*
Cellini *54s/Mad-Park*
Chianti *2A/54-5s*
Chola *58s/2-3A*
Cinquanta *50s/Mad-Park*
Clarke's, P.J. *3A/55s*
Coco Pazzo Café *59s/5A-Mad*
Columbus Bakery *1A/52-3s*
Cosi Sandwich *56s/Mad-Park; 52s/Lex-3A*
Da Antonio *55s/Lex-3A*
Dawat *58s/2-3A*
DeGrezia *50s/2-3A*
Della Femina *54s/Lex-Park*
Deniz *57s/1A-Sutton Pl.*
Divine Bar *51s/2-3A*
Eros *1A/58-9s*
Ess-a-Bagel *3A/50-1s*
Europa B&G *Lex/53s*
Felidia *58s/2-3A*
57 57 *57s/Mad-Park*
Four Seasons *52s/Lex-Park*
Fresco by Scotto *52s/Mad-Park*
Fresco on the Go *52s/Mad-Park*
Giambelli *50s/Mad-Park*
Haikara Grill *2A/53-4s*
Harry Cipriani *5A/59-60s*
Houston's *3A/54s*
Il Menestrello *52s/5A-Mad*
Il Nido *53s/2-3A*
Il Valentino *56s/1-2A*
Istana *Mad/51s*
Jubilee *54s/1-2A*
Kaplan's *59s/Mad-Park*
King Cole Bar *55s/5A-Mad*
Kokachin *52s/5A-Mad*
Korea Palace *54s/Lex-Park*
La Gioconda *53s/2-3A*
La Grenouille *52s/5A-Mad*
La Mangeoire *2A/53-4s*
La Mediterranée *2A/50-1s*
Le Cirque 2000 *Mad/50-1s*
Le Colonial *57s/Lex-3A*
L'Entrecote *1A/57-8s*
Leopard *50s/2-3A*
Le Perigord *52s/1A-FDR Dr.*
Lespinasse *55s/5A-Mad*

Les Sans Culottes *2A/57-8s*
Le Train Bleu *3A/59-60s*
Luna Piena *53s/2-3A*
Lutèce *50s/2-3A*
Maloney & Porcelli *50s/Mad-Park*
March *58s/1A-Sutton Pl.*
Meltemi *1A/51s*
Metropolitan Cafe *1A/52-3s*
Monkey Bar *54s/Mad-Park*
Montebello *56s/Lex-Park*
Mr. Chow *57s/1-2A*
Mr. K's *Lex/51s*
Neary's *57s/1A*
Nippon *52s/Lex-3A*
Oceana *54s/Mad-Park*
Oikawa *3A/50s*
One 51 *50s/Lex-3A*
Oscar's *50s/Lex*
Otabe *56s/Mad-Park*
Our Place *55s/Lex-3A*
Pamir *1A/58s*
Paper Moon Exp. *59s/Mad-Park*
Paper Moon Mil. *58s/Mad-Park*
Pescatore *2A/50-1s*
Raffaele *1A/57-8s*
Rosa Mexicano *1A/58s*
San Pietro *54s/5A-Mad*
Scarabée *51s/2-3A*
Serafina on Run *58s/Mad-Park*
Seryna *53s/5A-Mad*
Shun Lee Palace *55s/Lex-3A*
Simply Caviar *Park/51s*
Solera *53s/2-3A*
Soma Park *56s/Lex-Park*
Sono *57s/Lex-Park*
Starbucks *Mad/55-6s*
Sushi Rose *52s/2-3A*
Sushisay *51s/Mad-Park*
Tatany 52 *52s/2-3A*
Tea Box *5A/54-5s*
Teodora *57s/Lex-3A*
Townhouse *58s/2-3A*
Tratt. Pesce/Pasta *1A/59s*
Tse Yang *51s/Mad-Park*
Typhoon *54s/5A-Mad*
Vong *54s/3A*
Zarela *2A/50-1s*

East 40s

(East of Fifth Avenue)
Ambassador Grill *UN Plaza/1-2A*
Blackbird *49s/Mad-Park*
Bobby Van's *Park/46s*
Box Tree *49s/2-3A*
Bukhara Grill *49s/2-3A*
Bull & Bear *Lex/49s*
Burger Heaven *Mad/40-1s;
  49s/5A-Mad*
Cafe Centro *45s/Lex-Vanderbilt*
Café de Paris *2A/49s*

Cafe S.F.A. *5A/49-50s*
Captain's Table *2A/46s*
Chiam *48s/Lex-3A*
Chikubu *44s/5A-Mad*
Chin Chin *49s/2-3A*
Cibo *2A/41-2s*
Comfort Diner *45s/2-3A*
Cosi Sandwich *45s/Mad-Vanderbilt*
Daily Soup *43s/Lex-3A; 3A/48-9s*
da Mario *1A/49-50s*
Delegates' Din. Rm. *1A/46s*
Dishes *44s/Mad-Vanderbilt*
Diwan Grill *48s/Lex-3A*
Docks *3A/40s*
Domingo *49s/2-3A*
Ferrara *Mad/45-46s*
Flower Drum *2A/45-6*
Grifone *46s/2-3A*
Hale & Hearty *47s/5A-Mad*
Hatsuhana *48s/5A-Mad; Park/46s*
Heartbeat *49s/Lex-3A*
Il Postino *49s/1-2A*
Inagiku *49s/Lex-Park*
Katsuhama *47s/5A-Mad*
Kuruma Zushi *47s/5A-Mad*
Little Italy Pizza *Vanderbilt/45-6s*
Luna Blu *44s/2-3A*
Mangia *48s/5A-Mad*
Marichu *46s/1-2A*
Menchanko-tei *45s/Lex-3A*
Mezze *44s/5A-Mad*
Michael Jordan's *Vanderbilt/44s*
Morton's *5A/45s*
Nanni *46s/Lex-3A*
Naples 45 *45s/Lex-Vanderbilt*
Osteria Laguna *42s/2-3A*
Oyster Bar *42s/Lex-Vanderbilt*
Palm *2A/44-5s*
Palm Too *2A/44-5s*
Patroon *46s/Lex-3A*
Peacock Alley *Park/49-50s*
Peking Park *Park/40s*
Pershing Sq. *42s/Park*
Phoenix Garden *40s/2-3A*
Pietro's *43s/2-3A*
San Giusto *2A/49-50s*
S. Dynasty *Lex/48s*
Shinbashi *Park/48s*
Sichuan Palace *44s/1-2A*
Smith & Wollensky *3A/49s*
Sparks *46s/2-3A*
Starbucks *Mad/42s; Park/48s*
Sushiden *49s/5A-Mad*
T.G.I. Friday's *5A/48-9s;
  42s/Mad-Vanderbilt*
Thady Con's *2A/48-9s*
Top of the Tower *Mitchell Pl.:1A/49s*
Tropica *45s/Lex-Vanderbilt*
Tudor Grill *Tudor City Pl./1-2A*

Wolf & Lamb *48s/5A-Mad*
Wollensky's Grill *49s/3A*
Zócalo *42s/Vanderbilt*

West 90s & Up
(West of Fifth Avenue)
Alouette *Bway/97-8s*
Bleu Evolution *187s/Ft. Wash. Ave.*
Cafe Con Leche *Amst./95-6s*
Cafe St. John *110s/Amst.*
Carmine's *Bway/90-1s*
Copeland's *145s/Amst.-Bway*
Empire Szechuan *Bway/100s;*
  Bway/97s; Bway/170-1s
Fish Rest. *Bway/108s*
Flor de Mayo *Bway/100-1s*
Gabriela's *Amst./93s*
Gennaro *Amst./92-3s*
Hunan Park *Col./95s*
Kismat *Ft. Wash. Ave./187s*
Krispy Kreme *125s/8A*
La Cocina *Bway/98-9s*
Le Monde *Bway/112-3s*
Lemongrass Grill *Bway/94-5s*
Londel's *8A/139-40s*
Mamá Mexico *Bway/101-2s*
Mary Ann's *Bway/90-1s*
Métisse *105s/Amst.-Bway*
Ollie's *Bway/116s*
Pampa *Amst./97-8s*
Papaya King *125s/Lenox-7A*
Starbucks *125s/Lenox*
Sylvia's *Lenox/126-7s*
Terrace *119s/Amst.-Morningside*
Tomo Sushi/Sake *Bway/110-1s*
V&T Pizzeria *Amst./110-1s*
Well's *7A/132-3s*
Zula *Amst./122s*

West 80s
(West of Central Park)
Avenue *Col./85s*
Barney Greengrass *Amst./86-7s*
Bella Luna *Col/88-9s*
Brother Jimmy's *Amst./80-1s*
Burritoville *Amst./81-2s*
Cafe Con Leche *Amst./80-1s*
Cafe Lalo *83s/Amst.-Bway*
Calle Ocho *Col/81-2s*
Columbus Bakery *Col./82-3s*
Delphini *Col./85s*
Docks *Bway/89-90s*
Edgar's Cafe *84s/Bway-W. End*
EJ's Lunch. *Amst./81-2s*
Flor de Mayo *Amst./83-4s*
Fred's *Amst./83s*
French Roast *Bway/85s*
Fujiyama Mama *Col./82-3s*
Good Enough to Eat *Amst./83-4s*
Haru *Amst./80-1s*

Jackson Hole *Col./85s*
Kitaro *Amst./84-5s*
La Cocina *85s/Amst.-Bway*
La Mirabelle *86s/Amst.-Col.*
La Rocchetta *Col./84-5s*
Lemongrass Grill *Amst./84s*
Les Routiers *Amst./87-8s*
Little Jezebel *Col./86s*
Louie's Westside *Amst./81s*
Luzia's *Amst./80-1s*
Merchants *Col./85-6s*
Ollie's *Bway/84s*
Pizzeria Uno *Col./81s*
Polistina's *Bway/81-2s*
Popover Cafe *Amst./86-7s*
Puccini *Col./83s*
Rain *82s/Amst.-Col.*
Roppongi *Amst./81s*
Saigon Grill *Bway/87s*
Salt *Col./84-5s*
Sarabeth's *Amst./80-1s*
Silk Rd. Palace *Amst./81-2s*
Starbucks *Bway/87s*
Time Cafe *Bway/85s*
Viva Brasil *Col./82-3s*

West 70s
(West of Central Park)
Baluchi's *Col./73-4s*
Bruculino *Col./70-1s*
Burritoville *72s/Amst.-Col.*
Café Frida *Col./77-8s*
Cafe Luxembourg *70s/Amst.-W. End*
Cafe Mozart *70s/Bway-Col.*
China Fun *Col./71-2s*
Citrus B&G *Amst./75s*
City Grill *Col./72-3s*
Coppola's *79s/Amst.-Bway*
Dallas BBQ *72s/Col.-CPW*
Dining Room/Columbus *Col./78s*
Emack & Bolio's *Amst./78-9s*
Empire Szechuan *72s/Bway-W. End*
Epices du Traiteur *70s/Bway-Col.*
Ernie's *Bway/75-6s*
Freddie & Pepper's *Amst./74-5s*
Gray's Papaya *Bway/72s*
Hunan Park *Col./70-1s*
Isabella's *Col./77s*
Josie's *Amst./74s*
Krispy Kreme *72s/Amst.-Col.*
La Caridad 78 *Bway/78s*
La Grolla *Amst./79-80s*
La Vela *Amst./77-8s*
Mormando's *71s/Col.-CPW*
Niko's *Bway/76s*
North West *Col./79s*
Ocean Grill *Col./78-9s*
Pappardella *Col./75s*
Pasha *71s/Col.-CPW*
Patsy's Pizza *74s/Col.-CPW*

Penang *Col./71s*
Planet Sushi *Amst./78s*
Pomodoro Rosso *Col./70-1s*
Provi Provi *72s/Bway-W. End*
River *Amst./76-7s*
Ruby Foo's *Bway/77s*
Sambuca *72s/Col.-CPW*
Sandoval *Col./72-3s*
Savann *Amst./79-80s*
Scaletta *77s/Col.-CPW*
Sesso *Col./73-4s*
Shark Bar *Amst./74-5s*
Spazzia *Col./77s*
Sugar Bar *72s/Bway-W. End*
Two Two Two *79s/Amst.-Bway*
Vinnie's Pizza *Amst./73-4s*
Zen Palate *Bway/76-7s*

West 60s
(West of Fifth Avenue)
Br. Americaine *64s/Bway-CPW*
Café des Artistes *67s/Col.-CPW*
Cafe Fiorello *Bway/63-4s*
Coco Opera *65s/Col.-CPW*
Empire Szechuan *Col./68-9s*
Gabriel's *60s/Bway-Col.*
Jean Georges *CPW/60-1s*
John's Pizzeria *65s/Col.-CPW*
Josephina *Bway/63-4s*
La Boite en Bois *68s/Col.-CPW*
Levana *69s/Bway-Col.*
Merlot B&G *63s/Bway-Col.*
Nick & Toni's *67s/Bway-Col.*
Ollie's *Bway/67s*
O'Neals' *64s/Bway-CPW*
Picholine *64s/Bway-CPW*
Saloon *Bway/64s*
Santa Fe *69s/Col.-CPW*
Sapphire *Bway/60-1s*
Shun Lee *65s/Col.-CPW*
Shun Lee Cafe *65s/Col.-CPW*
Starbucks *Bway/60s*
Tavern on Green *CPW/66-7s*
Vince & Eddie's *68s/Col.-CPW*
West 63rd Steak *63s/Bway-Col.*

West 50s
(West of Fifth Avenue)
Adrienne *5A/55s*
Afghan Kebab Hse. *9A/51-2s*
André *56s/Bway-8A*
Angelo's Coal Oven *57s/6-7A*
Aquavit *54s/5-6A*
Artusi *52s/5-6A*
Atlas *CPS/5-6A*
Azuri Cafe *51s/9-10A*
Baluchi's *56s/Bway-8A*
Bangkok Cuisine *8A/52-3s*
Bay Leaf *56s/5-6A*
Beacon *56s/5-6A*

Bello *9A/56s*
Ben Benson's *52s/6-7A*
Benihana *56s/5-6A*
Bistro Latino *Bway/54s*
Bombay Palace *52s/5-6A*
Bricco *56s/8-9A*
Broadway Diner *Lex/52s*
Brooklyn Diner *57s/Bway-7A*
Café Botanica *CPS/6-7A*
Caffe Cielo *8A/52-3s*
Carnegie Deli *7A/55s*
Castellano *55s/6-7A*
Chanpen Thai *9A/51s*
Chez Louis *50s/6A*
Chez Napoléon *50s/8-9A*
China Fun *Bway/51s*
China Grill *53s/5-6A*
Christer's *55s/6-7A*
Churr. Plantation *CPS/6-7A*
Ciao Europa *54s/5-6A*
Circo *55s/6-7A*
Cité *51s/6-7A*
Cité Grill *51s/6-7A*
Cosi Sandwich *Bway/51s*
Daily Soup *54s/Bwy-8A*
Dakshin Indian *9A/50s*
Da Tommaso *8A/53-4s*
Druids *10A/50-1s*
Ellen's Stardust *Bway/51s*
Ferrara *Bway/53-4s*
Fontana di Trevi *57s/6-7A*
Gallagher's *52s/Bway-8A*
Giovanni *55s/5-6A*
Halcyon *54s/6-7A*
Hale & Hearty *56s/5-6A*
Hard Rock *57s/Bway-7A*
Harley Davidson *6A/56s*
Heartland Brewery *6A/51s*
Iguana *54s/Bway-8A*
Il Tinello *56s/5-6A*
Island Burgers *9A/51-2s*
Jekyll & Hyde *6A/57-8s*
Joe's Shanghai *56s/5-6A*
JUdson Grill *52s/6-7A*
Julian's *9A/53-4s*
Kabul Cafe *54s/Bway-8A*
Keewah Yen *56s/5-6A*
Kiiroi-Hana *56s/5-6A*
La Bonne Soupe *55s/5-6A*
La Caravelle *55s/5-6A*
La Côte Basque *55s/5-6A*
La Vineria *55s/5-6A*
Le Bar Bat *57s/8-9A*
Le Bernardin *51s/6-7A*
Le Biarritz *57s/8-9A*
Le Bouchon *51s/8-9A*
Le Quercy *55s/5-6A*
Les Pyrénées *51s/Bway-8A*
Les Sans Culottes *51s/8-9A*

Limoncello *7A/50-1s*
Mangia *57s/5-6A*
Mangia e Bevi *9A/53s*
Manhattan Chili *Bway/53-4s*
Manhattan Ocean *58s/5-6A*
Mars 2112 *Bway/50-1s*
Menchanko-tei *55s/5-6A*
Michael's *55s/5-6A*
Mickey Mantle's *CPS/5-6A*
Milos *55s/6-7A*
Mi Nidito *8A/51-2s*
Molyvos *7A/55-6s*
Nirvana *CPS/5-6A*
Nocello *55s/Bway-8A*
Norma's *57s/6-7A*
Oak Room *5A/CPS*
Old San Juan *9A/51-2s*
Onigashima *55s/5-6A*
Oyster Bar/Plaza *58s/5-6A*
Palette *6A/55-6s*
Palio *51s/6-7A*
Palm Court *5A/59s*
Palm West *50s/Bway-8A*
Patsy's *56s/Bway-8A*
Petrossian *58s/7A*
Planet Hollywood *57s/6-7A*
Puttanesca *9A/56s*
Redeye Grill *7A/56s*
Red Garlic *8A/54-5s*
Remi *53s/6-7A*
René Pujol *51s/8-9A*
Rice 'n' Beans *9A/50-1s*
Rinconcito Peru *9A/53-4s*
Rino Trattoria *8A/52-3s*
Route 66 *9A/55-6s*
Russian Samovar *52s/Bway-8A*
Russian Tea Room *57s/6-7A*
Ruth's Chris *51s/6-7A*
San Domenico *CPS/Bway-7A*
Seeda Thai *50s/8-9A*
Seppi's *56s/6-7A*
Sette MoMA *53s/5-6A*
Siam Inn *8A/51-2s*
Soup Kitchen *55s/Bway-8A*
Stage Deli *7A/53-4s*
Starbucks *57s/8-9A*
Sugiyama *55s/Bway-8A*
Sushiya *56s/5-6A*
Tang Pavilion *55s/5-6A*
Tapika *8A/56s*
Ten Kai *56s/5-6A*
T.G.I. Friday's *Bway/52s; 51s/5-6A; 7A/50s*
Tino's *56s/5-6A*
Topaz Thai *56s/6-7A*
Tout Va Bien *51s/8-9A*
Tratt. Dell'Arte *7A/57s*
Trionfo *51s/Bway-8A*
Tuscan Square *51s/5-6A*

'21' Club *52s/5-6A*
Uncle Nick's *9A/50-1s*
ViceVersa *51s/8-9A*
Victor's Cafe *52s/Bway-8A*
Wondee Siam *9A/52-3s*
Zenith Vegetarian *8A/52s*

West 40s
(West of Fifth Avenue, including
Theater District)
Afghan Kebab Hse. *46s/6-7A*
Algonquin *44s/5-6A*
Amarone *9A/47-8s*
Amy's Bread *9A/46-7s*
Bali Nusa Indah *9A/45-6s*
Barbetta *46s/8-9A*
Becco *46s/8-9A*
Brasilia *45s/5-6A*
Bryant Park Cafe *42s/5-6A*
Bryant Park Grill *40s/5-6A*
B. Smith's *8A/47s*
Burritoville *9A/44-5s*
Cabana Carioca *45s/6-7A*
Cafe 1 2 3 *44s/Bway-6A*
Cara Mia *9A/45-6s*
Carmine's *44s/Bway-8A*
Casa Di Meglio *48s/Bway-8A*
Charley O's *45s/Bway-8A*
Charlotte *44s/Bway-6A*
Chez Josephine *42s/9-10A*
Chez Suzette *9A/46-7s*
Chimichurri Grill *9A/43-4s*
Churr. Plataforma *49s/8-9A*
Coco Pazzo Teatro *46s/Bway-8A*
Cosi Sandwich *48s/5-6A; 42s/5-6A*
Daily Soup *8A/43-4s*
Dallas BBQ *43s/Bway-6A*
Delta Grill *9A/48s*
Dish of Salt *47s/6-7A*
Don Giovanni *44s/8-9A*
Edison Cafe *47s/Bway-8A*
ESPN Zone *Bway/42s*
FireBird *46s/8-9A*
Foley's Fish *7A/47-8s*
44 *44s/5-6A*
Frankie & Johnnie's *45s/Bway-8A*
Frico Bar *43s/9A*
Garrick Bistro *49s/Bway-8A*
Hale & Hearty *42s/5-6A*
Hourglass Tavern *46s/8-9A*
Ipanema *46s/5-6A*
Island Spice *44s/9-10A*
Jewel of India *44s/5-6A*
Jezebel *9A/45s*
Joe Allen *46s/8-9A*
John's Pizzeria *44s/Bway-8A*
Katen *Bway/45s*
Krispy Kreme *8A/40-1s*
La Cocina *8A/46-7s*
Lakruwana *44s/8-9A*

Landmark Tavern *11A/46s*
La Primavera *48s/Bway-8A*
La Réserve *49s/5-6A*
La Rivista *46s/8-9A*
Lattanzi *46s/8-9A*
Le Beaujolais *46s/8-9A*
Le Madeleine *46s/9A*
Le Marais *46s/6-7A*
Le Rivage *46s/8-9A*
Les Sans Culottes *46s/8-9A*
Little Italy Pizza *45s/6A*
Local *47s/Bway*
Lotfi's *46s/8-9A*
Luxia *48s/8-9A*
Manhattan Chili *Bway/43s*
Meskerem *47s/9-10A*
Mezzanine *46s/Bway-8A*
Nation *45s/5-6A*
New World Grill *49s/8-9A*
Official All Star *Bway/45s*
Ollie's *44s/Bway-8A*
Orso *46s/8-9A*
Osteria al Doge *44s/Bway-6A*
Palladin *49s/Bway-8A*
Pierre au Tunnel *47s/Bway-8A*
Pietrasanta *9A/47s*
Pomaire *46s/8-9A*
Pongsri Thai *48s/Bway-8A*
Rachel's *9A/43-4s*
Rio de Janeiro's *43s/Bway-6A*
Rosa's Place *48s/8-9A*
Sardi's *44s/Bway-8A*
Sea Horse Grill *8A/48s*
Shaan *48s/5-6A*
Soul Cafe *42s/9-10A*
Starbucks *9A/47s*
Supper Club *47s/Bway-8A*
Sushiden *49s/6-7A*
Sushi Zen *46s/5-6A*
Tennessee Mtn. *45s/Bway-6A*
Torre di Pisa *44s/5-6A*
Tratt. Dopo Teatro *44s/Bway-6A*
Via Brasil *46s/5-6A*
View *Bway/45-6s*
Virgil's BBQ *44s/Bway-6A*
Wally's & Joseph's *49s/Bway-8A*
West Bank Cafe *42s/9-10A*
World Yacht *41s/Hudson River*
Wu Liang Ye *48s/5-6A*
Yamaguchi *45s/5-6A*
Zen Palate *9A/46s*
Zuni *9A/43s*

Murray Hill
(40th to 30th Sts., East of Fifth)
Abigael's *37s/5A-Mad*
Asia de Cuba *Mad/37-8s*
Bellew *33s/3A*
Belluno *Lex/39-40s*
Bienvenue *36s/5A-Mad*

Cinque Terre *38s/Mad-Park*
Coach House *32s/5A-Mad*
Da Ciro *Lex/33-4s*
El Parador *34s/1-2A*
El Pote *2A/38-9s*
Evergreen Shanghai *38s/5A-Mad*
Fino *36s/5A-Mad*
Garden Cafe *38s/Park*
Hangawi *32s/5A-Mad*
Jackson Hole *3A/35s*
La Giara *3A/33-4s*
Lemongrass Grill *34s/Lex-3A*
Marchi's *31s/2-3A*
Mishima *Lex/30-1s*
Morgan Ct. *36s/Mad*
Mosaico *Mad/33-4s*
Nadaman Hakubai *Park/38s*
Nicola Paone *34s/2-3A*
Notaro *2A/34-5s*
Pasticcio *3A/30-1s*
Patoug Manhattan *30s/5A-Mad*
Patsy's Pizza *3A/34-5s*
Porta Rossa *Lex/31s*
Rive Gauche *3A/37s*
Rosehill *32s/Mad-Park*
Rossini's *38s/Lex-Park*
Salute! *Mad/39s*
Sarge's Deli *3A/36-7s*
Sonia Rose *34s/Lex-3A*
Sonora *39s/2-3A*
Stella del Mare *Lex/39-40s*
Sushi Sen-nin *34s/Mad-Park*
Tivoli *3A/34-5s*
Toledo *36s/5A-Mad*
Tratt. Alba *34s/2-3A*
Villa Berulia *34s/Lex-Park*
Water Club *30s/East River*
Waterfront Ale *2A/30s*
Wu Liang Ye *Lex/39-40s*

Gramercy Park
(30th to 24th Sts., East of Fifth Ave.,
and 24th to 14th Sts., East of
Park Ave. S.)
Casa Mia *24s/2-3A*
Cavaliere *3A/17-8s*
Choshi *Irving Pl/19s*
Coppola's *3A/27-8s*
Da Beco *2A/28-9s*
Daily Soup *Park S./24-5s*
Eleven Mad. Pk. *Mad/24s*
Empire Szechuan *3A/27-8s*
Enoteca I Trulli *27s/Lex-Park S.*
Ess-a-Bagel *1A/21s*
Friend of Farmer *Irving Pl/18-9s*
Gamut *25s/Lex-Park*
Globe *Park S./26-7s*
Houston's *27s/Park S.*
I Trulli *27s/Lex-Park S.*
Jai Ya Thai *3A/28s*

Joanie's *28s/Lex-Park S.*
Lady Mendl's *Irving Pl./17-8s*
Lamarca *22s/3A*
L'Annam *3A/28s*
La Petite Auberge *Lex/27-8s*
Les Halles *Park S./28-9s*
Mad 28 *Mad/27-8s*
Mavalli Palace *29s/Mad-Park S.*
Moreno *Irving Pl./18s*
Noodles on 28 *3A/28s*
Novitá *22s/Park S.*
Old San Juan *2A/26s*
Park Bistro *Park S./28-9s*
Paul & Jimmy's *18s/Irv.-Park S.*
Pete's Tavern *18s/Irving Pl.*
Pitchoune *3A/19s*
Pongal *Lex/27-8s*
Pongsri Thai *2A/18s*
Rodeo B&G *3A/27s*
Rolf's *3A/22s*
Rungsit Thai *23s/Lex-3A*
Saffron *Lex/26s*
Sal Anthony's *Irving Pl./17-8s*
Sam's Noodle *3A/29s*
Scopa *28s/Mad-Park S.*
Spencer *18s/Irv. Pl.-Park S.*
Tabla *Mad/25s*
Tatany *3A/27-8s*
Turkish Kitchen *3A/27-8s*
27 Standard *27s/Lex-Park S.*
Union Pacific *22s/Lex-Park S.*
Vatan *3A/29s*
Verbena *Irving Pl./17-8s*
Yama *17s/Irving Pl.*

Garment District & Chelsea
(40th to 24th Sts., West of Fifth
Ave., and 24th to 14th Sts.,
West of Sixth Ave.)
Abigael's *Bway/38-9s*
Alex & Max's *39s/5-6A*
Alley's End *17s/8-9A*
Amy's Bread *9A/15-6s*
Bateaux NY *23s/Hudson River*
Bendix Diner *8A/21s*
Ben's Kosher Deli *38s/7A*
Biricchino *29s/8A*
Bongo *10A/27-8s*
Bottino *10A/24-5s*
Bright Food Shop *8A/21-2s*
Burritoville *39s/8-9A; 23s/7-8A*
Cafeteria *7A/17s*
Chelsea Bistro *23s/8-9A*
Chelsea Grill *8A/16-7s*
Chelsea Lobster *7A/19-20s*
Chelsea Rist. *8A/15-6s*
Chez Gnagna Koty's *9A/39-40s*
Cho Dang Gol *35s/5-6A*
Christina's Kitchen *10A/37-8s*

Cupcake Cafe *9A/39s*
Daily Soup *7A/36-7s*
Daniella *8A/26s*
Da Umberto *17s/6-7A*
Don Giovanni *10A/22-3s*
East of Eighth *23s/7-8A*
Eighteenth & Eighth *8A/18s*
El Cid *15s/8-9A*
El Quijote *23s/7-8A*
Emack & Bolio's *34s/Herald Sq.*
Empire Diner *10A/22s*
Francisco's Centro *23s/6-7A*
Frank's Rest. *10A/15s*
Gascogne *8A/17-8s*
Grand Sichuan Int'l *9A/24s*
Gus' Figs Bistro *27s/7-8A*
Hale & Hearty *9A/15-6s; 7A/35-6s*
Havana Chelsea *8A/19-20s*
JB *9A/22-3s*
Kang Suh *Bway/32s*
Keens Steakhse. *36s/5-6A*
Krispy Kreme *Penn Plaza/33s;*
  23s/7-8A
Kum Gang San *32s/Bway*
La Bergamote *9A/20s*
La Lunchonette *10A/18s*
La Taza de Oro *8A/14-5s*
Lo Gamin *9A/21s*
Le Madri *18s/7A*
Le Singe Vert *7A/19-20s*
Le Zie *7A/20-1s*
Lot 61 *21s/10-1A*
Markt *14s/9A*
Maroons *16s/7-8A*
Mary Ann's *8A/16s*
Merchants *7A/16-7s*
Meriken *7A/21s*
Metro Grill *35s/5-6A*
Moran's *10A/19s*
Negril *23s/8-9A*
Old Homestead *9A/14-5s*
147 *15s/6-7A*
O Padeiro *6A/19-20s*
Oriont *14s/9-10A*
Pepe Giallo *10A/25s*
Petite Abeille *18s/6-7A*
Raymond's *7A/15-6s*
Red Cat *10A/23-4s*
Reg'l Thai Taste *7A/22s*
Rocking Horse *8A/19-20s*
Royal Siam *8A/22-3s*
Siena *9A/22-3s*
Soul Fixins' *34s/8-9A*
Spice *8A/20-1s*
Spirit Cruises *23s/Hudson River*
Starbucks *8A/39s; 8A/35s; 7A/35s*
Sunny East *39s/5-6A*
Tazza *8A/20s*
Tello's Rist. *19s/7-8A*

T.G.I. Friday's *8A/34s*
Tir Na Nóg *8A/33-4s*
Tonic *18s/6-7A*
Trois Canards *8A/19-20s*
T.S. Ma *Penn Pl.: 8A/33s*
Tupelo Grill *Penn Pl.: 33s/7-8A*
Veronica *38s/7-8A*
Viceroy *8A/18s*
Vox *8A/18-9s*
Won Jo *32s/Bway-5A*
Woo Chon *36s/5-6A*

Flatiron District/ Union Square

(Between Chelsea & Gramercy
Park, bounded by 24th and
14th Sts., between 6th Ave.
and Park Ave. S.)
ABC Parlour Cafe *19s/Bway-Park S.*
Alva *22s/Bway-Park S.*
America *18s/Bway-5A*
Angelo & Maxie's *Park S./19s*
Basta Pasta *17s/5-6A*
Bella Donna *23s/Mad*
Blue Water Grill *Union Sq. W./16s*
Bolo *22s/Bway-Park S.*
Bondí *20s/5-6A*
Bricco *22s/5-6A*
Cal's *21s/5-6A*
Campagna *21s/Bway-Park S.*
Candela *16s/Irving Pl.-Park S.*
Chat 'n Chew *16s/5A-Union Sq. W.*
City Bakery *17s/Bway-5A*
City Crab *Park S./19s*
Coffee Shop *Union Sq. W./16s*
Colina *18s/Bway-Park S.*
Cosi Sandwich *17s/Bway-5A*
Daily Soup *17s/Bway-5A*
Eisenberg *5A/22-3s*
Follonico *24s/5-6A*
Giorgio's *21s/Bway-Park S.*
Gramercy Tavern *20s/Bway-Park S.*
Hamachi *20s/Bway-Park S.*
Heartland Brew. *Union Sq. W./16-7s*
Hush *19s/5-6A*
Justin's *21s/5-6A*
L'Acajou *19s/5-6A*
La Griglia *20s/Bway-5A*
La Pizza Fresca *20s/Bway-Park S.*
Lemon *Park S./19s*
L'Express *Park S./20s*
Live Bait *23s/Mad*
Lola *22s/5-6A*
Mayrose *Bway/21s*
Medusa *Park S./19-20s*
Mesa Grill *5A/15-6s*
Metronome *Bway/21s*
Old Town Bar *18s/Bway-Park S.*
Park Avalon *Park S./18-9s*
Patria *Park S./20s*

Periyali *20s/5-6A*
Privé *19s/Bway-Park S.*
Punch *Bway/20-1s*
Republic *Union Sq. W./16-7s*
Ribollita *Park S./20-1s*
Shaffer City *21s/5-6A*
Silver Swan *20s/Bway-Park S.*
Starbucks *6A/22s*
Steak Frites *16s/5A-Union Sq. W.*
Tossed *Park S./22-3s*
Tratt. I Pagliacci *Park S./19-20s*
T Salon *20s/Bway-5A*
Union Sq. Cafe *16s/5A-Union Sq. W.*
Veritas *20s/Bway-Park S.*
Zen Palate *Union Sq. E./16s*

Greenwich Village

(14th to Houston Sts., West of Fifth)
Anglers & Writers *Hudson/St. Luke's*
Antonio *13s/6-7A*
Arturo's Pizzeria *Houston/Thompson*
Astray Café *Horatio/Greenwich s*
Au Troquet *12s/Greenwich s*
Babbo *Waverly Pl./MacDougal-6A*
Baluchi's *6A/Washington Pl.-W4*
Bar Cichetti *Houston/6A-7A*
Bar Pitti *6A/Bleecker-Houston*
Bar Six *6A/12-3s*
Bel Villagio *Bleecker/Carmine-6A*
Benny's Burritos *Greenwich A/Jane*
Blue Ribbon Bake. *Downing/Bedford*
Bombay City *7A S./Bedford-Morton*
Boughalem *Bedford/Downing-Houston*
Brothers BBQ *Varick/Clarkson*
Burritoville *Bleecker/Grove-7A S.*
Cafe Asean *10s/Greenwich A-6A*
Café de Bruxelles *Greenwich A/13s*
Cafe Español *Carmine/7A S.;*
  Bleecker/MacDougal-Sullivan
Café Fès *4s/Charles*
Café Loup *13s/6-7A*
Cafe Milou *7A S./Bleecker-Grove*
Caffe Rafaella *7A S./Charles-10s*
Caffe Rosso *12s/8A-4s*
CamaJe *MacDougal/Bl-Houston*
Campo *Greenwich A/Bank-12s*
Caribe *Perry/Greenwich s*
Casa *Bedford/Commerce*
Cent'Anni *Carmine/Bedford-Bleecker*
Chez Brigitte *Greenwich A/Bank-7A*
Chez Jacqueline *MacDougal/*
  Bleecker-Houston
Chez Michallet *Bedford/Grove*
Choga *Bleecker/La Guardia-Thompson*
Cornelia St. Cafe *Cornelia/Bleecker-4s*
Corner Bistro *4s/Jane*
Cowgirl Hall *Hudson/10s*
C3 *Waverly Pl./MacDougal*
Cucina Fontana *Bleecker/Charles*
Cucina Stagionale *Bleecker/6A-7A S.*

Cuisine de Saigon *13s/6-7A*
Da Andrea *Hudson/11s-Perry*
Da Silvano *6A/Bleecker-Houston*
Delícia *11s/Greenwich s-Washington*
Drovers *Jones/Bleecker-4s*
EJ's Lunch. *6A/9-10s*
El Charro *Charles/Greenwich A-7A*
El Faro *Greenwich s/Horatio*
Emack & Bolio's *7A/13-4s*
Empire Szechuan *7A S./11s-Perry; Greenwich A/6A-10s*
Eq *4s/Perry*
Fish *Bleecker/6A-7A S.*
Florent *Gansevoort/Greenwich s*
Focacceria *MacDougal/Bl-Houston*
French Roast *11s/6A*
Fressen *13s/9A-Washington*
Garage *7A S./Barrow-Grove*
Gene's *11s/5-6A*
Grand Ticino *Thompson/Bleecker-3s*
Grange Hall *Commerce/Barrow*
Grano Trattoria *Greenwich A/10s*
Gray's Papaya *6A/8s*
Grey Dog's *Carmine/Bedford*
Grove *Bleecker/Grove*
Gus' Place *Waverly Pl./Christopher s*
Hog Pit *9A/13s*
Homo *Cornelia/Bleecker-4s*
Il Mulino *3s/Sullivan-Thompson*
Indigo *10s/Greenwich A-Waverly Pl.*
'ino *Bedford/Downing-6A*
Ithaka *Barrow/Bedford-Bleecker*
Joe's Pizza *Bleecker/Carmine; Carmine/6A*
John's Pizzeria *Bleecker/6A-7A S.*
Junno's *Downing/Bedford-Varick*
La Boheme *Minetta Ln./Bleecker-3s*
La Focaccia *Bank/4c*
La Lanterna/Vitt. *MacDougal/3-4s*
La Metairie *10s/4s*
La Nonna *13s/6-7A*
La Ripaille *Hudson/Bethune-12s*
L'Attitude *6A/11-2s*
Le Gans *Gansevoort/Greenwich s*
Le Gigot *Cornelia/Bleecker-4s*
Lemongrass Grill *Barrow/7A S.*
Les Deux Gamins *Waverly Pl./Grove*
Les Deux Lapins *Thompson/Bl-3s*
Le Zoo *11s/Greenwich s*
Little Basil *Greenwich A/Charles*
Little Havana *Cornelia/Bleecker-4s*
L-Ray *10s/5-6A*
Lupa *Thompson/Bleecker-Houston*
Malatesta *Washington/Christopher*
Marylou's *9s/5-6A*
Mary's *Bedford/Carmine-Leroy*
Massimo *Thompson/Bleecker-3s*
Mexicana Mama *Hudson/Charles*
Mi Cocina *Jane/Hudson*

Minetta Tavern *MacDougal/Bl-3s*
Miracle Grill *Bleecker/Bank-11s*
Mitali E/W *Bleecker/7A S.*
Moomba *7A S./Charles-10s*
Moustache *Bedford/Barrow-Grove*
Nadine's *Bank/Greenwich s*
One if by Land *Barrow/4s-7A S.*
Paris Commune *Bleecker/Bank-11s*
Peanut Butter *Sullivan/Bleecker-3s*
Pearl Oyster Bar *Cornelia/Bl-4s*
Pepe Verde *Hudson/11s-Perry*
Petite Abeille *14s/9A; Hudson/Barrow*
Philip Marie *Hudson/11s*
Piadina *10s/5-6A*
Piccolo Angolo *Hudson/Jane*
Pink Tea Cup *Grove/Bedford-Bleecker*
Pizzeria Uno *6A/8s-Waverly Pl.*
Place *4s/Bank-12s*
Pó *Cornelia/Bleecker-4s*
Porto Bello *Thompson/Bleecker-3s*
Quantum Leap *3s/Sullivan-Thompson*
Rafaella *Bleecker/Charles-Perry*
Rice 'n' Beans *3s/MacDougal-6A*
Rinçon España *Thompson/Bl-3s*
Rio Mar *9A/Little W. 12s*
Rocco *Thompson/Bleecker-Houston*
Salam Cafe *13s/6-7A*
Sammy's Noodle *6A/11s*
Sapore *Greenwich A/Perry*
Sevilla *Charles/4s*
Shopsin's *Bedford/Morton*
Sud *10s/Bleecker-4s*
Sung Chu Mei *Hudson/Jane-12s*
Surya *Bleecker/Grove-7A S.*
Taka *Grove/Bleecker-7A S.*
Tanti Baci *10s/7A S.-Waverly Pl.*
Taq. Mexico *Greenwich A/Bank 12s*
Tartine *11s/4s*
Tavern on Jane *8A/Jane*
Thali *Greenwich A/Charles-10s*
Tibet on Houston *Houston/MacDougal-Sullivan*
Tio Pepe *4s/6A-7A S.*
Titou *4s/Charles-Perry*
Tomoe Sushi *Thompson/Bl-Houston*
Toons *Bleecker/Bank*
Tortilla Flats *Washington/12s*
Tratt. Pesce/Pasta *Bleecker/6A-7A S.*
Treehouse *Hudson/Morton*
Two Boots *11s/7A S.*
Uguale *West St./10s*
Veg. Paradise *4s/MacDougal-6A*
Velli *Houston/MacDougal-Sullivan*
Villa Mosconi *MacDougal/Bl-Houston*
Vittorio Cucina *Bleecker/Grove-7A S.*
Volare *4s/MacDougal-6A*
Waterloo Brass. *Charles/Washington*
White Horse *Hudson/11s*

Yama *Carmine/Bedford-Bleecker;*
  Houston/La Guardia-Thompson
Ye Waverly Inn *Bank/Waverly Pl.*
Zutto *Greenwich A/7A-11s*

Central Village/NoHo
(14th to Houston Sts., Fifth to
Third Aves.)
Acquario *Bleecker/Bowery-Elizabeth*
Alaia *5A/12-3s*
Arté *9s/5A-Univ Pl.*
Asti *12s/5A-Univ Pl.*
Belgo *Lafayette/Astor Pl.-E4s*
Black & White *10s/3-4A*
Bond Street *Bond/Bway-Lafayette*
Bop *Bowery/2s*
Borgo Antico *13s/5A-Univ Pl.*
Cafe Spice *Univ. Pl./10-1s*
Clementine *5A/8s*
Dallas BBQ *Univ Pl./8s*
Danal *10s/3-4A*
Dojo *4s/Bway-Mercer*
Dolphins *Cooper Sq./5-6s*
Emerald Planet *Gr. Jones/Bway*
Ennio & Michael *La Guardia/3s*
Five Points *Gr. Jones/Lafayette*
Gotham B&G *12s/5A-Univ. Pl.*
Great Jones *Gr. Jones/Bowery*
Il Buco *Bond/Bowery-Lafayette*
Il Cantinori *10s/Bway-Univ. Pl.*
Indochine *Lafayette/Astor Pl.-4s*
Japonica *Univ. Pl./12s*
Johnny Rockets *8s/Bway-Univ. Pl.*
Knickerbocker B&G *Univ. Pl./9s*
Krispy Kreme *8s/Greene-Univ. Pl.*
La Belle Epoque *Bway/12-3s*
Lan *3A/10-1s*
Lemongrass Grill *Univ. Pl/11s*
Marquet Patisserie *12s/5A-Univ. Pl.*
Marumi *La Guardia/Bleecker-3s*
NoHo Star *Lafayette/Bleecker*
Patsy's Pizza *Univ. Pl/10-1s*
Pintaile's Pizza *4A/12-3s*
Pizza Borgo *13s/5A-Univ Pl.*
Pop *4A/12-3s*
Quake *Bway/10s*
Riodizio *Lafayette/Astor Pl.-4s*
Sala *Bowery/Gr. Jones*
Starbucks *Astor Pl./Lafayette*
Temple Bar *Lafayette/Bl-Houston*
Thé Adoré *13s/5A-Univ. Pl.*
Time Cafe *Lafayette/Gr. Jones*
Two Boots *Bleecker/Bway*
Zutto *Greenwich A/6-7A*

East Village
(14th to Houston Sts., East of
Third Ave.)
Angelica Kitchen *12s/1-2A*
Avenue A *Ave. A/6-7s*

Bagatelle *St. Marks Pl./2-3A*
Baluchi's *2A/6s*
Bambou *14s/2-3A*
Bendix Diner *1A/10-1s*
Benny's Burritos *Ave. A/6s*
Boca Chica *1A/1s*
Briam *14s/1-2A*
Burritoville *2A/8-9s*
Cafe Margaux *Ave. B/11s*
Casimir *Ave. B/6-7s*
Chez Es Saada *1s/1-2A*
Christine's *1A/12-3s*
Circa *2A/6s*
Cloister Cafe *9s/2-3A*
Col Legno *9s/2-3A*
Coup *6s/Aves. A-B*
Cucina Pesce *4s/2-3A*
Cyclo *1A/12-3s*
Dallas BBQ *2A/St. Marks Pl.*
Dojo *St. Marks Pl./2-3A*
Dok Suni's *1A/7s-St. Marks Pl.*
Elephant *1s/1-2A*
First *1A/5-6s*
Flea Market *Ave. A/9s-St. Marks Pl.*
Flor's Kitchen *1A/9-10s*
Frank *2A/5-6s*
Frutti di Mare *4s/2A*
Galapagos *1A/7-8s*
Global 33 *2A/5-6s*
Hasaki *9s/2-3A*
Haveli *2A/5-6s*
Holy Basil *2A/9-10s*
I Coppi *9s/Ave. A-1A*
Il Bagatto *2s/Ave. A-B*
Iso *2A/11s*
Jeollado *4s/1-2A*
John's of 12th St. *12s/2A*
Jules *St. Marks Pl./1-2A*
Khyber Pass *St. Marks Pl./2-3A*
Kiev *2A/7s*
La Gould Finch *Ave. B/6s*
Lanza *1A/10-1s*
La Paella *9s/2-3A*
Lavagna *5s/Aves. A-B*
Le Gamin *5s/Aves. A-B*
Lemongrass Grill *Ave. A/4s*
Léon, Resto *12s/1-2A*
Le Tableau *5s/Aves. A-B*
Lhasa *2A/5-6s*
Luca Lounge *Ave. B/13-4s*
Lucien *1A/1s*
Lucky Cheng's *1A/1-2s*
Mama's Food *3s/Aves. A-B*
Marion's *Bowery/4s-Gr. Jones*
Mary Ann's *2A/5s*
Mekka *Ave. A./Houston-2s*
Mesopotamia *Ave. B/6-7s*
Mingala Burmese *7s/2-3A*
Miracle Grill *1A/6-7s*

Mitali E/W *6s/1-2A*
Monk *5s/1-2A*
Moustache *10s/Ave. A-1A*
Mugsy's Chow *2A/1-2s*
Odessa *Ave. A/7s-St. Marks Pl.*
O.G. *6s/Aves. A-B*
Oggi *Ave. A/13s*
Old Devil Moon *12s/Aves. A-B*
Opaline *Ave. A/5-6s*
Orologio *Ave. A/10-1s*
Pangea *2A/11-2s*
Passage to India *6s/2A*
Penang B&G *3A/11s*
Pepe Rosso *St. Marks Pl./Ave. A-1A*
Pierrot Bistro *Ave. B/2-3s*
Pisces *Ave. A/6s*
Pizzeria Uno *3A/10-1s*
Radio Perfecto *Ave. B/11-2s*
Raga *6s/Ave. A-1A*
Roettele *7s/Ave. A-1A*
Rose of India *6s/1-2A*
Sapporo East *10s/1A*
Second Ave. Deli *2A/10s*
Settanta Sette *St. Marks Pl./1-2A*
Shabu-Tatsu *10s/1-2A*
Sobaya *9s/2-3A*
St. Dymphnas *St. Marks/Ave. A-1A*
Stingy Lulu's *St. Marks/Ave. A-1A*
Takahachi *Ave. A/5-6s*
Teresa's *1A/6-7s*
Tsampa *9s/2-3A*
26 Seats *Ave. B/10-11s*
Two Boots *Ave. A/3s; Ave. A/2-3s*
Ukrainian *2A/9s-St. Marks Pl.*
Veniero's *11s/1-2A*
Veselka *2A/9s*
Windows on India *6s/1A*
Xunta *1A/10-1s*

Lower East Side
(Houston to Canal Sts., East
of Bowery)
Katz's Deli *Houston/Ludlow*
Ratners *Delancey/Norfolk-Suffolk*
Sammy's Roumanian *Chrystie/Delan.*
Torch *Ludlow/Rivington-Stanton*

SoHo – Little Italy
(Houston to Canal Sts., West
of Bowery)
Alison *Dominick/Hudson-Varick*
Angelo's *Mulberry/Grand-Hester*
Aquagrill *Spring/6A*
Bacco *Spring/W. Bway-Wooster*
Balthazar *Spring/Bway-Crosby*
Baluchi's *Spring/Sullivan-Thompson*
Bari *Bway/Spring*
Barolo *W. Bway/Broome-Spring*
Bistro Les Amis *Spring/Thompson*
Bistrot Margot *Prince/Elizabeth-Mott*

Blue Ribbon *Sullivan/Prince-Spring*
Blue Ribbon Sushi *Sullivan/Prince*
Boom *Spring/W. Bway-Wooster*
Broome St. Bar *W. Bway/Broome*
Cafe Colonial *Elizabeth/Houston*
Café Habana *Prince/Elizabeth*
Cafe Noir *Grand/Thompson*
Can *W. Bway/Houston*
Canal House *W. Bway/Grand*
Casa La Femme *Wooster/Prince*
Caviarteria *W. Bway/Canal-Grand*
Cendrillon *Mercer/Broome-Grand*
Clay *Mott/Kenmare-Spring*
Country Cafe *Thompson/Broome-Spr*
Cub Room *Sullivan/Prince*
Cub Room Cafe *Prince/Sullivan*
Cupping Rm *W. Bway/Broome-Grand*
Da Nico *Mulberry/Broome-Grand*
Denizen *Thompson/Broome-Spring*
Diva *W. Bway/Broome-Grand*
Downtown *W. Bway/Broome-Spring*
Emilio Ballato *Houston/Mott-Mulb*
Fanelli's Cafe *Prince/Mercer*
Félix *W. Bway/Grand*
Ferrara *Grand/Mott-Mulberry*
Frontière *Prince/MacDougal-Sullivan*
Ghenet *Mulberry/Houston-Prince*
Holianthus *MacDougal/Houst-Prince*
Herban Kit. *Hudson/Dominick-Spring*
Honmura An *Mercer/Houston-Prince*
Ideya *W. Bway/Broome-Grand*
Il Corallo *Prince/Sullivan-Thompson*
Il Cortile *Mulberry/Canal-Hester*
Il Fornaio *Mulberry/Grand-Hester*
Il Palazzo *Mulberry/Grand-Hester*
I Tre Merli *W. Bway/Houston-Prince*
Jean Claude *Sullivan/Houston-Prince*
Jerry's *Prince/Greene-Mercer*
Kelley & Ping *Greene/Houston-Prince*
Kin Khao *Spring/Thompson-W. Bway*
Kitchen Club *Prince/Mott*
La Jumelle *Grand/W. Bway-Wooster*
La Mela *Mulberry/Broome-Grand*
L'Ecole *Bway/Grand*
Le Gamin *MacDougal/Houston-Prince*
Le Jardin *Cleve. Pl./Kenmare-Spring*
Le Pain Quotidien *Grand/Mercer*
Le Pescadou *King/6A*
Little Italy Pizza *Varick/Charlton-King*
Lombardi's *Spring/Mott-Mulberry*
L'Orange Bleue *Broome/Crosby*
Lucky Strike *Grand/W. Bway-Wooster*
L'Ulivo *Spring/Sullivan-Thompson*
Lupe's East L.A. *6A/Watts*
Match *Mercer/Houston-Prince*
MeKong *Prince/Mott-Mulberry*
Mercer Kitchen *Prince/Mercer*
Mezzogiorno *Spring/Sullivan*
Novecento *W. Bway/Broome-Grand*

Ñ 33 Crosby *Crosby/Broome-Grand*
Nyonya *Grand/Mott-Mulberry*
Omen *Thompson/Prince-Spring*
Once Upon a Tart *Sullivan/Prince*
O'Nieal's Grand *Grand/Ctr-Mulberry*
Oro Blu *Hudson/Charlton*
Palacinka *Grand/6A-Thompson*
Pão! *Spring/Greenwich s*
Patrissy's *Kenmare/Lafay-Mulberry*
Pellegrino's *Mulberry/Grand-Hester*
Penang *Spring/Greene-Mercer*
Pepe Rosso *Sullivan/Houston-Prince*
Pho Bang *Mott/Broome-Grand*
Pintxos *Greenwich s/Canal-Spring*
Pravda *Lafayette/Houston-Prince*
Provence *MacDougal/Prince*
Quilty's *Prince/Sullivan-Thompson*
Raoul's *Prince/Sullivan-Thompson*
Rialto *Elizabeth/Houston-Prince*
Rice *Mott/Prince-Spring*
Sal A's SPQR *Mulberry/Grand-Hester*
Savore *Spring/Sullivan*
Savoy *Prince/Crosby*
Shanghai Tang *Houston/W. Bway*
Soho Kitchen *Greene/Prince-Spring*
Soho Steak *Thompson/Prince-Spring*
Spring St. Nat. *Spring/Lafayette*
Starbucks *Spring/Crosby*
Taormina *Mulberry/Grand-Hester*
Tennessee Mtn. *Spring/Wooster*
Triplets Old NY *Grand/6A*
Vandam *Varick/Vandam*
Va Tutto! *Cleve. Pl./Kenmare-Spring*
Velvet *Mulberry/Prince-Spring*
Woo Lae Oak *Mercer/Prince*
Zoë *Prince/Bway-Mercer*

Chinatown

(South of Hester St., East of
Lafayette St.; west of Allen &
Pike Sts.)
Ba Ba *Bayard/Bowery-Mott*
Big Wong *Mott/Bayard-Canal*
Bo-Ky *Bayard/Mott-Mulberry*
Canton *Division/Bowery-Market*
Evergreen Sh. *Mott/Bayard-Canal*
Excell. Dumpling *Lafay/Canal-Walker*
Golden Unicorn *E. Bway/Catherine*
Goody's *E. Bway/Chatham Sq.*
Grand Sichuan *Canal/Bowery*
Great Shanghai *Division/Bowery*
HSF *Bowery/Bayard-Canal*
Jing Fong *Elizabeth/Bayard-Canal*
Joe's Shanghai *Pell/Bowery-Mott*
Kam Chueh *Bowery/Bayard*
Little Szechuan *E. Bway/Chatham*
Mandarin Court *Mott/Bayard-Canal*
New Green Bo *Bayard/Eliz-Mott*
New Pasteur *Baxter/Bayard-Canal*
New York Noodle *Bowery/Bayard*

Nha Trang *Baxter/Bayard-Canal*
Nice Rest. *E. Bway/Catherine-Market*
Oriental Garden *Eliz/Bayard-Canal*
Peking Duck *Mott/Chatham Sq.-Pell*
Pho Bang *Chatham Sq./Mott;*
   Pike/Canal-Division
Pho Viet Huong *Mulberry/Canal*
Ping's *E. Bway/Catherine-Market*
Shanghai Cuisine *Bayard/Mulberry*
Shanghai Gourmet *Mott/Bayard*
Sweet-n-Tart *Mott/Chatham Sq.-Pell;*
   Mott/Canal
Tai Hong Lau *Mott/Bayard-Canal*
Thailand *Bayard/Baxter-Mulberry*
Triple Eight *E. Bway/Division-Market*
Veg. Paradise *Mott/Pell*
Vietnam *Doyers/Bowery-Pell*
Wong Kee *Mott/Canal-Hester*

TriBeCa – Downtown

(South of Canal Street, including
Wall St. area)
Acappella *Hudson/Chambers*
American Park *Battery Park/State*
Arqua *Church/White*
Au Mandarin *WFC: Vesey/West*
Bayard's *Hanover Sq./Pearl-Stone*
Bouley Bakery *W. Bway/Duane-Reade*
Bridge Cafe *Water/Dover*
Bubby's *Hudson/N. Moore*
Burritoville *Water/Broad;*
   Chambers/Greenwich s-W. Bway;
   John/Bway-Nassau
Capsouto Frères *Washington/Watts*
Chanterelle *Harrison/Hudson*
City Hall *Duane/Church-W. Bway*
Coco Marina *WFC/Liberty-West*
Cosi Sandwich *WFC: Vesey; Pine/William;*
   Broad/Beaver-Exchange Pl.
Daily Soup *Rector/Trinity Pl.;*
   John/Dutch-Nassau; Broad/Beaver
Danube *Hudson/Duane*
Delmonico's *Beaver/William*
Divine Bar *Liberty/Nassau*
Duane Park *Duane/Hudson-W. Bway*
Ecco *Chambers/Church-W. Bway*
El Teddy's *W. Bway/Franklin-White*
F.illi Ponte *Desbrosses/W. Side Hwy.*
Flor de Sol *Greenwich s/Harrison*
14 Wall St. *Wall/Broad-Bway*
Franklin Station *W. Bway/Franklin*
Fraunces Tavern *Pearl/Broad*
Gemelli *WTC: Church/Dey*
Gigino *Greenwich s/Duane-Reade*
Giovanni's Atrium *Wash/Rector*
Grill Room *WFC: Liberty/West*
Hale & Hearty *WTC: Vesey*
Harbour Lights *Seaport/Pier 17*
Harry's *Hanover Sq./Pearl-Stone*
Hudson Riv. Club *WFC: Vesey/West*

Il Giglio *Warren/Greenwich s*
Independent *W. Bway/Leonard*
i Rest. *Church/Franklin-White*
Juniper Café *Duane/Greenwich s*
Kitchenette *W. Bway/Warren*
Kori *Church/Franklin-Leonard*
Krispy Kreme *WTC/Church*
Laight Street *Laight/Greenwich s*
Layla *W. Bway/Franklin*
Lemongrass Grill *Liberty/Church*
Little Italy *Park Pl./Bway-Church*
Mangia *Wall/Broad-William*
Menchanko-tei *WTC Concourse*
Montrachet *W. Bway/Walker-White*
Morton's *West St./Albany-Cedar*
Nam Phuong *6A/Walker-White*
Nobu *Hudson/Franklin*
Nobu, Next Door *Hudson/Franklin*
Obeca Li *Thomas/Church-W. Bway*
Odeon *W. Bway/Duane-Thomas*
Petite Abeille *W. Bway/Duane*
Pizzeria Uno *Seaport/Pier 17*
Rosemarie's *Duane/W. Bway*

Roy's NY *Washington/Albany-Carlisle*
Salaam Bombay *Greenwich s/Duane*
Scalini Fedeli *Duane/Greenwich s*
Screening Room *Varick/Canal-Laight*
Seaport Soup *Fulton/Gold*
Sosa Borella *Greenwich s/Watts*
Souperman *Pearl/Stone*
SouthWest NY *WFC: Liberty*
Spartina *Greenwich s/Harrison*
Starbucks *State/Pearl; Broad/Beaver;*
  Wall/Pearl-William
St. Maggie's *Wall/Front-South*
T.G.I. Friday's *Bway/Exchange Pl.*
Thai House *Hudson/Hubert*
Tiffin *Murray/Bway-Church*
Toons *Greenwich s/Franklin-Harrison*
Tribeca Grill *Greenwich s/Franklin*
Walker's *N. Moore/Varick*
Wild Blue *WTC/Liberty-Vesey*
Windows on World *WTC/West*
Yaffa's *Greenwich s/Harrison*
Yaffa's Tea Room *Harrison/Greenwich s*
Zutto *Hudson/Harrison-Jay*

BRONX

Bellavista *235s/Johnson-Oxford*
Dominick's *Arthur/187s*
Jimmy's *W. Fordham/Mjr. Deegan*
Le Refuge Inn *City Is./Sutherland*
Liebman's *235s/Johnson*

Lobster Box *City Is./Belden*
Mario's *Arthur/184-6s*
Roberto's *186s/Belmont*
Starbucks *E. Fordham/Elm Pl.*

BROOKLYN

Bay Ridge
Areo *3A/85s*
Baci Italian *3A/71-2s*
Chadwick's *3A/89s*
Chianti *3A/86s*
Eliá *3A/86-7s*
Embers *3A/95-6s*
Goodfella's *3A/96-7s*
Lento's *3A/Ovington*
Omonia Cafe *3A/76-7s*
101 *4A/101s*
Pizzeria Uno *4A/92s*
Short Ribs *3A/91s*
St. Michel *3A/75-6s*
Tuscany Grill *3A/86-7s*

Bensonhurst
Tommaso's *86s/14-5A*

Boerum Hill
Brawta Carib. *Atlantic/Hoyt*
Moustache *Atlantic/Bond-Nevins*
Saul *Smith/Bergen*
Two Toms *3A/President-Union*

Brighton Beach
Rasputin *Coney Is. A/Ave. X*

Brooklyn Heights
Acadia Parish *Atlantic/Clinton-Henry*
Caffe Buon Gusto *Montague/Henry*
Gage & Tollner *Fulton/Jay*
Grimaldi's *Old Fulton/Front-Water*
Hale & Hearty *Court/Remsen*
Heights Cafe *Montague/Hicks*
Henry's End *Henry/Cranberry*
La Bouillabaisse *Atlantic/Henry*
Le Gamin *Main/Plymouth*
Noodle Pudding *Henry/Middagh*
Pete's Dtwn. *Water/Cadman Plaza W.*
Petite Crevette *Atlantic/Clinton-Henry*
Queen *Court/Livingston-Schermerhorn*
River Cafe *Water/Bklyn Bridge*
Teresa's *Montague/Hicks*
Tin Room Cafe *Front/Old Fulton*
Waterfront Ale *Atlantic/Clinton-Henry*

Carroll Gardens
Ferdinando's *Union/Col.-Hicks*
Marco Polo *Court/Union*
Mignon *Court/Carroll-1st Pl.*

Monte's Italian *Carroll/Nevins-3A*
Patois *Smith/DeGraw-Douglass*
Sur *Smith/Butler-Douglass*
Uncle Pho *Smith/DeGraw*

Cobble Hill
Harvest *Court/Warren*
Kalio *Court/Butler-Kane*
Osaka *Court/DeGraw-Kane*
Sweet Melissa *Court/Butler*

Coney Island
Gargiulo's *15s/Mermaid-Surf*
Totonno Pizzeria *Neptune/15-6s*

Downtown
Archives *Adams/Willoughby*
Junior's *Flatbush Ext./DeKalb*
New City *Lafayette/Ashland Pl.*

Fort Greene
Cambodian Cuis. *S. Elliot Pl./Fulton*
Chez Oskar *DeKalb/Adelphi*
Lucian Blue *Lafayette/Fulton*
Sol *DeKalb/Adelphi-Clermont*

Gravesend
Fiorentino's *Ave. U/McDonald-West*
Sahara *Coney Island/T-U*

Greenpoint
Thai Cafe *Manhattan A/Kent*

Ocean Parkway
Ocean Palace *Ave. U/14-5s*

Park Slope
Al Di La Trattoria *5A/Carroll*

Coco Reef *7A/5s*
Coco Roco *5A/6-7s*
Cucina *5A/Carroll-Garfield Pl.*
Lemongrass *7A/Berkeley-Lincoln Pl.*
Lento's *Union/6-7A*
Max & Moritz *7A/14s*
Mike & Tony's *5A/Carroll*
Sweet Mamas *7A/1s-Garfield Pl.*
12th St. B&G *8A/12s*
Two Boots *2s/7-8A*

Prospect Heights
Garden Cafe *Vanderbilt/Prospect Pl.*
New Prospect *Flatbush A/Plaza*
Tom's *Washington/Sterling Pl.*

Sheepshead Bay
Lundy Bros. *Emmons/Ocean A*

Sunset Park
Jade Plaza *8A/60-1s*
Nyonya *8A/54s*
Ocean Palace *8A/55s*

Williamsburg
Bamonte's *Withers/Lorimer-Union*
Black Betty *Metropolitan/Havemeyer*
Diner *Bway/Berry*
Miss Williamsburg *Kent/3s*
Oznot's Dish *Berry/9s*
Peter Luger *Bway/Driggs*
Planet Thailand *7s/Bedford-Berry*
Seasons *Driggs/7s*
Vera Cruz *Bedford/6-7s*

QUEENS

Astoria
Christos Hasapo *23A/41s*
Elias Corner *31s/24A*
Esperides *30A/37s*
Karyatis *Bway/35-6s*
Omonia Cafe *Bway/33s*
Piccola Venezia *28A/42s*
Ponticello *Bway/46-7s*
S'Agapo *34A/35s*
Taverna Kyclades *Ditmars/33-5s*
Taverna Vraka *31s/23-24A*
Telly's Taverna *23A/28-9s*
Tierras Colombianas *Bway/33s*
Tratt. L'incontro *31s/Ditmars*
Ubol's Kitchen *Steinway/25A*
Uncle George's *Bway/34s*

Bayside
Ben's Kosher Deli *26A/Bell*
Caffé on Green *Cross Is. P'way*
Frankie & Johnnie's *Northern/194s*
Marbella *Northern/220-221s*
Pier 25A *Northern/215s*

Pizzeria Uno *Bell/39-40A*
Uncle Jack's *Bell/40A*

Corona
Green Field *Northern/108s*
Park Side *Corona/51A*

Elmhurst
Jai Ya Thai *Bway/81-2s*
Joe's Shanghai *Bway/45A-Whitney*
Pho Bang *Bway/Elmhurst*
Ping's *Queens Blvd/Goldsmith s*

Flushing
East Lake *Main/Franklin*
Golden Monkey *Roosevelt/Prince*
Jade Palace *38A/Main*
Joe's Shanghai *37A/Main-Union*
K.B. Garden *39A/Main-Union*
Kum Gang San *Northern/Main-Union*
Master Grill Int'l *College Pt./34-5A*
Penang *Prince/Main*
Pho Bang *Kissena/Main*
Shanghai Tang *40 Rd./Main s*

Silver Pond *Main/56A*
Sweet-n-Tart *38A/Main*
Tierras Colombianas *Roosevelt/83s*
Woo Chon *Kissena/Main*

Forest Hills
Bistro Metro *Metropolitan/Ascan*
Cabana *70 Rd./Austin-Queens*
Cho-Sen Garden *108s/64-65A*
Krispy Kreme *Queens/Continental*
Mardi Gras *Austin/70 Rd.*
Nick's Pizza *Ascan/Austin-Burns*
Pizzeria Uno *70 Rd./Austin-Queens Bl.*
Q, a Thai Bistro *Ascan/Austin-Burns*

Fresh Meadows
Quantum Leap *Fr. Meadow Ln./67A*

Glendale
Gebhardt's *Myrtle/65 Pl.-65 s*
Zum Stammtisch *Myrtle/Cooper*

Jackson Heights
Afghan Kebab Hse. *37A/74-5s*

Delhi Palace *74s/Roosevelt-37A*
Jackson Diner *74s/Roosevelt-37A*
Jackson Hole *Astoria/70s*

Little Neck
La Baraka *Northern/Little Neck P'way*

Long Island City
Manducatis *Jackson/47A*
Water's Edge *44 Dr.-East River/Vernon*

Middle Village
Niederstein's *Metropolitan/69s*

Ozone Park
Don Peppe *Lefferts/149A*

Rego Park
Goody's *63 Dr./Booth-Saunders*
London Lennie's *Woodhaven/63 Dr.*

Sunnyside
Dazies *Queens/39-40s*

Whitestone
Cooking w/Jazz *154s/12A*

STATEN ISLAND

Aesop's Tables *Bay/Maryland*
Angelina's *Jefferson/Annadale*
Carol's *Richmond/4 Corners-Seaview*
Denino's *Pt. Richmond/Hooker Pl.*
Goodfella's *Hylan/Garretson*
Historic Bermuda Inn *Arthur Kill/Rossville*

Killmeyer's *Arthur Kill/Sharrotts*
Marina Cafe *Mansion/Hillside*
Parsonage *Arthur Kill/Clarke*
South Shore *Huguenot/W. Shore Expy*
Tratt. Romana *Hylan/Benton*

SPECIAL FEATURES AND APPEALS

AYCE
(All you can eat; call ahead
for times and prices)
Bangkok Cuisine
Bay Leaf
Becco
Bombay Palace
Brother Jimmy's
Bukhara Grill
Chola
Churr. Plantation
Churr. Plataforma
Green Field
Master Grill Int'l
Rio de Janeiro's
Riodizio
Shaan
Tennessee Mtn. (Mon.)

Breakfast
(All hotels and the
following standouts)
ABC Parlour Cafe
An American Place
Anglers & Writers
Balthazar
Barney Greengrass
Bendix Diner
Broadway Diner
Brooklyn Diner
Cafeteria
Café Word/Mouth
Carlyle
Carnegie Deli
Chez Louis
City Bakery
Coffee Shop
Columbus Bakery
E.A.T.
EJ's Lunch.
Empire Diner
57 57
Florent
Fraunces Tavern
French Roast
Friend of Farmer
Good Enough to Eat
Heartbeat
Home
Jackson Hole
Jean Georges
Lespinasse
Mark's
Mayrose
Mercer Kitchen
Michael's
Payard Pâtisserie
Pershing Sq.
Regency
Sarabeth's
Veselka
Viand

Brunch
(Best of many)
ABC Parlour Cafe
Ambassador Grill
America
American Park
An American Place
Anglers & Writers
Aquagrill
Aquavit
Atlantic Grill
Bateaux NY
Bistro du Nord
Blue Ribbon Bakery
Bridge Cafe
Bryant Park Grill
B. Smith's
Bubby's
Butterfield 81
Café Botanica
Café de Bruxelles
Café des Artistes
Cafe Luxembourg
Capsouto Frères
Carlyle
Chez Michallet
Copeland's
Cornelia St. Cafe
Cowgirl Hall
Docks
Emily's
Ferrier
Fireman's of B'klyn
First
Five Points
Florent
Friend of Farmer
Globe
Good Enough to Eat
Grange Hall
Grove
Gus' Place
Harbour Lights
Historic Bermuda Inn
Hudson Riv. Club
Independent
Isabella's
Island
Joe Allen
La Goulue
Landmark Tavern
Le Bilboquet
Lenox Room
Le Régence
Lola
Maison
Mark's
Markt
Marylou's
Matthew's
Metropolitan Cafe

Miracle Grill
Nadine's
Ocean Grill
Odeon
Park Avalon
Park Ave. Cafe
Park Bistro
Park View/Boathse.
Petaluma
Popover Cafe
Redeye Grill
River Cafe
Russian Tea Room
Saloon
Sarabeth's
Screening Room
Sylvia's
Tavern on Green
Time Cafe
Tratt. Dell'Arte
Treehouse
Tribeca Grill
Trois Jean
Verbena
Viceroy
Water Club
Well's
Windows on World
World Yacht
Zoë

BYO

(Recommended; also check
for newcomers awaiting
liquor licenses)
Acadia Parish
Afghan Kebab Hse.
Bendix Diner
Big Wong
Brawta Carib.
Cucina Stagionale
East Lake
El Ombú
Flor's Kitchen
Freddie & Pepper's
Goody's
Grand Sichuan Int'l
Havana Chelsea
Island Burgers
Jackson Diner
K.B. Garden
Kiev
Kitchenette
Lakruwana
Lamarca
Le Gamin
Mama's Food
Marquet Patisserie
Mignon
Miss Williamsburg
Patoug Manhattan
Pepe Rosso
Petite Crevette
Phoenix Garden

Ping's Seafood
Pink Tea Cup
Pintaile's Pizza
Quantum Leap
Rinconcito Peru
Rose of India
Rungsit Thai
Saffron
Soul Fixins'
Tartine
Tiffin
Veg. Paradise
Wong Kee
Yura & Co.
Zen Palate (beer only)

Corkage Fee

(Following leading restaurants
permit patrons to bring wine
after phoning in advance;
although the practice is not
common, these places do not
discourage it, especially for
rare bottles not on their list –
customary corkage fee per
bottle is noted)
Aquavit ($20)
Blue Ribbon Sushi ($15)
Chanterelle ($35)
Gotham B&G ($35)
Gramercy Tavern ($15)
Il Mulino (varies by vintage)
Jean Georges ($45)
La Caravelle ($20)
Le Perigord ($15-20)
Nobu ($15-20)
Nobu, Next Door ($15-20)
Oceana ($20)
Picholine ($35)
Sushi of Gari ($15)
Tabla ($15)
Union Pacific ($30)
Union Sq. Cafe ($15)

Cheese Trays

Alva
Aureole
Babbo
Cello
Chanterelle
Circo
Colina
Drovers
Eleven Mad. Pk.
Eq
Fred's at Barneys
Gramercy Tavern
Herban Kitchen
I Trulli
Jean Georges
JUdson Grill
La Caravelle
La Grenouille
Lenox Room

Lespinasse
Milos
Picholine
Solera
Veritas

Cigar Friendly
American Park
Angelo & Maxie's
Asia de Cuba
Bar Six
Bayard's
Ben Benson's
Bobby Van's
Bravo Gianni
Bruno
Bull & Bear
Campagna
Clarke's, P.J.
Club Macanudo
Delmonico's
Fanelli's Cafe
F.illi Ponte
Frankie & Johnnie's
Frank's Rest.
Gallagher's
Harry's/Hanover Sq.
Hudson Riv. Club
Jimmy's Bronx
Keens Steakhse.
King Cole Bar
Knickerbocker B&G
Landmark Tavern
Lemon
Maloney & Porcelli
Manhattan Grille
Michael Jordan's
Michael's
Morton's
Old Homestead
Old Town Bar
Patroon
Rao's
Ruth's Chris
Smith & Wollensky
Soho Steak
Sparks
Top of the Tower
Torre di Pisa
Tupelo Grill
'21' Club
Typhoon
Uncle Jack's
Water Club
Waterfront Ale
West 63rd Steak
Wollensky's Grill

Coffeehouses/Desserts
(See *Hotels & Teas*, plus the
following best bets)
ABC Parlour Cafe
Anglers & Writers
Blue Ribbon Bakery
Café des Artistes (annex)

Cafe Lalo
Cafe Mozart
Café Word/Mouth
Caffe Rafaella
Carlyle
Columbus Bakery
Cupcake Cafe
Cupping Room
DT•UT
Edgar's Cafe
Emack & Bolio's
Ferrara
Grey Dog's
Krispy Kreme
Le Gamin
Marquet Patisserie
Omonia Cafe
Once Upon a Tart
Palm Court
Payard Pâtisserie
Pershing Sq.
Pink Tea Cup
Sant Ambroeus
Serendipity 3
Starbucks
Sweet Melissa
Trois Jean
T Salon
Veniero's

Dancing/Entertainment
(Check days, times and
performers for entertainment;
D=dancing; best of many)
Algonquin (cabaret)
Asti (opera)
Bateaux NY (D/jazz)
Bistro Latino (D/Latin)
Blue Water Grill (jazz)
B. Smith's (jazz)
Chez Josephine (jazz/piano)
Cooking w/Jazz (jazz)
Cornelia St. Cafe (jazz/poetry/theater)
FireBird (cabaret/harp/piano)
Iguana (D)
Jimmy's Bronx (D/merengue/salsa)
Jules (jazz)
Knickerbocker B&G (jazz)
La Belle Epoque (cabaret/jazz/opera)
Live Bait (jazz)
Londel's (jazz/pop/R&B)
Lucky Cheng's (drag/karaoke)
Mardi Gras (blues/jazz)
Metronome (D/jazz)
One 51 (D)
Oriont (D)
Palm Court (harp/piano/violin)
Rasputin (D/cabaret/international)
Russian Samovar (vocals)
Screening Room (jazz/movies)
Spirit Cruises (D/band/vocals)
Supper Club (D/cabaret/swing)
Sylvia's (gospel/jazz)
Tavern on Green (D/jazz/piano)

Tommaso's (opera/piano)
Top of the Tower (piano/vocals)
27 Standard (jazz)
World Yacht (D/bands/piano)

Delivers*/Takeout
(Nearly all Asians, coffee
shops, delis, diners and
pasta/pizzerias deliver or do
takeout; here are some
interesting possibilities;
D=delivery, T=takeout; *call
to check range and charges,
if any)
ABC Parlour Cafe (T)
Aquavit (T)
Barney Greengrass (D,T)
Bay Leaf (D,T)
Ben Benson's (D,T)
Bice Rist. (D,T)
Bistro du Nord (D,T)
Brooklyn Diner (D,T)
Brother Jimmy's (D,T)
Burritoville (D,T)
Café Word/Mouth (D,T)
Campagnola (D)
Carnegie Deli (D,T)
Chin Chin (D,T)
Columbus Bakery (D,T)
Cosi Sandwich (D,T)
Daily Soup (D,T)
Dallas BBQ (D,T)
Dawat (D,T)
Dishes (D,T)
E.A.T. (D,T)
Eisenberg (D,T)
EJ's Lunch. (D,T)
El Pollo (D,T)
Frank's Rest. (D,T)
Fresco on the Go (D,T)
Hale & Hearty (D,T)
Harry's/Hanover Sq. (D,T)
'ino (T)
Jackson Hole (D,T)
Joe's Shanghai (D,T)
John's Pizzeria (T)
Junior's (D,T)
Le Madri (T)
Lemongrass Grill (D,T)
Levana (D,T)
Lombardi's (D,T)
Lusardi's (D,T)
Mangia (D,T)
Matthew's (T)
Mitali E/W (D,T)
Our Place (D,T)
Pamir (D,T)
Park Bistro (D,T)
P.J. Bernstein Deli (D,T)
Rain (D,T)
Ratners (D,T)
Remi (D,T)
Second Ave. Deli (D,T)
Serafina Fab. Pizza (D,T)

Shun Lee (D,T)
Shun Lee Palace (D,T)
Sushi Hana (D,T)
Sylvia's (D,T)
Turkish Kitchen (T)
Uncle Nick's (D,T)
Viand (D,T)
Vinnie's Pizza (D,T)
Virgil's BBQ (D,T)
Zarela (T)

Dining Alone
(Other than hotels, coffee
shops, sushi bars and places
with counter service)
ABC Parlour Cafe
Amy's Bread
Anglers & Writers
Aquagrill
Aquavit
Bouterin
Café Botanica
Café de Bruxelles
Café M
Cafe S.F.A.
Carlyle
Caviar Russe
City Hall
Cosi Sandwich
Drovers
EJ's Lunch.
Eleven Mad. Pk.
Emerald Planet
FireBird
Fred's at Barneys
Good Enough to Eat
Gotham B&G
Gramercy Tavern
Gray's Papaya
Gus' Place
Hudson Riv. Club
JUdson Grill
La Caravelle
Lespinasse
Le Train Bleu
Mangia
Mme. Romaine
Naples 45
Nick & Toni's
Nobu, Next Door
Oceana
Ollie's
O Padeiro
Oyster Bar (Gr. Cent.)
Park View/Boathse.
Pearl Oyster Bar
Petite Abeille
Petrossian
Republic
Sarabeth's
Sette MoMA
Souperman
Soup Kitchen
Sushisay

Sushiya
Tabla
T Salon
Tuscan Square
Union Sq. Cafe
Vinnie's Pizza
Zen Palate

Dining at the Bar
(Best of many; see also sushi bars)
Aquagrill
Atlantic Grill
Avenue
Babbo
Bistro Les Amis
Bolivar
Bricco
Campagnola
China Grill
Christer's
Circo
City Hall
Daniel
Delmonico's
Eleven Mad. Pk.
Fanelli's Cafe
Four Seasons
Gotham B&G
Gramercy Tavern
Gus' Place
Lobster Club
Lupa
Maratti
Mesa Grill
Molyvos
Monkey Bar
Old Town Bar
Oyster Bar (Gr. Cent.)
Palio
Patria
Patroon
Pearl Oyster Bar
Periyali
Petrossian
Pravda
Rain
Redeye Grill
Tabla
Tapika
Tribeca Grill
Union Sq. Cafe
Veritas
Zoë

Family Style
Asia de Cuba
Becco
Brother Jimmy's
Canton
Carino
Carmine's
Chiam
Chianti (Bklyn.)
China Grill

Chin Chin
Churr. Plantation
Churr. Plataforma
Copeland's
Dawat
Drovers
Green Field
Jackson Diner
John's Pizzeria
Kum Gang San
Le Colonial
Lemongrass Grill
Marchi's
Master Grill Int'l
Orienta
Oriental Garden
Penang
Rao's
Rio de Janeiro's
Riodizio
Sambuca
Siam Inn
Tony's Di Napoli
Ulrika's

Fireplaces
(Best of many)
American Park
Arté
Asia de Cuba
Barbetta
Bolivar
Box Tree
Briam
Cafe Centro
Cafe Milou
Caffé on Green
Chelsea Bistro
Christer's
Circus
Cornelia St. Cafe
Demi
Dining Room/Columbus
Divine Bar
Fraunces Tavern
Gage & Tollner
I Trulli
Keens Steakhse.
La Gondola
La Lanterna/Vittorio
Landmark Tavern
Lot 61
Maratti
March
Marylou's
Mary's
Merchants
Moran's
O'Neals'
One if by Land
Paris Commune
René Pujol
Russian Tea Room
Savoy

Shaffer City
Thady Con's
Tivoli
Vittorio Cucina
Vivolo
Water Club
Ye Waverly Inn

Game in Season
(The following are
recommended)
Acacia
Al Di La Trattoria
An American Place
Aquavit
Atlas
Aureole
Babbo
Balthazar
Barbetta
Beacon
Bondí
Borgo Antico
Bouley Bakery
Café Boulud
Cafe Centro
Café Crocodile
Café des Artistes
Capsouto Frères
Chanterelle
Christer's
Circo
Danube
Da Umberto
Della Femina
Erminia
Europa B&G
Felidia
Four Seasons
Frontière
Gabriel's
Gramercy Tavern
Grande Mela
Grano Trattoria
Henry's End
Hudson Riv. Club
Il Cantinori
I Trulli
Jean Georges
Jo Jo
Keens Steakhse.
L'Absinthe
La Caravelle
La Grenouille
La Griglia
La Réserve
Léon, Resto
Le Perigord
Limoncello
Lx
March
Mark's
Massimo
Mazzei Osteria

Nino's
Oriont
Palette
Palio
Picholine
Pó
River Cafe
San Domenico
Scalini Fedeli
Silver Swan
Sonia Rose
Swifty's
Tello's Rist.
Terrace
Tonic
'21' Club
Two Two Two
Veritas

Health/Spa Menus
(Most places cook to order
to meet any dietary need;
call in advance to check;
besides Asians, the following
are good bets)
Acacia
Adrienne
Cafe Fiorello
Café Pierre
Candle Cafe
Daily Soup
Istana
Jean Georges
Josie's
Korea Palace
Le Cirque 2000
Lobster Club
Lutèce
Mangia
Mark's
Marylou's
Mr. K's
Nirvana
Nobu
Persepolis
Popover Cafe
Quantum Leap
Shun Lee
Shun Lee Palace
Tratt. Dell'Arte
Trionfo
Tuscan Square
Vong
Zen Palate

Holiday Meals
(All hotels and the following
standouts)
Aquavit
Box Tree
Café Botanica
Café des Artistes
Café Pierre
Carlyle
Charlotte

Destinée
Duane Park
57 57
FireBird
44
Four Seasons
Fresco by Scotto
Gotham B&G
Halcyon
Historic Bermuda Inn
Hudson Riv. Club
JUdson Grill
Le Régence
Lespinasse
Lobster Box
Mark's
Neary's
Oak Room
Ocean Grill
One if by Land
Park Ave. Cafe
Peacock Alley
Petrossian
Regency
River Cafe
San Domenico
Soma Park
Sonia Rose
Tavern on Green
Terrace
Trois Jean
View
Water Club
Ye Waverly Inn

Hotel Dining

Algonquin Hotel
  Algonquin
Avalon Hotel
  Coach House
Beekman Tower
  Top of the Tower
Belvedere Hotel
  Churr. Plataforma
Benjamin Hotel
  An American Place
Box Tree
  Box Tree
Carlyle Hotel
  Carlyle
Delmonico Hotel
  Caviarteria
Eastgate Tower
  Sonora
Essex House
  Café Botanica
Four Seasons Hotel
  57 57
Hotel Edison
  Edison Cafe
Hotel Elysée
  Monkey Bar
Hotel Lexington
  S. Dynasty

Hotel Plaza Athénée
  Le Régence
Hotel Wales
  Sarabeth's
Inn at Irving Place
  Lady Mendl's
Kitano Hotel
  Garden Cafe
  Nadaman Hakubai
Le Parker Meridien
  Norma's
  Seppi's
Le Refuge Inn
  Le Refuge Inn
Lombardy Hotel
  Soma Park
Lowell Hotel
  Post House
Mark, The
  Mark's
Marriott Fin. Ctr.
  Roy's NY
Marriott Marquis
  Katen
  View
Mayfair Hotel
  Garrick Bistro
Mercer Hotel
  Mercer Kitchen
Michelangelo Hotel
  Limoncello
Millennium Broadway
  Charlotte
Morgans Hotel
  Asia de Cuba
NY Marriott Brooklyn
  Archives
NY Palace Hotel
  Istana
  Le Cirque 2000
Omni Berkshire Pl.
  Kokachin
Paramount Hotel
  Coco Pazzo Teatro
  Mezzanine
Peninsula Hotel
  Adrienne
Pierre Hotel
  Café Pierre
Plaza Hotel
  Oak Room
  Oyster Bar/Plaza
  Palm Court
Radisson Empire Hotel
  Merlot B&G
  West 63rd Steak
Ramada Inn (Queens)
  Marbella
Regal UN Plaza Hotel
  Ambassador Grill
Regency Hotel
  Regency
Renaissance Hotel
  Foley's Fish

Rihga Royal Hotel
  Halcyon
Royalton Hotel
  44
Sherry Netherland
  Harry Cipriani
Shoreham Hotel
  La Caravelle
SoHo Grand Hotel
  Canal House
  Caviarteria
Stanhope Hotel
  Café M
St. Regis Hotel
  King Cole Bar
  Lespinasse
Surrey Hotel
  Café Boulud
Sutton Hotel
  Il Valentino
Time Hotel
  Palladin
Trump Int'l Hotel
  Jean Georges
Waldorf-Astoria
  Bull & Bear
  Inagiku
  Oscar's
  Peacock Alley
Warwick Hotel
  Ciao Europa
Washington Sq. Hotel
  C3
W New York
  Heartbeat

"In" Places
Alaia
Amaranth
Aquagrill
Asia de Cuba
Atlantic Grill
Babbo
Balthazar
Beacon
Blue Ribbon
Blue Water Grill
Bond Street
Café Boulud
Calle Ocho
Chez Es Saada
Circo
City Hall
Danube
Della Femina
Divine Bar
Eleven Mad. Pk.
44
Fressen
Gabriel's
Gramercy Tavern
Junno's
La Grenouille
Le Cirque 2000

Le Colonial
Markt
Mercer Kitchen
Milos
Nobu, Next Door
Odeon
One 51
Oriont
Patroon
Rain
Rao's
Red Cat
Ruby Foo's
Tabla
Torch
212
Union Pacific
Veritas

Jury Duty
(Best bets near the
courthouses)
Arqua
Bo-Ky
Bouley Bakery
Bridge Cafe
City Hall
Da Nico
Danube
Duane Park
Ecco
Excellent Dumpling
Il Cortile
Il Fornaio
Il Palazzo
Joe's Shanghai
Kitchenette
Layla
Little Szechuan
Lombardi's
Nam Phuong
New Pasteur
New York Noodle
Nha Trang
Nobu
Odeon
Oriental Garden
Pho Viet Huong
Sal A's S.P.Q.R.
Souperman
Sweet-n-Tart
Taormina
Thailand
Vietnam
Wong Kee

Late Late – After 12:30
(All hours are AM)
Alva (2)
Arturo's Pizzeria (1)
Avenue A (1:45)
Ba Ba Malaysian (2)
Balthazar (2)
Bar Six (2)
Blue Ribbon (4)

Blue Ribbon Bakery (2)
Blue Ribbon Sushi (2)
Broome St. Bar (1:30)
Cafe Lalo (2)
Cafe Mozart (1)
Cafe Noir (4)
Casa La Femme (3)
Chez Es Saada (1)
Chez Josephine (1)
Choga (4)
City Grill (1)
Clarke's, P.J. (4)
Clementine (1:30)
Club Macanudo (1)
Coffee Shop (5:30)
Corner Bistro (4)
Denizen (2)
Diva (2)
Divine Bar (1)
Dojo (1)
East Lake (2)
Edgar's Cafe (12:45)
Elaine's (2)
El Teddy's (1)
Empire Szechuan (1,2)
Fanelli's Cafe (2)
Ferrier (2)
First (2)
Fish (2)
Five Points (2)
Florent (24 hrs.)
Frank (1)
Garage (2)
Global 33 (1)
Harbour Lights (1:30)
HSF (3)
Il Buco (1)
'ino (2)
I Tre Merli (1)
Jackson Hole (1)
Jade Palace (5)
Jekyll & Hyde (1)
Jeollado (1)
J.G. Melon (2:30)
Jimmy's Bronx (2)
Joe's Pizza (4)
Jules (1)
Junior's (1)
Kam Chueh (4:30)
Kang Suh (24 hrs.)
Klev (24 hrs.)
Knickerbocker B&G (1)
Kum Gang San (24 hrs.)
La Caridad 78 (1)
La Jumelle (2)
La Lanterna/Vittorio (3)
Le Charlot (1)
Lemon (1)
Le Monde (2)
Live Bait (1)
Lot 61 (1)
Lucien (2)
Lucky Strike (3)
Marion's (2)

Markt (1)
Match (2)
Medusa (2)
Merchants (2)
Mesopotamia (1)
Mezzogiorno (1)
Neary's (1:30)
New York Noodle (4)
Nirvana (1)
Ñ 33 Crosby (1:30)
Ocean Palace (2)
Odeon (2)
Odessa (24 hrs.)
Official All Star (1)
Ollie's (2)
Omonia Cafe (4)
Opaline (2)
Oriental Garden (1:30)
Penang (1)
Pierrot Bistro (1)
Ping's Seafood (2,3)
Pizzeria Uno (1,1:30)
Planet Hollywood (1)
Planet Sushi (2)
Planet Thailand (1)
Pravda (2:45)
Raoul's (2)
Rio Mar (1:30)
Sahara (1:30)
Sapporo East (12:45)
Seppi's (2)
Serafina Fab. Grill (2)
Shanghai Gourmet (1)
Silver Pond (2)
Stage Deli (1)
Stingy Lulu's (4)
Sushihatsu (3:30)
Takahachi (12:45)
Tatany (3:30)
Tavern on Jane (1)
Tio Pepe (1)
Torch (1)
Two Boots (1)
Uncle George's (24 hrs.)
Walker's (1)
Waterloo Brass. (1)
West Bank Cafe (1)
White Horse (1)
Wollensky's Grill (2)
Won Jo (24 hrs.)
Woo Chon (24 hrs.)
Yaffa's (3)

Meet for a Drink
(Most top hotels and the
following standouts)
Algonquin
Amaranth
America
Balthazar
Bar Six
Bella Blu
Blackbird
Blue Water Grill

Brown's
B. Smith's
Café Pierre
Cal's
Carlyle
Charley O's
Circo
City Hall
Clarke's, P.J.
Clementine
Cub Room
Danube
Eleven Mad. Pk.
Fanelli's Cafe
57 57
FireBird
44
Four Seasons
Fred's at Barneys
Fressen
Gotham B&G
Gramercy Tavern
Harbour Lights
Heartbeat
Heartland Brewery
i Rest.
I Tre Merli
JB
Jean Georges
Jimmy's Bronx
JUdson Grill
Junno's
Keens Steakhse.
King Cole Bar
Landmark Tavern
Le Cirque 2000
Le Colonial
Lemon
Lenox Room
Local
Lot 61
Mark's
Markt
Maxx
Mercer Kitchen
Merchants
Metronome
Michael Jordan's
Monkey Bar
Oak Room
Old Town Bar
O'Neals'
One 51
Oriont
Palladin
Palm Court
Patroon
Peacock Alley
Pershing Sq.
Pete's Tavern
Pravda
Punch
Red Cat
Regency

Ruby Foo's
Shark Bar
Soul Cafe
SouthWest NY
Sugar Bar
Temple Bar
Tonic
Top of the Tower
'21' Club
27 Standard
Union Sq. Cafe
Velvet
West 63rd Steak
Windows on World

Noteworthy Newcomers (274)
(Name, *cuisine*; *Not open at press time, but looks promising)

Acacia, *French*
Acquario, *Mediterranean*
Ada*, *Indian*
Alaia, *American/Med.*
Al Di La Trattoria, *Italian*
Alex & Max's, *American*
Amaranth, *Mediterranean*
André, *French*
Arté Café*, *Italian*
Artie's*, *Deli*
A Table*, *French*
Atlas, *American*
Az*, *Asian*
Ba Ba Malaysian, *Malaysian*
Bagatelle, *American/Irish*
Bari, *Mediterranean*
Bateaux NY, *American*
Bayard's, *French*
B.B. King's*, *American*
Beacon, *American*
Belgo, *Belgian*
Bellew, *American/Irish*
Bel Villagio, *Italian*
Beppe*, *Italian*
Berkeley B&G, *Californian*
Black & White, *American*
Black Betty, *Middle Eastern*
Blackbird, *American*
Bleu Evolution, *Eclectic*
Bombay City, *Indian*
Bongo, *Seafood*
Brasserie*, *French*
Brasseriebit*, *French*
Brasserie 8½*, *French*
Brasserie Julien, *French*
Briam, *Greek*
Brown's, *American*
Bruculino, *Italian*
Bukhara Grill, *Indian*
Café Frida, *Mexican*
Café Guy Pascal, *French*
Café Habana, *Latin Amer.*
Cafe Lafayette*, *French*
Cafe Nicholson*, *Continental*

Calle Ocho, *S. American/Carib.*
Campari*, *Italian*
Canteen*, *American*
Capital, *Middle Eastern*
Casimir, *French*
Celadon, *American/Asian*
Cello, *Seafood*
Central Park Grill*, *Med./Asian*
Chevy's*, *Mexican*
Chez Gnagna Koty's, *Senegalese*
Chez Louis, *French*
Chinghalle*, *American/Cont.*
Chow Bar & Grill*, *Asian*
Churr. Plantation, *Brazilian*
Cibi Cibi, *Italian*
Citarella*, *Seafood*
Clinton Fresh Food*, *American*
Club Guastavino*, *French/Italian*
Coach House, *American*
Coco Reef, *Malaysian/Singaporean*
Colina, *Italian*
Cool Hse. of Loo, *Asian*
Coup, *American*
Cuba Libre*, *Cuban*
Da Andrea, *Italian*
Dakshin Indian, *Indian*
Danube, *Viennese*
Del Frisco's*, *Steakhouse*
Della Femina, *American*
Deux Amis*, *French*
Diner, *American/French*
Dining Room/Columbus, *Eclectic*
Dishes, *Eclectic*
Do Hwa*, *Korean*
Dolphins, *Seafood*
Edwardian Room*, *American*
El Fogoncito*, *Mexican*
Eliá, *Greek*
Eli's Manhattan, *American*
El Ombú, *Argentine*
Esca*, *Italian Seafood*
ESPN Zone, *American*
Europa B&G, *Mediterranean*
Evergreen Shanghai, *Chinese*
Feinstein's*, *American*
Fireman's of B'klyn, *American*
Fish, *Seafood*
Five Points, *American/Med.*
Florentine*, *Italian Steakhouse*
Flor's Kitchen, *Venezuelan*
Flynn's*, *Irish*
Fresco on the Go, *Italian*
Fressen, *organic American*
Gabriela's Kitchen*, *Mexican*
Galapagos, *Seafood/S. American*
Gamut, *Eclectic*
Grace*, *American*
Grande Mela, *Italian*
Grocery, The*, *American*
Guastavino*, *French/Italian*
Guernica*, *Eclectic*
Gus' Figs Bistro, *Mediterranean*
Guy Reuge*, *French*
Heartbeat, *organic American*

Honey*, *American*
Hush, *American*
Hydra*, *American*
Hyotan Nippon*, *Japanese*
Icon NY*, *French*
Iguana, *Tex-Mex*
Il Gatto/La Volpe, *Italian*
Il Riccio, *Italian*
Imagin-Hallo Berlin*, *German/Carib.*
'ino, *Italian*
i Rest., *Eclectic*
Isla*, *Cuban*
Jack's Fifth*, *American*
JB, *American*
Jeollado, *Korean/Japanese*
Jerry's B/G*, *American*
Joe Franklin's*, *American*
Johnny Rockets, *Hamburgers*
Junno's, *Japanese*
Komodo*, *Mexican/Asian*
Kori, *Korean*
La Gondola, *Italian*
La Gould Finch, *Cajun/Creole*
La Griglia, *Italian*
La Grolla, *Italian*
Laight Street, *Seafood*
La Nonna, *Italian*
La Rocchetta, *Italian*
La Tour, *French*
L'Attitude, *French*
Lavagna, *Italian*
Le Gans, *French*
Le Monde, *French*
Léon, Resto, *French*
Le Zie, *Italian*
Le Zinc*, *French*
Lili's Noodle Shop, *Chinese*
Little Basil, *Thai*
Little Dove*, *American*
L'Ivre*, *French*
Local, *American*
Lucian Blue, *American*
Lucien, *French*
Lupa, *Italian*
Lx, *Argentine*
Maison, *American/French*
Mangia Tutto*, *Italian*
Maratti, *Italian*
Marché Movenpick*, *Int'l*
Maritime*, *Seafood*
Markt, *Belgian*
Maroons, *Jamaican/Southern*
Matrix*, *American*
Maxx, *French*
Medi*, *Italian/French*
Metrazur*, *Mediterranean*
Mexicana Mama, *Mexican*
Mignon, *French/Mediterranean*
Minton's Playhouse*, *American*
Miss Williamsburg, *Italian*
Mormando's, *Steakhouse*
Morrell Wine Bar/Cafe*, *American*
Mortimer's*, *French*
New City B&G, *American*

New Green Bo, *Chinese*
Nicole's, *Med./Eclectic*
Nina's*, *Italian*
North West, *American*
Odyssey*, *Greek Seafood*
Oggi, *Italian*
One 51, *Eclectic*
Oriont, *Asian/French*
Osaka, *Japanese*
Outback*, *Steakhouse*
Palette, *Mediterranean*
Palladin, *French*
Pastis*, *French*
Patoug Manhattan, *Persian*
Peanut Butter, *Amer./Sandwiches*
Pepe Giallo, *Italian*
Pershing Sq., *American*
Phebe's*, *American*
Philip Marie, *American*
Pintxos, *Spanish/Tapas*
Pizza Borgo, *Pizzeria*
Pop, *French/American*
Quake, *Asian*
Quantum*, *American*
Quince*, *American*
Radio Perfecto, *American*
Rainbow Grill*, *Italian*
Red Cat, *Mediterranean*
Rino Trattoria, *Italian*
Rive Gauche, *French*
Roppongi, *Japanese*
Rose Hall*, *Jamaican/Cuban*
Rosehill, *Seafood*
Rothmann's*, *Steakhouse*
Roy's NY, *Asian/Euro Fusion*
Ruby Foo's, *Asian*
Ruby Foo's Times Sq.*, *Asian*
Rue 57*, *French*
Russian Tea Room, *Russian*
Rx*, *American*
Saci*, *Brazilian*
Saffron, *Indian Vegetarian*
Sala, *Spanish*
Sandoval, *Southwestern*
Sapphire, *Indian*
Saul, *American*
Scalini Fedeli, *Italian*
Scopa, *Italian*
Scozzari*, *Italian*
SeaGrill*, *Seafood*
Seppi's, *French*
Serafina on Run, *Italian*
Settanta Sette, *Italian*
Slipper Room*, *French*
SMF*, *American*
Sol, *Asian/Caribbean*
Soma Park, *American*
Sono, *American/Japanese*
SouthWest NY, *Southwestern*
Spazzia, *Mediterranean*
Spencer, *American*
Steak au Poivre, *French Steakhse.*
Sugiyama, *Japanese*
Sultan, *Turkish*

Sur, *Argentine*
Sweet Mamas, *Southern*
Swifty's, *American*
Taperia Madrid, *Spanish/Tapas*
Tello's Rist., *Italian*
Thalia*, *French/Calif.*
Tibet on Houston, *Tibetan*
Tiffin, *Indian/Vegetarian*
Tir Na Nóg, *Irish*
Tivoli, *American*
Tomo Sushi/Sake, *Japanese*
Toqueville*, *American*
Trata, *Greek Seafood*
Tratt. L'incontro, *Italian*
26 Seats, *American*
212, *American*
Uguale, *Italian*
Ulrika's, *Scandinavian*
Uncle Pho, *French/Vietnamese*
Unico*, *Latin Amer.*
Utsav*, *Indian*
Valentino Chelsea*, *Italian*
Vandam, *French/S. American*
Va Tutto!, *Italian*
Veritas, *American*
ViceVersa, *Italian*
Village*, *American*
Vine*, *American*
Viva Brasil, *Brazilian*
Vox, *International*
Wall Street*, *American*
Wild Blue, *American*
Wolf & Lamb, *Kosher Steakhouse*
Wolf's*, *Deli*
Woo Lae Oak, *Korean*
WWF-NY*, *American*
Zuccherino, *Italian*
Zucchero e Pomodori, *Italian*

Noteworthy Closings (96)

Across the Street
Akbar
Akroyiali
American Festival Cafe
Amici Miei
Angelo's Fish Corner
Aperitivo
Aria
Asiana
Barocco
Bellissima
Blue Star
Bondini
Busby's
Caffe Popolo
Casa Brasil
Cena
Cipriani Wall St.
City Wine & Cigar Co.
Club Raleigh at The Oaks
Comedy Nation
Commons Wine Bar & Restaurant
Contrapunto
Cookie's

Copal
Cucina della Nonna
D'Amici
D'Angelo, Osteria
David Ruggerio
85 Down
Fashion Cafe
Flowers
Gertrude's
Grills
Hosteria Fiorella
Hurley's
Hynes Bros. Cafe & Bar
King Crab
Kiosk
KPNY Cafe
Kreischer Mansion
La Cigale
La Colombe d'Or
La Maison Japonaise
La Terrazza
Le Grenadin
Le Relais
Les Célébrités
Le Solex
Liam
Lookout, The
Louisiana Community Bar & Grill
Mare Mare
Marko
Mingala West
Mirezi
Momo Yama
Monzu
Motown Cafe
Mythos
No. 18
One 3
Oona
Osteria del Mezzaluna
Pacific East
Pacifico
Paggio
Panarella's
Parioli Romanissimo
Park Restaurant
Peaches
Pearson's Texas Barbecue
Phil's Kosher Deli
Picasso Cafe
Pondicherry
Primula Rossa Caffe
Raphaël
Rendezvous
Rose Cafe
Rosina's Bistro
Royal Canadian Pancake
Salient
Song
Souperdog
Soup Nutsy
Soup Pot
Sushi Bar, The
Swiss Inn

Sydney B.
Tatou
Tin Angel, The
Tramps Cafe
20 Mott Street Restaurant
Uzie & Marco's
Washington Place
Zinno, Tredeci at

Offbeat
Acadia Parish
Alley's End
Azuri Cafe
Ba Ba Malaysian
Ben's Kosher Deli
Boca Chica
Bongo
Cabana Carioca
Casa
Casa La Femme
Chez Es Saada
Chez Gnagna Koty's
Cool Hse. of Loo
Copeland's
Cowgirl Hall
Delta Grill
Deniz
Dominick's
Druids
Elephant
Elias Corner
Eli's Vinegar Factory
El Pollo
Florent
Franklin Station
Green Field
Havana Chelsea
Jeollado
Jimmy's Bronx
Juniper Café
Katen
La Caridad 78
La Taza de Oro
Le Bar Bat
Lucky Cheng's
Marion's
Mars 2112
Master Grill Int'l
Monk
Mugsy's Chow
New York Noodle
Pintxos
Rasputin
Rodeo B&G
Rolf's
Shopsin's
Sosa Borella
Stingy Lulu's
Sugiyama
Sultan
Sylvia's
Tabla
Tibet on Houston
Tino's

Uguale
Ulrika's
Uncle George's
Well's
Zula

Old New York
(50+ yrs.; year opened;
*building)

1716 Historic Bermuda Inn*
1726 One if by Land*
1763 Fraunces Tavern
1794 Bridge Cafe*
1853 Moran's*
1855 Parsonage*
1863 City Hall*
1864 Pete's Tavern
1868 Landmark Tavern
1868 Old Homestead
1870 Billy's
1872 Fanelli's Cafe
1875 Harry's/Hanover Sq.
1879 Gage & Tollner
1880 White Horse
1885 Keens Steakhse.
1887 Peter Luger
1888 Katz's Deli
1889 Niederstein's
1890 Clarke's, P.J.
1890 Walker's*
1892 Ferrara
1892 Old Town Bar
1894 Veniero's
1896 Rao's
1900 Bamonte's
1902 Algonquin
1902 Angelo's Mulberry
1904 Ferdinando's
1904 Lanza
1905 Ratners
1906 Barbetta
1906 Monte's Italian (Bklyn.)
1907 Gargiulo's
1907 Oak Room
1907 Palm Court
1908 Barney Greengrass
1908 John's of 12th St.
1913 Oyster Bar (Gr. Cent.)
1917 Café des Artistes
1919 Caffé on Green*
1919 Gene's
1919 Grand Ticino
1919 Mario's
1920 Marchi's
1920 Ye Waverly Inn
1921 Sardi's
1922 Rocco
1924 Totonno Pizzeria
1925 El Charro
1926 Frankie & Johnnie's
1926 Palm
1927 El Faro
1927 Gallagher's
1929 Eisenberg

1929 John's Pizzeria
1929 '21' Club
1930 El Quijote
1931 Café Pierre
1931 Peacock Alley
1932 Pietro's
1933 Gebhardt's
1933 Lento's
1934 Papaya King
1934 Tavern on Green
1936 Tom's
1937 Carnegie Deli
1937 Denino's Pizzeria
1937 Le Veau D'Or
1937 Minetta Tavern
1937 Patrissy's
1937 Stage Deli
1938 Well's
1939 Heidelberg
1941 Sevilla
1944 Patsy's
1945 Gino
1945 V&T Pizzeria
1946 Lobster Box
1947 Delegates' Din. Rm.
1949 King Cole Bar
1949 Tout Va Bien
1949 Two Toms

Outdoor Dining
(G=garden; S=sidewalk;
T=terrace; best of many)

Aesop's Tables (G)
American Park (T)
Aureole (G)
Barbetta (G)
Barolo (G)
Bistrot Margot (G)
Bondí (G)
Bottino (G)
Bryant Park Cafe (G,T)
Bryant Park Grill (G,T)
Cello (G)
Chelsea Grill (G)
Churr. Plantation (G)
Dolphins (G)
Druids (G)
East of Eighth (G)
Ennio & Michael (S)
Friend of Farmer (S)
Garage (S)
Gascogne (G)
Grove (G)
Harbour Lights (T)
Harvest (G)
Historic Bermuda Inn (G,T)
Home (G)
I Coppi (G)
Il Cortile (G,S,T)
Il Palazzo (G,S)
I Trulli (G)
Jean Georges (T)
Julian's (G,S)
Killmeyer's (G)

La Nonna (G)
Lanza (G)
Lattanzi (G)
Le Jardin Bistro (G)
Le Madri (S,T)
Le Petit Hulot (G)
Le Refuge (G)
Luca Lounge (G)
Lupa (G)
March (G)
Marichu (T)
Markt (S,T)
Metropolitan Cafe (G)
Miracle Grill (First Ave.) (G,T)
New City B&G (G)
Park View/Boathse. (T)
Provence (G)
Radio Perfecto (G,S)
Redeye Grill (S)
Rialto (G)
Sahara (G)
Saloon (S)
St. Dymphnas (G)
Sugar Bar (G)
Surya (G)
Tavern on Green (G,T)
Terrace (T)
Va Tutto! (G)
Verbena (G)
Vittorio Cucina (G,T)
White Horse (S)

Parties & Private Rooms
(Any nightclub or restaurant charges less at off-times; the following lists the best of many; an * means the place has private rooms)
ABC Parlour Cafe
An American Place*
Anglers & Writers
Aquavit*
Asia de Cuba
Barbetta*
Barolo*
Bateaux NY*
Bayard's*
Becco*
Blue Water Grill*
Brother Jimmy's
Brothers BBQ*
Bryant Park Grill*
B. Smith's*
Carlyle*
Cello*
Chez Es Saada
Chez Josephine*
Churr. Plantation*
Churr. Plataforma
Club Macanudo
Colina*
Cornelia St. Cafe
Cowgirl Hall
Daniel*

Eleven Mad. Pk.*
Eli's Vinegar Factory*
El Teddy's*
Espn Zone*
FireBird*
First
Four Seasons*
Fressen
Gabriel's*
Gallagher's*
Giambelli*
Giovanni's Atrium*
Global 33
Golden Unicorn*
Gramercy Tavern*
Grange Hall
Il Buco*
Il Vagabondo
Independent
I Tre Merli
Jezebel
Jimmy's Bronx*
Jo Jo*
Keens Steakhse.*
Killmeyer's
Kings' Carriage Hse.*
La Belle Epoque
La Côte Basque*
La Fourchette
La Grenouille*
Landmark Tavern*
La Réserve*
La Soirée d'Asie*
Le Bar Bat*
Le Bernardin*
Le Cirque 2000*
Le Colonial*
Lenox Room
Leopard*
Local*
Lola*
Lombardi's
Londel's*
Lot 61*
Lucky Cheng's
Lupa*
Lutèce*
Maloney & Porcelli*
Maratti*
Marion's
Marylou's
Mary's*
Metronome*
Milos*
Miracle Grill
Moomba*
Moran's
Nirvana
Oceana*
Official All Star*
O'Neals'*
One 51*
147*
Palio*

238

Park Ave. Cafe*
Patroon*
Peking Park*
Picholine*
Planet Hollywood*
Pravda*
Primavera*
Rasputin
Redeye Grill*
Remi*
René Pujol*
River Cafe*
Ruby Foo's*
Russian Tea Room*
Sal A's S.P.Q.R.*
Sammy's Roumanian*
San Domenico*
Savoy
Screening Room*
Second Ave. Deli*
Serendipity 3
Shun Lee Palace
Spirit Cruises
St. Maggie's
Supper Club
Sylvia's
Tavern on Green*
Tennessee Mtn.
Thady Con's*
Tonic*
Tratt. Dopo Teatro
Tribeca Grill*
'21' Club*
27 Standard*
212*
Two Toms
Typhoon
Union Pacific*
Verbena*
Virgil's BBQ
Vivolo
Water Club*
Water's Edge*
Well's
Willow
Windows on World*
World Yacht
Zarela

People-Watching
Alaia
Amaranth
Atlantic Grill
Atlas
Babbo
Balthazar
Bar Pitti
Bice Rist.
Blue Ribbon
Blue Ribbon Sushi
Blue Water Grill
Bond Street
B. Smith's
Cafe Fiorello

Campagna
Chez Es Saada
China Grill
Cibi Cibi
Clementine
Club Macanudo
Coffee Shop
Coup
Danube
Elio's
Ferrier
FireBird
44
Fressen
Gotham B&G
Harry Cipriani
Henry's Evergreen
Independent
Indochine
La Grenouille
Le Bar Bat
Le Colonial
Lot 61
Lx
Markt
Match
Nobu
Nobu, Next Door
Odeon
One 51
Orienta
Oriont
Park Avalon
Patria
Patroon
Pravda
Rain
Rasputin
Redeye Grill
Ruby Foo's
Russian Tea Room
Saloon
Serafina Fab. Grill
Stingy Lulu's
Tabla
Tonic
212
Veritas
Vox
Waterloo Brass.

Power Scenes
Ambassador Grill
Bayard's
Ben Benson's
Café Boulud
Carlyle
Cello
Daniel
Della Femina
Eleven Mad. Pk.
Elio's
FireBird
Four Seasons

Fresco by Scotto
Gabriel's
Gallagher's
Hudson Riv. Club
Il Nido
La Caravelle
Le Bernardin
Lespinasse
Maloney & Porcelli
Milos
Morton's
Oceana
Ocean Grill
Park Ave. Cafe
Patroon
Peter Luger
Rao's
Regency
Smith & Wollensky
Sparks
Tratt. Dell'Arte
'21' Club

Pre-Theater/Prix Fixe Menus

(See pages 21–22, plus the following additional good buys; call to check prices, days and times; B=brunch, L=lunch, D=dinner, *indicates dinner prix fixe is pre-theater only)

Adrienne (B,L,D)
Algonquin (D)*
Alva (D)*
Barbetta (D)*
Belgo (B,L,D)
Bouley Bakery (L)
Bryant Park Grill (B,D)*
Caviar Russe (L,D)
Chez Napoléon (D)
China Fun (L,D)
Churr. Plantation (L,D)
Cité Grill (D)
Country Cafe (L,D)*
Cucina Pesce (D)
Demarchelier (L,D)
Demi (B,L,D)
Downtown (L,D)
Fraunces Tavern (L,D)
Gage & Tollncr (L,D)
Green Field (L,D)
Hourglass Tavern (D)
Jewel of India (D)
Josephina (D)*
La Grenouille (L,D)
La Mangeoire (L,D)
L'Ardoise (D)
Le Bernardin (L,D)
Le Biarritz (L,D)
Le Bistrot de Maxim (L,D)
Le Boeuf à la Mode (D)
Le Cirque 2000 (L)
Le Refuge (L,D)*

Les Sans Culottes (L,D)
Lucien (B,L,D)
Lundy Bros. (B,L,D)
March (D)
Metronome (L,D)*
Mitali E/W (B,D)
Oceana (L,D)
Old Homestead (L,D)
Patsy's (L,D)
Paul & Jimmy's (D)
Pierre au Tunnel (L,D)
Pietro's (L)
Pisces (D)*
Ribollita (L,D)
River Cafe (D)
Sal Anthony's (L,D)
Simply Caviar (L)
Tazza (B,D)*
Tino's (L,D)
Tout Va Bien (D)*
Tuscan Square (L,D)
27 Standard (L)
Ulrika's (L)
View (D)
Ye Waverly Inn (L,D)
Zarela (L,D)

Pubs/Bars/Microbreweries

(See also upcoming *Zagat Nightlife Survey* for more listings)

Amaranth
Bar Six
Broome St. Bar
Charley O's
Cité Grill
Clarke's, P.J.
Corner Bistro
Fanelli's Cafe
Ferrier
Gramercy Tavern
Heartland Brewery
Hog Pit
J.G. Melon
Joe Allen
Keens Steakhse.
Killmeyer's
King Cole Bar
Knickerbocker B&G
Landmark Tavern
Markt
Match
Monkey Bar
Neary's
Oak Room (bar)
Old Town Bar
O'Neals'
Oyster Bar (Gr. Cent.)
Palio (downstairs)
Pete's Tavern
Pravda
Shark Bar
St. Dymphnas
Tavern on Jane

Thady Con's
'21' Club
Typhoon
Walker's
Waterfront Ale
White Horse
Windows on World
Wollensky's Grill

Quiet Conversation
ABC Parlour Cafe
Alley's End
Aquavit
Atlas
Barbetta
Bellini
Box Tree
Café Botanica
Café Pierre
Cafe Trevi
Carlyle
Caviar Russe
Cello
Chanterelle
Chelsea Bistro
Chez Michallet
City Hall
Daniel
Danube
Della Femina
Destinée
Domingo
Eleven Mad. Pk.
FireBird
Four Seasons
Gramercy Tavern
Gus' Place
Honmura An
Hudson Riv. Club
Il Giglio
Il Monello
Il Tinello
Jean Georges
Keens Steakhse.
Kings' Carriage Hse.
La Caravelle
La Grenouille
La Réserve
La Soirée d'Asie
Le Bernardin
Le Boeuf à la Mode
Le Cirque 2000
Le Régence
Lespinasse
Lutèce
March
Mark's
Montrachet
Morton's
Oak Room
One if by Land
Palio
Palm Court
Park View/Boathse.

Peacock Alley
Petrossian
Picholine
Primavera
Regency
San Domenico
Seryna
Tea Box
Temple Bar
Terrace
Top of the Tower
T Salon
Tse Yang
Union Pacific
Union Sq. Cafe
Veritas
Water's Edge
West 63rd Steak
Wild Blue
Zen Palate

Raw Bars
(Best of many)
American Park
Aquagrill
Atlantic Grill
Avenue
Balthazar
Blue Ribbon
Blue Water Grill
Bongo
Brasserie Americaine
Candela
Circa
City Crab
City Hall
Coco Marina
Cooking w/Jazz
Docks
Europa B&G
Fireman's of B'klyn
Fish
Galapagos
Garage
Globe
Go Fish
Harbour Lights
Hatsuhana
Independent
Kuruma Zushi
Laight Street
Lenox Room
Live Bait
Local
London Lennie's
L-Ray
Lundy Bros.
Mercer Kitchen
Nobu
Nobu, Next Door
Oceana
Ocean Grill
Oyster Bar (Gr. Cent.)
Palette

Pearl Oyster Bar
Pisces
Redeye Grill
Rosehill
Shaffer City
T.S. Ma

Renovated or Moved
(Recently renovated or moved, but not yet reflected in decor ratings)
An American Place (moved)
Aureole
Bouley Bakery
Chelsea Bistro
Chianti (Manh.)
Da Ciro
Demi
Eq
Eros
Henry's Evergreen
Historic Bermuda Inn
Il Buco
Kalio
La Réserve
Le Perigord
Les Deux Lapins (moved)
March
Marco Polo
Mazzei Osteria (moved)
Meriken
Mi Cocina
Mi Nidito
Pappardella
Peking Duck (moved)
Pig Heaven
Planet Thailand (moved)
Roberto's
Sahara
Sarge's Deli
Steak au Poivre
Terrace
Tin Room Cafe (moved)

Romantic Spots
Alison on Dominick
Barbetta
Bateaux NY
Bottino
Box Tree
Café des Artistes
Candela
Casa La Femme
Caviar Russe
Cello
Chez Es Saada
Chez Josephine
Chez Michallet
Danal
Danube
Delphini
Demarchelier
Domingo
Erminia
FireBird

Five Points
Grove
Harbour Lights
Historic Bermuda Inn
I Trulli
Jezebel
King Cole Bar
Kings' Carriage Hse.
La Belle Epoque
Lady Mendl's
La Goulue
La Grenouille
La Ripaille
Le Colonial
Le Gigot
Le Jardin Bistro
Le Refuge
Maison
Maratti
March
Marichu
Mark's
Match
Mercer Kitchen
Merchants
Metronome
Nirvana
One if by Land
Palm Court
Park View/Boathse.
Provence
Quilty's
Rafaella
River Cafe
Rosemarie's
Scalini Fedeli
Soma Park
Spirit Cruises
Tavern on Green
Temple Bar
Terrace
Top of the Tower
Torch
ViceVersa
Water's Edge
Windows on World
World Yacht

Saturday – Best Bets
(B=brunch; L=lunch; best of many)
ABC Parlour Cafe (B)
Acacia (B,L)
American Park (B)
An American Place (B)
Anglers & Writers (B,L)
Aquavit (L)
Arqua (L)
Atlas (B,L)
Babbo (L)
Balthazar (B,L)
Baraonda (B,L)
Barbetta (L)
Barolo (B,L)

Bice Rist. (L)
Blue Ribbon Bakery (B,L)
Blue Water Grill (L)
Bouley Bakery (L)
Broome St. Bar (B,L)
Bryant Park Grill (B,L)
B. Smith's (L)
Butterfield 81 (B)
Café Botanica (L)
Café Boulud (L)
Café de Bruxelles (B,L)
Café des Artistes (B,L)
Cafe Luxembourg (B)
Capsouto Frères (B)
Carlyle (L)
Carnegie Deli (L)
Chanterelle (L)
Circo (L)
Daniel (L)
Da Silvano (L)
Dawat (L)
Docks (B,L)
E.A.T. (B,L)
Fanelli's Cafe (L)
FireBird (L)
Five Points (B,L)
Fressen (L)
Gallagher's (L)
Gramercy Tavern (L)
Honmura An (L)
Houston's (L)
Il Monello (L)
Il Nido (L)
Japonica (L)
Jean Georges (L)
Joe Allen (L)
Jo Jo (L)
Junior's (B,L)
La Boheme (B)
L'Absinthe (B)
La Côte Basque (L)
La Goulue (L)
La Grenouille (L)
Landmark Tavern (L)
Le Bilboquet (L)
Le Cirque 2000 (L)
Le Refuge (B,L)
Lespinasse (L)
Maloney & Porcelli (B,L)
Markt (B)
Mary Ann's (B)
Matthew's (B,L)
Mayrose (B,L)
Mesa Grill (B)
Miracle Grill (B)
Mitali E/W (B,L)
O'Neals' (B,L)
Oriental Garden (B,L)
Orso (L)
Payard Pâtisserie (L)
Pershing Sq. (B,L)
Petaluma (B,L)
Petrossian (B)
Picholine (L)

Pig Heaven (L)
Provence (B,L)
Quatorze Bis (B,L)
Quilty's (B)
Rain (B,L)
Redeye Grill (B)
René Pujol (L)
River Cafe (B)
Second Ave. Deli (B,L)
Serafina Fab. Pizza (L)
Serendipity 3 (L)
Shark Bar (B)
Spartina (L)
Steak Frites (B,L)
Sushi Hana (L)
Sushiya (L)
Sylvia's (B,L)
Table d'Hôte (B)
Tartine (B,L)
Tavern on Green (B,L)
Tonic (B)
Trata (B,L)
Tratt. Dell'Arte (B)
Uncle Nick's (L)
Union Sq. Cafe (L)
Veselka (B,L)
Vox (L)
Walker's (B)
Water Club (L)
Well's (B,L)
White Horse (B,L)
Windows on World (L)
Wollensky's Grill (L)

Sunday – Best Bets

(All restaurants that are open on Sunday have an S following their names in the body; this is a list of top recommendations; B=brunch; L=lunch; D=dinner; plus all hotels and most Asians)
Ambassador Grill (B,L,D)
America (B,L,D)
An American Place (B,D)
Anglers & Writers (B,L,D)
Aquagrill (B,D)
Atlantic Grill (B,D)
Atlas (B,L,D)
Avenue (B,L,D)
Babbo (L,D)
Balthazar (B,L,D)
Barney Greengrass (B,L)
Barolo (B,L,D)
Bateaux NY (B,D)
Bella Blu (B,L,D)
Bistro du Nord (B,D)
Blue Ribbon Bakery (B,L,D)
Blue Water Grill (B,D)
Broome St. Bar (B,L,D)
B. Smith's (B,L,D)
Butterfield 81 (B,D)
Café Botanica (B,D)
Café Boulud (D)

Café de Bruxelles (B,L,D)
Café des Artistes (B,L,D)
Cafe Luxembourg (B,D)
Capsouto Frères (B,D)
Carlyle (B,L,D)
Carmine's (L,D)
Carnegie Deli (D)
Cello (D)
Chez Michallet (B,D)
Chiam (L,D)
Circa (B,D)
Cité (B,L,D)
Copeland's (B,L,D)
Dallas BBQ (L,D)
Da Silvano (L,D)
Docks (B,L,D)
Dominick's (L,D)
EJ's Lunch. (B,L,D)
Five Points (B,L,D)
Fressen (L,D)
Friend of Farmer (B,D)
Gabriela's (B,L,D)
Globe (B,D)
Good Enough to Eat (B,D)
Gotham Bar & Grill (D)
Gramercy Tavern (L,D)
Grand Ticino (B,L,D)
Gus' Place (B,L,D)
Heights Cafe (B,L,D)
Historic Bermuda Inn (B,D)
Il Cortile (L,D)
Independent (B,D)
Isabella's (B,D)
Jean Georges (B,D)
Joe Allen (B,L,D)
John's Pizzeria (L,D)
Jubilee (B,D)
Junior's (B,L,D)
L'Absinthe (B,D)
La Fourchette (B,D)
La Goulue (B,D)
Le Madri (B,D)
Le Marais (L,D)
Lenox Room (B,D)
Le Régence (B,L,D)
Les Halles (B,L,D)
Lombardi's (L,D)
Lx (B,D)
Maloney & Porcelli (B,L,D)
Manhattan Grille (B,D)
Mark's (B,D)
Markt (B,D)
Marylou's (B,D)
Matthew's (B,L,D)
Metropolitan Cafe (B,D)
Miracle Grill (B,D)
Molyvos (L,D)
Moreno (L,D)
Mr. K's (L,D)
New City B&G (B,D)
Nobu (D)
Ocean Grill (B,D)
Odeon (B,D)
Oggi (B,D)

Old Town Bar (L,D)
O'Neals' (B,L,D)
Orienta (D)
Oriental Garden (B,L,D)
Park Avalon (B,D)
Park Ave. Cafe (B,D)
Park Side (L,D)
Peter Luger (L,D)
Petrossian (B,D)
Piccola Venezia (L,D)
Picholine (D)
Provence (B,L,D)
Quatorze Bis (B,L,D)
Queen (L,D)
Rain (B,L,D)
Redeye Grill (B,D)
Ruby Foo's (B,D)
Russian Tea Room (B,D)
Second Ave. Deli (B,L,D)
Serafina Fab. Grill (L,D)
Sette Mezzo (L,D)
Sharz Cafe (B,D)
Shun Lee (L,D)
Shun Lee Palace (L,D)
Sistina (L,D)
Spring St. Nat. (B,L,D)
Sylvia's (B,L,D)
Table d'Hôte (B,D)
Tavern on Green (B,L,D)
Tratt. Dell'Arte (B,D)
Tratt. Pesce/Pasta (L,D)
Treehouse (B,D)
Tse Yang (L,D)
212 (B,D)
Union Sq. Cafe (D)
Va Tutto! (B,D)
Veselka (B,L,D)
Vico (B,L,D)
Water Club (B,L,D)
Zoë (B,D)

Senior Appeal

Asti
Aureole
Barbetta
Billy's
Box Tree
Café Botanica
Café des Artistes
Cafe Greco
Cafe Trevi
Carlyle
Christer's
Coco Opera
Daniel
Danube
Della Femina
Duane Park
Eleven Mad. Pk.
Felidia
FireBird
Four Seasons
Gallagher's
Giovanni

Girasole
Grande Mela
Il Menestrello
Il Monello
Il Nido
Il Tinello
Jewel of India
La Caravelle
La Grenouille
La Mangeoire
La Mediterranée
La Petite Auberge
La Réserve
Le Bernardin
L'Ecole
Le Perigord
Le Régence
Lespinasse
Levana
Lutèce
Manhattan Grille
Maratti
March
Mark's
Mr. K's
Neary's
Nippon
Oak Room
Oceana
Otabe
Oyster Bar (Gr. Cent.)
Palm
Palm Court
Peacock Alley
Peter Luger
Picholine
Primavera
Remi
Rosa Mexicano
Russian Samovar
Russian Tea Room
S. Dynasty
Shun Lee
Shun Lee Palace
Solera
Soma Park
Sushisay
Tavern on Green
Tse Yang
'21' Club
Vivolo
West 63rd Steak
Wilkinson's

Singles Scenes
(See also upcoming *Zagat Nightlife Survey* for more listings)
Alaia
Amaranth
Angelo & Maxie's
Aquagrill
Atlantic Grill
Balthazar

Bar Six
Benny's Burritos
Blackbird
Blue Water Grill
Boca Chica
Canal House
Charley O's
Chez Es Saada
Cité Grill
Clarke's, P.J.
Clementine
Coconut Grill
Cub Room
Docks
Dt•ut
El Teddy's
Ernie's
Ferrier
First
Fressen
Grande Mela
Heartland Brewery
Hush
Independent
Isabella's
I Trulli
JUdson Grill
Jules
La Goulue
Le Bar Bat
Live Bait
Marion's
Markt
Match Uptown
Merchants
Miracle Grill
Monkey Bar
North West
Oak Room (bar)
Ocean Grill
Old Town Bar
One 51
147
O'Nieal's Grand
Oriont
Park Avalon
Pershing Sq.
Pete's Tavern
Pravda
Ruby Foo's
Serafina Fab. Grill
Shark Bar
Tabla
Thady Con's
Tortilla Flats
Tribeca Grill
212
Vandam
Viceroy
Vox
Walker's
Waterloo Brass.
White Horse
Zarela

Sleepers

(Good to excellent food, but little known)

Archives
Bellew
Chez Gnagna Koty's
Da Andrea
Dolphins
Domani
Eliá
Gamut
Havana Chelsea
Il Valletto, Sofia
Istana
Jeollado
Joanie's
Kam Chueh
Katen
Killmeyer's
La Bergamote
La Grolla
La Rocchetta
Le Bouchon
Londel's
Lucian Blue
Maratti
New Green Bo
Oro Blu
Pintxos
Ponticello
Porta Rossa
Reg'l Thai Sa-Woy
Rinconcito Peru
Rino Trattoria
Sachi
S'Agapo
Seaport Soup
Serafina on Run
Simply Caviar
Soma Park
Sushi Sen-nin
Tiffin
Tir Na Nóg
Veronica
Zula

Teflons

(Very popular, despite so-so food, i.e. other attractions prevent criticism from sticking)

America
Bendix Diner
Broadway Diner
Burger Heaven
Cowgirl Hall
Dallas BBQ
Elaine's
Fanelli's Cafe
French Roast
Hard Rock
Harley Davidson
Heartland Brewery
Jekyll & Hyde

Le Bar Bat
Lemon
Live Bait
Lucky Cheng's
Mars 2112
Mayrose
Mickey Mantle's
Official All Star
Old Town Bar
Pete's Tavern
Pizzeria Uno
Planet Hollywood
Saloon
Starbucks
Stingy Lulu's
Viceroy
White Horse
World Yacht

Tasting Menus

Aquavit ($85)
Babbo ($49 & up)
Balthazar ($45)
Bond Street ($60 & up)
Bouley Bakery ($68 & up)
Café Pierre ($72)
Caviar Russe ($55 & up)
Cello ($110)
Chanterelle ($89)
Circo ($60)
Coco Pazzo Teatro ($65)
Cub Room ($65)
Daniel ($105 & up)
Danube ($80)
Della Femina ($59)
Destinée ($69)
Eq ($75 & up)
Gramercy Tavern ($78)
Jean Georges ($115)
Jo Jo ($43 & up)
JUdson Grill ($78)
La Caravelle ($90 & up)
La Côte Basque ($90)
La Grenouille ($110)
La Réserve ($85)
Le Bernardin ($120)
Le Cirque 2000 ($90)
Le Perigord ($75)
Lespinasse ($125)
Lutèce ($85)
March ($90)
Mark's ($78)
Nadaman Hakubai ($80 & up)
Nobu ($60)
Oceana ($90 & up)
One if by Land ($68)
Patria ($79)
Picholine ($70 & up)
River Cafe ($90)
Roy's NY ($55 & up)
San Domenico ($60)
Savoy ($48)
Seppi's ($70)
Solera ($70 & up)

Sono ($78)
Sushisay ($50 & up)
Tabla ($65 & up)
Tonic ($85)
Tse Yang ($75)
'21' Club ($85)
Union Pacific ($85 & up)
Verbena ($65)
Vong ($68)

Teas
(See also *Hotels* and
Coffeehouses/Desserts; the
following are highly touted)
ABC Parlour Cafe
Adrienne
Anglers & Writers
Café M
Café Pierre
Cafe S.F.A.
Café Word/Mouth
Carlyle
Caviar Russe
C3
Danal
Garden Cafe
Jean Georges
Kings' Carriage Hse.
Lady Mendl's
Le Train Bleu
Limoncello
Mark's
Morgan Ct.
Palm Court
Payard Pâtisserie
Russian Samovar
Russian Tea Room
Sarabeth's
Sweet Melissa
Tea Box
Treehouse
Trois Jean
T Salon
Yaffa's

Teenagers & Other Youthful Spirits
America
Bendix Diner
Benny's Burritos
Ben's Kosher Deli
Bridge Cafe
Brother Jimmy's
Bryant Park Cafe
Cafe Lalo
Carmine's
Carnegie Deli
Cowgirl Hall
Dallas BBQ
EJ's Lunch.
Empire Diner
Ernie's
ESPN Zone
Globe
Good Enough to Eat

Goodfella's
Gray's Papaya
Grimaldi's
Hard Rock
Harley Davidson
Houston's
Island Burgers
Jackson Hole
Jerry's
Johnny Rockets
John's Pizzeria
Katz's Deli
Krispy Kreme
Landmark Tavern
Le Tableau
Lupe's East L.A.
Mangia
Mars 2112
Master Grill Int'l
Maya
Mickey Mantle's
Nirvana
NoHo Star
Ollie's
Papaya King
Pig Heaven
Pizzeria Uno
Planet Hollywood
Sammy's Roumanian
Screening Room
Second Ave. Deli
Shun Lee Cafe
Stage Deli
Sylvia's
Tavern on Green
Tennessee Mtn.
Totonno Pizzeria
Tuscan Square
Uncle Nick's
Vinnie's Pizza
Virgil's BBQ
Windows on World
World Yacht
Zarela

Theme Restaurants
(† Not open yet)
Brooklyn Diner
Ellen's Stardust
ESPN Zone
Hard Rock
Harley Davidson
Jekyll & Hyde
Joe Franklin's†
Johnny Rockets
Le Bar Bat
Lucky Cheng's
Mars 2112
Mickey Mantle's
Official All Star
Planet Hollywood
WWF-NY†

Transporting Experiences

ABC Parlour Cafe
Anglers & Writers
Aquavit
Balthazar
Barolo
Bateaux NY
Bouterin
Box Tree
Café des Artistes
Candela
Caribe
Casa La Femme
Chez Es Saada
Chez Josephine
Chez Michallet
Colina
FireBird
Gramercy Tavern
Heidelberg
Honmura An
Il Buco
Jezebel
Keens Steakhse.
Kelley & Ping
Kings' Carriage Hse.
La Belle Epoque
La Côte Basque
La Goulue
La Grenouille
Landmark Tavern
La Petite Auberge
Le Colonial
Le Refuge
Mark's
Nirvana
Nobu
Obeca Li
Palm Court
Park View/Boathse.
Pravda
Provence
Rao's
Raoul's
Tavern on Green
Temple Bar
Thady Con's
Top of the Tower
Union Pacific
Vatan
Windows on World
Zen Palate

Visitors on Expense Accounts

Aquavit
Atlas
Aureole
Balthazar
Beacon
Bice
Bouley Bakery

Cafe Centro
Café des Artistes
Carnegie Deli
Cello
Chanterelle
Chin Chin
Daniel
Danube
Da Umberto
Downtown
Eleven Mad. Pk.
Felidia
FireBird
Four Seasons
Gotham B&G
Gramercy Tavern
Harry Cipriani
Hudson Riv. Club
Il Cantinori
Il Mulino
Il Nido
Jean Georges
Jo Jo
Kuruma Zushi
La Caravelle
La Côte Basque
La Grenouille
La Réserve
Le Bernardin
Le Cirque 2000
Lutèce
Manhattan Ocean
Maratti
March
Mesa Grill
Milos
Montrachet
Nadaman Hakubai
Nobu
Oceana
One if by Land
Palio
Palm
Park Ave. Cafe
Patria
Patroon
Periyali
Peter Luger
Remi
River Cafe
San Domenico
Shun Lee Palace
Smith & Wollensky
Soma Park
Sparks
Sushisay
Tavern on Green
Terrace
Tribeca Grill
'21' Club
Two Two Two
Union Sq. Cafe
Veritas

Vong
Water Club
Windows on World

Wheelchair Access

(Recommended on the basis of overall quality and ease of access. The data re access comes from the restaurants and has not been verified by personal inspection. Thus, you should call in advance.)

America
American Park
Asia de Cuba
Balthazar
Barolo
Ben Benson's
Billy's
Bolo
Bouley Bakery
Bryant Park Cafe
Bryant Park Grill
B. Smith's
Café Botanica
Café Boulud
Cafe S.F.A.
Calle Ocho
Cal's
Carlyle
Chanterelle
Chiam
Churr. Plataforma
Circo
Cité
Cité Grill
City Hall
Coco Pazzo
Daniel
Docks
Eleven Mad. Pk.
Ernie's
57 57
F.illi Ponte
Frank's Rest.
Gabriel's
Gramercy Tavern
Heartbeat
Hudson Riv. Club
Il Postino
Istana
Jean Georges
Kokachin
La Caravelle
La Côte Basque
Le Bernardin
Lespinasse
Lundy Bros.
Milos
Morton's
Palio
Park View/Boathse.
Patroon
Peacock Alley

Remi
Republic
River Cafe
Roy's NY
Sette MoMA
Sparks
Starbucks
Tavern on Green
Tribeca Grill
Vong
Wild Blue
Windows on World
Woo Lae Oak
Yura & Co.

Winning Wine Lists

Alison on Dominick
Aquagrill
Aquavit
Atlantic Grill
Aureole
Babbo
Balthazar
Barbetta
Barolo
Bayard's
Becco
Ben Benson's
Blue Ribbon
Blue Water Grill
Bouley Bakery
Bull & Bear
Cafe Centro
Café des Artistes
Capsouto Frères
Carlyle
Chanterelle
Chelsea Bistro
Chiam
Circo
Cité
City Hall
Coco Pazzo
Cucina
Daniel
Divine Bar
Docks
Eleven Mad. Pk.
Felidia
57 57
F.illi Ponte
Follonico
Four Seasons
Fresco by Scotto
Gabriel's
Gotham B&G
Gramercy Tavern
Halcyon
Harry's/Hanover Sq.
Henry's End
Hudson Riv. Club
I Coppi
Il Cantinori
Il Mulino

I Tre Merli
I Trulli
Jean Georges
Jo Jo
JUdson Grill
La Caravelle
La Côte Basque
La Grenouille
La Réserve
La Vineria
Le Bernardin
Le Cirque 2000
L'Ecole
Le Madri
Lenox Room
Le Perigord
Les Halles
Lespinasse
Lobster Club
Lutèce
Maloney & Porcelli
Manhattan Ocean
March
Mark's
Mercer Kitchen
Merlot B&G
Mesa Grill
Michael Jordan's
Michael's
Milos
Monkey Bar
Montrachet
Moomba
Nicola Paone
Ñ 33 Crosby
Oceana
Ocean Grill
One if by Land
Orso
Oyster Bar (Gr. Cent.)
Palio
Palm
Park Ave. Cafe
Patria
Patroon
Peacock Alley
Peter Luger
Piccola Venezia
Picholine
Post House
Provence
Raoul's
Remi
René Pujol
River Cafe
Ruby Foo's
San Domenico
San Pietro
Savoy
Sharz Cafe
Shun Lee Palace
Smith & Wollensky
Soho Kitchen
Sparks

Tabla
Tavern on Green
Terrace
Tommaso's
Tratt. Dell'Arte
Tribeca Grill
Trois Jean
Tropica
Tse Yang
'21' Club
Union Pacific
Union Sq. Cafe
Verbena
Veritas
Water Club
Windows on World
Wollensky's Grill
Zoë

Young Children
(Besides the normal fast-food places; * indicates children's menu available)
ABC Parlour Cafe
America
Anglers & Writers*
Arqua
Avenue*
Barking Dog
Barney Greengrass
Bateaux NY
Bella Luna*
Benihana
Ben's Kosher Deli*
Brooklyn Diner
Brother Jimmy's*
Bryant Park Cafe
B. Smith's*
Bubby's
California Pizza*
Calle Ocho*
Carnegie Deli
Churr. Plataforma*
Comfort Diner*
Cowgirl Hall*
Dallas BBQ
EJ's Lunch.*
Eli's Manhattan
Eli's Vinegar Factory*
Ernie's*
ESPN Zone
57 57*
Friend of Farmer*
Gabriela's*
Gebhardt's*
Gene's
Go Fish*
Good Enough to Eat*
Grand Ticino*
Green Field
Harbour Lights*
Hard Rock*
Harley Davidson*
Heidelberg*

Historic Bermuda Inn*
Il Vagabondo
Jackson Hole*
Jekyll & Hyde*
John's Pizzeria
Junior's*
Katz's Deli
Kelley & Ping
Lobster Box*
London Lennie's*
Lundy Bros.*
Manhattan Chili*
Mars 2112*
Mary Ann's*
Master Grill Int'l*
Mickey Mantle's*
Odeon*
Odessa*
Official All Star*
O'Neals'*
Oscar's*
Park View/Boathse.*
Patsy's Pizza

Peanut Butter*
Pizzeria Uno
P.J. Bernstein Deli
Planet Hollywood*
Polistina's
Popover Cafe*
Saloon*
Sarabeth's
Second Ave. Deli
Stage Deli*
Sylvia's*
Tavern on Green*
Tennessee Mtn.*
Time Cafe
Treehouse*
Tribeca Grill*
Two Boots*
V&T Pizzeria*
Vinnie's Pizza
Virgil's BBQ
Ye Waverly Inn
Zum Stammtisch*

Wine Vintage Chart 1985-1998

This chart is designed to help you select wine to go with your meal. It is based on the same 0 to 30 scale used throughout this *Survey*. The ratings (prepared by our friend **Howard Stravitz**, a law professor at the University of South Carolina) reflect both the quality of the vintage and the wine's readiness for present consumption. Thus, if a wine is not fully mature or is over the hill, its rating has been reduced. We do not include 1987, 1991 or 1993 vintages because, with the exception of cabernets, '91 Northern Rhônes and '93 red Burgundies and Southern Rhônes, those vintages are not especially recommended.

	'85	'86	'88	'89	'90	'92	'94	'95	'96	'97	'98
WHITES											
French:											
Alsace	25	20	23	28	28	24	28	26	24	25	24
Burgundy	24	25	19	27	22	23	22	27	28	25	24
Loire Valley	–	–	–	26	25	18	22	24	26	23	22
Champagne	28	25	24	26	28	–	–	24	26	24	–
Sauternes	22	28	29	25	26	–	18	22	23	24	–
California:											
Chardonnay	–	–	–	–	–	24	22	26	22	26	26
REDS											
French:											
Bordeaux	26	27	25	28	29	18	24	25	24	23	23
Burgundy	24	–	23	27	29	23	23	25	26	24	24
Rhône	26	20	26	28	27	15	23	24	22	24	26
Beaujolais	–	–	–	–	–	–	21	24	22	24	23
California:											
Cab./Merlot	26	26	–	21	28	26	27	25	24	25	26
Zinfandel	–	–	–	–	–	21	23	21	22	24	25
Italian:											
Tuscany	27	–	24	–	26	–	–	25	19	28	25
Piedmont	25	–	25	27	27	–	–	23	25	28	25

Bargain sippers take note: Some wines are reliable year in, year out, and are reasonably priced as well. They include: Alsatian Pinot Blancs, Côtes du Rhône, Muscadet, Bardolino, Valpolicella and inexpensive Spanish Rioja and California Zinfandel and are best bought in the most recent vintages.